# Marrakech

**timeout.com/marrakech**

**Published by Time Out Guides Ltd**, a wholly owned subsidiary of Time Out Group Ltd.
Time Out and the Time Out logo are trademarks of Time Out Group Ltd.

**© Time Out Group Ltd 2005**
Previous edition 2003

10 9 8 7 6 5 4 3 2 1

**This edition first published in Great Britain in 2005 by Ebury Publishing**
Ebury Publishing is a division of The Random House Group Ltd,
20 Vauxhall Bridge Road, London SW1V 2SA

**Random House Australia Pty Limited** 20 Alfred Street, Milsons Point, Sydney, New South Wales 2061, Australia
**Random House New Zealand Limited** 18 Poland Road, Glenfield, Auckland 10, New Zealand
**Random House South Africa (Pty) Limited** Endulini, 5A Jubilee Road, Parktown 2193, South Africa

Random House UK Limited Reg. No. 954009

**Distributed in the USA by Publishers Group West**
1700 Fourth Street, Berkeley, California 94710

**Distributed in Canada by Penguin Canada Ltd**
10 Alcorn Avenue, Toronto, Ontario, Canada M4V 3B2

For further distribution details, see www.timeout.com

ISBN 1-904978-45-2

A CIP catalogue record for this book is available from the British Library

Colour reprographics by Icon, Crowne House, 56-58 Southwark Street, London SE1 1UN

Printed and bound in Germany by Appl

Papers used by Ebury Publishing are natural, recyclable products made from wood grown in sustainable forests

**Time Out Guides Limited**
**Universal House**
**251 Tottenham Court Road**
**London W1T 7AB**
Tel + 44 (0)20 7813 3000
Fax + 44 (0)20 7813 6001
Email guides@timeout.com
www.timeout.com

## Editorial

**Editors** Andrew Humphreys, Dave Rimmer
**Listings Editor** Lynn Perez
**Proofreader** Marion Moisy
**Indexer** Jackie Brind

**Editorial/Managing Director** Peter Fiennes
**Series Editor** Ruth Jarvis
**Deputy Series Editor** Lesley McCave
**Business Manager** Gareth Garner
**Guides Co-ordinator** Holly Pick
**Accountant** Kemi Olufuwa

## Design

**Art Director** Scott Moore
**Art Editor** Tracey Ridgewell
**Senior Designer** Oliver Knight
**Designer** Josephine Spencer
**Junior Designer** Chrissy Mouncey
**Freelance Designer** Tessa Kar
**Digital Imaging** Dan Conway
**Ad Make-up** Pete Ward

## Picture Desk

**Picture Editor** Jael Marschner
**Deputy Picture Editor** Tracey Kerrigan
**Picture Researcher** Helen McFarland

## Advertising

**Sales Director** Mark Phillips
**International Sales Manager** Ross Canadé
**International Sales Executive** Simon Davies
**Advertising Sales (Marrakech)** Aniko Boehler
**Advertising Assistant** Lucy Butler

## Marketing

**Marketing Director** Mandy Martinez
**Marketing & Publicity Manager, US** Rosella Albanese

## Production

**Production Director** Mark Lamond

## Time Out Group

**Chairman** Tony Elliott
**Managing Director** Mike Hardwick
**Group Financial Director** Richard Waterlow
**Group Commercial Director** Lesley Gill
**Group General Manager** Nichola Coulthard
**Group Circulation Director** Jim Heinemann
**Group Art Director** John Oakey
**Online Managing Director** David Pepper
**Group Production Director** Steve Proctor
**Group IT Director** Simon Chappell

**This guide was researched and written by Andrew Humphreys and Dave Rimmer, except:**

**History** (*Darling, I want a riad* Maggie Perry). **Gardens** Andrew Humphreys, Maggie Perry. **Shops & Services** Additional reviews by Delphine Mottet, Carinthia West (*The souk for dummies* Delphine Mottet). **Children** Lynn Perez. **Film** Tom Charity, Andrew Humphreys. **Music** Garth Cartwright, Andrew Humphreys, Dave Rimmer. **Nightlife** Additional reviews by Pablo Ganguli (*Gay Marrakech* Graham Lye). **Sport & Fitness** Andrew Humphreys, Lynn Perez (*Lions of the Atlas* Peterjon Cresswell).

**Maps** JS Graphics (john@jsgraphics.co.uk). The following maps are based on data supplied by New Holland Publishers - Casablanca, Essaouira, Fès, Marrakech, Rabat and Tangier. Maps on pages 65, 67 and 248-51 are based by data supplied by Jean Louis Dorveaux.

**Photography** Elan Fleisher, except: page 10 Musee des Augustins, Toulouse, France, Giraudon/ Bridgeman Art Library; pages 13, 15 Getty Images; page 16 Time Life; pages 20, 21, 23, 93, 94, 96, 157, 158, 161, 201, 202 Hadley Kincade; pages 122, 123 Viviana Gonzales; page 141 Corbis; pages 190, 209, 213, 214, 215, 217 Dave Rimmer.
The following images were provided by the featured establishments/ artists: pages 39, 112, 114, 115, 179, 197, 222.

The Editors would like to thank Graham Carter, Mounat Charrat, Lara Cleminson, Kevin Cote, Peterjon Cresswell, Esther Dalitz, Gadi Farfour, Adil El Fatimy, John Fitzsimons, Viviana Gonzalez, Volker Hauptvogel, Beatrix Maximo, Joanna Monkhouse, Delphine Mottet, Lynn Perez, Clay Perry, Maggie Perry, Mark Reeder, Frederic Scholl, Neil Tennant, Emma Wilson and all contributors to previous editions of *Time Out Marrakech & the best of Morocco*, whose work forms the basis for parts of this book.

# Contents

| | | | |
|---|---|---|---|
| Introduction | 6 | Music | 145 |
| | | Nightlife | 148 |
| **In Context** | **9** | Sport & Fitness | 156 |
| History | 10 | **Essaouira** | **165** |
| Marrakech Today | 22 | | |
| Architecture | 28 | Essaouira | 166 |
| Marrakech Style | 32 | *Map: Essaouira* | *172* |

**Where to Stay** — **37**

**The High Atlas & Sahara** — **189**

| | | | |
|---|---|---|---|
| Where to Stay | 38 | Getting Started | 190 |
| | | *Map: The High Atlas & Sahara* | *192* |
| **Sightseeing** | **63** | Tizi-n-Test to Taroudant | 196 |
| | | The Ourika Valley | 201 |
| Introduction | 64 | Tizi-n-Tichka to Ouarzazate | 203 |
| Koutoubia Mosque & | | The Dadès Valley & the Gorges | 208 |
| Jemaa El Fna | 67 | The Tafilelt & Merzouga | 213 |
| *Map: Jemaa El Fna* | *68* | The Drâa Valley | 218 |
| The Souks | 72 | | |
| *Map: The Souks* | *73* | **Directory** | **223** |
| The Kasbah & Mellah | 82 | | |
| Guéliz | 87 | Getting Around | 224 |
| Gardens | 90 | Resources A-Z | 227 |
| | | Vocabulary | 238 |
| **Eat, Drink, Shop** | **95** | Further Reference | 241 |
| | | Index | 243 |
| Restaurants & Cafés | 96 | Advertisers' Index | 248 |
| Shops & Services | 117 | | |

**Maps** — **249**

| | | | |
|---|---|---|---|
| **Arts & Entertainment** | **135** | Marrakech Overview | 250 |
| | | Marrakech Medina – North | 252 |
| Children | 136 | Marrakech Medina – South | 254 |
| Film | 139 | Guéliz/Hivernage | 256 |
| Galleries | 142 | | |

# Introduction

With its deep Islamic faith but parallel belief in everyday magic, a Medina organised around craft guilds and medieval methods, doggedly independent mountain tribesmen and ancient urban cultures, Marrakech is the city for which the word exotic was invented. It's the place where all the clichés come true. It's where the beggars really are blind and snakes are thoroughly charmed, where mounds of food are delivered on platters as bare-navelled bellydancers shimmy by the table, where herbalists in the souk sell jars of scorpions and exorcists with wildly darting eyes know what to do with them.

There is nowhere so close to Europe that gives such a strong sense of foreigness and mystery as Marrakech does, something that neither four and a half decades of French colonial occupation, nor the subsquent influence of tourism, has managed to erode. It's a place where the colourful and sensual fantasy of Oriental life can be indulged to the full – with a soothing herbal oil massage and cocktails afterwards.

The current passion for ethnicity and colour has conspired to make Marrakech the destination du jour. But that's nothing new. It was abfab in the 1930s when Charlie Chaplin and Rita Hayworth dropped in to play, in the '40s when Winstons Churchill frequented the Mamounia and in the '60s when it became drop-out central for assorted Beats, bohemians, heirs and heiresses. OK, so it went a little quiet for a while but these days such is the parade of A-list names swanning across the concourse of the city's rather modest international airport that one travel agency imposes a ten per cent surcharge on all celebrity bookings.

Marrakech's hip status has been further cemented in recent times by a string of absurdly stylish accommodations. Tailor-made for days of blissed-out indolence, they are completely addictive. Bearing in mind the cheap price of property here, more than a few visitors have returned home to tell friends, 'We liked the hotel so much, we bought one just like it.'

## ABOUT THE TIME OUT CITY GUIDES

This is the second edition of *Time Out Marrakech, Essaouira & the High Atlas*, one of an expanding series of Time Out guides produced by the people behind the successful listings magazines in London, New York and Chicago. Our guides are all written by resident experts who have striven to provide you with all the most up-to-date information you'll need to explore the city or read up on its background, whether you're a local or a first-time visitor.

## THE LIE OF THE LAND

Marrakech is a small city that neatly divides into two: the Medina, or old city, which is contained within the city walls, and the new city, which is everything outside the city walls. For a map showing the different city areas and how they relate to each other, *see pp250-51*. We've divided the Medina into two main areas, which are north of the main square and south of the main square; the square (Jemaa El Fna) and its surrounding neighbourhood also gets a chapter of its own. These area designations are a simplification of the city's geography and are not official names you'll see on signposts, we hope they'll help you to understand the city's layout and to find its most interesting sights. For consistency, the same areas are used in addresses throughout the guide. We've included map references in our addresses that point to our street maps at the back of the guide. For further orientation information, *see p64*.

## ESSENTIAL INFORMATION

For all the practical information you might need for visiting the area – including visa and customs information, details of local transport, a listing of emergency numbers, information on local weather and a selection of further reference material – turn to the **Directory** at the back of this guide. It begins on page 223.

## THE LOWDOWN ON THE LISTINGS

We have tried to make this book as easy to use as possible. Addresses, phone numbers, opening times and admission prices are all included in the listings. However, businesses can change their arrangements at any time. Before you go out of your way, we'd strongly advise you to phone ahead to check opening times and other particulars. While every effort and care has been made to ensure the accuracy of the information contained in this guide, the publishers cannot accept responsibility for any errors it may contain.

Introduction

## PRICES AND PAYMENT

We have noted where venues such as shops, hotels, restaurants and theatres accept the following credit cards: American Express (AmEx), Diners Club (DC), MasterCard (MC) and Visa (V). Many will also accept travellers' cheques. However, for important information regarding the use of credit cards, *see p233*.

The prices we've listed in this guide should be treated as guidelines, not gospel. If prices vary wildly from those we've quoted, ask whether there's a good reason. If not, go elsewhere. Then please let us know. We aim to give the best and most up-to-date advice, so we want to know if you've been badly treated or overcharged.

## TELEPHONE NUMBERS

The country code for Morocco is 212; the area code for Marrakech is 044. You must dial area codes with all numbers, even when calling a number within the same area code – but drop the zero if calling from abroad. For more on telephones and codes, *see p234*.

## LET US KNOW WHAT YOU THINK

We hope you enjoy the *Time Out Marrakech, Essaouira & the High Atlas Guide*, and we'd like to know what you think of it. We welcome tips for places that you consider we should include in future editions and take note of your criticism of our choices. You can email us your comments at guides@timeout.com.

# Advertisers

We would like to stress that no establishment has been included in this guide because it has advertised in any of our publications and no payment of any kind has influenced any review. The opinions given in this book are those of Time Out writers and entirely independent.

There is an online version of this book, along with guides to over 45 other international cities, at **www.timeout.com**.

# HEURE BLEUE
## PALAIS

A beautifully and sensitively renovated ancient fondouq in the heart of Essaouira that recreates the perfect atmosphere of a genuine ryad

A rooftop terrace offering an exceptional 360° view of the historic port of Essaouira and beyond, complete with swimming pool, solarium and bar

16 elegant rooms and 19 luxury themed suites designed in African, Oriental, Portuguese and English styles, all fully air-conditioned, complete with DVD players and fireplaces

Library • Billiards Room
Restaurant • Patio • Private
Screening Room
Turkish Baths

2 rue Ibn Batouta - Essaouira-Morocco
Tel: +212 44 78 34 34 - Fax: +212 44 47 42 22
e-mail: info@heure-bleue.com - web: www.heure-bleue.com

# In Context

History                              10
Marrakech Today                      22
Architecture                         28
Marrakech Style                      32


## Features

Winston's winter retreat             15
Portrait gallery                     18
Thanks God and the big
  white tent                         20
Darling, I want a riad               23
24-hour party people                 25

Moulay Abdel Rahman, The Sultan of Morroco by Eugène Delacroix.

# History

Founded by tribesmen, loved by the international jetset.

In the beginning, were the Berbers. Long before anyone thought of building a place called Marrakech, they were already here – before the Arabs came bearing Islam, before the rise and fall of Carthage and Rome, even before the Phoenicians. A Caucasian people, often light-skinned with fair hair and high cheekbones, their origins are lost in time. One theory is that they're descendants of the neolithic culture that stretched along Europe's Atlantic coast – a stone circle at Mzoura, near Asilah, is in similar style, and in a similar heathland location, to circles in Portugal, Brittany and southern England.

Over the centuries, the Berbers developed a complex clan system and dug into the Rif and Atlas mountains. There they remained unconquered, no matter what happened down on the plains. The Romans couldn't dislodge them. Neither could the Arabs, who ended up living alongside them. But though the Berbers had been unimpressed by Christianity, Islam took their fancy. The eighth-century Muslim conquest of Iberia was almost certainly achieved with an army of Berber converts.

Islam proved to be the cultural glue that would hold Morocco together. It condemned petty interests and local loyalties, and enabled a central authority to draw legitimacy from respect for its teachings. From here on, the history of Morocco is one of dynastic rule, but also of tension between central government and tribal independence, between the relatively orderly plains and coast – known as the *Bled El Makzhen* – and the ungovernable areas of mountain and desert – the *Bled Es Siba*. And as tribe after tribe forayed out of the Atlas or Sahara to found dynasties in the north, Marrakech would watch history from the border between the two.

### THE ALMORAVIDS (1062-1147)

The first such was the Almoravid dynasty. In the ninth and tenth centuries, trans-Saharan trade routes were established, mostly for gold – exchanged for salt in the Niger region. The main staging-post at this end was Sijilmassa, which stood near present-day Rissani in the Tafilelt oasis and thrived until the 14th century. There was ferocious competition for control of the caravan routes, but one tribe of nomadic Berbers came out on top. They ranged across the western Sahara from fortified religious settlements, known as *ribat*, and this gave them their name – El Mourabitoun, or Almoravids.

One of their leaders went off to Mecca and returned preaching against palm wine and having more than four wives. Newly fired with missionary fervour, the Almoravids subdued the south, crossed the Atlas and paused for breath. Being nomads, they'd never done much in the way of founding cities, but as their dominions grew they saw the wisdom in having a central store of weapons and food, and as a pious people they wanted somewhere to build a great mosque. It was 1062. At a location offering control of the most important Atlas passes, they founded Marrakech.

It began as a military outpost – no more than an encampment circled by thornbush – but, well placed on the route between Sahara and Atlantic, it soon also became a trading post. The original name was Marra Kouch. No one knows what it meant but the name lives on in both 'Marrakech' and 'Morocco'.

From this new base, the Almoravids quickly went on to conquer the whole of Morocco. In 1086 they landed in Spain, defeated the Christians and absorbed much of the Iberian peninsula. By the early 12th century their empire stretched from Lisbon to West Africa and from the Atlantic to Algeria.

Back in Marrakech, the Almoravids built what was by all accounts a spectacular city. Sadly, nothing survives except one little piece of their great big mosque – the small but exquisite **Koubba El Badiyin** (*see p75*). How grand must the Ali Ben Youssef Mosque have been if this was just its ablutions fountain?

The Almoravid legacy in Marrakech can still be felt in the city walls they erected and the palm groves they planted. They used their Saharan expertise to establish the water supply, building long underground pipes that conveyed Atlas meltwater to the fountains, pools and gardens of Marrakech.

### THE ALMOHADS (1147-1269)

By the mid 12th century, the Almoravids had overstretched themselves. There were reverses in Spain and unrest at home. A rival confederation of Berber tribes, the Almohads, scented blood.

The Almohads had their own *ribat*, the mountain fastness of Tin Mal (*see p198*) in the High Atlas. Armed with interpretations of Islam even more strict than their predecessors, the Almohads, whose name means 'unitarians', galloped out of the hills and placed Marrakech under siege. It took 11 unpleasant months, but in 1147 the city was theirs.

## 'The original name was Marra Kouch. No one knows what it meant.'

So they knocked it all down and rebuilt it – and, to be fair, did a beautiful job. The monumental architecture of this period still dominates Marrakech. The most stunning achievement was their own big mosque, the **Koutoubia** (*see p67*). Other significant period pieces include the **Kasbah Mosque** and **Bab Agnaou** (for both *see p82*) and the **Agdal** and **Menara gardens** (*see pp90-94*).

The greatest Almohad leader, Abdel Moumen, reconquered southern Spain and was victorious in Tunis, Tripoli and southern Algeria. During his reign, Marrakech became a bastion of Islamic civilisation and culture, a haven for scholars and philosophers.

### THE MERENIDS (1248-1554)

Like the Almoravids before them, the Almohads had overreached, losing their religious drive and running into trouble in Spain. And of course yet another nomadic Berber tribe was waiting to charge in, this one the Beni-Merens – Merenids – from the empty lands between Tafilelt and Algeria. Fès fell to them in 1248; Marrakech in 1269.

The Merenids ruled from Fès and, compared to the glory of the Almohad period, Marrakech fell upon hard times, reduced to the status of provincial outpost. This is the era of the great Muslim geographers and explorers such as Ibn Khaldun and Ibn Batuta (the Muslim Marco Polo). But it was a golden age in which Marrakech played little part except as a bastion against attacks from the south.

Following the pattern established by previous dynasties, by the 15th century the Merenids too were in decline and Europe was on the attack. This was the epoch of the great discoveries. The Portuguese explored the African coast, grabbing Mogador (present-day Essaouira) and other ports. With maritime routes opening up to the 'gold coast', the overland trans-Saharan trade routes, and with them the whole south of Morocco, were declining in importance. And the Christian incursions, which the Merenids had proved unable to resist, spawned a new kind of Islamic movement, based around leaders called *cherifs*, who claimed descent from the Prophet. The Saadians were one such movement.

### THE SAADIANS (1549-1668)
The Saadians arrived from Arabia in the 12th century and settled in the Drâa Valley. They lived peacefully among the palm groves and bothered no one for several hundred years. But when the 16th century rolled around, with the Portuguese all over the coast, rebellious Berber tribes roaming the interior and the Merenids pretty much confined to Fès and Marrakech, the Saadians decided it was time to restore order and repel the Christians.

They needed time to establish themselves. In 1510 they took the Sous valley and used the south of the Atlas city Taroudant as their capital. In 1541 they defeated the Portuguese at nearby Agadir. And in 1549 they dethroned the Merenids at Fès.

The Saadians returned the court to Marrakech and essentially refounded the city, which once more acquired the atmosphere of an imperial capital. Sultan Moulay Abdellah built a new Ali Ben Youssef Mosque and developed the similarly named *medresa* (*see p74*) into North Africa's biggest Koranic school. He gave the Jews their own quarter (*see p85* **Exodus**), the Christians their own trading centre at the heart of the Medina (roughly where Club Med is today), and sprinkled the city with fountains and hammams.

To celebrate victory over the Portuguese at Battle of the Three Kings (1578) – remembered as such because that's how many rulers lost their lives before it was over – the succeeding Sultan Ahmed El Mansour ('the Victorious'; 1578-1603) oversaw the construction of the lavish **Badii Palace** (*see p83*), importing 50 tons of marble from Italy. Another extravagance was the opulent mausoleums now known as the **Saadian Tombs** (*see p82*).

Much of this was paid for with gold from the Niger. In 1590 Ahmed led an army across the Sahara, reviving the trade routes, securing the salt mines, grabbing the gold and enslaving the locals. The whole area of the Western Sahara, Mauritania and Mali became a protectorate run by the Saadian pashas from Timbuktu.

### ENTER THE ALAOUITES
After Ahmed died in 1603, Morocco descended into civil war. Saadian rulers clung on to the Sous and Marrakech, while another tribe grabbed Fès and the strange pirate republic of the Bou Regreg briefly flourished in Rabat and Salé. It was clearly time for another dynasty to enter from the south.

The Alaouites were *cherifs* from Rissani in the Tafilelt, the same oasis that 600 years previously had nurtured the Almoravids. Like the Saadians before them, the Alaouites' route to power was a slow one; they took Taza and Fès before seizing Marrakech in 1668. Moulay Rachid was the first Alaouite Sultan, and though his reign was uneventful, his legacy lives on: the Alaouites still rule Morocco today.

> **'Sultan Moulay Ismail is said to have personally killed 30,000 people.'**

As in any family, there are the members no one likes to talk about – in this case, Rachid's younger brother and successor Moulay Ismail (1672-1727). Ismail hated Marrakech and built a new imperial capital at Meknès. He stripped the Badii Palace and, such was the wealth there, this took a team of labourers 12 years to complete. Marrakchis must have been glad to see the back of him, particularly as he turned out to be one of the most cruel and depraved rulers in the whole of Moroccan history. He is said to have personally killed 30,000 people, chopping off heads and doing a bit of disembowelling whenever the fancy took him. He also sired 888 children, ensuring succession problems. But there was method as well as madness. He kept at bay both the Europeans and the Ottomans, by now camped next door in Algeria, and one way or another made Morocco strong again.

Until, after a 54-year reign, he died. Ismail's authority had been enforced by his Black Guard, an army of descendants of slaves taken by the Saadians on their Timbuktu

Colonial adminstrator **Maréchal Lyautey** (*see p14*) dining with Sultan Moulay Youssef.

expeditions. With Ismail gone this force owed loyalty to no one and spent 30 years on the rampage, rendering Morocco ungovernable.

Somehow the Alaouite ruler Sidi Mohammed Ben Abdellah (1757-90) managed to get the Black Guard under control. He also rebuilt the Atlantic port of Mogador and renamed it Essaouira – its rational, almost rectilinear medina dates from his reign – and invited English, French and Jewish merchants to set up shop. But chaos resumed as soon as he died, followed by a period of isolationism towards Europe.

### THE 1800s: NO PROGRESS

By the early 19th century, Marrakech still hadn't progressed much beyond the Middle Ages. Dynasties had come and gone and it still made its living the same way it had done for 1,000 years, trading olive oil, corn, livestock, tanned leather, slaves and woven goods.

Meanwhile, the end of the Napoleonic Wars left European powers free to get on with colonial expansion. The French moved into Algeria in 1830, leaving Morocco under pressure and isolated from the rest of the Islamic world. France then defeated the

Moroccan army at the Battle of Isly in 1944, the Spanish added Tetouan to their conquests on the Mediterranean coast and grabbed the area that is now Western Sahara, and the British forced Sultan Abdel Rahman (1822-59) to sign a preferential trade treaty in 1857. But amazingly, as the 19th century drew to a close, Morocco remained just about the only bit of Africa that wasn't under some form of colonial rule.

Sultan Moulay Hassan (1873-94), the last pre-colonial ruler with any real power, used Marrakech as his southern capital. By this time the city had long been in decline – the 1875 *Encyclopaedia Britannica* noted holes in the walls big enough for a horseman to ride through and a Medina 'defaced by mounds of rubbish and putrid refuse'.

But Moulay Hassan was a moderniser. He tried to stabilise the currency, play off the Europeans against each other and shore up national defences. For funds he had no recourse save the traditional *harka* – the Sultan would set off somewhere with an army and entourage, collecting tribute in the manner of a swarm of locusts. In 1893, he returned from such an expedition in the Tafilelt dying and with his forces in disarray. Crossing the Atlas towards Marrakech via the Tizi-n-Tichka pass, he was offered sanctuary at Telouet, fortress of the Glaoua tribe.

Hassan's arsenal included an aged but still functional Krupp assault cannon. Such weapons had acquired a bizarre symbolic role as representative of the Sultan and his *cherifian* powers. People swore by them, prayed to them, kissed their barrels, brought them offerings of severed enemy heads, and believed them to possess healing powers.

Madani El Glaoui somehow fed and sheltered the Sultan's entire army for several days. In gratitude, Hassan declared him his personal representative in the Atlas and Sahara and left behind most of his armoury, including the 77mm bronze Krupp cannon. The Glaoua tribe thus acquired both a weird legitimacy and a fearsome arsenal. They set about subjugating the South.

## EUROPEAN INTERVENTION

Moulay Hassan died soon afterwards. He was succeeded by his young son, Abdel Aziz (1894-1908), but for the first few years Hassan's powerful vizier, Ba Ahmed Ben Moussa, carried on pulling the strings. He also spent the next six years building for himself the **Bahia Palace** (*see p85*). When Ba Ahmed died in 1900, Abdul Aziz was barely 20 years old.

Walter Harris, the *Times* correspondent whose *Morocco That Was* is a court insider's account of this period, paints a vivid picture of a country ripe for imperialist plucking. While his advisers feathered their nests, and the European powers contemplated a colonial carve-up of North Africa, the Sultan Abdel Aziz amused himself with games of cricket and bicycle polo, frittering away millions on toys and gadgets. These included a lift for a one-storey palace and a state coach for a country with no roads. Morocco was now heavily in debt to European banks.

European powers met to discuss matters at the 1906 Conference of Algeciras. This established Tangier's status as an international free port and affirmed the independence of the Sultan, but it also paved the way for the Protectorate by giving Spain and France a mandate to restore order, if necessary.

In 1907 Dr Emile Mauchamp, the first European doctor in Marrakech, made the mistake of attaching a radio aerial to his roof. Believing it to be black magic, a crowd chased him into an alley and killed him. Europeans were also lynched in Casablanca. This was all the excuse France needed to step in and occupy the city. Aziz was deposed by his brother, Moulay Hafid (1908-12), but faced with unrest, crippling debts and European aggression, Hafid

had little choice but to accept the imposition of French rule, formalised in the 1912 Treaty of Fès. He abdicated soon afterwards.

## FRENCH PROTECTORATE

The first French Résident Général (later Maréchal) of Morocco was one Louis Lyautey. He was to have an enormous effect on the country, building roads and railways, the ports of Casablanca and Kenitra, and adding new French-style towns to the old Medinas of Rabat, Fès, Meknès and Marrakech. The French basically dragged Morocco into the 20th century – except some of it didn't want to come along.

The old Bled El Makzhen became what the French called *Maroc Utile* – the useful bits of Morocco whose resources they would set about exploiting. The rest of the country – the old *Bled Es Siba* of mountains and desert – remained recalcitrant and unruly. Hardly was the ink dry on the Treaty of Fès than a tribal warlord called El Hiba appeared from the South and camped an army of 12,000 outside the walls of Marrakech. The French turned up to massacre them with modern machine-guns and mortars.

Machine-guns and mortars would soon also be firing in Europe, and the likelihood of war with Germany meant Lyautey would never have the forces needed to subdue the South. Instead, to keep a lid on the region, he struck a deal with the ruler of the powerful Glaoua tribe, Thami El Glaoui, who, along with his brother Madani, had recently backed the coup that placed Moulay Hafid on the throne. Thami was installed as *bacha* (lord) of Marrakech, while Madani was given command of all lands and tribes of the South. They were allowed to rule as they saw fit and in return gave their full support to the occupying power. Madani died in 1918, but Thami was to carry on for the next 42 years.

## LORD OF MARRAKECH

Ensconced in the lavish palace known as Dar El Bacha ('House of the Lord'), Thami El Glaoui took his place among the leading despots of Moroccan history, ruling Marrakech as would a Mafia boss. He hung the heads of his enemies from the gates, while his secret agents briefed him each evening on the goings-on in the Medina and brought in parades of suspects to be tried in his own personal *salon de justice*.

As the dungeons filled with prisoners and the coffers with cash, the Glaoui threw sumptuous banquets for European dignitaries while his henchmen combed the countryside for girls to stock the harem. The Glaoui funded his extravagant lifestyle by grabbing local

# Winston's winter retreat

It was January 1943. The Casablanca Conference had just ended and British Prime Minister Winston Churchill and US President Franklin D Roosevelt were tidying away their declarations of unity and commitment. Roosevelt intended to head straight back to America, but Churchill had other ideas: 'You cannot come all the way to North Africa without seeing Marrakech,' he told the President. And so, with an escort of armoured cars and fighter planes, the two war leaders drove south.

Soon after their arrival at Villa Taylor, a Guéliz mansion leased by the US Consul, two servants made a chair of their arms and carried wheelchair-bound Roosevelt up to the roof terrace. Reclining on a divan, taking in the scene of setting sun and snowy mountains, he was moved to remark, 'I feel like a sultan; you may kiss my hand, my dear.' We don't know whether Winston obliged, but his doctor's diary records that as the party watched twilight settle over Marrakech, Churchill murmured: 'It's the most lovely spot in the world.'

Churchill had discovered Marrakech on holiday in December 1935. First he'd visited Tangier, where his ancestor John Churchill served as a lieutenant in 1668. Then on 26 December he joined former PM Lloyd George at the Mamounia (*see p42* **Mamounia**). It was the start of a long-running relationship with the hotel; between 1935 and 1959 Churchill came to Marrakech six times and the Mamounia was his headquarters on all peacetime visits.

'I am captivated by Marrakech,' he wrote in the *Daily Mail* of his first visit. 'Here in the spacious palm groves rising from the desert the traveller can be sure of perennial sunshine, of every comfort and diversion, and can contemplate with ceaseless satisfaction the stately and snow-clad panorama of the Atlas mountains. The sun is brilliant and warm but not scorching; the air crisp, bracing without being chilly; the days bright, the nights cool and fresh.'

He was here twice during World War II. Later, out of power, and with doctors prescribing warmer climes in winter, Churchill returned in December 1947. Mornings and late nights were devoted to his wartime memoirs (most of *Volume I: The Gathering Storm* was written in Marrakech), while

afternoons were reserved for painting, his favourite hobby. Apart from on his balcony or in the Mamounia gardens, he'd also set up his easel by the ramparts or in a corner of the Medina. Some evenings he would be entertained by the Glaoui, Winnie's patience tested by interminable dinners at the Dar El Bacha.

His last visit was in January 1959, when he flew in accompanied by his wife Clementine and three dozen bottles of Pol Roger. King Mohammed V was here to greet him and the French airbase changed its flying schedules to avoid waking the great man too early. Churchill checked out of the Mamounia on 18 February 1959 and travelled with Aristotle Onassis to Safi, where he boarded the magnate's ship, the *Christina*, for a Canary Island cruise. He would never return to Morocco. The only legacy of his relationship with Marrakech is the dozen or so oils he painted of his 'loveliest spot', and the suite named after him at the Mamounia.

'Lord of the Atlas' **Thami El Glaoui**. *See p14*.

monopolies in hemp, olives, almonds, saffron, dates, mint and oranges. Soon, he enjoyed greater power than the puppet Sultan and Marrakech rivalled in importance the new capital, Rabat.

But there was one snag. Madani had handed control of the lands beyond the Atlas to his son-in-law, Hemmou, who now sat in Telouet between Thami and the rest of the South. Wealthy, ruthless and equipped with an arsenal

greatly expanded since the original Krupp cannon, he was also obstinately anti-French. For this reason the South was never 'pacified' – and the Protectorate not fully established – until after his death in 1934. It's also why the French Foreign Legion built the Tizi-n-Tichka road over a difficult route avoiding Telouet.

But despite all this, the Glaoui enjoyed the wholehearted support of the French administration. His despotic regime left them free to exploit Morocco's phosphates, iron, anthracite, manganese, lead and silver. Agriculture also flourished, as French companies turned traditional olive groves and orchards into industrialised enterprises.

## NATIVES AND TOWN-PLANNING

Lyautey was on a civilising mission. 'I have always had two passions,' he said, 'policies regarding the natives and town-planning'. Thus Marrakech acquired a *nouvelle ville* just outside the Medina, later to become known as Guéliz. Lyautey was explicit that this new quarter – like similar projects in other Moroccan cities – had to be separate from the Medina in order to 'protect the autonomy of each'. This can be read two ways: on the one hand, a respect for Moroccans and a commendable desire not to interfere with the traditional organisation of their cities; on the other, an enforced segregation with nice new quarters for the white folks and the natives confined to crowded and insanitary medinas.

For the new Marrakech a town planner named Henri Prost laid out a scheme of large *rondpoints* connected by broad, leafy avenues. Camp Guéliz, a military fort on a rocky outcrop just north of the new town, provided security. Almost as significantly, Prost was one of the architects behind the opulent new Mamounia hotel, built in 1922 by the Moroccan national rail company. Thus Guéliz received all the roads, railway connections, hospitals and schools; the Medina remained in squalor.

Lyautey's town-planning formalised the gulf between Moroccans and Europeans. By the 1930s there were 325,000 of the latter in the country. The staggering inequality between the 'colos' and the locals was a major factor in stoking support for a nationalist movement. This found political voice in the Istiqlal (Independence) Party, formed in Rabat and Fès. World War II provided further momentum. The French army had included 300,000 Moroccan soldiers. These acquitted themselves so ably that Franklin D Roosevelt, who had travelled to Casablanca to meet Churchill for a conference (*see p15* **Winston's winter retreat**), hinted to the new Sultan, Mohammed V, that, after the war, the country would become independent.

## TOWARDS INDEPENDENCE

Mohammed V had succeeded his father in 1927. He was young but in no way content to be a puppet. After the war, he began to press for independence. With membership of the Istiqlal Party mushrooming, the French began to get nervous. In 1953, with the help of the Glaoui (who imprisoned his own son for nationalist sympathies), they sent Mohammed V into exile. This proved a mistake, confirming him as a nationalist figurehead. His expulsion sent the country into turmoil, triggering riots in Marrakech and Casablanca. There was a clampdown on both cities, with curfews, arrests and interrogation under torture. A week after the Sultan's expulsion, 13,000 Moroccans had been arrested for treason.

By the summer of 1955 a campaign for the Sultan's return had escalated into armed rebellion. Terrorists tossed a bomb into a Casablanca café, killing seven Europeans. In Marrakech, a bomb was lobbed into the Berima Mosque where Ben Arafa, France's new puppet Sultan, was praying.

The Glaoui advised the French to 'do as the British did with the Mau Mau' – a reference to the particularly brutal campaign in Kenya, where nationalists had been slaughtered in their thousands. Given such an attitude towards his fellow Moroccans, it's perhaps not surprising that, when being driven around in his Bentley, the Glaoui only felt safe on the floor with a submachine gun clutched to his chest.

Hands already full with a bloody nationalist revolt in Algeria, the French decided to cut their losses in Morocco. In November 1955 Mohammed V was permitted to return. The Glaoui was furious, but kissed the Sultan's feet and begged for mercy. Punitive measures were unnecessary as the Glaoui was dying of cancer. He succumbed on 30 January 1956.

> **'Allies of the Glaoui were dragged outside the city walls to be doused in petrol and set alight.'**

What should have been a joyous occasion for Marrakech quickly turned ugly – as if even in death the Glaoui could bring terror to the streets. A rampaging mob chanted 'Death to the traitors!'. Old allies of the Glaoui were hunted down, stripped, stoned and dragged outside the city walls to be doused in petrol and set alight. Children gathered around, laughing and cheering as victim upon victim was thrown on to the bonfires.

The new governors of Marrakech did nothing to halt the rioting but placed guards round the smouldering bodies so that women could not take pieces of them for black magic. The corpse of the Glaoui himself was spared any indignities and interred, with full French military honours, at the Shrine of Sidi Ben Slimane. Three months later, with France fully engaged in a bloody war against the nationalists in Algeria, Morocco was granted its independence.

## SOVEREIGN MOROCCO

It was March 1956. The first act of the Sultan was to restyle himself as King Mohammed V, a modern constitutional monarch. But not too modern: the monarchy was still at the centre of political life, and the King kept the military on a short leash. He was rightly worried that the jubilation following independence would be short-lived; the nationalist movement quickly disintegrated into rival factions. The left-wing of the Istiqlal Party broke away to form the socialist UFSP, with the King lending his support to the more moderate Mouvement Populaire.

Mohammed V never lived to see the first democratic election. Presided over by his son, King Hassan II, in 1963, it was won by a coalition of royalists and the Mouvement Populaire. The socialists claimed that the polls had been rigged. Their leader, Ben Barka, denounced the monarchy and was exiled to Paris, where he was assassinated by secret agents. So much for the new Morocco.

Much of the period's civil unrest was the result of poverty compounded by a series of natural disasters. In 1961 locusts devastated crops around Marrakech. Severe drought added to the country's woes, as did the catastrophic

# Thanks God and the Big White Tent

In 1972, Maggie Perry, her husband Clay and eight-year-old daughter Sarah travelled to Marrakech for the first time. They returned in 1999 and now own a riad, a farm, a donkey, a horse and two chameleons there. Perry's account of sharing her life with Morocco, *Thanks God and the Big White Tent*, will be published in 2006.

'A friend, Sydney Bigman, had invited us to visit him in Marrakech. A small windfall meant we had some money and we were going to be his house guests for a month.

We were on a low budget so we had flown to Spain and taken the ferry to Tangier. From the port we took the train to Marrakech – the "Marrakech Express" of the Crosby, Stills and Nash song, which had arrived in London just a couple of years back. We sped through a landscape of small isolated villages, tin roofs glinting in the sun, the plains between scattered with cactus hedges, wild narcissus and irises. Horsemen would suddenly appear to gallop alongside the train. On the train, strange, hooded, hobbit-like figures shuffled along the corridor as the lights flickered on and off, worked by a dynamo I think. And every carriage was pungent with the heavy smell of *kif*.

At one point in the night, the train lurched to a halt somewhere close to the middle of nowhere. Clay announced that he'd get off and go and find us some food. Terrified that he'd be left behind, Sarah and I went with him. A short distance away, in the pool of light cast by a kerosene lamp, a man in a pointy hood was hunched over a charcoal grill cooking brochettes. We bought and ate and returned to the train that I was so sure was going to disappear into the night without us.

We arrived at Marrakech at five in the morning, far too early to arrive at someone's house. We found our way to the place Jemaa El Fna, the square at the heart of the Medina, and took refuge at the only place open, the "Wimpy bar" – the name of the British snackbar chain shamelessly nicked and attached to a rickety coffeeshop.

The waiter at the Wimpy knew where Sydney's house was – we later found that everybody knew where Sydney's house was. He led us to an enormous studded wooden door, which was opened to admit us into the most beautiful riad. A riad is a courtyard house, all the rooms face inwards and from the outside in the narrow street it's impossible to know what the doors conceal. Sydney's riad had a fountain courtyard with orange and apricot trees. The rooms were beautiful with tiles and low beds buried under Moroccan rugs.

Sydney's house was doubly enchanting because it acted as a sort of cultural salon. A troupe of gnawa dancers and musicians would appear most evenings to entertain the almost constant presence of assorted writers and painters that were encouraged by Sydney to drop by. We were there one night when one of the Beat poets, Ted Joans, arrived. He announced that he'd just come back from Timbuktu and regaled us with tales of his journey through the desert by camel. He'd bought a house there cheap simply so that when people asked where he came from he could reply, "I'm from Timbuktu". This wasn't the first time we'd met Joans, we'd met him before in Shakespeare & Co, the Left Bank bookshop in Paris. But how unexciting and mundane Paris seemed from where we were sitting now.'

1961 earthquake in Agadir, which killed 15,000. Hassan II nationalised much of the economy, expropriating land from French companies. But most of this land was reserved for export crops and did nothing to feed the domestic population. By the mid 1960s Morocco – once called 'the bread basket of the Roman Empire' – had become a net importer of cereals.

As poverty increased, mass migration to the cities followed. Sprawling, overcrowded shanty towns – known as *bidonvilles* – sprang up on the edge of Marrakech and other major cities. A whole uncontrolled economy developed. Marrakech was soon packed with illegal taxi drivers, street peddlers and hustlers. The rise of hashish farming also fuelled the black economy and helped spawn a new kind of tourism.

### SEX AND DRUGS AND ROCK 'N' ROLL
North Africa had long held romantic resonance for European intellectuals: a haven for 19th-century bohemians, it had been a source of inspiration for writers and painters from Gustave Flaubert and Eugène Delacroix to André Gide and Henri Matisse.

The bohemian tradition continued into the 20th century when the licentious enclave of Tangier – designated an International Zone under the joint rule of France, Spain, Britain, Portugal, Sweden, Holland, Belgium, Italy and the USA – attracted the likes of Paul Bowles and William Burroughs. In 1956 the International Zone was absorbed into independent Morocco and the expats began drifting south to Marrakech, lured by its balmy climate and colourful exoticism.

In accordance with Beat philosophy, the spiritual went hand in hand with the sexual. The Marrakech brothels were infamous, particularly among gays (sun and sex in Marrakech remains a favourite with ageing American and European queens to this day). And, of course, there was the *kif*, or cannabis, which was smoked openly.

Brian Jones of the Rolling Stones made his first trip in 1966 with his girlfriend Anita Pallenberg. He brought the rest of the band with him on the next visit; they drove from Tangier to Marrakech and checked into the Hotel Es Saadi. There they tripped on LSD and ran into Cecil Beaton, who photographed Mick and Keith by the pool. At the centre of the scene were the American oil heir John Paul Getty Jr and his wife Talitha. The Gettys owned a place in the Medina, where they were famously photographed in kaftans up on the roof terrace against a backdrop of Koutoubia and the Atlas Mountains. Here they hosted parties that went on for days at a time. An entry in John Hopkins's *The Tangier Diaries* for 1 January

1968 reads: 'Last night Paul and Talitha Getty threw a New Year's Eve party at their palace in the Medina. Paul McCartney and John Lennon were there, flat on their backs. They couldn't get off the floor let alone talk. I've never seen so many people out of control.'

### THE UNKILLABLE KING
While the foreigners carried on, members of the royal court were plotting to get rid of their ruler. In 1971 the King's 42nd birthday party was gatecrashed by 1,400 army cadets who loosed machine-gun fire at the 800 or so diplomatic guests lounging around the pool. The coup leader was accidentally killed in the crossfire and the cadets panicked, at which point the King, who had hidden in a bathroom, emerged and coolly stared down his would-be assassins, who dropped their weapons and rushed to kiss his hands and feet. The failed coup had left 98 guests dead.

> **'As the King and his party ran for cover three more rebel aircraft continued to strafe the runway.'**

Thirteen months later the King's Boeing 727 was attacked in the air by six F5 fighters from his own airforce. One of the jet's engines was destroyed but the pilot managed to land at Rabat. As the King and his party ran for cover three more rebel aircraft continued to strafe the runway and the officials who had been waiting to greet the King on the ground were killed and close to 50 wounded. The minister of defence committed suicide, there were summary executions, the pilot was promoted and the King got back to ruling the country.

In 1975 he seized the Spanish colony of Rio del Oro in the Western Sahara. He did so by organising the 'Green March', in which 350,000 citizens marched into the territory from Marrakech. General Franco had just died and Spain relinquished the colony without much fuss. But the colony's residents had other ideas. Polisario, a nationalist group comprised of the indigenous Sahrawi tribe, proclaimed a republic. Backed by the Algerians, they waged a guerrilla war of independence against Morocco until a ceasefire in 1991. The situation remains unresolved today.

The same year as the Polisario ceasefire, the King dispatched 1,200 troops to Saudi Arabia as a gesture of support to the US-led Gulf War operation. It was not a popular move – Arab versus Arab – and resulted in rioting and worse: in 1994 Islamic extremists attacked a

# Portrait gallery

Portraits of leaders are a feature of authoritarian societies, where the nation is supposedly embodied in the person of a charismatic leader. Hanging one up on the wall is a sign of loyalty. Or conformism. Or simply because to do otherwise would be to invite unwelcome attention from the secret police. You might not particularly want to put up a picture of the King, but if you don't then people might talk.

The days are probably gone when ordinary Moroccans need worry about being dragged off to some dungeon. The heavy-handed Hassan II inspired considerable fear, but Mohammed VI is clearly a more liberal-minded fellow. Still, you'll see his likeness everywhere, on roadside banners and billboards, in both government offices and private businesses. On some hillsides in the South, white stones are laid to spell out in giant letters: 'God, Country, King'. Moroccans, like Britons, are subjects, not citizens. And here the King still rules OK.

But there aren't really official portraits in the way there were in, say, Communist-era Russia or China. A Mao or Stalin was represented by a unitary, approved image that – as Andy Warhol twigged – was more of a graphic icon than a human likeness. Portraits of Mohammed VI are as varied as can be, and seem to show a human being rather than an idealised symbol of authority.

The game in shops and businesses, given that they more or less have to have one, is finding a picture appropriate to their enterprise. A café might show Mohammed VI drinking a coffee. In a kaftan shop, he'll be wearing traditional garb. At the fake Ray-Ban stall, he'll be sporting designer shades. Even the humble shoeshine guy might pin on his

wooden box of brushes a picture of the King shod in something highly polished. You see it immediately at the airport. At the kiosk of car-rental company First-Car – logo: blue and yellow – the King is pictured wearing blue tie and yellow lapel badge. And in the nearby teléboutique, Hassan II is pictured talking on the phone.

hotel in Marrakech, spraying the lobby with machine-gun fire and killing two Spanish tourists. Hassan II reacted with the ruthless suppression characteristic of his reign, involving arbitrary arrests, 'disappearances' and widespread abuses of human rights and judicial norms. It's a darker side to the King's rule that has only recently been aired in public, most notably in the furore surrounding 2004's publication of a novel by Moroccan writer Tahar Ben Jelloun (*see p241*) that focused on the fate of detainees in Hassan II's desert concentration camps.

## THE KING OF COOL

Hassan II died of a heart attack in July 1999 and was succeeded by his then 36-year-old eldest son, who became King Mohammed VI. Popular approval greeted his pledge to a multiparty political system, respect for human rights and improved rights for women. Some progress has been made towards these goals. Early in his reign the King dismissed his father's much-feared interior minister, political exiles were allowed to return and political detainees were released. In 2004 a Justice and Reconciliation Authority was set up to

Portraits of Hassan II are still common, and comparing pics of father and son you can see a distinct shift in style. When Hassan II was shown riding a stallion or teeing up at the 18th hole, it was to present him as master of everything, first Moroccan in all things. The more informal pictures of Mohammed VI, holding his baby or laughing

at something off-camera, are saying that he shares these ordinary human things with everyone, that he is close to the people.

If you feel like hanging one at home or in your workplace, pictures of Mohammed VI can be found at stationery or photographic shops, and on book and newspaper stalls around the Jemaa El Fna.

investigate the human rights abuses of the past. The same year, the rights of women were improved by a rewriting of the *moudawana* (the laws governing personal rights) to restrict polygamy and give women equal rights to men in marriage, divorce and the care of children.

Marrakech has definitely prospered under the influence of the new King. Although the official royal residence is in Rabat, Mohammed VI spends as much time as he can in the Pink City – said to be his favourite place in Morocco. He removed the red tape obstructing foreign investment, triggering the current property

boom in the Medina, and cracked down on the touts and hustlers. He was also instrumental in launching the Marrakech film festival in 2001.

The young King is a genuinely popular ruler, despite recent press revelations that he costs Moroccan taxpayers £144.6 million a year – 18 times more than Britain's Queen Elizabeth II. But it's hard not warm to someone who speaks with such frankness: *Time* magazine asked him what advice his father gave him; the King answered, 'He told me that the most important thing was "to last." I do not know what he meant.' Well, good luck to him anyway.

# Marrakech Today

## Was that George Clooney on the back of that donkey? In Marrakech it might well be.

There's this club, right. It's a private members' affair in beautiful surrounds, with several lounging salons, a restaurant, bar, library and a handful of bedrooms for overnighters. The list of persons who belong to this most exclusive of establishments reads like an international who's who of former newspaper editors, gallery owners, news-network vice presidents, writers, filmmakers and artists. At the club a G&T costs £8 and annual membership is a sweet £5,000. *Wallpaper** magazine garlanded the place as simply 'the best club' (January 2005). And where is this most fabulous of hangouts? Why, in Marrakech, of course.

Meanwhile, there's Colin Farrell draining the bar at Le Meridien, the Beckhams in town renewing their vows, Tracey Emin scooting through the back alleys of Mouassine, Scarlett Johansson accessorising her outfit in the leather souk, Angeline Jolie looking for more waifs to adopt... So how did a small, provincial, near-dry (in all senses) city in North Africa get to be such an international jetsetting hotspot?

Fast rewind to the 1960s. It was back then that the foundations were laid for the Western fantasy of Marrakech, a city where all eccentricities are permitted, solitude is not considered antisocial, genuinely individual style has room to flourish and lassitude is never out of season. There were Mick and Keith being

photographed by the pool while bright young hope of the fashion world Yves Saint Laurent came house-hunting, along with Diana Vreeland of *Vogue*, the Gettys, the odd Rothschild, and sundry rich and famous. It was the alter ego of London and Paris, a place where the fast-living jetset went to shed their social skins and professional identities. As Saint Laurent described it, the city was a 'place out of time' – but that was probably just the *majoun*.

In fact, Marrakech had been fulfilling much the same role since the 1920s, when the same mixture of local colour, Orientalist mystique and a liberating remove from the West captured the imagination of an earlier generation of millionaires and aristos. The social circle then revolved around the Villa Taylor, built in 1923 by the Taylors of Newport, Rhode Island, who came to Morocco on a steam yacht. Its guest rooms played host to Rita Hayworth and Charlie Chaplin, Winston Churchill (*see p15* **Winston's winter retreat**) and Franklin D Roosevelt. The story goes that when Mrs Taylor learned that FDR had spent the night at her house, she refused ever to set foot in it again and the place was sold to the Countess Boul de Breteuil (who, according to John Hopkins' *The Tangier Diaries*, had a seamstress who'd undergone a mastectomy and used her false breast as a pincushion). Anyway, for all those

'60s *arrivistes*, a homage-paying stop at the Villa Taylor was an essential part of the Marrakech social itinerary.

When the scene moved on, as scenes do, and everything went a bit *Hideous Kinky* – all tie dyes and patchouli oil – not all of the seasonal migrants departed. Figures such as American interior designer Bill Willis, French designer Jacqueline Fossaic and Yves Saint Laurent stayed on. Having settled on Marrakech, they wanted to make their homes in traditional style rather than heading for the new city (location of Villa Taylor), so many began restoring houses in the Medina.

## FLIGHT TO THE MEDINA

It seems obvious now that the Medina is where anyone would want to live, but during the French Protectorate, which ended only in 1956, the old walled city suffered. In their respect for indigenous life, the French authorities left the Medina well alone and built their new European quarters outside the city walls. What nobody perhaps foresaw was that the Moroccans also preferred to live in the new European neighbourhoods, where houses had modern amenities such as plumbing and the streets were surfaced and wide enough for cars. Money began moving out of the Medina, a trend that continued long after the French had gone.

However, that first European and American incursion into the Medina set in motion a sea change from which the city is currently reaping the benefits. Where Willis and Co went others followed. Their numbers were small but the investment was significant, not just in terms of hard cash but also in revitalising traditional skills like tiling, stucco-carving and woodworking. The market for high-quality craftsmanship boomed, and soon local Marrakchis began to pick up on what was going on.

In 1990 entrepreneur Abdelatif Ben Abdellah bought his first riad, renovated it with the help of young Belgian architect Quentin Wilbaux, and sold it on. While searching for other suitable properties, Ben Abdellah and Wilbaux became alarmed by the state of houses they were seeing, so they went to the Ministry of Culture to talk about what could be done to preserve the city's heritage. 'What heritage?' said the Ministry. So the pair set up Marrakech Medina, a company devoted to restoring as much of the Medina as two driven individuals could possibly manage.

To date, the number of old houses worked on by Abdelatif is into double figures but along the way the whole scenario acquired momentum beyond anyone's imaginings. The catalyst can be pinpointed with absolute accuracy: a French

# Darling, I want a riad

A month spent in Marrakech in the 1970s kicked off the affair. I fell in love with the place. My husband sighed and hoped it would pass. For a while it did and I flirted with Crete, but then a return visit to Morocco in 1996 on a quest for winter warmth rekindled the flame and the 'Marrakech project' took hold. In 1999 we began combing the ancient alleys of the Medina. We were looking for a house that we could also run as a B&B to cover costs. Aided by two local friends, over the course of three visits we looked at around 100 different properties. Nothing was suitable. We were on the verge of giving up when we walked into the courtyard of one last riad and knew instantly that it was the one.

The house was in a state of total neglect but the structure was sound. We swiftly agreed a price and visited the *notaire*. The notaire's job is to establish that deeds are 'clean' – that is, that everybody who owns the house agrees to sell. Because of the laws of inheritance Marrakech houses are typically owned by dozens of family members and

every last one of them has to agree to the sale. It can take weeks, months or even years to track them all down. Fortunately, that wasn't the case with our house.

The riad needed complete restoration. We had architect friends in the UK draw up plans and located a local builder in Marrakech. Foolishly, we paid the builder in three tranches according to an agreed contract, and as soon as the third payment was made work fizzled out well short of completion. We turned to another friend, a local, who called in builders from his neighbourhood mosque, as well as assorted relatives to make curtains and mattresses. The work was completed on schedule. The riad was kitted out by local craftsmen (five brothers handcrafted the furniture) and from the neighbouring souks.

From start to finish the project took around a year. We now have a gorgeous second home, which is also a thriving little business and, best of all, a whole bunch of loyal Marrakech friends.

*By Maggie Perry, of Riad Magi (see p55).*

Marrakech: "A place out of time".

TV feature on Morocco screened in the mid 1990s, during which the presenter reported that for the price of a small flat in Paris one could buy a palace in Marrakech. The next day Ben Abdellah's phone went mad with excited calls from France wanting to know if he'd got any palaces he could sell them.

A little over five years on and at last count over 600 houses in the Medina had been bought by foreigners, mainly French, although the Italians and Brits are fast catching up. Prices have skyrocketed and, for a Moroccan, real estate is the business to be in (although they are no longer interested in selling to locals because foreigners pay so much more). Even at the most inflated rates, a pretty little Marrakchi *dar* (house) or *riad* (a house with courtyard garden) still represents an attractive buy. A property with perhaps three bedrooms and a couple of spare salons arranged around a planted inner court open to the sky probably sets you back around £40,000. What's that in London terms, a garden shed in Dagenham? Most of the foreign-bought properties are converted into guest accommodation, either rented out whole or run as *maisons d'hôtes*.

Riad fever has made Marrakech a staple of the glossy travel porn spreads. *Elle Decoration, Homes & Gardens* and *Wallpaper\** are read more avidly in Guéliz coffeeshops than any daily newspapers. This brings problems, as each new arrival on the Marrakech scene now has to outdo its predecessors to be sure of coverage (proud owners carry the clippings in top pockets). Sleek and stylish is no longer enough. New properties have to razzle and dazzle with stage-set decor: a central water basin the size of a football pitch; waterways snaking round the property; re-creations of Alhambran courts. They have to up the ante on services offered, adding cigar lounges, 'house' camels or pick-ups from the airport in an air-conditioned London Hackney cab.

With the architecture of many new developments teetering towards parody – 'traditional' Moroccan via the filter of West Coast America – Marrakech has come to resemble a kind of North African Las Vegas.

**FOREIGNERS WELCOME**

All those Manola Blahniks tottering through the dusty alleys of the Medina – you have to wonder what the locals make of it. More to the point, 600 foreign-owned residences represents about five per cent of Old City occupancy. On some streets there is barely a single Moroccan family remaining. But on the whole locals see this mild foreign infestation as a good thing.

# 24-hour party people

A ten-minute drive south of central Marrakech is a small factory complex used until recently for processing sugar cane. It's an attractive set of brick buildings and it's surrounded by acres of open land. In Europe or America some smart property developer would snap it up for conversion into a chic, post-industrial office space or some apartment housing. Alternatively, it might make the perfect shell for a small museum or arts complex. But this is Marrakech, and so the empty building has been filled with designer chairs and tables and assorted high campery and is now available for hire as a party venue.

Partying is big business in this town. Ever since Sting's much-publicised big bash at the Amanjena – which got called off in the wake of 9/11 – anyone with a cause to celebrate and money to burn heads for the Pink City. Colonel Qaddafi's son hired out the Sugar Factory; P Diddy cut loose at Comptoir.

But it's not just celebs. The pocket-sized nature of Marrakech's myriad riads makes them perfect for exclusive hire. Almost any riad is happy to rent out the property in its entirety. These can range from four bedrooms (sleeping eight) to 20 or more. For your money (starting from as little as £1,000 for a whole riad for a week) you'll get staff and a cook thrown in. Most riad owners can also organise extras such as in-house entertainment – belly-dancers, musicians, snake charmers (*see p70* **Those charming men**) – or restaurant and club bookings.

Requests can and do go far beyond those norms. Joanne Penny, a UK-based events planner (www.destinationmarrakech.co.uk) has fielded requests for 40 people to go boar hunting, while in-demand party planner Lynn Perez (lynnperez@menara.ma) has been asked in the past to provide elephants for a bride and groom to ride, and for a military guard of honour to escort a birthday boy to his table. Nothing, she says, is impossible, it just might cost a hell of a lot of money – as in the case of elephants, which are not native to North Africa, and which, in the end, were replaced by camels.

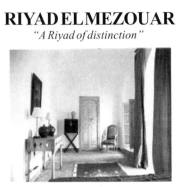

Koutoubia Gardens. *See p68.*

There's the odd instance of cultural clash – topless Spaniards on the terraces, boozy English singalongs with the call to prayer – but ask around and most locals will tell you that the majority of foreigners are properly respectful of Moroccan ways and traditions.

Not that any great concessions have to be made. Morocco might be Islamic but in terms of severity it's closer to Bradford than Tehran, while Marrakech is so far removed from the national centres of political power (Rabat) and religion (Fès) that it enjoys an even greater degree of liberalism.

Any gulf between foreign residents and locals is going to focus not on religion but on money. The country as a whole suffers from widespread poverty, illiteracy and more than 20 per cent unemployment. Moroccans are pinning their hopes on their new king. Under 40 and dynamic, Mohammed VI (M6 to his young fans) won great initial approval when soon after ascending to the throne in 1999 he sacked scores of government officials to make way for reform. Then, when the story got round that after dining at the Mamounia the King pulled out his wallet to settle the tab, his popularity went through the ceiling.

The King also happens to like Marrakech and his patronage is the other major factor in the city's current high profile. His intentions were signalled when he built himself a new modestly sized residence just inside the city walls as a more homely alternative to the rambling palace favoured by his predecessors, and by his appointment of the new *wali*. The wali is the governor and the guy who actually runs the city. The person that the King chose for the job is, like his boss, relatively young and has a reputation for getting things done; he is also an ex-chairman of Royal Air Maroc – that is, someone who understands tourism. This is

important given that the king has stated his wish to see the present figure of 2.5 million visitors to Morocco per year boosted to ten million by 2010.

Together, M6 and the wali are on the right track. One of their first initiatives, for example, was to snip away at the red tape and make it easier for foreigners to acquire property. This was aimed specifically at encouraging the growth of riad-style accommodation, creating jobs while helping to preserve the Medina. After a survey showed that few first-time visitors to Marrakech would ever consider coming back, the dynamic duo also cracked down on the legions of aggressive touts who used to make trips into the souk unbearable.

Not all the changes are for the better. In 2004 the Jemaa El Fna was paved over and the ragtag chain of orange-sellers' carts that ringed the square were replaced by uniform, coach-like barrows. It's a misguided attempt to impose order on a phenomenon whose very appeal lies in chaos.

There are other worrying portents too. Accommodation has to be found for the King's additional 7.5 million visitors. To this end a 100-hectare site on the southern outskirts of town has been set aside as an 'international hotel and restaurant' zone, a building site reserved for a threatened slew of five-star chain properties. This is where a massive new 3,000-capacity super club Pacha (*see p154*) opened in Frebruary 2005 – the jury is still out on that one.

All of which begs the question, what happens when a city that thrives on exclusivity and vicarious tourism becomes inundated? Can Marrakech sustain its niche appeal in the face of a possible onslaught of Hiltons, Inter-Continentals and Best Westerns? Our advice: book that flight now.

Koubba El Badiyin.

# Architecture

Arab artisans and Berber mud builders conspire
to create high art.

When the Arab commander Oqba Ben Nafi
spurred his horse into the surf of the
Atlantic in AD 682 and swore, 'O God, I take
you to witness that there is no ford here. If there
was I would cross it', it marked the completion
of the Islamic conquest of North Africa,
confirmed when Idris II established the wholly
Islamic city of Fès. In 818 a failed rebellion in
Córdoba sent a flood of Arab refugees to Fès,
and a decade later a similar rebellion in Tunisia
brought more. In just a few decades Morocco
had gained its defining architectural influences
and the communities of craftsmen that would
give it shape and form.

### GAINS FROM SPAIN

Morocco became the inheritor of the
architectural and craft traditions of Muslim
Spain and the Córdoban empire (whose glory
was enshrined in the glorious Mezquita,
Córdoba's Great Mosque). The Almoravids
(1062-1147), who were the next dynasty to
reunite Morocco after the country dissolved into
principalities on the death of Idris II, further
opened the doors to the influx of Spanish
Muslim culture. They founded Marrakech

(1062) as their capital and, under the influence
of the Spanish, built some monumental
structures, importing into Morocco for the first
time the horseshoe arch and cusp arch (the one
that looks like a broccoli section). Under the
Almoravids the fine carving of stucco also first
appears. Incredibly, some of those earliest
designs (stylised, paisley-like flowers), which
appear in the *mihrab* (prayer niche) of the
Karawiyin Mosque in Fès and are reproduced
in the erudite *A Practical Guide to Islamic
Monuments in Morocco* by Richard Parker,
are still being reproduced in Marrakech in 2003
by young craftsmen furiously chiselling swirls
and flourishes into bands of damp plaster
before it sets.

In terms of surviving monuments, the only
complete Almoravid building in the whole of
Morocco is Marrakech's **Koubba El Badiyin**
(*see p75*), which displayed for the first time
many of the elements and motifs that have
since come to characterise Moorish building.

During the reign of the successors to the
Almoravids, the Almohads (1147-1269), the
Spanish-Moorish synthesis reached its peak.
Moroccan architectural styles were developed

dramatically. Building materials of choice remained mud brick and *pisé* (reinforced mud), but stone was employed for certain structures, notably the splendid Marrakech gate known as the **Bab Agnaou** (*see p82*). Decoration was simplified and made more masculine; according to Parker, whereas the Almoravids went in for flowers, their successors favoured geometric patterns. However, even these austere rulers seemed to have eventually softened to some degree, as can be seen in the lovely trellis-like brickwork and faience tiling lavished on the minarets of the **Koutoubia Mosque** (*see p67*) and the **Kasbah Mosque** (*see p82*).

Under the Merenids (1276-1554), Marrakech may have languished as attention switched to the northern imperial cities of Fès, Meknes and Salé, but artistic interchange continued with Spain. Some of the Merenids' finest monuments – including the Karaouiyine Mosque and Bou Inania Medersa, both in Fès – share similarities with the other great Moorish architectural achievement of the time, the extraordinary Alhambra palace complex, just across the Strait in Granada.

### DECORATIVE REFINEMENTS

It was the Merenids who introduced most of the familiar interior design repertoire into Morocco, including carved stucco (previously largely confined to the outside of buildings) and carved wood, as well as *zelije*, the creation of intricate mosaic design using hand-cut tiles.

Islamic tradition forbids any representation of living things, a policy defined in the formative years of the religion when the

**Kasbah Mosque.**

Prophet Mohammed first started preaching against the idol worshippers of his home town of Mecca. Hence, with very few exceptions, creativity flourished in more abstract forms. The tradition of tiling was carried west by the Arabs, who had been inspired by the bright turquoise domes and mausoleums of ancient Persia and Samarkand. The Central Asians, in their turn, had picked up the idea from Chinese porcelain, hence the devotion to blue. The Moors of Morocco and Andalucía took the art form into a whole new area by widening the colour palette courtesy of the influence of the Berbers. Tribal inhabitants of the Atlas Mountains that separate Morocco from the rest of Mediterranean North Africa, the Berbers added pink, purple, orange, red and yellow to the existing blue, green and white palette of Islamic culture.

> **'The Berbers added pink, purple, orange, red and yellow to the existing blue, green and white palette of Islamic culture.'**

Zelije takes the form of complex geometrical patterns executed in small glazed tiles like a massive jigsaw puzzle. The tiles are formed in large, not small, sizes and have to be cut to shape. This remains the case even today. Visit a building under construction and there will be a group of craftsmen employed to do nothing but cut tiles, which are then stockpiled awaiting the attention of the *zelayiya*, the zelije master craftsman, who will assemble them according to designs passed from father to son and retained in memory only.

There are, it is claimed, 360 different shapes of cut-clay pieces, called *fourma*, and the permutations of colour and pattern are endless. The craft has always been a speciality of the artisans of Fès where the best examples of work are to be found, but Marrakech has no shortage of kaleidoscopic tiling either, exhibited in its various palaces and religious monuments.

The other great Merenid addition to the architectural repertoire is woodworking. Wood has rarely been used as a primary structure (walls and floors are made of stone and mudbrick) but it was frequently employed for ceilings, lintels, capitals and, of course, doors – frequently massive and imposing pieces of work, and typically decorated with carving, incising and inlays.

Unfortunately, much of the best wood-working has traditionally been reserved for holy institutions such as mosques, shrines and *medersas* (Koranic schools; a building type also introduced by the Merenids), all of which are, with very few exceptions, off-limits to non Muslims. However, some impressive examples of historic craftsmanship can be seen in Marrakech at the engrossing **Dar Si Said Museum** (*see p86*).

## PALACES AND HOUSES

Post Merenid, Moroccan architecture went into a period of stagnation. The Moors had retreated from southern Spain in the late 15th century and the Moroccan empire had collapsed inwards. Under the Saadians (1549-1668), Marrakech became the capital again and was embellished with grand new monuments, including the delightful **Ben Youssef Medersa** (*see p74*) and the dazzling **Saadian Tombs** (*see p82*). The former is notable for its acres of carved stucco and wood, the latter for floor-to-ceiling zelije. In the opinion of architectural historians these buildings are of little importance and are dismissed as inferior repetitions of earlier techniques and motifs, created by artisans rather than architects. That may be so, but at least through them the visitor gains an idea of the glories of previous buildings which have since been lost.

What the Saadians excelled at were palaces. Sultan Ahmed El Mansour (1578-1607) took 25 years over the building of the **Badii Palace** (*see p83*). Unfortunately, throughout history Moroccan dynasties have not only had a habit of shifting the centre of power around and constructing new monuments of grandeur, they've also been inclined to destroy whatever had been created by their predecessors. So, right at the start, the Almohads pulled down the original founding fortress of Marrakech to replace it with the Koutoubia Mosque, and, later, Moulay Ismail, who succeeded the Saadians, dismantled the Badii Palace – all that remains are impressive ruins.

Essentially the palaces echoed the design of a traditional house or *dar*. Both followed the principle of an anonymous exterior of blank walls with an entrance leading via a passage – kinked so that anyone at the door or gate couldn't see directly inside – to a central open-air court. The whole palace or house looks inward rather than outward, with windows and terraces addressing the courtyard, which serves to introduce both light and air into the rooms set around it. On the ground floor these are public reception rooms and salons; the private quarters are above.

The central open spaces are also rooms in themselves, used for eating and entertaining. In larger houses the courts often have *bahou*, small recessed seating areas. A *douiriya*, or annex,

contains the kitchens and servants' rooms. At roof level, flat terraces provide additional space for storage, drying washing or keeping goats and chickens.

## KASBAHS AND KSOUR

All that has been described so far is essentially Arab architecture, imported into Morocco since the arrival of Islam. But Marrakech is different to the imperial cities of the north because of the influence of the indigenous Berbers.

These desert and mountain tribal people were the original inhabitants of Morocco long before the Arabs and their city of Fès, long even before the Romans established their outpost at Volublis. Their architecture is quite literally of the earth. The typical fortified Berber village, known as a *ksar*, or *ksour* in the plural, has traditionally been built of soil reinforced with lime, straw and gravel, mixed into a thick mud paste and applied by hand to a wooden frame. It dries so hard that it takes a hammer and chisel to mark it. At the same time, it has a beautifully organic quality; if another home or extension is needed it's simply welded on and the village grows like a bees' nest.

> ## 'With French rule came a new style of architecture, a mix of European modernistic and Moorish, dubbed "Mauresque".'

Similar to the ksour is the *kasbah*, which can be described variously as a castle, a fortress, a palace or a garrison – the key to its definition is that it is the residence of a tribal ruler. These ancient structures predominate in southern Morocco, built as much to protect the Berbers from one another as from outside invaders. They are often sited on a hill or other strategic feature of the landscape, with towers at each corner serving as lookout posts. The interiors are simple, often claustrophobic, with narrow windows, so rely on terraces and courtyards to bring in light. They might rise to four or five storeys, with the living quarters and grander reception rooms on the upper floors. Decoration is in the form of bold geometric motifs – the Berbers were early converts to Islam so share the Arab aversion to figurative representation. At the same time, they held on to many pre-Islamic superstitions and commonly adorned walls with simple motifs carved into the drying mud that were designed to ward off evil.

A guaranteed way to breach the defences of a kasbah was to reroute a river and let the water to wash away the fortification's foundations.

Ever more kasbahs are being restored for use as hotels, as here at **Skoura**. *See p208*.

Sadly, many kasbahs and ksours have been abandoned over the decades as tribal power has waned. The south of Morocco, especially the High Atlas region, is studded with grandly decaying hilltop ruins, most spectacularly at **Telouet** (*see p204*), the former stronghold of the Glaoui tribe. On a birghter note, there are also impressive partially and wholly restored kasbahs at **Aït Benhaddou** (*see p205*), **Skoura** (*see p208*), **Taouirt** (*see p205*) and **Tiffoultoute** (*see p206*).

**UNTIL TODAY**

Following the Saadian dynasty, Marrakech and Morocco as a whole endured a succession of weak, ineffectual imperial figureheads who were largely unable to halt the country's descent into intermittent civil war. Architecture rarely flourished. Marrakech briefly grew wealthy during the reign of free-trade fan Sultan Abdel Rahman (1822-59), with the wealth accrued resulting in the building of the **Bahia Palace** (*see p85*). Half a century later the Glaoui's rapacious taxes financed the **Dar El Bacha** (*see p79*). However, if the Saadian monuments were just imitations of greater glories past then these later buildings are third-hand pastiche, only sporadically enlightened by the skills of local artisans.

The arrival of the French in 1912 drew a line under all that had gone before. With foreign rule came a new style of architecture, a mix of European modernistic and Moorish, dubbed 'Mauresque'. Marrakech gained a new town but few buildings of distinction.

In Marrakech, the Protectorate was a mixed blessing. The city was introduced to new architectural ideas, but traditional forms and crafts were largely sidelined in the process. It's only recently, almost 50 years after the departure of the French, that architecture in the city has begun to move on. Gratifyingly, the inspiration for much of what is happening is Berber simplicity, with current high-profile architects such as Charles Boccara and Elie Mouyal looking to the logic, economy and organic-stylings of mud building.

According to Boccara, when he first began working in Marrakech in the 1980s there was 'no competition'; now he estimates there are maybe more than 50 small architectural practices. He singles out for attention Mohammed Amine Kabbaj, originally from Casablanca, trained in Strasbourg with a diploma from Paris and resident in Marrakech since 1980. Along with two partners, Kabbaj operates out of a hi-tech basement office in the New City, balancing big-bucks projects like a new factory for Coca-Cola with riad rebuilds in the Medina and a personal project to revitalise the small Berber town of Tamesloht and conserve its kasbah.

At the same time, thanks to the patronage of a new wave of designers and decorators, the traditional skills of the city's artisans – zelije workers, the wood and stucco carvers – are also back in vogue. After what has been the best part of four centuries of lassitude, a new Marrakech style looks set to shake things up.

# Marrakech Style

How Marrakech took over the style mags.

Every so often some magazine lifestyle pundit says that Moroccan as a style is 'over'. Really? Tell that to Mourad Mazouz, whose Sketch restaurant recently opened in London to the staccato clatter of a collective dropping of jaws, and which makes more than a nod to Moroccan mod. That's not to mention his signature restaurant Momo, still one of the hottest dinner reservations in London and totally Maghrebi. Tell that to leading interiors guru Jonathan Amar, designer of Paris' OTT Moroccan-themed Nirvana Lounge, haunt of the film and fashion crowd. Tell that to American restaurateur Terry Alexander who hired designer Suhail to create a trippy Moroccan fantasy for his chic Chicago eatery Tizi Melloul.

Now check out some of the titles down at your local bookstore: *Moroccan Interiors*, a huge doorstopping catalogue of Oriental homes to die for published by Taschen; *Morocco: Decoration, Interiors, Design*, published by Conran Octopus (complete with an appendix of home accessories stockists); and *Morocco Modern*, published way back in 1996 by Thames & Hudson and written by one Herbert Ypma before he moved on to hip hoteldom. Is it too fanciful to suppose that the hotels Herbert saw in Morocco (Villa Maroc in Essaouira; Dar Tamsna, Les Deux Tours and the Tichka Salam in Marrakech) and described in his first book

gave him the inspiration for his bestselling series? Could it be that this quartet of southern Moroccan hotels are the prototype of the 'hip'? Quite possibly.

If there's one thing that Marrakech has in abundance it is natural style and effortless flair. Fès is too fussy, the walls of its buildings frequently garish with glazed tiles. Tangier is overly Andalucian, overwrought with curling iron and rendered extra chintzy by pastel baby hues. Casablanca suffers a colonial hangover, eager to imitate past masters and prove that it can do everything independently, including erect its own carbuncles in concrete.

Only Marrakech seems to have the self-possession to cut its own cloth, and do so in the most elegant of fashions. Why? It's a Berber thing. It's the combination of simplicity of form – itself dictated by the materials (mud, mudbrick, tree trunks and branches) – with the addition of the vibrant colours of the Atlas: red earth, fruity orange, rose pink, lemon yellow, cobalt sky blue.

But for Berber traditions to come to the attention of the likes of the mass international DIYing public picking up their earth-glazed dishes at Habitat, terracotta kitchen tiles from Fired Earth and metalwork lanterns from Ikea required some form of intermediary. Step forward Bill Willis.

## AN AMERICAN IN MARRAKECH

If anyone can claim credit for reigniting interest in traditional Marrakchi styles it would be Willis. He claims credit for other discoveries too. 'I discovered cocaine in Italy, turned Robert [Fraser] on to that and then he turned the Rolling Stones and the Beatles on to it,' (from *Groovy Bob: The Life and Times of Robert Fraser* by Harriet Vyner). Willis was an interior designer and architect hanging out in '60s London with Jagger and Marianne Faithfull, Groovy Bob and the whole hippy deluxe crowd. He first travelled to Marrakech in 1968, accompanying Paul Getty Jr and his wife, who were looking for a house. He found himself mesmerised by 'a rhythm of life I used to know as a child growing up in Memphis, Tennessee,' he explained in a 1986 magazine interview. 'I was fed up with big cities. Paris, Rome, New York – I'd tried them all. Here it was very slow and easy-going, a sleepy gracious, Southern kind of thing.' Once Getty had found his house, Willis went to work.

Through a string of subsequent clients, including the Rothschilds, Yves Saint Laurent (*see p92* **Saint Laurent of Arabia**) and sundry local industrialists, Willis developed a style based on traditional Moroccan references (arches, painted woodwork, geometric patterns in tiling, plaster carving), but imbued with a wry, almost camp sense of humour of his own. Just take a look at his dandy, candy-striped, onion-domed fireplaces at Dar Yacout (*see p99*), the Felliniesque salons at the Trattoria Giancarlo (*see p111*) or the tongue-in-cheek palm tree columns at the Tichka Salam hotel (*see p57*).

### 'If there's one thing that Marrakech has in abundance it is natural style and effortless flair.'

While his particular twists are wholly modern, the techniques employed in achieving the finished result are age-old, involving intricate mosaic work, wood carving and stone masonry. Because of the demands placed on local *maalim* (master craftsmen), forcing them to adapt, relearn and stretch themselves, Willis's interiors are credited with almost single-handedly reviving artisan traditions in Marrakech. This may not be entirely true; according to Herbert Ypma's book, an ambitious programme of palace restoration by Hassan II, the father of the present king, boosted the number of *zelije* (tiling) artisans in Fès from 50 to 700, while the construction of the mammoth

mosque in Casablanca, which employed 30,000 artisans, also played a major part in the renaissance of Moroccan craftsmanship. What is amazing, though, is that at the end of the 20th century these essentially medieval crafts were still around to be revived. Can you imagine in Britain trying to put together a bunch of builders to kit out your mansion with sculpted stone spandrels and coffered ceilings in oak?

The difference is that Marrakech is a city of artisans. It remains largely a pre-industrial city that still gets by on trade, commerce and small-scale manufacturing – plus, these days, tourism, which in itself is another perpetuator of handicrafts. The ability of its craftspeople astounds. One local furniture designer tells the story of how he took a prototype lantern in tin to a metalworker to have it refashioned in copper. Less than 48 hours later the model was all over the souk after being copied in a dozen workshops or more. Capitalising on such infinite and ingenious creative skills, an American woman, Dana Schondelmeyer, has set up a company, Made in Marrakech, supplying costumes and props to Hollywood. Here in the Medina her artisans have manufactured Tibetan sandals for Martin Scorsese's *Kundun*, US-style military flak jackets for *Blackhawk Down* and all-leather attire for the Egyptian armies of *The Mummy Returns*.

### THE TADELAKT KING

Bill Willis still lives in the holy heart of the northern Medina, between a mosque and a cemetery, in the harem section of an 18th-century palace, but he rarely accepts commissions any more. Charles Boccara, sometime partner of Willis (they worked on the Tichka hotel together), makes up for both with his prolificacy. While Willis is a decorator, Boccara is an architect. Born in Tunisia, educated in Morocco and trained in Paris at the Ecole des Beaux-Arts, he's a force of nature, a big bear of a man, who packs Italian, French and English all into the same sentence. Like Willis, he has seized on traditional elements of local design. He constructs in concrete but plasters in *pisé* (mud). His interiors make stunning use of *tadelakt*, the polished wall finish traditionally employed in *hammams* (bathhouses), where heat and moisture are a problem. It's a technique to create steam-proof walls. Surfaces are trowelled in a plaster of powdered limestone with a small amount of coloured dust mixed in to provide the desired colour. After the plaster is set, it's painstakingly polished with flat stones approximately the size of a hand, which makes it as hard as marble. To seal the material further, the surface is painted with a glaze of egg whites. Finally, there's one

last polish with a cake of locally made back soap. The finished result looks like soft leather and is as smooth as lather to the touch.

Boccara is the man credited with bringing tadelakt out of the steam room and into style. His buildings make great use of it in almost every room. Since the example set by his signature Les Deux Tours (*see p61*), completed in the early 1990s, Marrakech has gone tadelakt mad. The mantra now seems to be that if an interior surface is flat, it gets tadelakt'd.

But Boccara's architecture goes far beyond surface. He's a man who values surprise and even folly, who believes that getting lost is one of the real pleasures of a house. At Les Deux Tours his bathrooms are astounding, featuring soaring ceilings of mudbrick domes pierced by round holes that emit shafts of light. Ceilings in other rooms are panelled with oleander branches and then brightly painted in vivid geometric patterns like backgammon boards.

With projects like hotels Les Deux Tours and the Tichka Salam, and the as-yet-unfinished Royal Opera House (*see p88*), Boccara has managed to create an architecture that conveys a strong sense of place while striking an unmistakably modern pose. It combines the comforts of modern life – plumbing, bathrooms, fully fitted kitchens – with the mood, texture and ambience of Marrakech's history and culture.

### MUD MODERN

Transplanted Parisian Jacqueline Fossaic arrived around the same time as Bill Willis, although she has far more in common with Charles Boccara. She's mud mad, and over the past three decades has taken the traditional peasant clay or mud house and turned it into something quite sophisticated.

'Dar Tamsna, the prototype boho-chic villa, introduced Marrakech to the pages of the international life-style press.'

She shares her passion with a protégé of Charles Boccara, native Moroccan Elie Mouyal, and the two have worked together on a number of projects, including several houses for Fossaic in the Palmeraie. The dwellings are constructed entirely of handmade mudbricks echoing the traditional Berber *kasbahs* and *ksours* (*see p30*) of southern Morocco. Far from appearing primitive, the buildings are pure rustic chic with high vaulted ceilings, domes and cupolas. They are entirely terracotta in tone, inside and

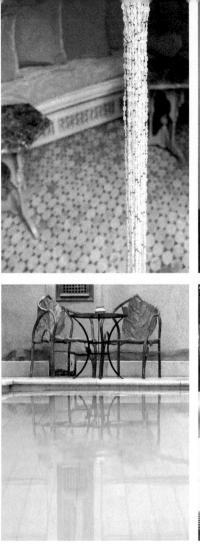

out, enlivened with weavings, painted doors and windows, and white-canvas hangings to provide shade on the terraces. Fossaic now works for clients on restoration projects in the Medina, as well as on more new-build houses in the Palmeraie. Mouyal has moved onwards and upwards and the building he's now most closely associated with is the gleaming white, 30-storey-plus Twin Towers Centre (not, we should point out, made of mudbrick) at the heart of Casablanca. However, the duo's experiments in raw-earth construction have made a lasting impression and continue to be an inspiration – for instance, in the development of

Caravanserai and Tigmi (*see p62* for both): two almost organic Berber-style hotel complexes that blend seamlessly into their local village settings.

## MOROCCAN MINIMALISM

French-Senegalese Meryanne Loum-Martin first came to Marrakech from Paris in the late 1980s in search of a holiday property that would be accessible to her and her scattered relatives. She found a half-built concrete shell in the Palmeraie and decided to finish the job. Throughout the early '90s she made frequent trips to Morocco and enrolled on a self-taught crash course in the country's traditional crafts and building methods. The result was Dar Tamsna, perhaps the prototype boho-chic villa and the place that introduced Marrakech to the pages of the international lifestyle press – with eight pages in *Condé Nast Traveller*, no less.

An architect by training, a lawyer in practice and a perfectionist by nature, in Dar Tamsna Loum-Martin came as close as any, according to style arbiter Herbert Ypma, to 'providing the essential Moroccan experience'. As Bill Willis before, she adapted local ingredients and reinterpreted them. In the instances where she instructed her craftsmen to use zelije she kept the tiling to a single colour; similarly the tadelakt, which is a deep and lustrous tobacco tone throughout. The Moroccan rugs and carpets are uniformally deep red and the wood work and *mashrabiyas* (fretworked wooden screens) all stained dark. Walking into one of the stately rooms the initial effect is of coolness and restraint, but look closer and the micro detail and intricacy are mesmerising.

In 2002 Loum-Martin completed a new hotel project, Jnane Tamsna (*see p59*), but this time the whole complex was built from scratch. It refines the MLM formula even further with architecture that's grounded in southern Morocco by its absolute simplicity and clarity of form, but with the added zest of some sublimely understated flourishes, such as Moorish keyhole arches and cloister-like arcades. The colours are mango, sand and tan. No surprise that the place is constantly in demand as a location for international fashion shoots.

In the few years between Dar Tamsna and Jnane Tamsna the whole riad scene in the Medina exploded. All of a sudden it seemed that behind every door in the Old City artisans were beavering away fashioning ever more neo-Moroccan fantasies. Each took as its starting point the same set of references, but the beauty of the whole modern Marrakech thing is how readily the architecture and traditional crafts lend themselves to experimentation and innovation. Hence hotels Riad Enija (*see p43*), which takes trad Moroccan into the realm of gothic fantasy; Riad Kaiss (*see p50*), which plays heavily on colour and patterning; Riad Malika, fashioned by designer/owner Jean-Luc Lemée as a unique fusion of Moorish and art deco – tadelakt meets bakelite! And there are countless, countless others. Despite the variations on the theme, there is now an established riad design checklist. Tadelakt walls. Tick. Carved stucco trim. Tick. Beaten copper handbasins. Tick. Zelije tiled basin surrounds. Tick. Funny-shaped shower cubicles. Tick. Kilims and rugs, walls only.

Tick. Bare terracotta flooring. Tick. White canvas sun canopies. Tick. Lanterns and tea candles. Tick. But when a formula works this beautifully, it would be truly perverse not to pay heed.

Another trend common to *the style* is to utilise older elements, such as aged wooden doors and window frames, marble washbasins, wooden columns or even plumbing fixtures from the 1920s, to create intriguing juxtapositions. Some of the elements become transformed from their original function, such as wooden columns from a baldaquin bed re-employed to hold up a roof terrace pergola. For all would-be designers (and there's something about the air here that effects a transformation; three days in Marrakech and even the most cack-handed and colour-blind suddenly come over all Laurence Llewelyn-Bowen) the local equivalent of Habitat is the Souk El Khemis (*see p131*), an open-air flea market in the northern Medina that is home to a great many architectural salvage merchants.

## THE PROFESSIONALS

Not everybody wants to go it alone and there's a decent living to be made in Marrakech as a designer-for-hire. That is now one of the labels worn by former Italian *Vogue* editor Alessandra Lippini. Arguably the most glamorous lady in the Medina, she trips through the souk in kitten heels and a party dress on her way each day to the Ministerio del Gusto (*see p128 and p144*), the delirious gallery-cum-workspace she shares with partner Fabrizzio Bizzarri. The pair design trippy interiors for a roster of wealthy clients, mainly from the Italian fashion world. If there's one word that characterises their work together it's 'fun'. Their shared Medina home is a riot of star-studded floorings, spidery chandeliers, Arabic stencils, Fauvist colour schemes and Flintstone furniture – so totally batty and bold that it made the perfect location for Bryan Ferry's video to 'Mamouna'. One of their recent works is a riad just off rue Dar Doukkala completely done out in geometric black and white – with a ceiling-high, leopard-skin bed headboard, just for the hell of it.

And that's the thing about Marrakech style. Flexibility. It's not about lanterns or tassles or dressing up in fezzes; it's a style based on indigenous values of simplicity and practicality. At root it's about basic building materials and using them to strike a harmonious balance between outside and in, by use of courtyards, terraces and gardens. Beyond that, architects and designers can be as imaginative and creative as they like. Now how can that ever go out of fashion?

# Where to Stay

**Where to Stay**          38

## Features
**The best** Hotels         38
Mamounia         42
The chain gang         57

# Where to Stay

Not so much lodgings as lifestyle locations.

If your city is low on conventional sights then make the accommodation the destination. Not a completely novel concept but few places have taken the idea as far as Marrakech, which probably boasts more boutique hotels per square mile than any other city in the world. Most of these properties are conversions of a type of local Medina house known as a *riad*, or garden house. Except for 'garden', in most cases, read courtyard. The houses are organised around one or more of these courtyards, reflecting the traditions of Moroccan domestic architecture, which are inward-looking with thick blank walls to protect the inhabitants from heat, cold and the attentions of the outside world. Grander riads involve two or more

houses knocked together but many consist of just half a dozen or so rooms around a single courtyard. Most are privately operated affairs, which generally means excellent personal service and a great degree of individuality.

In all but the cheapest riads, rooms have en suite bathrooms, but air-conditioning, TVs and telephones and other mod cons are typically dispensed with in the name of authenticity. Breakfast is commonly taken on a roof terrace shielded from the sun under tent-like awnings. Lunch and dinner are provided on request. Several of the riads have truly excellent cooks producing food as good as, if not superior to, anything dished up in the local restaurants.

In deference to local aesthetics, most riads forgo any kind of tell-tale frontage, signboard or even nameplate and, given that they often lie deep within the obscure twists of narrow alleys, this makes them an absolute swine to locate. Guests are met at the airport (for which there may or may not be an additional charge in the region of $10-$15) but after that it's just you and your sense of direction. It's wise to carry your riad's business card to show locals in case you get lost.

Gaining in favour is the idea of the out of town retreat. There are a growing number of villas and new-build compounds on the outskirts of town – scattered throughout the Palmeraie and further afield – that serve as semi-private retreats dedicated to indolence and pampering, with teams of cooks, masseurs, manicurists, maids and assorted flunkies to obviate the need for any exertion on the part of the guest. Marrakech is on hand simply to provide blasts of colour and exoticism between early afternoon waxings and evening cocktails. The ideal holiday is perhaps to spend a couple of days at a riad in the Medina followed by a couple of days in self-indulgent retreat. Independent tour operators are now pushing this sort of package.

Whichever way you choose to go, we highly recommend pushing the budget. Marrakech is not a place to scrimp on the accommodation, not when your hotel could so easily turn out to be the highlight of the trip.

### RATES & BOOKING

There are significant seasonal variations in room rates, with prices at some hotels rising by up to 25 per cent at peak periods. What

## The best **Hotels**

### For artful posing
**Jnane Tamsna** (*see p59*) and **Riad Enija** (*see p43*) often double as sets for fashion-shoots.

### For foodies
The man in the kitchen at **Casa Lalla** (*see p47*) is Michelin-starred chef Richard Neat.

### For artists in retreat
**Riad Ifoulki** (*see p49*) has strong literary connections; **Riad El Fenn** (*see p43*) is favoured by the Brit art set thanks to owner Vanessa Branson's art-world connections.

### For health and beauty
**Kasbah Agafay** (*see p62*) and the **Sultana** (*see p45*) come with full spa facilities.

### For water babies
The biggest pools are at the **Hotel Es Saadi** (*see p59*), **Sultana** (*see p45*) and **Tichka Salam** (*see p57*). The cheapest pool is at the **Grand Tazi** (*see p55*).

### For eco friendliness
Ethnobotanist Gary Martin grows his own kitchen produce at **Jnane Tamsna** (*see p59*); **Riad El Fenn** (*see p43*) has its own organic farm.

Gorgeous design, immaculate service at **Riad Farnatchi**. *See p41.*

www.maroc-selection.com
Office in Marrakech : 00 212 44 44 65 65

# MAROC SELECTION
LUXURY TRAVEL

100 finest Riads, Villas & Hotels in Morocco
Tailor-made : golf, spa, desert, car, 4&4

constitutes peak period varies by establishment but generally speaking you'll pay considerably more for a room any time over Christmas/New Year and Easter, plus from late September through to October, when the fierceness of the summer heat has abated and temperatures are near perfect. Rooms are scarce at peak times and booking well in advance is a must.

When it comes to making a reservation, even though most hotels boast websites bear in mind that Moroccan servers are prone to meltdown. Book through the website by all means but be sure to follow up with a phone call.

We've divided this chapter by area, then price: **deluxe** from 3,200dh (currently around £200); **expensive** 1,950dh-3,200dh (£120-£200); **moderate** 970dh-1,950dh (£60-£120); and **budget** up to 970dh (£60). Breakfast is usually included. Payment is typically cash only and it must be made in local currency. Even those places that purport to take credit cards usually prefer cash in practice – you might too, given that a five per cent surcharge may be added on top to cover the transaction costs.

## Medina

Aka the Old City. A room here puts you right in among the souks and sights, and the nearer to the ground zero of Jemaa El Fna the better. Remember that much of the Medina is inaccessible by car, so accommodation close to a taxi-friendly main street is always preferable.

## Deluxe

### Riad Farnatchi

*2 Derb Farnatchi, Kat Benahid (044 38 49 10/ fax 044 38 49 13/www.riadfarnatchi.com/ riadfarnatchi@menara.ma).* **Rates** *Jan, June-July* 3,100dh-3,800dh suite. *Feb-May, Sept-Dec (excluding Xmas)* 3,400dh-4,100dh suite. **Credit** MC, V. **Map** p253 D4.

Farnatchi is the creation of Jonathan Wix (42 The Calls in Leeds, the Scotsman in Edinburgh and Hotel de la Tremoille in Paris). Originally intended as his private residence, it's now an intimate and highly personal five-class hotel. Five suites are arrayed off two small courtyards, one of which has a modestly sized heated pool. The suites are vast and supremely luxurious with large sunken baths, shower rooms, under-floor heating, desks and armchairs and private balconies. The design throughout is a striking update of the local aesthetic, with stark black and white as a neutral backdrop to intricate woodworked screens and finely carved stucco. All the furniture has been specially designed and manufactured in Marrakech, except for bathroom fittings by Philippe Starck. The hotel is superbly run (Canadian manageress Lynn is a walking directory of Marrakech) and the location puts you right in the middle of the Medina, just north of the Musée de Marrakech and Ben Youssef Medersa; taxis can get to within 200 metres. Rates include complimentary hotel transfers. The hotel is closed annually during August. **Hotel services** *Cook. DVD library. Hammam. Massage. Plunge pool (outdoor). Safe.* **Room services** *Air-conditioning. Heating. Telephone. TV: DVD, satellite.*

### Villa des Orangers

*6 rue Sidi Mimoun, place Ben Tachfine (044 38 46 38/fax 044 38 51 23/www.villadesorangers.com/ message@villadesorangers.com).* **Rates** 2,900dh-3,800dh double; 4,000dh-6,800dh suite. **Credit** MC, V. **Map** p254 B7.

Built in the 1930s as the residence of a judge, the Villa des Orangers was acquired by a French husband-and-wife team with a successful hotel business in Paris and, after gaining an additional storey, it opened to paying guests in December 1999. The style is Moorish palatial and it has 19 rooms and suites arranged around three beautiful courtyards – one of them filled with the eponymous orange trees, the other two lavishly decorated with lacy carved plasterwork. Six suites have private upstairs sun terraces, although all rooms have access to the roof with matchless views of the nearby Koutoubia minaret – doubly enchanting when the storks come wheeling round at dusk. The service is outstanding and airport transfers are included in the price. **Hotel services** *Babysitting. Bar. Internet (wi-fi enabled). Laundry. Massage. Pool (2, outdoor). Restaurant. Safe. Solarium.* **Room services** *Air-conditioning. Heating. Minibar. Safe. Telephone. TV: satellite.*

## Expensive

### Jardins de la Koutoubia

*16 rue de la Koutoubia (044 38 88 00/fax 044 44 22 22/hoteljardinkoutoubia@menara.ma).* **Rates** 1,750dh-2,300dh single; 1,950dh-2,500dh double; 3,200dh mini-suite; 4,500dh-5,000dh junior suite. **Credit** Amex, MC, V. **Map** p252/254 B5.

If you want to be in the Medina but prefer the relative impersonality of a hotel over the intimacy of a *maison d'hôte*, or have work to do and need a desk and telephone more than radical curtains and a four-poster bed, then this comfortable, well-run five-star is the place. It's brilliantly located, two minutes from the Jemaa El Fna in one direction, two minutes from the Koutoubia mosque and a steady stream of taxis in the other. The courtyard pool is heated, they can shake a proper cocktail in the Piano Bar (*see p151*), the patio restaurant (*see p105*) is a fine spot for lunch, and everything is nicely spacious. The faux traditional design may be nothing for the style supplements, but it isn't too shabby and both beds and bathrooms are big and welcoming. As we went to press a huge extension – as big as the original hotel – was under construction to bring the total number of rooms up to around 100 and add another garden, a couple more swimming pools and a subterranean

# Mamounia

Almost since opening in 1923, the Mamounia has been so famous as to be practically synonymous with Marrakech. It was the palace of the crown prince of Morocco when the French administration annexed it for a hotel. During that romantic era of early travel, the Mamounia was not just a hotel, it was a way of life, where a small and exclusive community of expats, colonial rulers and adventurers would lazily sip Scotch in the hotel's well-watered gardens. In post-war years it was a favourite haunt of Winston Churchill, who declared the views from its roof to be 'paintaceous' and executed a number of watercolours to prove his point (there's now a 15,000dh-a-night suite named after him).

The place seems to have had great appeal for rotund and jowly Englishmen: Alfred Hitchcock checked in to film *The Man Who Knew Too Much* (in which James Stewart and Doris Day occupy room 414). But in 1986 when a conference centre was added and the hotel was refitted, the cool elegance of the past was sacrificed in a kitsch makeover. This was doubly unfortunate in that it was around this time that the first of Marrakech's famed hip hotels appeared, and the grande old dame began to find herself outclassed.

Its rooms (of which there are now 230) remain spacious, particularly the various suites, but the theming – 19th-century, Orient Express, 1930s, nuptial, Moroccan – is pure Las Vegas (one suite has a seven-foot harp, another a toy parrot in the bathroom). By contrast, the endless expanses of blank carpeted corridors are corporate characterless. Far more objectionable are supercilious staff and unnecessarily haughty service.

Do visit for the excellent poolside buffet **Trois Palmiers** (*see p107*), the **Churchill Piano Bar** (*see p150*) and to admire the lobby's custom-made furniture and peek at the fine marquetry in the lifts. But beware the hotel's erratically enforced no-jeans policy. Rumours also abound that the hotel is set to close some time in 2005 for several months of refurbishment.

## Mamounia

*avenue Bab Jedid, Medina (044 38 86 00/ fax 044 44 44 09/www.mamounia.com/ resa@mamounia.com).* **Rates** *20 June- 11 Sept 2,300dh-4,300dh standard room; 3,300dh-14,000dh suite. 12 Sept-19 June 3,300dh-5,300dh standard room; 4,300dh- 18,000dh suite.* **Credit** AmEx, MC, V. **Map** p254 A6.
**Hotel services** *Air-conditioning. Art gallery. Bars (4). Beauty centre: hairdresser, massage room, sauna. Business centre. Casino. Conference rooms. Fitness centre. Nightclub. Pool (outdoor). Restaurants (5). Safe. Shops. Tennis courts.* **Room services** *Airconditioning. Safe. Telephone. TV: satellite.*

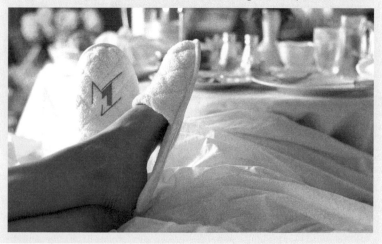

fitness centre. The new rooms will apparently all have balconies, internet sockets and DVD players, and should be finished in late summer 2005. **Hotel services** *Bar. Hammam. Restaurants (3). Pool (outdoor).* **Shop.** **Room services** *Air-conditioning. Heating. Minibar. Safe. Telephone. TV: satellite.*

### Maison Arabe

*1 Derb Assehbe, Bab Doukkala (044 38 70 10/ fax 044 38 72 21/www.lamaisonarabe.com/ maisonarabe@iam.net.ma).* **Rates** *14 June-15 Aug* 1,500dh-2,000dh double; 2,500dh-4,800dh suite. *16 Aug-13 June* 1,900dh-2,500dh double; 3,000dh-6,000dh suite. **Credit** MC, V. **Map** p252 A4.
Maison Arabe began life in the 1940s as a restaurant run by two raffish French ladies. It rapidly gained fame through popularity with patrons such as Winston Churchill. The last tajines were served in 1983 and the place lay dormant for more than a decade before reopening under new, Italian ownership in January 1998 as the city's first *maison d'hôte*. There are nine rooms and eight suites set around two flower-filled courts. The prevailing style is Moroccan classic with a French colonial feel – lots of Orientalist paintings and antiques, high-backed armchairs and a cedarwood library. The rooms are supremely comfortable, most with their own private terraces and a couple with fireplaces. Our favourite is Sabah (the rooms all have names), which is ingeniously fitted around the curve of a dome. The hotel pool may be a 20-minute drive away on the outskirts of town (serviced by hourly shuttles) but it does have a lovely garden setting where lunch is also served. The hotel restaurant (*see p101*) is excellent, there's a fine house bar, Le Club (*see p150*), and guests can also take cookery courses (*see p116*). **Hotel services** *Babysitting. Bar. Car park. Hammam. Internet (free). Pool (outdoor). Restaurant. Safe.* **Room services** *Air-conditioning. Heating. Minibar. Safe. Telephone. TV: satellite.*

### Riad El Fenn

*2 Derb Moulay Abdallah Ben Hezzian, Bab El Ksour, Medina (044 44 12 10/www.riadelfenn.com/ riadelfenn@menara.ma).* **Rates** 2,000dh children's room; 2,700dh-3,500dh double; 4,500dh douiria. **Credit** MC, V. **Map** p252/254 B5.
The most high-profile of recent Marrakech riad openings, the media attention Fenn has received is partly down to it being co-owned by Vanessa Branson (sister of Richard) and partly down to it being such a fine place. Two historic houses have been joined to create nine spacious sorbet-coloured bedrooms. Clutter free, each room is dominated by an Egyptian cotton-swathed imperial-sized bed. There's also a split-level suite (the *douiria*) that is arguably the most striking room for rent in the whole of Marrakech. Despite the grandeur of the architecture and some serious modern art on the walls, the mood is relaxed, with plenty of private spaces and the obligatory rooftop terrace. A garden in the foothills of the Atlas provides organic produce for the kitchen. Top-rank facilities include a sweet

little azure-blue pool, a DVD screening-room and an excellent library, although arguably the greatest assets are managers Frederic and Viviana, who ably live up to the riad's name: 'fenn' being local slang for 'cool'. Airport transfers are complimentary. **Hotel services** *Cook. DVD room. Hammam. Library. Massage room. Pool (outdoor).* **Room services** *Air-conditioning. CD player. Heating.*

### Riad Enija

*9 Derb Mesfioui, off rue Rahba Lakdima (044 44 09 26/fax 044 44 27 00/www.riadenija.com/ riadenija@iam.net.ma).* **Rates** 2,300dh-3,500dh double. **Credit** MC, V. **Map** p253/255 D5.
Anyone lacking the pose and hauteur of a Karl Lagerfeld model risks being made to look shabby by comparison with the drop-dead gorgeousness of their surrounds at Riad Enija. Its 12 rooms and suites variously boast glorious old wooden ceilings, beds as works of art (wrought-iron gothic in one, a green muslin-wrapped four-poster in another), some striking furniture (much of it designed by artist friends of Swedish/Swiss owners Björn Conerding and Ursula Haldimann) and bathrooms resembling subterranean throne chambers. Central to the three adjoined houses (which originally belonged to a silk trader from Fès and 64 members of his family) is a Moorish courtyard garden gone wild where maroon-uniformed staff flicker through the greenery. Distractions like TV and telephones are dispensed with – although there is a sweet little 'internet salon' – but alternative services include anything from a visiting aromatherapist and masseurs to cookery classes (*see p116*) and heli-skiing excursions (in season). Service and food are both excellent and the riad is just a few minutes' walk from Jemaa El Fna. It can be a nuisance, though, having the latest fashion shoot going on outside your window. **Hotel services** *Beauty treatments. Cook. Cooking classes. Garden (courtyard). Internet. Massage. Plunge pool (outdoor). Safe.*

### Riad Lotus Ambre

*22 Fhal Zefriti, Bab Laksour (044 44 14 05/fax 044 44 14 07/www.riadslotus.com/info@riadslotus.com).* **Rates** *Jan, June-Aug* 1,550dh-2,200dh double; 2,700dh suite. *Feb-May, Sept-Dec* 1,850dh-2,550dh double; 3,000dh suite. **Credit** MC, V. **Map** p252/254 B5.
In contrast to most riads, where the gone-native aesthetic means you're lucky to get a table lamp in your bedroom let alone a TV, the Lotus lays on the extras big time. The four doubles and one suite all come with logo'd bed linen, towels and toiletries, high-speed internet access and a Bang & Olufsen plasma screen, sound system and DVD player. Not to mention the huge Warhol-copy Pop Art pieces (Jackie O, Marilyn, Goethe and Mao) that dominate each room. All the lighting is touch-sensitive B&O, the crystalware comes from Italy and there's a jacuzzi on the roof. If bling's your thing, then here's your Marrakech home from home. Rooms, however, vary greatly in size (Marilyn, in particular, is a bit mean).

Owner Reda Ben Jelloun, Marrakech-born but previously a travel agent working in Florence, says his aim is to offer five-star service in intimate stylish surroundings. Riad Lotus Ambre had only just opened when we visited, but by the time you read this he should have added a second property, the Riad Lotus Perle, up in the Dar El Bacha neighbourhood, with a grand riad in Essaouira to follow in summer 2006.

**Hotel services** *Baby sitting. Cook. Hammam. Jacuzzi. Library (CDs, DVDs). Massage.* **Room services** *Air-conditioning. CD player. Heating. Internet portal. Minibar. Safe. Telephone. TV: DVD, satellite.*

## Sultana

*Rue de la Kasbah, Kasbah (044 38 80 08/ fax 044 38 77 77/lasultanamarrakech.com/ contact@lasultanamarrakech.co).* **Rates** 2,100dh-4,100dh double; 2,950dh-6,950dh suite. **Credit** MC, V. **Map** p254 B8.

Opened in 2004, the Sultana is astonishing in that it's a completely new-build hotel of considerable size and scale slapped down in the middle of the Medina. And you'd never know it was there. It has no frontage to speak of but beyond the arched street door are 11 guestrooms and 10 suites of varying degrees of largeness connected by seemingly acres of arcaded corridors, courtyards, landings and galleries and serviced by 62 staff. There's a good-sized swimming pool, a full spa complex (*see p164*), a row of boutiques and a vast roof terrace that directly overlooks the gardens of the Saadian Tombs. The hotel boasts all the facilities and amenities of a five-star but is packaged to look like a *maison d'hôte*. The architecture (Moorish-Gothic) and decoration is sumptuous going on camp (check out the life-size bronze of a camel beside the pool), piling Indian, African and Oriental on the Moroccan. The restaurant (French and Moroccan cuisines) is open to non-guests who reserve in advance but unfortunately not

Riad El Fenn. *See p43.*

The full-blown oriental excess of the **Sultana**. *See p45.*

so the basement bar that's kitted out to resemble a ship's cabin complete with envelope-screen window into the deep-end of the swimming pool.

**Hotel services** *Bar. Beauty treatments. Boutiques. Fitness room. Hammam. Library. Massage. Restaurant. Spa. Swimming pool (outdoor). Safe.* **Room services** *Air-conditioning. CD player. Heating. Internet portals. Minibar. Telephone. TV: satellite, DVD.*

## Moderate

### Casa Lalla

*16 Derb Jamaa, off Riad Zitoun El Kedim (044 42 97 57/fax 044 42 97 59/www.casalalla.com/ contact@casalalla.com).* **Rates** 972dh-1,242dh double. **Credit** MC, V. **Map** p254 C6.

Lalla is a beautiful little guesthouse with eight rooms ranged on two floors around its central courtyard. It's elegant yet homely, with lots of attractive *tadelakt* surfaces in prevailing tones of off-white, mushroom and chocolate. Some of the rooms have fireplaces and a couple of the suites have their own mezzanine areas. There's a lounge area off the courtyard with a fireplace, small library and dog (usually), and a couple of tables set up for chess. All of which is great: comfortable, relaxed and value for money. But what really sets Casa Lalla apart is that it's run by Richard Neat and wife Sophie. Neat is the British chef awarded two Michelin stars for his first restaurant Pied-à-Terre in London and a further star for his Neat Restaurant in Cannes. He cooks six nights a week for his guests, only offering a table to non-guests if space allows. Of course, you aren't obliged to eat in every night but the food is extraordinary (*see p101*) and dining here is one of the highlights of a trip to Marrakech. Free airport transfers are provided.

**Hotel services** *CD player. Hammam. Library. Massage room. Plunge pool/jacuzzi (outdoor). Restaurant.* **Room services** *Air-conditioning. Heating (fireplaces).*

### Dar Atta

*28 rue Jebel Lakhdar, Bab Laksour (044 38 62 32/fax 044 38 62 41/www.daratta.com/ daratta@menara.ma).* **Rates** 650-750dh double; 1,250dh suite. **No credit cards**. **Map** p252 B4.

At first sight it seems an unprepossing location – a not very picturesque part of the Medina, opposite the gaudy Alanbar. But you can get a taxi right to the door, or walk to the Jemaa El Fna or Koutoubia in ten minutes, and once you're inside, this Italian-owned *maison d'hôte* reveals itself to be a very pleasant place indeed. Seven stylish double rooms and three spacious suites are ranged around a sunken patio and two terraces. We liked the big, faintly ramshackle-looking wooden partitions that separate the comfortable double beds from the wardrobe areas, and the generally unobtrusive design – it's cool, but it's not in your face. Staff are equally discreet, drifting around in black uniforms. There's also a charming small hammam and massage area and a

restaurant that serves Moroccan and Italian dishes. And when it's time to leave, you're on the right side of town for a quick dash to the airport.

**Hotel services** *Hammam. Restaurant.* **Room services** *Air-conditioning. Heating (fireplaces).*

### Dar Attajmil

*23 rue Laksour, off rue Sidi El Yamami (044 42 69 66/www.darattajmil.com/darattajmil@iam.net.ma).* **Rates** 700dh-1,200dh double. **Credit** MC, V. **Map** p252/254 B5.

Just four bedrooms small, Dar Attajmil is nothing if not cosy. It's run by the lovely (English-speaking) Italian Lucrezia Mutti and her small body of staff, which includes two slothful black cats. There's a tiny courtyard filled to bursting with banana trees and coconut palms that throw welcome shade on to a small recessed lounge and a library. Bedrooms overlook the courtyard from the first floor; they're all beautifully decorated in warm rusty tones with dark-wood ceilings and lovely *tadelakt* bathrooms. Best of all is the astonishingly peaceful roof terrace, scattered with cushions, wicker chairs and sofas. Dinner – trad Moroccan with Italian leanings – is available on request (150dh per person). It's an easy six-minute walk from the house to the Jemaa El Fna, Mouassine and the main souks.

**Hotel services** *Cook. Hammam. Library. Massage.*

### Dar les Cigognes

*108 rue Berima, Berima (044 38 27 40/fax 044 38 47 67/www.lescigognes.com/info@lescigognes.com).* **Rates** *15 June-15 Sept* 1,400dh-1,900dh double; 2,400dh suite. *16 Sept-14 June* 1,700dh-2,200dh double; 2,700dh suite. **Credit** MC, V. **Map** p255 D7.

Facing the eastern ramparts of the Badii Palace where the storks (in French, 'cigognes') stand sentinel, this was originally a merchant's home and dates in part back to the 17th century. Restoration (overseen by architect Charles Boccara) has been sensitive and walls of white and muted tones serve to highlight fine carved dark wood details around the two central courts. Each of the ten rooms (plus there's a single suite) has its own distinct character. Decor ranges from the sublimely chic (the Berber room with its beautiful painted ceiling; the Safi room with a pistachio-coloured fireplace inset with shards of broken Safi pottery) to the wonderfully ridiculous (the Sahara room with a painted desert landscape complete with camels; the Silver room with all-over silvery-grey *tadelakt* and carved plasterwork glitzed up to look like a wedding cake doily). Best of all is the extensive terrace that occupies the roofs of two buildings and bridges the alley below.

**Hotel services** *Boutique. Cook. Hammam. Jacuzzi. Library. Massage.* **Room services** *Air-conditioning (some rooms). Heating (some rooms).*

### Dar Doukkala

*83 Arset Aouzal, off rue Bab Doukkala (044 38 34 44/fax 044 38 34 45/www.dardoukkala.com/ dardoukkala@iam.net.ma).* **Rates** 1,600dh-1,800dh double; 2,100dh-2,400dh suite. **Credit** MC, V. **Map** p252 B4.

# Jnane Tamsna
*Country Guesthouse*
17 Bedrooms ~ 3 Pools ~ Tennis court
Restaurant ~ Art Gallery ~ Boutique
5 acres of organic gardens
Tel: 212 44 329423     Fax: 212 44 329884
Email: meryanne@jnanetamsna.com
www.jnanetamsna.com
www.diversity-excursions.co.uk

A bizarre mix of English country mansion and Moroccan townhouse, Dar Doukkala is like the home of some demented Victorian explorer-inventor with an obsession for the Orient. Its four bedrooms and two suites are filled with gorgeous period details and furnishings, including claw-foot tubs and pedestal basins in the bathrooms. Other wonderfully eccentric touches include Guimard-like glass canopies projecting into the central garden courtyard, and an artful array of lanterns patterning the wall behind the terrace-level pool. It's one of the most fun and delightful *maisons d'hôtes* in town. Both suites have two extra beds each for kids, while one of the doubles also comes with an extra bed. The location is good too, opposite the wonderland warehouse of Mustapha Blaoui (*see p128*) and close to the taxis ranked outside the Dar Marjana restaurant.
**Hotel services** *Cook. Hammam. Library. Masssage room. Pool (outdoor). TV: satellite.* **Room services** *Air-conditioning. CD player. Heating. Safe.*

### Riad Azzar

*94 Derb Moulay Abdelkader, off Derb Debbachi (061 15 81 73/fax 044 38 90 91/www.riadazzar.com/ info@riadazzar.com).* **Rates** 1,188dh-1,400dh double; 2,160dh suite. **No credit cards. Map** p253/255 D5.
Owned by a friendly, English-speaking Dutch couple, Azzar is a neat little six-room riad with the feel of a B&B. It's distinguished by a small, emerald green, heated plunge pool in the middle of the courtyard – nice, but if the riad is full it could be a bit like bathing in the main lobby. Walls are whitewashed and the decor is restrained: it's a very tasteful place. Three of the rooms are suites and come with fireplaces and air-conditioning (as does one of the doubles); of these, the Taznarth suite also boasts a beautiful *moucharabieh* (wooden lattice) window overlooking the courtyard and a particularly lovely grey-*tadelakt* bathroom. The owners admit with admirable honesty that the hammam is of a size suitable only for petite French ladies. Also admirable is Riad Azzar's support of a local orphanage; guests are encouraged to contribute by bringing children's toys or clothing or school materials for donation.
**Hotel services** *Cook. CD player. Hammam. Massage. Plunge pool (outdoor).* **Room services** *Air-conditioning (4 rooms). Heating (4 rooms).*

### Riad El Cadi

*87 Derb Moulay Abdelkader, off Derb Debbachi (044 37 86 55/fax 044 37 84 78/www.riyadelcadi.com/ info@riyadelcadi.com).* **Rates** 1,230dh single; 1,476dh-1,845dh double; 2,460dh-2,950dh suite. **Credit** MC, V. **Map** p253/255 D5.
Comprising eight (!) interconnected houses, El Cadi is a rambling maze of a residence in which getting lost is a joy. Its 12 supremely comfortable suites and bedrooms, as well as the various salons, corridors and landings, also double as gallery spaces for an outstanding collection of art and artefacts gathered by former owner Herwig Bartels, who sadly died in 2003. The reception area alone gathers an ancient Berber textile with a Bauhaus chair and a Rothko-like abstract. Despite the rich details, the overall feel is uncluttered, cool and contemporary. Bartels's daughter Julia now runs the riad with the assistance of the dapper and charming general manager Ahmed El Amrani. Standards remain high, especially in the kitchen. Extensive roof terraces with tented lounging areas further add to the appeal of what, for the money, is some of the classiest accommodation in town.
**Hotel services** *Boutique. Cook. Hammam. Library. Plunge pool (outdoor). TV.* **Room services** *Air-conditioning. Heating. Telephone.*

### Riad Hayati

*27 Derb Bouderba, off Derb El Bahia, Riad Zitoun El Jedid (UK 07770 431 194/www.riadhayati.com/ info@riadhayati.com).* **Rates** 1,500dh double. **Credit** V. **Map** p255 D7.
Could this be the most tasteful riad in town? It's a little piece of visual perfection, with three all-white bedrooms ranged around the galleried first floor of an all-white courtyard. If necessary, the ground-floor study can serve as a fourth bedroom, with its own en suite bathroom. Complementing the classic Moorish architecture are small references to Ottoman Turkey, Persia and Arabia (a mirror modelled on one seen in Istanbul's Dolmabahçe Palace, a fountain from Damascus), memoirs of the British owner's many years in news broadcasting from the Middle East (*hayati* means 'my life'). The location, near the Bahia Palace, is extremely peaceful but still only six or seven minutes' walk from the Jemaa El Fna. Evening aperitifs are included, ideally taken on the roof terrace with Atlas views.
**Hotel services** *Cook.* **Room services** *Fan. Heating (fireplace). Safe.*

### Riad Ifoulki

*11 Derb Moqqadem, Arset Loghzail (tel/fax 044 38 56 56/www.riadifoulki.com/ riadifoulki@riadifoulki.com).* **Rates** 800dh single; 1,500dh double; 3,000dh suite. **Credit** MC, V. **Map** p255 D6.
This may be the only riad in town at which Latin is spoken; Latin and nine other languages, in fact, including Danish, which is the nationality of owner Peter Berg. The property is a former palace (or at least, four-fifths of one) with a total of 14 rooms arranged on several levels around numerous whitewashed courtyards, large and small. For all its imperial origins and size, this is one of the least showy and 'designed' of riads; rooms are simple, with big beds swathed in translucent shimmery fabrics. Parts of the residence are self-contained with their own doors, ideal for families, and with gates at the top of stairs for child safety. There's a small library with volumes on Morocco in various languages, some of which are signed by their authors with gratitude to the erudite Berg. Guests can take lessons in the arts of *tadelakt* (plastering), *zelije* (tiling) and caligraphy, and are welcome to accompany the kitchen staff on shopping expeditions and help cook. Airport transfers are free.

**Hotel services** *Babysitting. Cook. Fitness room. Hammam. Library. Massage. Plunge pool (outdoor). TV.* **Room services** *Safe.*

## Riad Kaiss

*65 Derb Jedid, off Riad Zitoun El Kedim (tel/fax 044 44 01 41/www.riadkaiss.com/riad@riadkaiss.com).* **Rates** 1,770dh-2,355dh double. **Credit** MC, V. **Map** p254 C7.

Renovated, owned and managed by architect Christian Ferré, who lives on the premises, Kaiss is small (eight rooms) but exquisite. Its Rubik's Cube layout has rooms linked by galleries, multi-level terraces and tightly twisting stairs all around a central court filled with orange, lemon and pomegranate trees. Decor is trad Moroccan: earthy ochre walls with chalky Majorelle-blue trim, stencilled paintwork (including some gorgeous ceilings), jade *zelije* tiling and frilly furniture (including four-poster beds). Guests are greeted by red rose petals sprin-

kled on their white linen pillows. It's the Merchant Ivory of riads. Modern tastes dictate a cool plunge pool on the roof and a well-equipped fitness room – it's worth a workout for the ache-relieving pleasures of the in-house hammam that comes afterwards. **Hotel services** *Cook. Fitness room. Hammam. Plunge pool (outdoor).*

## Riad Mabrouka

*56 Derb El Bahia, off Riad Zitoun El Jedid (tel/fax 044 37 75 79/www.riad-mabrouka.com/info@riad-mabrouka.com).* **Rates** 1,200dh single; 1,400dh double; 1,800dh suite. **Credit** MC, V. **Map** p255 D6.

The Mabrouka is a vision of cool elegance. Architect Christophe Siméon has gone for a Moroccan minimalist look with whitewashed walls, billowing canvas in place of doors and some fabulous painted ceilings and shutters plus kilims adding selective splashes of colour. The result is stylish, but also very comfortable. Bathrooms are seductively sensuous,

Raid Kaiss.

all soft corners and rounded edges looking like they've been moulded out of coloured clay. With just two suites, three doubles and a single single it's very intimate. There's a pleasant cactus-potted roof terrace, with a canvas-shaded breakfast area, and a good kitchen turning out Moroccan, Mediterranean, French and Italian cuisine.

**Hotel services** *Beauty treatments. Boutique. Cook. Library. Massage. Pool (outdoor).*

## Riad Noga

*78 Derb Jedid, Douar Graoua (044 38 52 46/ fax 044 38 90 46/www.riadnoga.com/ riadnoga@menara.ma).* Rates 1,451dh-2,121dh double. **Credit** MC, V. **Map** p255 D5.

One of the most homely of Marrakech riads. Behind salmon-pink walls is a bougainvillaea and orange tree-filled courtyard (complete with chatty grey parrot) serving as an antechamber to an inner, more private court centred on a shimmering green-tiled solar-heated swimming pool. Noga is very spacious (it's three old houses knocked into one) and shared by just seven bedchambers, all bright, bold and cheery, and displaying the hospitable touch (small libraries of holiday-lite literature, for instance) of the garrulous German owner, Gaby Noack-Späth. Expansive roof terraces filled with terracotta pots and lemon trees offer terrific views over the Medina and make for the perfect spot to enjoy aperitifs or fine cooking from the excellent in-house Moroccan chefs. Closed during August.

**Hotel services** *Cook. Pool (outdoor). Safe.* **Room services** *Air-conditioning. CD player. Heating. Internet sockets. Telephone. TV: satellite.*

## Riad 72

*72 Derb Arset Aouzal, off rue Bab Doukkala (tel 044 38 76 29/fax 044 38 47 18/www.riad72.com).* **Rates** *1 June-31 Aug* 1,000dh-1,400dh double; 2,000dh suite. *1 Sept-28 Feb* 1,200dh-1,600dh double;

**ALCS**
association
de lutte
contre
le sida

"AIDS exists in Morocco too...
so protect yourself as well as others"

Since its creation in 1988, the Moroccan Association in the Fight Against AIDS (ALCS), the first of its kind in the Arab world, has focused on two objectives: the prevention of HIV infection and the support of those whose lives are affected by HIV.

The very presence of those living with HIV at the ALCS has enabled us to become a focal point for helping all concerned with this virus, by providing access to all information, access to treatment, defending their right to work, their right to live.

In the domain of prevention, we have chosen to get much closer to the public, especially those groups most vulnerable to infection, by putting ourselves in a position to listen to their reality, to their differences, and to their needs.

Our volunteers constantly lead the fight, both day and night, against ignorance, prejudice and denial. Present in schools, cafés, factories, parks, nightclubs, and on the streets, they listen, explain and inform.

If you would like to support the work of the ALCS, then please email us at:
alcsmarrakech@menara.ma

2,500dh suite. *1 Mar-31 May* 1,440dh-1,920dh double; 3,000dh suite. **Credit** AmEx, MC, V.
**Map** p252 B4.

Italian owned and, boy, doesn't it show. This is one sleek and good-looking place – Marrakech has it away with Milan. The resulting union is a trad townhouse given a black, white and grey *tadelakt* makeover. The structure, spatials and detailing are Moroccan, the furniture and fittings imported. There are only four guest bedrooms, all up on the first floor arrayed around the central courtyard, including a master suite that's laugh-out-loud large, five metres or more high and crowned by an ornate octagonal fanlight. The roof terrace boasts one of the best views in town, with the green-tiled roofs of the Dar El Bacha in the foreground and beyond a cinemascopic jagged mountain horizon. Being that much higher than the neighbours means sunbathing is no problem (many other riads are overlooked so modesty can be an issue).

**Hotel services** *Babysitting. Cook. Hammam. Massage. Plunge pool (outdoor).* **Room services** *Air-conditioning. Heating. Safe.*

## Tchaikana

*25 Derb El Ferrane, Kaat Benahid (tel/fax 044 38 51 50/www.tchaikana.com/info@tchaikana.com).*
**Rates** *7 Jan-28 Feb, 1 July-31 Aug* 800dh double; 1,300dh suite. *1 Mar-30 June, 1 Sept-6 Jan* 900dh double; 1,500dh suite. **No credit cards.**
**Map** p253 D4.

Run by a young and charming (English-speaking) Belgian couple, Jean-François and Delphine, Tchaikana has just four rooms (a fifth, small single should be added some time in 2005). However, those four rooms are enormous, particularly the two suites, each of which measures 11 metres by five metres (36ft by 16ft). The decor is beautiful, with a sort of *Vogue* goes Savannah look, and the central courtyard, laid out for dining, is gorgeously lit at night. Rates are per room, and given that all have banquettes in addition to double beds, each could sleep four or more impecunious souls – Jean-François has no objections (although no more than four breakfasts per room). Soft drinks and orange juice are also free, and there's a library of *bandes dessinée*. Delphine is a buyer for several major UK high-street stores and so is the ideal person for advice on shopping the souk. In case you're wondering, a 'tchaikana' is a Central Asian teahouse.

**Hotel services** *Cook. Internet (wi-fi enabled). Library. Tortoise.* **Room services** *Air-conditioning. Heating.*

## Budget

Let's just reiterate this: Marrakech is not the place to scrimp on accommodation. But for those who just don't have the cash there are plenty of budget hotels between rue Bab Agnaou and Riad Zitoun El Kedim, south of Jemaa El Fna. The very best of the budget options are listed below.

## Dar Fakir

*16 Derb Abou El Fadal, off Riad Zitoun El Jedid (044 44 11 00/fax 044 44 90 42/darfakir@yahoo.fr).*
**Rates** 650dh-750dh double. **Credit** MC, V.
**Map** p254 C6.

The *Vogue* goes Savannah look of **Tchaikana**.

Opulence thy name is
**Ksar Char-Bagh**. *See p59.*

The riad for the clubbing generation. Its central courtyard and surrounding salons are layered with casually strewn rugs and scattered with glittery throw cushions. Incense hangs heavy in the air and tea candles serve for illumination. There's a bar counter and every corner and recess is filled with exotic plunderings from South-east Asia and the Levant. A chilled soundtrack adds to the Buddha Bar vibe. Of the eight guestrooms, two are on the ground floor and six upstairs; they're very simply done but attractive, including *tadelakt* bathrooms. Owner Noureddine Fakir, an ambitious young guy originally from Casablanca, also runs the nearby Marrakchi restaurant (*see p101*) and residents can order off its menu and have the food delivered within around 20 minutes. He's also the guy behind the Sunset Club (*see p111*) poolside lunch spot and nightclub at the Palmeraie Golf Palace, so anyone staying at Dar Fakir is exempt from the usual 200dh cover charge.

**Hotel services** *Bar. CD player. Cook. Fireplace. Restaurant.*

### Grand Tazi

*Corner of avenue El Mouahidine & rue Bab Agnaou (044 44 27 87/fax 044 44 21 52).* **Rates** 246dh single; 293dh double. **Credit** MC, V. **Map** p254 C6.

More accurately, the 'No Longer So Grand Tazi' – although we doubt it was ever particularly salubrious. It's a two-storey, two-star establishment that retains its popularity because of its plum location just a minute's walk from Jemaa El Fna, combined with cheap room rates plus swimming pool and bar. Rooms vary wildly in quality: some have ragged curtains only just hanging from the rails, greying towels that tear when used too vigorously and otherwise unpleasant bathrooms, but then some rooms are considerably nicer. Ask to view a few before settling. Up on the first floor, what must be the longest corridor in Marrakesh leads to the good-sized swimming pool with loungers. In the evening the area beside reception takes on a life of its own as a lounge bar of dubious reputation (*see p150*). You probably want to avoid eating at the house restaurant.

**Hotel services** *Bar. Car hire. Pool (outdoor). Restaurant.* **Room services** *Air-conditioning. Telephone. TV.*

### Hotel Gallia

*30 rue de la Recette, off rue Bab Agnaou (044 44 59 13/fax 044 44 48 53/www.ilove-marrakesh.com/ hotelgallia).* **Rates** 290dh single; 450dh double. **Credit** MC, V. **Map** p254 C6.

The lanes off rue Bab Agnaou – seconds from the Jemaa El Fna – are thick with budget options but Gallia comes top of the class. This small, French-owned operation gets ticks in all the right boxes: it's smack-bang central, impeccably clean and aesthetically pleasing. Nineteen en suite double rooms open on to two picture-pretty, flower-filled courtyards, where an excellent breakfast is served. Bathrooms are big, modern pink affairs with limitless hot water. The well-kept flowery roof terrace is an ideal spot for lounging. Unsurprisingly, Gallia is popular. Bookings should be made by fax and it is advisable to book at least one month in advance.

**Hotel services** *TV: satellite.* **Room services** *Air-conditioning. Heating. Telephone.*

### Jnane Mogador

*116 Riad Zitoun El Kedim (044 42 63 24/ fax 044 42 63 23/www.jnanemogador.com/ contact@jnanemogador.com).* **Rates** 260dh single; 300dh double; 380dh triple; 460dh quadruple. **Credit** MC, V. **Map** p254 C6.

Arguably the best value accommodation in town, the Mogador is a small riad with charm and warmth. And it's clean. And all this for an unbelievable 300dh (20 quid) a double with en suite bathroom. Just don't expect a power shower. The 17 rooms are simple and predominantly pink with light pine and wrought-iron furniture and *tadelakt* bathrooms. Public areas are much more ornate with fountain courtyards, stucco arches and a large roof terrace used for breakfast. Be prepared however, to dress warmly in winter as there is no heating. Advance reservations are essential as the place is permanently full. English may or may not be spoken but if the riad's website is anything to go by ('This supernatural riad opens to those that conjugate their dreams in the present') even if it is you are unlikely to understand anything.

### Riad Magi

*79 Derb Moulay Abdelkader, off Derb Dabbachi (tel/fax 044 42 66 88).* **Rates** 560dh single; 815dh-978dh double. **No credit cards. Map** p253/255 D5.

Petite, unpretentious and homely, Riad Magi has six carefully colour-coordinated rooms on two floors around its central orange-tree shaded courtyard. The first-floor blue room is particularly lovely with its step-down bathroom. Breakfast is taken on the roof terrace or in the courtyard (which may or may not sport tree-clinging chameleons); other meals are available by arrangement. When in town, English-owner Maggie Perry holds court from her corner table, organising guests' affairs and spinning stories of local absurdity – at such times Riad Magi becomes easily the most fun hangout in Marrakesh. Maggie, and husband Clay, also own a farm, complete with donkey and horse, down in the Ourika Valley, a 30-minute drive south of the city, and guests of the riad are invited to visit or even stay overnight on the property.

**Hotel services** *Cook. Massage.*

### Sherazade

*3 Derb Djama, off Riad Zitoun El Kedim (tel/ fax 044 42 93 05/www.hotelsherazade.com/ sharazade@iam.net.ma).* **Rates** *En suite bathroom* 210dh-510dh single; 260dh-610dh double. *Shared bathroom* 160dh single; 210dh double. **Credit** MC, V. **Map** p254 C6.

Probably the most popular budget accommodation in the Medina. Why so? Perhaps because it's so much better run than most of its competitors. The desk staff speak a variety of languages, English included, rooms come with meal menus, services and

# THE WORLD'S YOUR OYSTER

# The chain gang

A growing number of global chains have branches in Marrakech, with many more on the way. Don't, as a rule, expect a great deal of individual character, but do rest assured that you'll get the same standard of service and level of comfort you last found at the same chain's outlets in Dallas, Kuala Lumpor, Zurich…

● **Le Meridien N'Fis** (avenue Mohammed VI, Hivernage, 044 44 87 72, www.lemeridien.com) offers 278 rooms including 12 suites, two restaurants, a bar, a tearoom, a pool and all the other usual amenities. It's a five-minute taxi ride from the Medina.

● The **Royal Mirage Marrakech** (avenue de la Menara, Hivernage, 044 44 89 98, www.royalmiragehotels.com) was formerly the Sheraton. It has 219 rooms, ten suites and a royal villa, plus five restaurants, a bar, a pool, a putting green and tennis courts. A poster on tripadvisor.com rates the place as the 'worst five-star hotel of all time'. It's also a taxi ride from the Medina.

● We rate the **Sofitel Marrakech** (rue Harroun Errachid, 044 42 56 00, www.sofitel.com) as the city's best chain hotel. It has a lovely garden with a big pool. It's also the closest to the Medina walls and within walking distance of Jemaa El Fna. There are 260 rooms and suites, each with private balcony or terrace (ask for one south-facing overlooking the garden with the mountains in the distance), as well as all the usual facilities.

trips out of town, the place is cleaned regularly, and there's a general air of competency, which isn't always a given down at this end of the market. Some rooms are better than others; those on the roof share toilets and get overly hot in summer, while only a handful of the most expensive have air-conditioning. Breakfast is charged extra at 50dh per person.

## Villa El Arsa

*18 Derb El Arsa, off Riad Zitoun El Jedid (tel/fax 044 42 63 26/susiescott451@hotmail.com).* **Rates** 815dh-978dh. **No credit cards. Map** p255 D6.
Owned by a British couple, David and Susie Scott, this is a modest little house, but utterly charming with it. There's a rustic, vaguely Spanish air about the place, suggested by whitewashed walls, potted plants, and bare, weathered wooden doors and furniture. There are two attractive cushion-filled lounging salons off a central courtyard that comes with a

tub-sized underlit plunge pool. The four bedrooms are ranged off the irregularly shaped upper gallery. Two of the rooms are on the small side, but the other pair are generous; all are rendered in calm neutral tones with splendid en suite bathrooms. One of the larger rooms contains an additional single bed and is air-conditioned. Plus, there's the ubiquitous roof terrace, in this case with an open fireplace for chill winter evenings. The Scotts have good connections with a pair of mountain guides and can arrange one-day or overnight trekking in the Atlas.
**Hotel services** *Cook. Plunge pool (outdoors).*

## Guéliz & Semlalia

Guéliz offers a continental-style café scene, boutique shopping, good eating and what passes locally for nightlife. It's a good antidote to the foreignness of the Medina, which is still only five minutes from central Guéliz by taxi. Semlalia is just a few minutes' north of Guéliz on the route de Casablanca.

## Moderate

### Tichka Salam

*Route de Casablanca, Semlalia (044 44 87 10/ fax 044 44 86 91/www.groupesalam.com/ tichkasalam@iam.net.ma).* **Rates** *6-31 Jan, 1 June-31 Aug, 1 Nov-21 Dec* 950dh single; 1,200dh double; 1,700dh-2,700dh suite. *1 Feb-15 Mar, 1 Apr-31 May, 1 Sept-31 Oct* 1,000dh single; 1,300dh double; 1,800dh-3,000dh suite. *16 Mar-30 Apr, 22 Dec-5 Jan* 1,100dh single; 1,300dh double; 2,000dh-3,300dh suite. **Credit** AmEx, MC, V. **Map** p250 B1.
Jaws dropped when the Tichka first opened in the 1970s. It's said that Jagger checked out of the Mamounia and executed a snake-hipped shimmy straight over here. The society-page people followed. The big wow was the design, courtesy of louche Texan Bill Willis (*see p32*). Since then, Marrakech has been hip-hotelled to excess and much of the sheen has come off the Tichka, but the public spaces are nevertheless still huge fun, particularly the bar and restaurants, which are a riot of rich colouring and tongue-in-cheek detail – dark-green tiling and column capitals. Plus, the back garden pool, complete with giant birdcage on stilts, remains arguably the best in town. Rooms (130, plus eight suites), though blessed with Willis furniture, are badly in need of a little TLC, especially the drab bathrooms.
**Hotel services** *Bar. Garden. Hammam. Laundry. Massage. Pool (outdoor). Restaurants (2). Safe. Shops.* **Room services** *Air-conditioning. Heating. Minibar. Safe. Telephone. TV: satellite.*

## Budget

### Hotel du Pacha

*33 rue de la Liberté, Guéliz (044 43 13 27/fax 044 43 13 26).* **Rates** 275dh single; 360dh double. **No credit cards. Map** p256 B2.

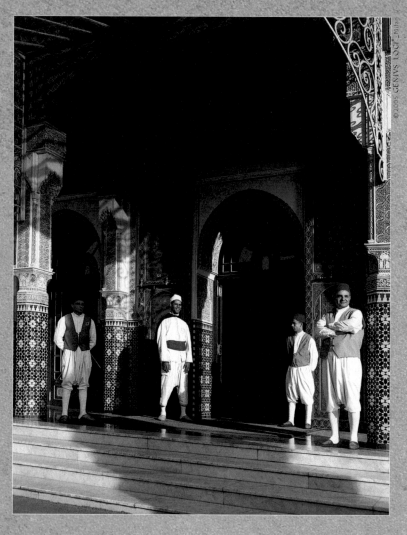

# LA MAMOUNIA

Avenue Bad Jdid   40 000 Marrakech (Maroc)
Tel. +212 44 44 44 09   +212 44 38 86 00   Fax +212 44 44 46 60
resa@mamounia.com   www.mamounia.com

*The Leading Hotels of the World*

CONCORDE
HOTELS

A standard two-star joint, nondescript and of a kind common to cities the world over. The only indication that this is Morocco is a handful of aged tourist office posters. The better rooms have small balconies overlooking a central courtyard. All are in need of a little investment, with worn furniture and broken fittings, but the beds are comfortable and the en suite bathrooms are kept clean. For the price it's a reasonable deal and one that has considerable appeal for independent tour groups, judging by the logo'd stickers on the door. The hotel business card announces that it has a 'restaurant gastronomique' but that's hardly the case – this is not a problem, though, as there are plenty of good dining options in the neighbourhood. Note that breakfast is charged extra (30dh).
**Hotel services** *Bar. Restaurant. Safe. TV lounge.*
**Room services** *Air-conditioning. Heating. Telephone. TV.*

## Hivernage

Aka the international enclave. Hivernage is between the airport and the walls of the Medina (five minutes from each), so the location is good, but the architectural neighbours are puffed-up villas and civic buildings and it's a taxi journey to get anywhere of interest. All the international five-star hotels are located in Hivernage: *see p57* **The chain gang**.

## Moderate

### Hotel Es Saadi
*avenue El Qadissia (044 44 88 11/fax 044 44 76 44/www.essaadi.com).* **Rates** *4-31 Jan, 7 June-20 Dec* 1,500dh-1,800dh double; 2,800dh-3,600dh suite. *1 Feb-6 June, 21 Dec-3 Jan* 1,800dh-2,100dh double; 3,100dh-3,900dh suite. **Credit** AmEx, MC, V.
**Map** p256 C5.
The Saadi has been around forever. Cecil Beaton snapped the Rolling Stones beside its pool back in the late 1960s. Undoubtedly, then it looked like the chicest thing on the planet; now it looks more like a municipal hospital. Guests tend to be of the same era as the hotel, that is a good few decades past their prime, but a lot of them are repeat customers, so folk are obviously well looked after here. Rooms (150 of them) are dated but comfortable, but be sure to get one south-facing, overlooking the gardens. We like how the glass rear wall of the lobby slides up during the day so that the hotel blends seamlessly with the poolside terrace – and the irregularly shaped pool remains one of the biggest and best in town. Even if you aren't staying here, the terrace is a good lunch option and house club Théatro (*see p154*) is currently one of the hippest nightspots in town.
**Hotel services** *Bar. Casino. Conference rooms. Golf driving range. Hairdressing salon. Hammam. Massage. Pool (outdoor). Restaurants (2). Sauna. Tennis courts.* **Room services** *Air-conditioning. Minibar. Radio. Telephone. TV: satellite.*

## Palmeraie

Location of choice for the moneyed and famous, accommodation among the palms is strictly select and top end. Personally, we find the 20-minute drive into town a drag (not to mention expensive if you have to take taxis), but if luxury isolation is your thing, look no further.

## Deluxe

### Jnane Tamsna
*Douar Abiad (044 32 94 23/fax 044 32 98 84/www. jnanetamsna.com/meryanne@jnanetamsna.com).*
**Rates** 2,800dh-4,500dh per room. **Credit** MC, V.
A creation of designer Meryanne Loum-Martin and her ethnobotanist husband Dr Gary Martin, Jnane Tamsna is a 'Moorish hacienda' with ten opulent rooms set around two central courtyard gardens. The architecture is vernacular chic, coloured in the palest tones of primrose, peppermint and clay and enhanced by Loum-Martin's own inspired furniture. Surrounding fruit orchards, herb and vegetable gardens provide fragrance and organic produce for the kitchen. A second kitchen is used for 'culinary adventure' programmes (*see p116*). Overflow from the main building is taken up at an adjacent villa complex of five double rooms, the decor of each inspired by a different Islamic culture. The combination of rural tranquillity, Zen-like aesthetics and ecological initiative makes for an almost utopian (no locks on the doors!) scenario. There's also an art gallery and boutique, open by appointment (061 24 27 17), and non guests are able to take advantage of 'pool, lunch and tennis' packages or visit for dinner, prepared by a former executive chef of the Quinta do Lago Four Seasons: call for details.
**Hotel services** *Art gallery. Boutique. Cook. Garden. Laundry. Massage. Pool (3, outdoor). Restaurant. Safe. Tennis courts. TV: satellite. Video library.*
**Room services** *Air-conditioning. Heating.*

### Ksar Char-Bagh
*Palmeraie (044 32 92 44/fax 044 32 92 14/ www.ksarcharbagh.com/info@ksarcharbagh.com).*
**Rates** 5,940dh-7,020dh suite; 9,180dh pool apartment. **Credit** MC, V.
Char-Bagh takes the whole Moroccan fantasy trip to its absolute extremes. A charming French couple (she in advertising, he publishing) have re-created an Alhambra palace court that defies belief. It's been built from scratch on a kasbah-sized scale. A moated gatehouse with six metre-high beaten metal doors fronts an arcaded central court with a central pool. Extensive grounds contain herb and flower gardens, an orchard, an open-air spa and the deepest of pools. OTT indoor amenities include a cigar salon (!) and wine cellar selected by the house sommelier (!!). The chef trained under Alain Ducasse. All this is shared by just a handful of sumptuous, not to mention spacious, suites, each with its own private garden or terrace, and one with its own exclusive

swimming pool. Guests are collected from the airport in a reconditioned London taxi, one of a pair shipped here via Casablanca.

**Hotel services** *Billiard room. Gardens. Gym. Hammam. Library (books, CDs, DVDs). Massage. Pool (outdoor). Restaurants. Safe. Tennis courts. Wine cellar.* **Room services** *Air-conditioning. CD player. Heating. Minibar. TV: DVD, satellite.*

## Expensive

### Les Deux Tours

*Douar Abiad (044 32 95 27/fax 044 32 95 23/ www.les-deuxtours.com/deuxtour@iam.net.ma).* **Rates** *5-31 Jan, 16 June-30 Sept, 1-19 Dec* 1,750dh double; 2,500dh deluxe; 4,000dh suite. *1 Feb-15 June, Oct, Nov, 20 Dec-4 Jan* 2,000dh double; 3,000dh deluxe; 4,000dh suite. **Credit** MC, V.

One of the longer established guesthouses in the Palmeraie, Les Deux Tours (named for its distinctive twin-towered gateway) is the sublime work of premier Marrakchi architect Charles Boccara. Approached via a cactus-lined driveway, it's a walled enclave of earthen-red villas that together offer 24 rooms and suites in a lush blossom and palm garden setting. No two rooms are the same but all feature glowing *tadelakt* walls and *zelije* tiling with stunning sculpturally soft bathrooms, several seductively lit via glassy punch-holes in pink mud-brick domes. Guests share the most attractive of outdoor pools, keyhole shaped and fringed by grassy lawns, as well as a stunning subterranean hammam. Breakfast is charged extra (100dh).

**Hotel services** *Cook. Hammam. Massage room. Pool (outdoor).* **Room services** *Air-conditioning.*

## Further afield

All of the places below are a 15- to 30-minute drive from the Medina – far enough away to be rural, close enough to pop to town for dinner.

## Deluxe

### Amanjena

*Route de Ouarzazate, km12 (044 40 33 53/ fax 044 40 34 77/www.amanresorts.com/ amanjenares@amanresorts.com).* **Rates** 7,000dh-11,675dh pavilion; 18,160dh-24,215dh maison. **Credit** AmEx, MC, V.

No creature comfort uncatered for at **Caravanserai**. *See p62.*

You did convert those prices right: rooms from $800 to $2,800. The Amanjena is part of the Amanresorts group, the world's most luxurious international hotel chain. It caters to a very specific and highly pampered clientele: Aman-junkies are not the kind to worry about a couple of hundred dollars here and there. What they get for their money is an exclusive gated complex a few miles south of town, well away from the masses (and secure from paparazzi). The architecture is low-rise palatial, rose pink and frilly, trimmed with green tiled roofs. At the heart of the resort is the bassin, a massive fish-filled reservoir of water that feeds two shallow canals running between the 34 'pavilions' and six 'maisons'. These are vast and lavish private residences, some of them with their own walled gardens, all of them filled with every conceivable luxury. Services range from spas and facials to hot-air ballooning and the loan of clubs for use on the Amelkis golf course next door. Yes, that might be Sting by the pool, but if you can afford to stay here you're probably every bit as rich and famous as he is.

**Hotel services** *Bar. Beauty centre. Bicycle rental. Car rental. Gym. Hammam. Library (books, CDs, DVDs). Massage. Pool (outdoor). Restaurants. Shops. Tennis courts.* **Room services** *Air-conditioning. CD player. Heating. Minibar. Room service (24hrs). Safe. Telephone. TV: cable, DVD, video.*

## Expensive

### Kasbah Agafay
*Route de Guemassa (044 36 86 00/fax 044 42 09 70/ www.kasbahagafay.com/info@kasbahagafay.com).* **Rates** 4,000dh doubles; 4,300dh-5,000dh suites. **Credit** MC, V.

A 150-year-old hilltop fort formerly owned by a local holy man, the Kasbah Agafay has been rescued from dereliction and transformed into a striking piece of fantasy accommodation. It appears as some sort of monastic retreat or convent, solitary on a hillock among sun-browned fields and olive groves. Inside, 18 minimally furnished (but highly stylish) rooms are grouped around small private courtyards, most with direct access to one of the kasbah's varied and gorgeous gardens. There are also four air-conditioned Caidal tents the size of pavilions, each with two double beds and grand bath and shower facilities. A new addition is the spa, offering, among other treatments, open-air massage and mud and algae baths. After that guests take herbal tea on the lawn overlooking the walled garden where vegetables, herbs and aromatic plants are grown for the kitchens and cookery courses (*see p116*). Lunch (a buffet for around 300dh per person) and dinner (à la carte) are ideally taken among the olive trees beside the generously sized garden pool. At 20 miles (32km) south-west of Marrakech, distance could be an issue; then again, you could look at Agafay as a destination in itself with the bonus of a rather nice city close by. Guests of the kasbah also get use of the Ksour Agafay private members' club in the Medina.

**Hotel services** *Cook. Cookery lessons. Gardens. Hammam. Pool (outdoor). Spa. Tennis courts.* **Room services** *Air-conditioning. Heating.*

### Tigmi
*Douar Tagadert El Cadi, km24 route d'Amizmiz (www.tigmi.com).* **Rates** *1 June-31 Aug* 1,795dh suite; *5 Jan-19 Mar, 5 Apr-31 May, 1 Sept-19 Dec* 2,038dh suite. *20 Mar-4 Apr, 20 Dec-4 Jan* 2,610dh suite. **Credit** MC, V.

The ultimate rural retreat, Tigmi is a mud-walled eight-suite haven of solitude lying in the middle of nowhere, halfway to the foothills of the Atlas, some 15 miles (24km) south of Marrakech. The architecture and interiors are rustically simple but fashionshoot stylish – lots of whitewashed arches, arcades and alcoves, covered walkways and terraces with beguiling views over raw, dusty pinkish landscapes (think Sergio Leone with citrus fruits). Most suites have courtyards (one has its own pool), terraced chill-out areas and simple, cosy bedrooms with fireplaces (lit in winter). There's a TV room, a pool, food (and wine) when you want it and a small Berber village for company, but no phones and otherwise little to do but kick back and relax. A rental car would extend your options but, then again, as David Byrne once sang, 'Heaven is a place where nothing ever happens'. Airport transfers are £20 each way.

**Hotel services** *Car rental. CD player. Cook. Garden. Hammam. Pool (outdoor). TV: cable, DVD.*

## Moderate

### Caravanserai
*264 Ouled Ben Rahmoun (044 30 03 02/ fax 044 30 02 62/www.caravanserai.com).* **Rates** 700dh-1,250dh single; 1,250dh-2,500dh double; 1,750dh-3,250dh suite; 3,250dh-3,500dh Majorelle suite; 3,750dh-4,000dh pool suite. **Credit** MC, V.

Outwardly indistinguishable among the compressed mudbrick walls that make up the small hamlet of Ouled Ben Rahmoun, but behind its wooden door Caravanserai offers a super-sophisticated take on rural life – right down to a water-mist cooling system. It's a seductive ensemble of pale pink walls, rough-hewn eucalyptus ceilings, earthenware fittings and plenty of white canvas-draped banquettes for indolent hours spent lounging. Best of all is the magnificent central swimming pool, framed by a massive gate-like structure escaped from *Waterworld*. There are 17 rooms and suites, including a couple that feature their own courtyards and pools. For guests who can tear themselves away, a minibus shuttles into central Marrakech three times a day (15 mins) and there's a 24-hour taxi service. Reservations recommended. Directrice Beatriz Maximo is an absolute sweetie and supremely well informed on all things from Marrakchi haute couture to Berber tribal life.

**Hotel services** *Bar. Beauty treatments. Boutique. Car park. Garden. Hammam. Massage. Pool (outdoor). Restaurant.* **Room services** *Air-conditioning. Fridge. Heating. Telephone.*

# Sightseeing

| | |
|---|---|
| Introduction | 64 |
| Koutoubia Mosque & Jemaa El Fna | 67 |
| The Souks | 72 |
| The Kasbah & Mellah | 82 |
| Guéliz | 87 |
| Gardens | 90 |

## Features

| | |
|---|---|
| **The best** Sightseeing | 65 |
| 200 towers by four legs | 66 |
| Those charming men | 70 |
| Jinn and tonics | 79 |
| Pretty in pink | 80 |
| Exodus | 85 |
| Saint Laurent of Arabia | 92 |

## Maps

| | |
|---|---|
| Jemaa El Fna | 68 |
| The Souks | 73 |

# Introduction

Before you begin, get your bearings here.

The pink city on the plains.

Marrakech is poor on conventional sights. In sum there are hardly more than a half-dozen mosques, palaces or museums to detain the tour bus crowds. Visitors on tight itineraries can scurry round the landmarks in a few hours and still have time to get fleeced in the souk before dinner. Poor them. This city doesn't work like that. Much of what's best is discreet or hidden and it takes time or luck to find it or figure it out. The more hours spent idly wandering, the greater the chance of stumbling on the kind of place or experience that you can't find in a guidebook – and that slow sense of discovery, of a city gently opening up like a flower, is what getting to know Marrakech is all about.

### THE MEDINA

The area in which to idle is the Medina, Arabic for the 'city', which is the name used for the area enclosed by the old walls. As a visitor this is where you will be spending most of your walking hours. Such monuments as the city can boast are all here, typically well hidden in warrenous quarters and down dead-end alleys, most of which don't bear names. There's little logic in the layout but navigation is at least

aided by two major landmarks: the vertical signpost that is the minaret of the **Koutoubia Mosque**, helpfully flagging the location of the adjacent central square, the **Jemaa El Fna**, also known simply as 'la place'. This is the sink-hole around which Marrakech swirls. Seemingly whichever way you walk, you laways end up here.

The open space of the main square also neatly divides the Medina into two zones: north of Jemaa El Fna is commercial, with a fibrous network of *souks* (bazaars), and beyond them a grouping of three of the city's moderately interesting monuments: the Musée de Marrakech, Koubba El Badiyin and Ben Youssef Medersa (all covered in our chapter **The souks**: *see pp72-81*). South of Jemaa El Fna is imperial, the quarter of the palaces and location of the melancholic Saadian Tombs (covered in our chapter **The Kasbah & the Mellah**: *see pp82-86*).

Away from well-trodden tourist paths, alleys become even more shambolic. Stray into the far northern or eastern neighbourhoods of the Medina to experience a little-seen, backstage world of Marrakech *au naturel*.

Although it's not always apparent, there is some kind of street etiquette: pedestrians stick to the right leaving the centre free for scooters, pushbikes and donkeys.

### BEYOND THE MEDINA

North-west of the old walls is the 'new city', a French colonial creation of the 1930s, which goes by the name of **Guéliz**. Old city and new are connected by the broad, tree-lined avenue Mohammed V (pronounced 'M'hammed Sanc'). Named for the king who presided over Morocco's independence, it's the main street of Guéliz. Few short-term visitors bother with this part of town but middle-class Marrakchis and serious expats favour it for car-friendly streets, modern apartment blocks and a semblance of 21st-century living. It's also home to a lot of the better dining and shopping, plus most of what passes for nightlife.

South of Guéliz and immediately west of the city walls, is **Hivernage** (drop the aitch), a small, low-density neighbourhood of villas and international five-star hotels. Also out this way, where Hivernage shades into Guéliz, are civic trappings such as the railway station, new Royal Opera House, Palais des Congrès and, beyond them all, the airport.

On the opposite (north-east) side of the Medina is a vast bare-earth oasis of well-spaced palm trees, known, prosaically enough, as the **Palmeraie**. While not particularly pretty, its distance from the hoi polloi, low population density (there are more trees than people) and opportunities for lavish construction have made it a favourite locale for the homes of the rich – both Moroccans and foreigners.

## Getting around

The only way to tackle the Medina is by foot. It looks daunting on the map but the area within the walls isn't that large. However, the miles do add up with all the wrong turns you're bound to make, and a lot of the streets are too narrow to accommodate cars, which means dodging swarms of motorcycles, scooters and pushbikes instead. Occasionally, a taxi might be necessary, but more for navigation purposes than for anything else – some restaurants and hotels are so well hidden that the only way to find them is to be chauffeured by a native, who at least has the language skills to ask the way when he too gets lost.

Taxis are necessary for shuttling between the Medina and Guéliz, which is only a five-minute ride (roughly 6dh by day, 10dh by night) but a half-hour walk. The green-painted horse-drawn carriages (known as *calèches*) are pretty impractical as a form of transport, but they are a pleasant way to go about sightseeing and aren't prohibitively expensive (*see p66* **200 towers by four legs**). Rental of a two-wheeler is also a fun option, especially for exploring around the city beyond the walls and the Palmeraie.

For more information on getting around the city, *see pp224-26*.

### GUIDES

Hotels all but push them on clients, warning of the dangers of unaccompanied exploration, but do you really need a guide? The answer is an unequivocal 'no'. Yes, you'll probably get lost a few times but you'll never stay that way for

## The best Sightseeing

### For the total tourist trip
Climb into a horse-drawn **calèche** for a circuit of the city walls. *See p66.*

### For imperial excess
Check out the apartments of the concubines at the **Bahia Palace**. *See p85.*

### For spiritual serenity
Cool white marble and a beautiful ablutions pool induce calm at the **Medersa Ben Youssef**. *See p74.*

### For oriental intensity
Main square **Jemaa El Fna** is chaotic and enthralling at any time, but doubly so by night. *See p70.*

### For haunting ruins
Muse on how the mighty fall at the stork-festooned **Badii Palace**. *See p83.*

### For time stood still
Manufacturing remains pre-industrial in many of the Medina's adapted old **fundouks**. *See p77.*

### For greenery (and blue)
Planted by a painter, nurtured by a couturier, the **Majorelle Gardens** mix horticulture with art. *See p92.*

### For time out
Gorgeous exhibition space **Dar Cherifa** serves mint tea to weary explorers. *See p76.*

Walls of mud and straw.

long – any local will graciously set you back on track. In any case, in a city of so many hidden surprises, there's no such thing as a wrong turn, only alternative routes.

However, if you have special interests or wish to hire someone whose knowledge goes beyond the confines of this book, then we can recommend **Ahmed Tija**, who's been guiding visitors for the best part of 50 years, and was a friend of author Gavin Maxwell, whose *Lords of the Atlas* is the definitive local history book. We've also heard good things about the other guides listed below, all of whom speak English. Expect to pay 200dh-300dh per half day.

Beware picking up unofficial guides (official guides carry accreditation) as they usually turn out to be an expensive waste of time.

**Ahmed Tija**
*044 30 03 37/mobile 061 08 45 57.*

**Moulay Youssef**
*Mobile 061 16 35 64.*

**Mustapha Chouquir**
*Mobile 062 10 40 99.*

**Mustapha Karroum**
*Mobile 061 34 07 78.*

# 200 towers by four legs

The Medina began life as a garrison camp in 1060, under the leadership of the Almoravid leader, Youssef Ben Tachfine. As the nomadic tent-dwellers converted to a settled lifestyle, the city grew. Around 1126, in the face of threat from the Almohads to the south, Sultan Ali Ben Youssef decided to encircle the new city with walls. Within a year he had completed a circuit of ten kilometres (six miles) of ten-metre (30-foot) high walls defended by 200 towers and punctuated by 20 gates. There have been constant repairs and some expansion, but the original walls probably followed roughly the same lines as the walls of today.

The wall are built with reddish *pisé* (dried mud mixed with lime). Although strikingly beautiful at times – especially when pinkly glowing under a setting sun – they are fairly featureless. There are no ramparts to ascend, and a walk around the whole circuit is a bit of a slog. It makes for a great whirl in a horse-drawn calèche, though. Drivers and their carriages wait in line on the north side of place de Foucault (just follow your nose). A complete circuit, heading north up avenue Mohammed V and right out of the Bab Nkob, will take the best part of an hour and costs around 80dh; state-fixed prices are posted on the carriages.

# Koutoubia Mosque & Jemaa El Fna

The heart and the soul of the city.

The most vertical element of Marrakech, the minaret of the **Koutoubla Mosque**.

Paris has the Eiffel Tower, London has Big Ben, and Marrakech has the Koutoubia. Its square, towering minaret is the city's pre-eminent landmark and most recognisable icon. Not only that, it's also one of the city's oldest structures and stands on the site of what is believed to be the very first thing ever built here. The mosque and its minaret are unquestionably the heart of Marrakech. The soul lies 200 metres west in the amorphous form of Jemaa El Fna, market place and forum to the city almost since its foundation.

## Koutoubia Mosque

At 77 metres (252 feet) the minaret of the Koutoubia Mosque is not actually that high (the Eiffel Tower stands over four times taller at 321 metres), but thanks to Marrakech's flat topography and a local ordinance that forbids any other building in the Medina to rise above the height of a palm tree, it towers majestically over its surroundings. As such, the minaret is the first thing that any visitor sees when approaching the city from afar. Unfortunately, up close the view still remains largely restricted to the outside of the tower because the mosque (and the interior of the minaret) is off-limits to non-Muslims.

The Koutoubia gets its name (Mosque of the Booksellers) from the cluster of Koran merchants, parchment dealers, binders and scribes that at one time filled the surrounding streets. They and the streets are all long gone and instead the shadow of the minaret falls across a small modern plaza where tour groups rub shoulders with the faithful on their way to pray. Glassed-over, sunken areas on the plaza are the remains of reservoirs that belonged to the **Dar El Hajar** (House of Stone), a fortress built by city-founder Youssef Ben Tachfine towards the end of the 11th century, and the first permanent structure in the encampment that became Marrakech. The fortress was short-lived, destroyed by the conquering Almohads who replaced it with a mosque in 1147.

The extensive ruins of that first mosque, in the form of the foundations of columns that supported the roof, cover a large area due west of the plaza. The Koutoubia Mosque was built in 1158 adjoining the Almohad mosque, presumably because the earlier structure was no longer big enough to accommodate the city's expanding population. The two would have functioned as one mosque through connecting doors until the Almohad mosque fell into disrepair and eventually collapsed following an earthquake in 1775.

The Koutoubia's celebrated minaret was added by Yacoub El Mansour, an architectural patron of vertical delights; El Mansour was also responsible for the Tour Hassan in Rabat and the Giralda in Seville. Like the Giralda, the Koutoubia Minaret contains an ascending ramp, broad and tall enough for the *muezzin* (whose job it is to call the faithful to prayer five times a day) to ride a horse up to the top. The pale brick façade was originally encased in ceramics and stucco but all that remains is

a single narrow blue-tiled frieze beneath the saw-tooth crenellations.

Legend has it that the four brass balls that top the domed lantern were originally made of solid gold, cast from the melted-down jewellery of the sultan's wife as her penance for eating four grapes during Ramadan. Hardly more credible is the claim that in times past only blind *muezzin*s were employed because from the summit a sighted individual would have been able to gaze into the royal harem. The gibbet beside the balls is used to hoist a white flag that indicates prayer time for the deaf.

The small white domed structure on the plaza is the **Koubba of Lalla Zohra**, a shrine that used to be open to the public until the inebriated son of a former city mayor ploughed his car into the structure and, as part of the repairs, the door was sealed up.

It's possible to walk around either side of the Koutoubia, clockwise between the main entrance and the wall that encloses the grounds of the **French Consulate**, or anti-clockwise along the top of the Almohad ruins. Either route leads into the rose-filled Koutoubia Gardens, which spread south and west of the mosque. Across avenue Houman El Fetouaki, south of the gardens, a high wall cuts from sight a modest crenellated building; this is the humble **Tomb of Youssef Ben Tachfine**, founder of Marrakech. A padlocked gate ensures that the great desert warrior rests in peace, his mausoleum off limits to the public.

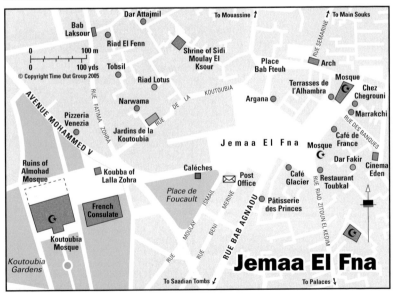

The **Jemaa El Fna**, setting for a daily carnival of Moroccan life. *See p70.*

## Jemaa El Fna

It's the main open space in Marrakech but to call Jemaa El Fna a public square is misleading. Uncontained, disorderly, untainted by grandeur or pomp, untamable by council or committee, Jemaa El Fna is nothing less than bedlam. It's an urban clearing, as irregular in shape as an accident of nature, and thronged day and night with a carnival of local life – totally at odds with its name, which roughly translates as 'Assembly of the Dead'.

The square is as old as Marrakech itself. It was laid out as a parade ground by the Almoravids in front of their royal fortress (the Dar El Hajar, see p68). When the succeeding Almohads built a new palace to the south, the open ground passed to the public and became what it remains today – a place for gathering, trading, entertainment and even the occasional riot. The name (pronounced with its consonants tumbling into each other to come out something like 'jemaf'na') refers to its former role as a venue for executions, with the decapitated heads put up on spikes for public display. The French put a stop to that.

In more recent times, during the 1970s, the municipality attempted to impose order with a scheme to tarmac the square and turn it into a car park. This was opposed and defeated. Since then, thanks in part to the lobbying efforts of Spanish writer Juan Goytisolo (who has lived just off the square since the late 1970s), Jemaa El Fna has been recognised by UNESCO as part of the 'oral patrimony of mankind' and its preservation is secured. There's still some tidying-up impulse at work, however. The design of the orange-juice carts has recently been regularised in a faux traditional style and over the last couple of years the whole square has been gradually paved over.

### A DAY IN THE LIFE

During the early part of the day the square is relatively quiet. The orange-laden carts of the juice-sellers line the perimeter, wagon-train fashion, but otherwise there's only a scattering of figures, seated on boxes or rugs, shaded under large shabby umbrellas. The snake-charmers are early starters with their black, rubbery reptiles laid out in front or sheltered under large tambourine-like drums (be careful what you kick). For a few dirhams visitors can have a photograph taken with a large snake draped over their shoulders; for a few more dirhams they can have it removed. Gaudily clad water-sellers wander around offering to pose for dirhams. Other figures may be dentists (teeth pulled on the spot), scribes (letters written to order), herbalists (good for whatever ails you) or beggars (to whom Moroccans give generously). Overlooking all, the prime morning spot for unhurried businessmen and traders is the patio of the landmark **Café de France** (see p114), which has been resident on the square for at least the last 50 years.

# Those charming men

Just as the gnawa musicians thrumming away on the Jemaa El Fna are pale imitations of the real thing, so too the square's snake charmers, who are a lethargic bunch almost as comatose as their reptiles. To see some real snake action you have to call in the professionals. They arrive – two strapping, mustachioed young blokes in flowing white robes – on a 50cc Yamaha. Strapped behind them above the rear wheel is a large box sheathed in a black plastic bin liner. The box is removed from the motorbike and placed in the courtyard where the performance is to take place. This is a birthday treat for a holidaying retired school teacher, a surprise arranged by the owner of the riad at which she's a guest. She has little idea of what's going on until one of the robed Moroccans reaches into his box and pulls out four foot of black, irritable cobra. It thashes, coils and spits until the charmer places his hand on its hooded head and it becomes still enough for him to lay the snake over the teacher's forehead. Then he puts it on the ground where it remains frozen until the charmer claps his hand and the snake instantly becomes animated and slithers at speed toward the shrieking observers. So begins 15 minutes of sheer terror. Scorpions are dropped in palms and down shirt fronts (thankfully this is only a sleight of hand), pythons are draped round necks and stuffed down trousers and a writhing spaghetti-ish mass of small snakes is brandished but quickly withdrawn possibly due to the hysterical alarm showing on the audience's faces. And then it's all over, thank God. The box is closed, put back in its bin liner and re-tied to the rear of the bike. The two charmers swing a leg over, give it a kickstart and they're off to a bring a little genuine terror to some other happy event.

Ringside seating at the **Argana**.

The action tends to wilt beneath the heat of the afternoon sun, when snake-charmers, dancers and acrobats can barely manage to stir themselves at the approach of camera-carrying tourists. It's not until dusk that things really kick off.

As the light and heat fade, ranks of makeshift kitchens set up with tables, benches and hissing flames, constituting one great open-air restaurant where adventurous eaters can snack on anything from snails to sheep's heads (*see p103* **Square meals**).

Beside the avenues of food stalls, the rest of the square takes on the air of a circus. Shoals of visiting Berber farmers from the surrounding plains and villages join Medina locals in crowding around the assorted performers. These typically include troupes of cartoon-costumed acrobats, musicians and their prowling transvestite dancers, storytellers and magicians, and boxing bouts between underage boys who can hardly lift their hands in the heavy leather gloves. The tourists and visitors who provided the *raison d'être* for the afternoon entertainers are now negligible in this far more surreal evening scene.

Approaching midnight the food stalls begin to pack up, the performers wind down, sending the contributions cap on one last round, and the crowds thin. Only the musicians remain, purveyors of seedy mysticisms, attended by small knots of wild-eyed devotees giddy on repetitive rhythms, helped along by hash. At the same time, the place becomes one great gay cruising ground, busy with tight-shirted, tight-trousered teens, sharp and cynical beyond their years.

## THE OVERVIEW

The best place to be at any time of the day is in among it all (watch your wallet and bags), but several of the peripheral cafés and restaurants have upper terraces with fine ringside seating, among them the **Argana** (*see p98*), **Café de France** (*see p114*), **Terrasses de l'Alhambra** (*see p106*) and – with the best view of the lot – the **Café Glacier**, which is above the Hotel CTM. Here, the purchase of one soft drink ('obligatoire') for 10dh allows you access to the café's *grand balcon* with its 270° sweeping panorama. According to a 1960 travel account, *By Road to Tangiers and Marrakech*, the snakecharmers used to perform up on this terrace during a temporary ban on snakes in the square.

Day or night, whether you choose stealthy observation from the terraces or a headlong plunge into the mêlée, Jemaa El Fna always remains somewhat elusive. 'All the guidebooks lie,' writes Juan Goytisolo, 'there's no way of getting a firm grasp on it.'

# The Souks

Need some bright yellow slippers, a chameleon and a couple of cheap daggers?

### Maps p252 & p253

Fanning north of Jemaa El Fna are the souks (markets), with alleyway upon alleyway of tiny retail cubicles – a hundred of them in a hundred metres. In the most densely touristed areas, the overwhelming number of shops is offset by the fact that most seem compelled to offer exactly the same non-essential goods; in particular, canary-yellow slippers (*babouches*), embroidered robes and etched brass platters the size of manhole covers. Slip away down the side alleys and you'll find that things improve; our **Shops & Services** chapter (*p117-34*) picks out some of the highlights.

The two main routes into the souks are rue Semarine and rue Mouassine; the former offers the more full-on blast of bazaar, the latter is a more sedate path leading to choice boutiques.

## Semarine & the Great Souk

Entrance to the rue Semarine (aka Souk Semarine) is via an elaborate arch one block north of Jemaa El Fna – reached via either the spice market or the egg market, both pungent experiences, one pleasant, the other not. Semarine is a relatively orderly street, broad and straight with overhead trellising dappling the paving with light and shadow. Every section of the souk has its own speciality and here it has traditionally been textiles, although these days cloth merchants have been largely supplanted by souvenir shops.

About 150 metres along, the first alley off to the east leads to a wedge-shaped open area known as the **Rahba Kedima**, or the 'old place'. (The way between Semarine and the Rahba Kedima is a perpetual crush because it also leads to a small court, the **Souk Laghzel**, formerly the wool market but now a car-boot-sale of a souk where women – and only women – come to sell meagre possessions such as a single knitted shawl or a bag of vegetables.) The Rahba Kedima used to be the city's open-air corn market but it's now given over to an intriguing mix of raffia bags and baskets, woollen hats and sellers of cooked snails. Around the edges are spice and 'magic' stalls – *see p79* **Jinn and tonics**.

The upper storeys of the shops on the northern side of the Rahba Kedima are usually hung with carpets and textiles, an invitation to search for the partially obscured passageway that leads through to the **Criée Berbère** (Berber Auction). These days this partially roofed, slightly gloomy section of the souk is the lair of the rug merchants, but until well into the 20th century it was used for the sale of slaves, auctioned here three times weekly. According to North African historian Barnaby Rogerson, the going rate was two slaves for a camel, ten for a horse and 40 for a civet cat.

Back on rue Semarine, just north of the turning for the Rahba Kedima, the street forks: branching to the left is the Souk El Attarin (*see below*), straight on is the **Souk El Kebir** (Great Souk). Between the two is a ladder of narrow, arrow-straight passages, little more than shoulder-width across and collectively known as the **Kissaria**. This is the beating heart of the souk. Stallholders here specialise in cotton, clothing, kaftans and blankets.

Further along the Souk El Kebir are the courtyards of carpenters and wood turners, before a T-junction forces a choice: left or right. Go left and then immediately right at the Meditel shop to emerge once again into streets that are wide enough for the passage of cars.

Just north is the dusty open plaza of the place Ben Youssef, dominated by the **Ben Youssef Mosque**, which is easily identifiable by its bright-green pyramidal roofs. The original mosque went up in the 12th century and was the grandest of the age, but what stands now is a third and lesser incarnation, dating from the early 19th century. Non-Muslims may not enter. However, in the immediate vicinity of the mosque is a cluster of tourist-friendly sights, including the decidedly average **Musée de Marrakech** (*see p75*), the enchanting **Ben Youssef Medersa** (*see p74*) and the venerable **Koubba El Badiyin** (*see p75*).

### DYERS' QUARTER

Back at the fork on rue Semarine, bearing left brings you on to **Souk El Attarin**, or the Spice Souk. Contrary to the name, this part of the souk no longer deals in the hot and flavoursome stuff. Instead its traders largely traffic in tourist tat, from painted wooden thingamies to leather whatjamacallits. Almost opposite the subdued entrance to a workaday mosque is the **Souk des Babouches**, a whole alley devoted to soft-leather slippers – and their almost identical synthetic counterparts.

Sightseeing

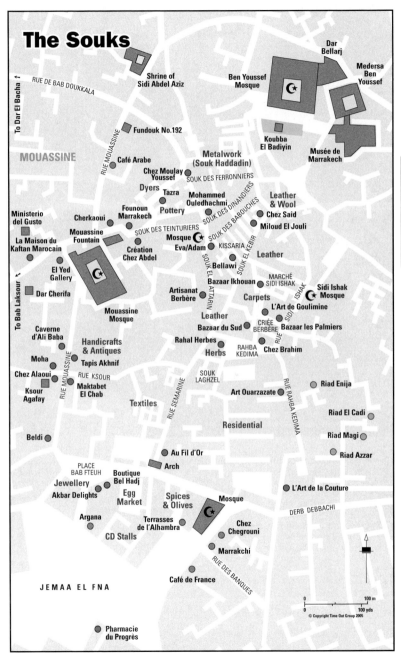

# The Souks

To Dar El Bacha ↑

RUE DE BAB DOUKKALA

Shrine of
Sidi Abdel Aziz

Dar
Bellarj

Ben Youssef
Mosque

Medersa
Ben
Youssef

Fundouk No.192

**MOUASSINE**

RUE MOUASSINE

Café Arabe

Metalwork
(Souk Haddadin)

Koubba
El Badiyin

Musée de
Marrakech

Chez Moulay
Youssef

SOUK DES FERRONNIERS

Dyers

Tazra

Mohammed
Ouledhachmi

Leather
& Wool

Pottery

SOUK DES DINANDIERS

Chez Said

Founoun
Marrakech

Cherkaoui

SOUK DES BABOUCHES

Miloud El Jouli

Ministerio
del Gusto

Mouassine
Fountain

SOUK DES TEINTURIERS

Mosque

SOUK EL KEBIR

La Maison du
Kaftan Marocain

Création
Chez Abdel

Eva/Adam

KISSARIA

Leather

El Yed
Gallery

Bellawi

MARCHÉ
SIDI ISHAK

Sidi Ishak
Mosque

Dar Cherifa

Artisanat
Berbère

Bazaar Ikhouan

SOUK EL ATTARIN

Carpets

L'Art de Goulimine

Mouassine
Mosque

Leather

CRIÉE
BERBERE

Bazaar les Palmiers

To Bab Laksour ↖

Caverne
d'Ali Baba

Handicrafts
& Antiques

Bazaar du Sud

RUE SIDI ISHAK

Rahal Herbes

Herbs

RAHBA
KEDIMA

Chez Brahim

Moha

Tapis Akhnif

RUE MOUASSINE

RUE KSOUR

Chez Alaoui

SOUK
LAGHZEL

Ksour
Agafay

Maktabet
El Chab

Textiles

RUE SEMARINE

Art Ouarzazate

RUE RAHBA KEDIMA

Riad Enija

Riad El Cadi

Beldi

Residential

Riad Magi

Au Fil d'Or

Riad Azzar

Arch

PLACE
BAB FTEUH

Boutique
Bel Hadj

L'Art de la Couture

Jewellery

Egg
Market

Spices
& Olives

Mosque

DERB DEBBACHI

Akbar Delights

Argana

Terrasses
de l'Alhambra

Chez
Chegrouni

CD Stalls

Marrakchi

RUE DES BANQUES

Café de France

**JEMAA EL FNA**

0 ————— 100 m
0 ————— 100 yds

© Copyright Time Out Group 2005

Pharmacie
du Progrès

Carpets, spices, sweets, whatever…

Further along Attarin, ringing hammer blows announce the **Souk Haddadin**, the quarter of the ironworkers. One of the most medieval parts of the souk, it's full of dark, cavern-like workshops in which firework bursts of orange sparks briefly illuminate tableaux of grime-streaked craftsmen like some scene by Doré.

West of Attarin three alleys run downhill into the **Souk des Teinturiers**, which is the area of the dyers' workshops. Labourers rub dyes into cured hides (to be cut and fashioned into babouches) and dunk wool into vats of dark-hued liquids. This results in brightly coloured sheafs of wool which are then hung over the alleyways in a manner irresistible to passing photographers. It also results in the labourers having arms coloured to their elbows. You know you're nearing this part of the souk when you start seeing people with blue or purple arms.

The three alleys converge into one, which then doglegs between a squeeze of assorted artisans' salesrooms (lanterns, metalwork and pottery) before exiting under an arch beside the Mouassine fountain and mosque (*see p76*).

### Ben Youssef Medersa

*place Ben Youssef (044 39 09 11)*. **Open** 9am-6.30pm daily. **Admission** 30dh. **No credit cards**. **Map** p73 & p253 D4.

A *medersa* is a Koranic school, dedicated to the teaching of Islamic scripture and law. This one was founded in the 14th century, then restored and enlarged to its current dimensions in 1564-5 by the Saadian sultan Abdellah El Ghalib. It was given a further polishing up in the late 1990s courtesy of the Ministry of Culture. Entrance is via a long, cool passageway leading through to the great courtyard, a place of serenity centred on a water-filled basin. The surrounding façades are decorated with *zelije* tiling,

**Sightseeing**

'Stork's House', so called because it was formerly a hospital for the big white birds. The stork is holy to Marrakech. There are countless tales to explain its exalted status, and the impression it gives of prayer-like prostration when at rest. The most commonly repeated is of a local *imam* (the Islamic priest), dressed in traditional Moroccan garb of white jellaba and black robe, drunk on wine, who then compounds the sin by climbing the minaret and blaspheming. Shazam! Man suffers wrath of god and is transformed into a stork. Even before the arrival of Islam, an old Berber belief also had it that storks are actually transformed humans. To this day the offence of disturbing a stork carries a three-month prison sentence. Restored in the 1990s, Dar Bellarj now serves as a local cultural centre hosting exhibitions, workshops and performances. Unless you're lucky enough to drop in on a happening there's little to see; the courtyard is attractive with seating and caged songbirds, and sweet tea is offered to visitors, but you may wonder exactly for what it was you paid admission. And despite the posted opening hours, the big door is sometimes firmly locked.

### Koubba El Badiyin

*place Ben Youssef (044 39 09 11).* **Open** *Apr-Sept* 9am-7pm daily. *Oct-Mar* 9am-6pm daily **Admission** 10dh. **Map** p73 & p253 C4.

Across from the Ben Youssef Mosque, set in its own fenced enclosure and sunk several metres below the current street level, is the Koubba El Badiyin (also known as the 'Qoubba Almoravide'). It looks unprepossessing but its unearthing in 1948 prompted one French art historian to exclaim that 'the art of Islam has never exceeded the splendour of this extraordinary dome'. It's the only surviving structure from the era of the Almoravids, the founders of Marrakech, and as such it represents a wormhole back to the origins of Moorish building history, presenting for the first time many of the shapes and forms that remain the basis of the North African architectural vocabulary. It dates to the reign of Ali Ben Youssef (1107-43) and was probably part of the ablutions complex of the original Ben Youssef Mosque. It's worth paying the slight admission fee to descend the brickwork steps and view the underside of the dome, which is a kaleidoscopic arrangement of a floral motif within an octagon within an eight-pointed star.

### Musée de Marrakech

*place Ben Youssef (044 39 09 11/www.museede marrakech.ma).* **Open** 9am-6.30pm daily. **Admission** 30dh. **No credit cards. Map** p73 & p253 D4.

Inaugurated in 1997, the Musée de Marrakech is a conversion of an opulent early 20th-century house formerly belonging to a Marrakchi grandee. Entering the outer courtyard, there's a pleasant café off to one side and a crap bookshop opposite. Within the museum exhibits rotate. On our last visit we found two rooms devoted to 20th-century Moroccan

stucco and carved cedar, all executed with restraint. At the far side is the domed prayer hall with the richest of decoration, notably around the *mihrab*, the arched niche that indicates the direction of Mecca. Back in the entrance vestibule, passageways and two flights of stairs lead to more than 100 tiny windowless students' chambers on two floors, clustered in sixes and sevens about small internal lightwells. Medieval as it all seems, the *medersa* was still in use until as recently as 1962. The building stood in for an Algerian Sufic retreat in Gillies Mackinnon's 1998 film *Hideous Kinky*.

### Dar Bellarj

*9 rue Toulat Zaouiat Lahdar (044 44 45 55).* **Open** 9am-6pm daily. **Admission** 15dh. **No credit cards. Map** p73 & p253 D4.

North of the entrance to the Ben Youssef Medersa is a large wooden door in the crook of the alley emblazoned with a bird's head: this is Dar Bellarj, the art and the rest filled with old ceramics from Fès. But the star attraction is the building itself, particularly the tartishly tiled great central court, roofed over and hung with an enormous chandelier like the mothership from *Close Encounters of the Third Kind*. The former hammam is lovely and makes a fine exhibition space for the prints and photos on show. If nothing else, the museum is a cool refuge from blazing heat outside. And as Joulia from Greece writes in the guest book, it has 'amazing toilets'. It is possible to get a combined 'three monuments' pass from the ticket office here, which is good for the museum, the Ben Youssef Medersa and the Koubba El Badiyin and costs 50dh. The ticket is valid for one day only.

## Mouassine

Although it's far from immediately apparent, **Mouassine** is rapidly becoming the most chic of Medina quarters. West of the main souk area and north of Jemaa El Fna, it's home to a growing number of smart boutiques, interesting galleries and hip *maisons d'hôtes*.

Immediately on entering rue Mouassine from place Bab Fteuh is **Beldi** (*see p121*), must-stop shop for the likes of Jean Paul Gaultier and sundry international fashion types. West of the junction with rue Ksour three elaborate brass lanterns above the alleyway mark the doorway of **Ksour Agafay**, Marrakech's own private members' club. If you ring the bell it's possible that they might allow you in to look around – it's a well-restored 19th-century house with, unusually, the courtyard up on the first floor.

At the point where the street widens to embrace the walls of the **Mouassine Mosque** (which lends its name to the quarter and was erected in the 1560s by Saadian sultan Abdellah El Ghalib) a side-street off to the west winds left then first right to reach a large wooden doorway with a signplate reading **Dar Cherifa**. Inside is a stunning late 16th-century riad with filigree stucco and beautiful carved cedar detailing. It operates as a gallery (*see p144*) and performance space, doubling as a café during the day.

Where rue Mouassine hits rue Sidi El Yamami, a dim little archway under a sign reading 'A la Fibule' jogs left and right to the fantastical façade of the **Ministerio del Gusto** (*see p144*), an extraordinary gallery-cum-sales space executed in an architectural style that co-creator Alessandra Lippini describes as 'delirium'.

Following rue Sidi El Yamami west leads to the city gate **Bab Laksour**, in the vicinity of which are the boutiques **Kulchi** (*see p125*) and **Kifkif** (*see p128*) and the Moroccan restaurants **Ksar Es Saoussan** (*see p99*) and **Tobsil** (*see p101*). In the opposite direction, a few paces east along Sidi El Yamami is the **Mouassine fountain** with quadruple drinking bays, three for animals and one – the most ornate – for people. It's here that the character Louis Bernard is fatally stabbed in Hitchcock's 1955 version of *The Man Who Knew Too Much* – although not so fatally that he can't first stagger half a mile to Jemaa El Fna to expire in the arms of Jimmy Stewart.

Ground zero for Moroccan architecture, the **Koubba El Badiyin**. *See p75.*

**Ben Youssef Medersa.** *See p74.*

Beside the fountain is an arched gateway beyond which is the Souk des Teinturiers (*see p74*). Some time in summer 2005 a couple of rooms within the gateway, above the arch, are due to open as a boutique run by Viviana Gonzalez of Riad El Fenn. North of the fountain at 184 rue Mouassine is **Café Arabe**. When it opened in 2004 this was welcome as a rare place in the souks where you could take tea or coffee and eat something small and snacky; now it has switched to serving full Moroccan meals only, which is little use to anybody.

Further up the street are a couple of good examples of *fundouk*s. The *fundouk* is the distant forerunner of the modern hotel. It was a merchant hostel, built to provide accommodation and warehousing for the caravan traders who had crossed the desert and mountains to the south to bring their wares into the marketplaces of Marrakech. A *fundouk* offered stabling and storage rooms on the ground floor, bedrooms off the upper galleries, and a single gated entrance to the street that was locked at night for security. Most of the city's surviving *fundouk*s now operate as ramshackle artisans' workshops, such as the one at No.192 rue Mouassine. This *fundouk* also featured in the film *Hideous Kinky* as the hotel where Kate Winslet and daughters lodged. Up on the first floor, the 'room' numbers painted by the film production crew remain – Winslet's was No.38, the only one with a bright new door. Another grand *fundouk* across the street is thought to be the oldest surviving example of this building type in Marrakech.

## SAINTS & SHRINES

A few steps north of the *fundouk*s is a cross-roads: go left for the Dar El Bacha and Bab Doukkala (*see p79*) or right for the dyers' quarter (*see p74*), but only adherents of Islam should proceed straight ahead, according to a sign that reads 'Non Moslem interdit'.

Up this particular alley is the **Shrine of Sidi Abdel Aziz**, resting place of one of the seven saints of Marrakech. Collectively known as 'El Sebti', this group of holy men have been venerated for centuries as guardians of the city. Each has a nice new shrine erected by Sultan Moulay Ismail in the 18th century. All the shrines are within, or just outside, the walls of the Medina and once a year they are the focus of an official seven-day *moussem* (pilgrimage).

Sidi Abdel Aziz's shrine can be skirted, zigging east then north, then east and north again on to rue Bab Taghzout, which runs north to the most renowned of the saintly resting places, the **Shrine of Sidi Bel Abbas**. (En route is a beautiful Marrakech cameo that brings together the stately **Chrob ou Chouf** – 'Drink and Look' – a monumental 18th-century fountain, and, directly opposite, a chickenshit amusement arcade where kids batter the hell out of pixilated Ninja warriors on gaming machines scarcely less ancient than the neighbouring water trough.)

Soon after widening to accommodate a local bus stop and scrubby park, the street narrows again to squeeze through the ornate gateway known as **Bab Taghzout**, with its six-inch thick wooden doors. This was one of the

They call them keyhole arches, for obvious reasons.

# Jinn and tonics

Abdelhamid Oulhiad wears a grey wool rollneck, canvas khakis and a black donkey jacket. He looks every inch the young (late thirtyish), stylish modern Moroccan. It's only when he removes his shades to display nervously darting, red-rimmed eyes that a note of the other-worldly creeps in. Abdelhamid battles *jinn*.

Created from fire, the *jinn* are souls without bodies and a tendency towards malice. Belief in these troublesome spirits is widespread throughout Morocco, even in the most urbane of social circles. On the occasion of a death in the house, a run of bad luck, uncharacteristically antisocial behaviour or inexplicable illness in a loved one, worried parties seek out Abdelhamid. Practitioners like him can often succeed where more conventional methods fail. He tells of a case where a woman was inexplicably paralysed following the death of her husband. The doctors couldn't understand it until an exorcist discovered she was being held captive for sex by the spirit of her recently deceased partner. A cure was effected. Honest.

The worst of the *jinn* is one-eyed Aicha Kandicha, a female spirit with a donkey's tail who plagues men. But the types and varieties are legion, with one set that operates exclusively by day and a whole other army that appears only by night.

To do battle, Abdelhamid relies on the Koran and a complex hand-drawn reference chart that takes into account numerology and astrology to indicate which are the best days to fight and when it's expedient to lay low. There are also myriad incenses and compounds required in different measures for each and every situation.

Herbalist Abdeljabbar Ait Chaib on the Rahba Kedima at the heart of the Medina stocks most ingredients, from jars of leeches to dried chameleons, good for warding off the evil eye: toss it into a small wood-fired oven and walk around it three times. If the chameleon explodes, it's bye-bye evil eye. But if the chameleon melts, you're still in the shit.

And the little black scorpions? Nothing to do with black magic – they're good against haemorrhoids, apparently.

original Medina gates until the walls were extended in the 18th century to bring the shrine within the city.

Through the *bab* and a few steps to the right is an even more elaborate arched gateway, executed in carved alabaster. Beyond is an arcade that would formerly have been lined with herbalists, faith healers and quack doctors here to minister to/prey on the sick and the ailing drawn to the tomb to bask in its saintly *baraka* (blessings). Such beliefs remain strong and the courtyard of the shrine – adorned with Marrakech's only sundial – is always filled with the crippled and infirm. If things don't work out, a shaded arcade on the south side harbours a decrepit gathering of largely blind characters, all of whom belong to a special sect of priesthood specialising in the ministering of last rites. The sanctuary itself is off limits; instead depart the courtyard on the western side where a large open plaza affords a photogenic view of the shrine's pyramidal green roofs.

Returning back through Bab Taghzout, a right turn leads down to the **Shrine of Sidi Ben Slimane El Jazuli**, another of the patron saints of Marrakech. Active in the 15th century, he was an important Sufi mystic and his *Manifest Proofs of Piety* remains a seminal mystical text.

## Dar El Bacha

West of the Mouassine quarter and the city's holy shrines is the high-walled former residence of the most unsaintly Thami El Glaoui, self-styled 'Lord of the Atlas' and ruler of Marrakech and southern Morocco throughout much of the first half of the 20th century; *see chapter* **History**. Known locally as Dar El Bacha ('House of the Lord'), and also as Dar El Glaoui, the residence is where the Glaoui entertained luminaries such as Churchill and Roosevelt, as well as the women his agents collected for him, scouring the streets for suitable prizes.

The complex dates from the early 20th century and is disappointingly dull to visit given all the spicy stories that came out of here. Visitors pass through several mundane administrative chambers (the complex now belongs to the Ministry of Culture) into a large courtyard, overwrought with carved plaster and woodwork, and excessive tiling. A passage snakes through to a second courtyard, which once served as the Glaoui's harem. Once again the decoration is laid on thick, but some of the work is impressive, particularly around the column capitals.

Sightseeing

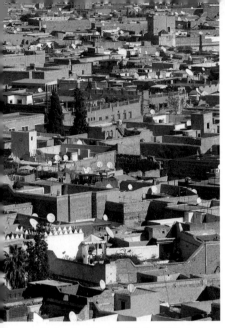

The major monument round here is the **Bab Doukkala Mosque**, built in 1558 by the mother of the Saadian sultans Abdel Malek and Ahmed El Mansour. It's fronted by the Sidi El Hassan fountain, now dry, fenced around and used as an occasional exhibition space. Across from the fountain, a small whitewashed building houses a 400-year-old hammam (men only) with a fantastic cedarwood ceiling in the reception area. Behind the fountain a faint hand-painted 'WC' signposts the city's oldest toilets, built at the same time as the Doukkala Mosque opposite. They're still in use.

The westernmost stretch of rue Bab Doukkala is the domain of the butchers and it verges on the macabre, with prominent displays of decapitated heads and mounds of glistening offal. Note that all the hanging bits of carcass display testicles: Moroccans don't eat female meat so butchers are mindful to prove the masculine provenance of their produce.

The massive Almoravid gate of **Bab Doukkala** is now bypassed by a modern road that breaches the city walls. There's a *petit taxi* rank at the foot of the gatehouse.

### Dar El Bacha (Dar El Glaoui)

*rue Dar El Bacha (no telephone).* **Open** 9am-2pm Mon-Fri. **Admission** 10dh. **Map** p252 B4.

## The tanneries

To experience Marrakech at its most raw, not to mention most pungent, take a taxi to the place du Moqf and walk east along rue de Bab Debbagh to the tannery district.

The tanners have been here since the city was founded, and the treatment of the skins remains a pre-industrial process. It begins with a softening soak, then the hair is scraped off by

Facing the side wall of the Dar El Bacha is another property with pedigree – owned previously by the chamberlain of the Glaoui, later by French *couturier* Pierre Balmain ('Dressmaking is the architecture of movement') and now, as a large sign announces, the premises of **Dar Moha** (*see p99*), one of the finest restaurants in Marrakech.

### BAB DOUKKALA

From Dar El Bacha, rue Bab Doukkala runs due west for around half a mile to the gate of the same name. At Nos.142-144 is **Mustapha Blaoui** (*see p128*), venue for some of the best shopping in the Medina.

# Pretty in pink

A bit of enlightened ordinance set down during the time of French rule specifies that all buildings in Marrakech must be painted pink. Except it's not really pink. The colour is ochre, natural hue of the earth on which the city is founded. Earth has always been the prime building material, mixed with crushed limestone and straw to make *pisé*. No painting required. It's already the right colour. It was only when the French began building the *nouvelle ville* now known as Guéliz in the early 20th century and introduced new building materials such as concrete that colour became an issue.

There's no prescribed paint number or swatches to match, and as a result the tones vary from pale flesh to fiery vermilion. It's all highly practical, as the colour takes much of the glare out of the often harsh sunlight (by contrast Casablanca, which frequently labours under overcast skies, is, as its name suggests, uniformly white).

Doors, woodwork and trim are usually done in some complementary shade of pale green – the minor term in the city's equation of colour. Some recent buildings in the new town, however, have begun contrasting Marrakech pink with Majorelle blue.

The tanneries.

hand. This is followed by more soakings in a variety of solutions to make the skins thinner, smoother and more supple, before they're scraped again in preparation for receiving the dyes. The animal hides are mostly sheep, goat and less often camel. At one time antelope hide was tanned to order, but no more, and the trade in lion skins has dwindled since the last Atlas lion was shot dead in 1912.

The tanneries can be tricky to find but some loitering youth will always approach unaccompanied foreigners and offer his services as a guide. The tanneries fill large yards and, with rows of lozenge-shaped pools of various hues, look like giant paintboxes. However, closer up the bubbling pits are more like cesspools with surfaces of floating, bubbling crud; the hides piled up beside look like rancid

tripe. Pity the poor labourers who wade in the noxious fluids up to mid-thigh ladling the skins from one pit to another. The work makes them prone to arthritis, and they often have to retire in their 40s, at which point their sons are inducted into the family trade. Guides sometimes hand out sprigs of mint to hold under your nose to block out the reek of pigeon shit (used to soften the hides) but it doesn't really help. Sensitive stomachs may rebel.

The results of the process can be seen and purchased at the leather shops near the gate, but you may prefer just to get the hell out of the quarter and go purge yourself in the nearest hammam. Taxis can be caught outside the **Bab Debbagh** (where a stair inside gives access to the roof of the gatehouse) on the route des Ramparts ringroad.

# The Kasbah & Mellah

Head to the southern Medina for sultans' palaces, the old Jewish quarter and museums full of wood.

**Maps p254 & p255**

Although little different in feel to the northern part of the Medina, almost since the founding of Marrakech the area south of the Jemaa El Fna has been the domain of the sultans and their retinues. The present Royal Palace is built on the site of the earliest Almohad palaces and covers an absolutely vast area, equivalent to a whole residential quarter. Youthful King Mohammed VI, however, has proved a little more modest in his requirements and has caused a much smaller bijou residence to be built nearby. Neither of these two royal precincts is open to the public but visitors are permitted to explore two 19th-century viziers' palaces, the Bahia and the Dar Si Said, as well as the impressive ruins of the grand Saadian-era Badii Palace.

Saadian Tombs.

## Saadian Tombs

Running south-west off Jemaa El Fna, pedestrianised **rue Bab Agnaou** is budget-tourist central, lined with banks, ATMs, moneychangers, téléboutiques, internet centres and too many dodgy eateries. At the far end is the famed roost for decades of impecunious travellers, the **Grand Tazi** (*see p55*) – also one of the few places in the Medina where it's possible to get a beer. South of the Tazi the street runs in the shadow of high walls: these are not the city walls, but a wall that formerly sectioned off the royal Kasbah (palace) from the rest of the Medina.

The traditional entrance to the Kasbah is via the gorgeous **Bab Agnaou** (Gate of the Gnawa), named after the black slaves brought from sub-Saharan Africa. The gate was built on the orders of the Almohad sultan Yacoub El Mansour in 1185. It's one of the very few stone structures in this otherwise mudbrick city, and has weathered in such a way that the aged limestone now resembles heavily grained wood.

Across the street from the Bab Agnaou is the original southern gate to the Medina, the **Bab Er Rob**, now filled by a pottery shop and bypassed by traffic, which exits through a modern breach in the walls.

A short distance inside the Agnaou gate is the **Kasbah Mosque**, constructed in 1190, again during the reign of Sultan Yacoub El Mansour (hence its alternative name of El Mansour Mosque). It has been renovated on numerous occasions since (most recently during the reign of Hassan II, father of the current king) but the cut-brick-and-green-tile decoration on the minaret is original. The plaza in front is usually busy with guide-led tourist groups. They're not here for the mosque, which, of course, they're forbidden to enter, but for what lies hidden in the lee of its southern wall: the **Saadian Tombs**.

In the early 1920s the French authorities noticed two green-tiled roofs rising above the shanty quarters. Inquiries made of the locals were met with evasive answers. The persistence of one curious official was eventually rewarded when he discovered a narrow, dark lane, wide enough for a single person, that ended in a tiny arched door. He pushed through to enter a courtyard garden and see what apparently no

Ah, but you should have seen it back in 1607: the ruined **Badii Palace**.

infidel had ever seen before – the holy tombs of the Saadian sultans. According to the account in a 1928 travelogue, *The Magic of Morocco*, the Frenchman was then accosted by a wizened guardian who said, 'You have discovered our secret, but beware what you do with the knowledge. You cannot make it a mere show for your people to come and gaze at'. Well, tough luck, pal, because that's exactly what has happened: the tombs are possibly the most visited site in Marrakech.

Entrance is via that same constricted passage first discovered 80 years ago and it gives access to an ancient walled garden, the use of which far predates the time of the Saadians. There are a great many early mosaic graves dotted around the shrubbery, of which the identity of the interred is long lost. Attention instead focuses on the three pavilions constructed during the reign of Saadian sultan Ahmed El Mansour. Despite drawing so many visitors, it's a far from spectacular ensemble, and the setting is so modest that it reminds of an English parish churchyard.

First on the left is the Prayer Hall, which was not intended as a mausoleum but nevertheless holds numerous graves, mainly of Alaouite princes from the 18th century. Their resting places are marked by what look like marble offcuts from a mason's yard. Next to it is the Hall of Twelve Columns, a far more ornate affair with three central tombs surrounded by a dozen marble pillars. The tomb in the middle is that of

Ahmed El Mansour, flanked by those of his son and grandson. A third, stand-alone pavilion has ornate Andalucian-style entrance portals.

Exiting the tombs, a left turn on to rue de Kasbah eventually leads to the **Grand Méchouar**, or parade grounds of the Royal Palace, but the way is closed when the king is in town. Iinstead it's perhaps more interesting to duck into the warren of alleys behind the tombs, where a small square at the conjunction of four alleys hosts a morning market of fruit, vegetable, meat and fish vendors.

### Saadian Tombs

*rue de Kasbah, Bab Agnaou.* **Open** 8.30-11.45am, 2.30-5.45pm daily. **Admission** 10dh. **Map** p254 C8.

## Badii Palace

Barely 400 metres east of the Saadian Tombs is the city's other great monument of that era, the Badii Palace. However, while secrecy preserved the sultans' mausoleums intact, the scale and ostentation of their triumphal residence marked it out for special attention and it survives only as a denuded ruin.

The palace was constructed during the reign of Sultan Ahmed El Mansour (1578-1607), funded by wealth accrued through victories over the Portuguese. Walls and ceilings were encrusted with gold from Timbuktu (captured by El Mansour in 1598), while the inner court had a massive central pool with an island, flanked by four sunken gardens filled with scented flowers

The **Mellah**.

and trees. At the centre of each of the four massive walls were four pavilions, also flanked by arrangements of pools and fountains. It took some 25 years for the labourers and craftsmen to complete the palace. Surveying the achievement, the sultan invited opinion from his fool and received the prophetic response that the palace 'would make a fine ruin'. And so it does. El Mansour was spared that vision because barely were the inaugural celebrations over before the ageing sultan passed away. His palace remained intact for less than a century before the Merenid sultan Moulay Ismail had it stripped bare and the riches carted north for his new capital at Meknès.

The palace is approached via the open plaza of place des Ferblantiers and a canyon-like space constricted between two precipitous walls, the outer one meant to keep the Medina at a respectful distance from the royal domains. The former main gate is collapsed and gone, and entrance is through a gaping hole in the fortifications directly into the great court. It's a vast empty space the size of a couple of football pitches, ringed around by pockmarked mudbrick walls that act as apartment blocks for pigeons and have stork nests along the battlements. The sunken areas that were once gardens still exist, as does the great dry basin that was the ornate central pool. On the west side are the ruins of the Pavilion of Fifty Columns; a small area of mosaic remains on the floor, but the colours are badly dulled by exposure to the elements.

In the south-east corner, a gate leads through to a newly reconstructed pavilion housing the **Koutoubia Mosque minbar** (20dh admission).

This was the original stepped pulpit in the city's great mosque. It was fashioned in the early 12th century by Cordoban craftsmen and the 1,000 decorative panels that adorn the sides supposedly took eight years to complete – the word 'ornate' falls somewhere short. It was removed from the mosque in the early 1960s for restoration and after a spell at the Dar Si Said Museum has ended up here. Next to the minbar pavilion are the excavated remains of troglodytic chambers and passages: a small underground labyrinth opened up for visitor exploration.

One of the palace bastions remains intact at the north-east corner of the great central court. Steps lead up to a rooftop terrace with fine views of the site and the surrounding quarter. You also get up close and personal with the many nesting storks.

The palace comes back to life once a year when a giant screen is set up on the central island for the International Film Festival (*see p141*).

### Badii Palace

*place des Ferblantiers (no phone).* **Open** 8.30-11.45am, 2.30-5.45pm daily. **Admission** 10dh; 20dh minbar pavilion. **Map** p254 C7.

## The Mellah

Hugging the eastern walls of the Badii Palace are the narrow gridded alleys of the Mellah, the old Jewish quarter. The name translates roughly as 'Place of Salt', a reference either to the Jews' historic monopoly on the trade in mineral salts from the Atlas Mountains, or to their landing the job of salting the heads of decapitees before they were hoisted up on spikes. Although the number of

Jews in Marrakech is now negligible (*see below* **Exodus**), evidence of Jewish heritage is abundant to anyone who knows where to look. In the nearby **Marché Couvert** (also known to locals as the Jewish Market), some of the signboards still bear Hebrew lettering. Several houses in the neighbourhood have external balconies, which in Morocco is peculiar to the Jews. Some have Hebrew letters on the metal grills above the doors. There's even an occasional Star of David.

Across the road from a newly laid-out **Rose Garden**, a green-painted arch leads through into the **Bab Es Salam market**. Following this south and east, past stalls of gaudy beaded necklaces (made in Hong Kong), bright pyramids of spices (the tallest of them actually clever cardboard fakes), and windows of the lurid sweets known as Pâte Levy, leads deep into the Mellah. The streets here are some of the narrowest and poorest in the Medina and in places crude scaffolding is required to stop the houses collapsing.

At the heart of the quarter is a small square, **place Souweka**, now disfigured by a badly sited concrete building. At No.36 along the street that runs north just beyond the square is one of the Medina's three last working synagogues (once there were 29). It occupies a large hall off the open courtyard of a well-maintained community centre. Judging by the plentiful supply of new prayer books and other contemporary trappings, the synagogue is kept alive by remittances from Marrakchi Jews abroad, but the advanced age of the congregation suggests that more than just money is needed to keep the community alive.

On the very eastern edge of the Mellah is the extensive Miâara Jewish cemetery; the sheer number of modestly marked graves (tens of thousands) is probably the best remaining testament to the one-time importance of Jewish life in Marrakech.

## Bahia Palace

On the northern edge of the Mellah is the Bahia Palace, built principally by Ba Ahmed Ben Moussa, a powerful vizier to the royal court in the 1890s and a man of 'no particular intelligence, but of indomitable will, and cruel' (*Morocco That Was*, Walter Harris; 1921). Entered via a long garden corridor, it's a charmless collection of paved courtyards, arcades, pavilions and reception halls constructed in a modern style but smothered in traditional Moroccan decoration (lots of unnecessary *zelije* tiling, sculpted stucco and carved cedarwood embellishments). It includes extensive quarters for Ba Ahmed's four wives and 24 concubines.

On Ba Ahmed's death – probably poisoned by the sultan's mother, along with his two brothers – the palace was completely looted by the sultan Abdel Aziz. Caravans of donkeys staggering under the weight of furniture, carpets and crates made their way the short distance from the Bahia to the Royal Palace. Between then and now it served as the living

# Exodus

Talk about population shifts: in the early years of the 20th century there were some 36,000 Jews living in Marrakech; best guess for a current total is 260, according to the keeper of one of three surviving synagogues.

Jews have been present in Morocco since Phoenician times. Later, protected by the walls and gates of their own quarter, and by the express patronage of the sultans (who valued their abilities in trade, linguistics and crafts), the Jews flourished as middlemen between visiting Christian merchants and local Muslims. Many of the latter viewed them with mistrust, especially in times of strife, but that didn't prevent the community from growing. However, from the end of the 19th century the pull of Zionism and the struggle for a homeland in Palestine (culminating in the creation of Israel in 1948) triggered mass emigration. King Mohammed V (who during World War II had resisted implementing the Vichy regime's anti-Semitic decrees) passed laws to prevent a mass exodus, fearing adverse effects on the economy. But Mossad, the Israeli secret service, smuggled out 18,000 Jews between 1958 and 1961. Arab-Israeli conflicts in 1956, '67 and '73 engendered such bad blood that even non-Zionists felt it expedient to relocate. Jews with money went to Canada, France and Israel. For many who arrived in the latter it was out of the frying pan and into the firing line – they were settled on the northern border with Lebanon to absorb mortar and missile attacks. Those less well off sought refuge in the more cosmopolitan climes of Casablanca, where the remaining Jewish community now thrives as part of the upper middle classes. The only Jews to stay in Marrakech were those too poor to move on, hence the decrepit state of the Mellah today.

Sightseeing

quarters of the French résident-généraux (Edith Wharton guested here at this time, described in her *In Morocco*; 1927) and it's still occasionally used by the current royal family – King Mohammed VI threw a party here for Puff Daddy in 2002.

### Bahia Palace

*Riad Zitoun El Jedid (044 38 92 21).* **Open** 8.30-11.45am, 2.30-5.45pm Mon-Thur, Sat, Sun; 8.30-11.30am, 3-5.45pm Fri. **Admission** 10dh. **Map** p255 D7.

## Dar Si Said Museum

Sightseeing

Connecting the Mellah with Jemaa El Fna (a distance of just under a kilometre) is **rue Riad Zitoun El Jedid**. The name means the 'new olive garden road' but the only olive trees in the area these days are in the modern Rose Garden at the very southern end of the street.

Also down at this end is the Préfecture de la Medina and, beside its guarded entrance, a narrow arch giving entrance to the Derb El Bahia and **Maison Tiskiwin**. Tiskiwin is a private house owned by Dutch anthropologist Bert Flint but open to display his interesting collection of crafts and decorative arts from southern Morocco and the Sahara. The exhibition is organised geographically, tracing influences along the old desert trade routes between Marrakech to Timbuktu. There's extensive documentation, but only in French.

A couple of twists to the north is the **Dar Si Said Museum**, the former home of the brother of Ba Ahmed, builder of the Bahia. This building is less grand in scale but more impressive in detail. It's home to a large collection of crafts and woodwork, beginning with a corridor lined with logs to represent the various trees of Morocco and including examples of just about anything that can be made out of wood. Among all the kitchen implements, weapons and musical instruments are numerous beautiful examples of carved cedar rescued from the city's lost dwellings – polychromic painted doors, window shutters, fragments of ceilings. There's also one room devoted to 'rural' woodwork that includes some primitively worked and painted Berber doors. Such items are very much in vogue with collectors these days and exchange hands for vast amounts of cash. The exhibits here are captioned in French only.

Also in the neighbourhood is **Riad Tamsna**, a restaurant of variable quality, a gallery, boutique and bookshop. It's also a beautiful building with a gorgeous central courtyard overlooked by high galleries. To find Riad Tamsna, coming along Riad Zitoun El Jedid look for a small, shabby pâtisserie next to an arched entrance (it's on the right approached from Jemaa El Fna); go down the arched passage, bear right and look for the black door with a No.23.

### Dar Si Said Museum

*Riad Zitoun El Jedid (044 38 95 64).* **Open** 9am-12.15pm, 3-6.15pm Mon, Wed-Sun. **Admission** 20dh. **Map** p255 D6.

### Maison Tiskiwin

*8 Derb El Bahia, off Riad Zitoun El Jedid (044 38 91 92).* **Open** 9.30am-12.30pm, 3.30-5.30pm daily. **Admission** 15dh. **Map** p255 D6.

The charmless **Bahai Palace**. *See p85.*

# Guéliz

The European quarter has its own particular charm – plus bars, bistros and a few bright lights.

Café les Négociants in the French *nouvelle ville. See p88.*

Café les Négociants in the French *nouvelle ville. See p88.*

Back in the 1970s the Medina was run-down and few visitors ventured far into its alleys from the carnival and cafés of the Jemaa El Fna. Foreigners would hang out mostly in the 'new city' of Guéliz (pronounced 'gileez', rhymes with please), with its broad avenues, European-style buildings, old-fashioned hotels and continental bistros. The hangout of choice was the Café Renaissance (now closed), especially its rooftop bar. The jetset dropped in on the Villa Taylor (*see p21*), while William Burroughs and Brion Gysin invoked demons in the Hotel Toulousain (still standing, just behind the site of the former Marché Central).

The rise of the riad hotel in the 1990s has made the Medina the place to stay, and with an increasing number of decent restaurants there too, Guéliz has been almost completely pushed off the tourist map. While the new city is small and devoid of big sights, we do like Guéliz for its unhurried but workaday atmosphere, its pavement café scene, and its disreputable bar life. This is the part of town where you can drink a beer, go to an art gallery, shop at fixed prices, find a liquor store, eat some non-Moroccan food and see one or two bright lights. It's particularly handy for a simulated European experience after a long sojourn in mountains or desert, or on one of those days where everything has been getting just a little bit too Moroccan. It's also a reminder that not all locals wear *jellaba*s and ride donkeys.

## HOLY BEGINNINGS

The 'new city' came into being shortly after December 1913 – the arrival date of Henri Prost, the young city planner imported to assist in the schemes of French résident général Marshal Lyautey. One of Prost's early sketches shows how he took the minaret of the Koutoubia as his focal point and from it extended two lines: one north-west to Jebel Guéliz, a rocky outcrop north-west of the Medina, the other south-west to the pavilion of the Menara Gardens. In the pie slice between these lines (which have since become avenue Mohammed V and avenue de la Menara) is the original nucleus of the new European city.

One of the first buildings was the church, or *église* – a word that was corrupted into the name Guéliz. This wasn't the first church in Marrakech; in 1908 a French priest consecrated a house in the Medina near what is now the Dar Si Said Museum. A Christian cross fashioned

Sightseeing

into the wrought-iron grill over one of the windows survives as evidence. The priest lasted nowhere near as long, murdered within two years of setting up shop.

The Guéliz *église* is now the Catholic **Church of St Anne**, barely a communion queue from the northern walls of the Medina. It's a modest affair with a bell tower very deliberately overshadowed by the taller minaret of a mosque built next door after independence. The notes for the congregation are printed in no less than six languages but Protestant services are relegated to the library.

## PARKS AND AVENUES

One block over from the church is the **Jnane El Harti** park, originally laid out as a French formal garden and a zoo. In a 1939 essay titled 'Marrakech', George Orwell writes of feeding gazelles here and of not being able to look at the animals' hindquarters without thinking of mint sauce. The park has only recently reopened after some serious re-landscaping and now boasts fountains, ponds and a children's play area with a big blue dinosaur.

The park's north-east corner connects with **place du 16 Novembre**, the hole in the middle of Guéliz's spider-web street pattern. Sadly, instead of developing as the grand *rondpoint* of Prost's vision, it has been disfigured by some plug-ugly structures, including a totalitarian central post office, two mammoth apartment blocks and a McDonald's.

Until the 1970s there were two lines of parking down the centre of the avenue, but the increase in traffic has done away with them. Shame, because standing in the middle of Mohammed V presents one of the city's best views: in one direction the Koutoubia minaret, sometimes with snowy Atlas mountains in the background; in the other a high rocky outcrop topped by the pink wall of a former French Foreign Legion fortress.

## CENTRAL GUELIZ

At the time of writing the focal point of Guéliz is its **Marché Central**, on avenue Mohammed V. This is where expats and middle-class Marrakchis come for groceries, of course, but also for booze, flowers, crockery, last-minute gifts. It's where they post flyers for lost Scottie dogs and ads for second-hand Renaults. However, in late spring 2005 it was scheduled for destruction. God knows why. A new market is promised just east of nearby place du 16 Novembre but residents fear that they are about to lose the social hub of the new city.

Diagonally across from the current/former market, at the junction of avenue Mohammed V and rue de la Liberté, is an elaborate colonial building with pavement arcades, art deco lines and Moorish flourishes. It dates to 1918 and is just about the oldest surviving building in Guéliz. This was the address (30 rue de la Liberté) of the city's first tourist office. A fading gallery of ancient hand-painted scenes of Morocco decorates the hallway.

The eastern stretch of rue de la Liberté is the local maid market, busy with poorly dressed women hanging around on the chance of some cleaning work. At the western end of the street, beyond current hipster magnet **Kechmara** (*see p151*) and where it meets rue de Yougoslavie, is a forgotten bit of Marrakech history: a narrow alley planted with mulberry trees and crammed with single-storey dwellings daubed in many colours (it may be the only non-pink street in Marrakech). This is the old **Spanish quarter**, a reminder of the city's once significant Hispanic population.

## BRIGHT LIGHTS, LITTLE CITY

Towards the northern end of Mohammed V is **place Abdel Moumen**, which is about as close as it gets to Piccadilly Circus. It's the hub of an area of cafés, bars, restaurants and nightclubs; it's even got neon. At **Café les Négociants** (*see p116*) grouchy uniformed waiters generate an air of efficiency while being brusquely indifferent to the customers. It's pleasing to find that almost 100 years on the ground rules laid by the French are still so lovingly adhered to. Across the intersection the **Café Atlas** is the place for beer with added entertainments (*see p151*). North of the Atlas is the boarded-up building that was formerly the infamous Café Renaissance.

From place Abdel Moumen, it's a 20-minute walk to the **Majorelle Gardens** (*see p92*), while to the west, Guéliz more or less peters out at the expanse of avenue Mohammed VI (formerly known, and still often referred to, as the avenue de France). There's an attractive little colonial-era **railway station**, which rises from its drowsy torpor a couple of times a day for the Casablanca train. The junction with avenue Hassan II is lorded over by the monumental **Royal Opera House**, designed by local star architect Charles Boccara. It's supposed to seat 1,200, but more than 12 years after it was begun the interiors have yet to be completed due to the spiralling costs.

Two blocks south is a similarly over-ambitious complex in the form of the **Palais des Congrès**. Constructed in 1989, it's a mammoth five-storey edifice used for the signing of GATT agreements in 1994. It has rarely been busy since. Still, if you should find yourself in need of a couple of halls the size of a modest Baltic state, you know where to look.

Looking down **avenue Mohammed V**
from the top of the Koutoubia minaret.

# Gardens

For a town on the edge of a desert, Marrakech is remarkably green.

Sightseeing

As if Marrakech wasn't pretty enough already, the municipality has embarked on a scheme to green the city. Large-scale planting of trees and flowers along the airport and Medina ring roads has already been completed and the ramparts are now surrounded by beds of roses, hibiscus and jasmine. The Jnane El Harti park (*see p88*) in Guéliz has been completely replanted and re-landscaped, as has the Arset Abdelsalam (*see below*) on the edge of the Medina.

But there have always been gardens here. Desert dwellers know how to manage water. When the Almoravids moved out of the Western Sahara to found Marrakech in the 11th century, they brought in water from the Ourika Valley by means of *khettra*, long irrigation pipes made of baked mud, the remains of which can still be found in the Palmeraie on the outskirts of the city. They used the water to nurture *jnane* (market gardens) and *agdal* (walled private gardens), as well as abundant public gardens.

The **Menara Gardens** (*see p93*), for instance, go right back to the 12th century and the era of the Almohads, as do the royal **Agdal Gardens** (*see below*). When the Saadian sultan Ahmed El Mansour built the show-stopping Badii Palace in the late 16th century, visitors marvelled at its architecture, but more than anything they were awestruck by its multi-level gardens and 700 fountains.

Neither were gardens the preserve of royals. Wealthy merchants, judges, master craftsmen and petty officials dwelt in riads, townhouses built around courtyard gardens. These were usually designed symmetrically: four beds planted with trees, underplanted with perfumed flowers, and arranged around the all-important central fountain. The microclimate thus created provided shade, cooled the air, gave off sweet smells and encouraged songbirds.

All credit to the French who continued the horticultural tradition under the Protectorate. In the *nouvelle ville* of Guéliz many of the boulevards are lined with jacaranda trees that bloom in electric blue each spring. Bougainvillaea and vines clothe the boundary walls of the villas and hibiscus flowers add spots of vibrant colour.

Then there are the orange trees. The streets of Guéliz are lined with them. The combination of blue sky, pink walls, green leaves and orange fruit is a knockout; it's like walking through a landscape by Matisse. All this and free fruit too? But that would be just too perfect and the oranges are in fact too sour to eat or juice. Instead, the prize is the blossom, highly valued for its scent. Every year the rights to a city-wide harvest are bought up by a major international perfume company and armies of local women are sent out to lay sheets under the trees and start banging the hell out of the branches.

## PUBLIC GARDENS

Besides the gardens described in this chapter, there are several other public gardens within the ramparts of the Medina. Most notable is the massed greenery of the **place de Foucault**, between Jemaa El Fna and the Koutoubia Mosque. It's a tight triangle of great palms soaring above the surrounding buildings, with benches at their bases. In spring these gardens are full of Candidum lilies.

Over the far side of the mosque are the **Koutoubia Gardens**, planted heavily with roses that are seemingly permanently in flower. Roses flourish in this climate, impervious to the heat of summer. Carefully shaped topiary hedges fringe the pathways.

To the north, flanking main avenue Mohammed V, is the **Arset Abdelsalam**, an extensive area of scrubby lawns, palms and pathways that are a favourite with promenading couples and civil servants from the town hall (Hôtel de Ville) opposite enjoying an open-air afternoon siesta. The park has recently been given a 21st-century upgrade with shopping kiosks and public internet booths sponsored by Maroc Télécom.

## Agdal Gardens

Laid out in 1156-7 by the Almohads, the royal Agdal Gardens are several hundred years older than those most celebrated of Islamic gardens at the Alhambra. They cover a vast 16 hectares (40 acres) stretching south for a couple of kilometres from the back door of the Royal Palace. At the centre of the Agdal is a massive pool, the Sahraj El Hana, so large that the sultan's soldiers used it for swimming practice. In 1873 Sultan Mohammed IV drowned in it while boating with his son; the servant who managed to swim to safety was executed on the spot for failing to save his lord. The rest of the area is divided into

Quiet reflection at the
**Menara Gardens**. *See p93*.

ardens,
yards, areas of
of walnut trees
veral ornamental
climb on to the
l Hana, beside the
of the gardens and

the path off the
south-weste... .e Méchouar Intérieur
(*see* map p255 D9).

### Agdal Gardens

**Open** irregularly but usually weekends; closed if the king is in residence at the Royal Palace. **Admission** free. **Map** p251 E5/F5.

## Majorelle Gardens

Now privately owned by Yves Saint Laurent (*see above* **Saint Laurent of Arabia**) – but open to the public – the gardens were created in the 1930s by two generations of French artists, Jacques and Louis Majorelle. Although small in scale and out on the edge of the New City, the glamour of the YSL connection ensures that the gardens are usually packed well beyond comfort by coachloads of visitors. The juxtaposition of colours is striking, plants sing against a backdrop of the famous Majorelle blue, offset with soft yellows and terracottas. Bamboo groves rustle in the soft breeze, great palms tower over all, sheltering huge ancient cacti. Rills lead into pools floating with water lilies and flashing with golden carp, terrapins paddle languidly and frogs croak. Great pots overflow with succulents and birds sing. For the botanically curious, everything is clearly labelled.

Jacques Majorelle's former studio has been turned into a fine little **Museum of Islamic Art**, recently renovated and reorganised to display a collection of traditional jewellery, fine embroidery, illuminated manuscripts, carved wooden doors and Majorelle lithographs of the High Atlas. Air-conditioned and dimly lit, the museum is a welcome refuge from the intensity of light and colour outside. There is English captioning of the exhibits. Beside the museum is a small boutique selling books, T-shirts, leather goods, babouche, pottery, cushions…

To get to the garden walk from central Guéliz (it's about two kilometres, or just over a mile, east along boulevard Mohammed Zerktouni) or take a petit taxi, which should cost around 6dh from Guéliz or 10dh from the Medina. Note that picnics, children and dogs are not allowed; it's a shame that the prohibitions don't extend to coach parties.

# Saint Laurent of Arabia

If Churchill was the totemic Marrakech visitor of the 1930s and '40s, then Yves Saint Laurent has been the name attached to the city since the 1970s. He and partner Pierre Bergé first visited in 1962, escaping the mixed reviews that followed the debut of the first YSL collection. The couple spent their days lounging around the Mamounia. Saint Laurent, who had been brought up in Oran, Algeria, revelled in his reacquaintance with the sun and colour of North Africa.

By 1967 YSL was established as the fashion figurehead for the Pop age and could contemplate buying a house in Marrakech. He and Bergé found a place in the Medina known as Dar El Hanch ('House of the Serpent'). Not surprisingly, the city made its influence felt in the next YSL collection, which featured transparent silk blouses and safari jackets.

Greater success equalled bigger Marrakech houses and a step up to a new villa. The Dar Es Saada ('House of Happiness') is a 1930s colonial building in the grounds of the family home of Jacques Majorelle. When rumours began that the adjacent gardens laid out by Majorelle were being sold to make way for an apartment complex, YSL and Bergé arranged to purchase them, reportedly through sources close to the royal family. They then groomed the gardens to a state of Rousseau-like feral picturesqueness and opened them to the public. Along with the gardens came another new house, the Villa Oasis. With the assistance of American decorator Bill Willis (*see p32*) the house was done over in an Orientalist style and filled with items from Paris auction houses.

Marrakech became Saint Laurent's escape, so much so that by around 1990 he was holed up in the Villa Oasis on two bottles of whisky a day, occasionally venturing into the Medina to scream hysterically if anyone broached the subject of going back to Paris. When his presence was absolutely required the fashion house had to fly someone to Marrakech to escort him back.

Saint Laurent still has the villa (it's the one behind the petrol station) and continues to spend part of the year in Morocco, but he is rarely seen in public these days.

Blue amid the greenery at the **Majorelle Gardens**. *See p92.*

## Majorelle Gardens

*avenue Yacoub El Mansour, Guéliz (no phone).*
**Open** 8am-5.30pm daily. **Admission** 30dh;
Museum of Islamic Art 15dh. **Map** p256 C1.

### Mamounia Gardens

The world-famous Mamounia hotel (*see p42*
**Mamounia**) takes its name from its gardens,
the Arset El Mamoun, which predate the hotel
by more than a century. They were established
in the 18th century by Crown Prince Moulay
Mamoun on land gifted to him by his father the
sultan on the occasion of his wedding. A
central pavilion served as a princely residence,
occasionally lent out to visiting diplomats. Ten
years after the imposition of French colonial
rule in Morocco, the gardens were annexed
and a 100-room hotel built on the site. Happily,
the gardens remain. They're designed in a
traditional style, on an axis, with walkways,
flowerbeds, orange groves and olive trees and
attended by 40 gardeners who, twice a year,
plant 60,000 new annuals. Non-guests can visit
but it's preferred that they do so in the context
of a buffet lunch at the poolside Trois Palmiers
restaurant (*see p107*) or afternoon tea at one
of the terrace cafés. Dress smartly (no jeans
or shorts) or you risk being sent packing.

## Mamounia Gardens

*Mamounia Hotel, avenue Bab Jedid, Medina (044 38
86 00/www.mamounia.com).* **Open** no set hours.
**Admission** see text. **Map** p254 A6.

### Menara Gardens

Coming in to land at Aéroport Marrakech
Menara, alert passengers may notice a large
rectangular body of water to the east. This is
the basin of the gardens from which the airport
takes its name. They've been there since around
750 years before man took to the air – like the
Agdal, the Menara Gardens were laid out by the
Almohads in the 12th century. Later they fell
into disrepair and their present form is a result
of 19th-century restoration by the Alouites.
The highly photogenic green tile-roofed picnic
pavilion that overlooks the basin was added
in 1869. Climb to the upper floor for a wonderful
view over the water or, better still, stroll around
to the opposite side for the celebrated view of
the pavilion against a backdrop of the Atlas.
Great ancient carp live in the basin; buy some
bread, toss it in and watch the water churn as
the fish go into a feeding frenzy.

   The bleachers that disfigure the view are
there to accommodate the evening audiences for
the 'Marvels and Reflections' sound and light

The Palmeraie.

show, which four nights a week presents the history of Morocco via the medium of contemporary dance and fireworks (which to us seems a bit like presenting Beethoven's oeuvre in mime). The show takes place year round apart from January and February, although our money is on the whole misguided enterprise folding before too long. The ticket office is at the entrance to the gardens.

To get to the Menara Gardens take a *petit taxi*, which should cost about 15dh from just about anywhere in the Medina. They'll try to charge you more coming back.

### Menara Gardens

*avenue de la Menara, Hivernage (044 43 95 80/ www.heritagevision.com).* **Open** 5am-6.30pm daily. *Marvels and Reflections box office* 9am-8pm daily; *show* 9.45pm Wed-Sat. **Admission** free; picnic pavilion 15dh. Marvels and Reflections 250dh. **Map** p250 A5.

## The Palmeraie

Legend has it that the huge Palmeraie north-west of the Medina was born of the seeds cast away by date-chomping Arab warriors centuries ago. A nice story but it fails to accord due credit to the clever minds that designed an underground irrigation system to carry meltwater all the way from the High Atlas and enable a palm oasis of several hundred thousand trees. The ancient *khettra* system now has only historical curiosity value because the water supply is guaranteed by several reservoirs and a network of artesian wells.

It's not what anybody would call a pretty oasis: many of the palms are worse for wear and the ground from which they sprout is dry, dusty and lunar-like. Even so, this is probably the most prime real estate in all North Africa. Ever since the 1960s, when King Hassan II granted the first permission for the sale of what is still fiercely protected by zoning regulations, Palmeraie land has been the plot of choice for the rich and even richer. This is the Beverly Hills of Morocco. Land is available only in parcels of more than one hectare and any building that takes place is not allowed to interfere with, damage or destroy any palms. Huge fines are levied for any tree disturbed. Narrow lanes carrying so little traffic that they're almost private drives slalom between copses, occasionally squeezing by high walls surrounding the typically massive grounds of highly discreet residences. It's sometimes possible to make out the turrets, spires and domes of upper storeys poking over the top.

Other than pricey accommodation, there isn't much to see in the Palmeraie (ramshackle villages, grazing camels, building sites). You might venture out here for a combination lunch and swim at the Sunset Club (*see p111*) at the Royal Golf Palace. It's also a good area for cycling. The ideal half-day ride is to head east out of town along the main route de Fès and take a left on to the route de Palmeraie (look for signs for the Tikida Gardens hotel), which winds through the oasis to exit north of the city on the Casablanca road. For details of where to hire bikes *see p226*.

# Eat, Drink, Shop

**Restaurants & Cafés**          96
**Shops & Services**          117

## Features

**The best** Restaurants          96
Square meals          103
The Moroccan (lack of a) menu          108
Marrakech without meat          113
Kitchen breaks          116
The hassle of haggling          119
The souk for dummies          122
To market, to market          131

# Restaurants & Cafés

Huge portions only sometimes compensate for a shortfall in creativity, but Marrakech dining is increasingly diverse.

A Marrakchi restaurateur once told us that Moroccan cuisine is the third greatest in the world after French and Italian. Erm, not really. It's not that Moroccan food isn't excellent but as served in local restaurants it is very limited in scope: tajine or couscous, couscous or tajine. Or quite often couscous *and* tajine, one after the other. It's a cuisine of diminishing returns: the first tajine is exquisite, the second very good, the third, well… We couldn't get a club sandwich could we?

The good news is that as Marrakech cements its reputation as a pit stop for well-heeled international weekenders, so the number and diversity of quality dining venues grows. French kitchens continue to prevail but the city now has its first Indian and Thai restaurants and a bona fide two-Michelin-star chef in Richard Neat, cooking at his own guesthouse, Casa Lalla.

Fine food's only part of the story, though. Dining in Marrakech is typically a full-blown multi-sensual experience. It starts with anticipation and intrigue – some of the restaurants are embedded so deep in the twists of the Medina that uniformed boys are posted at strategic locations to lead in guests. Interiors offer sumptuous visual feasts of tiling and stucco, courtyards open to starry skies, and everything is seductively textured and coloured with soft lighting and rich fabrics. Rose petals, jasmine and citrus blossom add scent, splashing fountains and lightly strummed *ouds* provide the soundtrack. In such sensuous surrounds, what the hell, bring on the tajine.

Also bear in mind that many of the riads and *maisons d'hôtes*, although not possessing a restaurant as such, do employ excellent cooks. Orders for lunch or dinner are usually taken in the morning; typically there's no menu, you're just told what's available. On the other hand, you can dictate *where* you'd like to eat – on your private terrace (if you have one), in the courtyard, up on the roof.

## RESERVATIONS & PAYMENT

Other than at the cheapest of places, reservations are always a good idea. At Casa Lalla, Comptoir, Dar Moha, Dar Yacout, Lollo Quoi and Tobsil you need to book at least several days in advance. The concierge at your hotel or the staff at your riad will be happy to take care of this.

Prices fluctuate between the unbelievably cheap (a handful of dirhams for a full meal at Restaurant Toubkal or Chez Chegrouni, for example) to the unpalatably expensive (£40

## The best Restaurants

### For going native
Chez Chegrouni (see p98); Jemaa El Fna (see p103 Square Meals); Restaurant Toubkal (see p101).

### For light lunching
Bar L'Escale (see p107); Jardins de la Koutoubia (see p105); Terrasses de l'Alhambra (see p106).

### For haute Moroccan
El Fassia (see p107); Maison Arabe (see p101); Marrakchi (see p101); Tobsil (see p101).

### For haute Française
Pavillion (see p106).

### For culinary innovation
Casa Lalla (see p101); Dar Moha (see p99).

### For outdoor dining
L'Abyssin (see p111); Alizia (see p111); Pizzeria Venezia (see p106); Rôtisserie de la Paix (see p109); Sunset Club (see p111).

### For seeing and being seen
Bô-Zin (see p113); Comptoir (see p111). Lollo Quoi (see p109).

### For anything but tajine
Catanzaro (see p108); Kechmara (see p109); Nawarma (see p105); Salam Bombay (see p109).

**Dar Yacout.** *See p99.*

per head at Dar Yacout). On average, expect to shell out around 200dh (roughly £13) per head for dinner with wine. The 'average' prices we give in the text are based on a two-course meal per person without drinks.

Tipping of around ten per cent is customary, although in more upmarket restaurants service is often included in the bill.

While many places display the symbols of major credit cards, management will commonly claim that the machine is broken. If you insist and are willing to endure a 20-minute stand-off, the machine may miraculously start working again, but it's a lot easier to make sure that you carry enough cash to cover the meal.

# Restaurants

## Medina

### Moroccan

#### Argana

*Jemaa El Fna (044 44 53 50)*. **Open** 5am-11pm daily. **Average** 90dh-140dh. **No credit cards**. **Map** p252/254 C5.
A no-frills (plastic tablecloths, garden furniture) eaterie on the edge of Marrakech's mayhemic main square, Argana's formula of pack-'em-in seating,

canteen catering and ringside views makes it a big hit with tour groups. A stair at the back of the ground-floor café (good ice-cream) leads up to two floors of restaurant terrace. Choose from a trio of three-course set menus (90dh, 100dh or 140dh), or order à la carte from a basic menu (in English) of salads, ten kinds of tajine, or meat from the grill. The quality is so-so, but portions are large. It makes for a good lunch spot, but the views are best at dusk.

#### Chez Chegrouni

*Jemaa El Fna (065 47 46 15)*. **Open** 6am-11pm daily. **Average** 30dh-50dh. **No credit cards**. **Map** p252/254 C5.
Everybody's favourite cheap restaurant in the Medina, Chegrouni has recently expanded upwards, adding a first- floor *salon à manger* and a rooftop terrace with a partial view of the Jemaa El Fna and an excellent panorama of rooftops and distant mountains. The ground-floor terrace is also a great vantage, though, for watching locals sweep in and out of the square on foot or on mopeds. Chegrouni is clean, well run and deservedly popular with both Marrakchis and tourists. All the usual dishes (salads 10dh-15dh, grills 30dh-40dh, couscous and tajines 50dh) are served briskly, accompanied by big baskets of fresh bread. Note to vegetarians: there is no meat stock in the vegetable couscous, while the vegetable soup (12dh) is excellent. Menus are in English and glasses on the tables contain paper napkins on which you scribble your order and then hand it to a waiter; it returns at the end as your bill.

**Foundouk.** *See p101.*

## Dar Moha

*81 rue Dar El Bacha (044 38 64 00/www.dar moha.ma).* **Open** noon-3pm, 7.30pm-late Tue-Sun. **Average** *Prix fixe* 220dh lunch; 420dh dinner (drinks not included). **Credit** AmEx, MC, V. **Alcohol served**. **Map** p252 B4.

Owner Moha Fedal, the self-styled 'Petit Prince de la cuisine Marrakech' is the closest the city comes to a home-grown celebrity chef. He learned his trade over 14 years in Switzerland and the result is a kind of Moroccan fusion cuisine – traditional dishes with a twist. We recommend sampling a standard tajine or couscous elsewhere first, then come here and delight in the difference. Both lunch and dinner are set-course affairs but there is some choice of dishes. Prime seating is outside beside the pool, with the overspill accommodated inside in premises that were once home to designer Pierre Balmain. Service is exemplary, the gregarious Moha usually flits from table to table, and the gnawa musicians who play every night are among the best we've encountered in Marrakech restaurants. Book well in advance.

## Dar Yacout

*79 rue Ahmed Soussi, Arset Ihiri (044 38 29 29).* **Open** 7pm-1am Tue-Sun. **Average** *Prix fixe* 700dh dinner. **Credit** AmEx, DC, MC, V. **Alcohol served**. **Map** p252 B3.

Yacout's fame rests as much on its art of performance as it does on cooking. The building itself is all show, a madcap mansion designed by Bill Willis (*see p32*) complete with flowering columns, candy striping, fireplaces in the bathrooms and a yellow crenellated rooftop terrace. Guests are led up to the latter on arriving or invited to take a drink (included in the price, so feel free) in the first-floor lounge, before being taken down, past the pool and across the courtyard, to be seated for dinner at great round tables inset with mother-of-pearl. On comes the food, delivered with pomp to the accompaniment of musicians, course after course, quickly passing the point where you'd wish it would stop. It's a feast fit to bursting for both eyes and belly, but one thing's for sure, your wallet will leave considerably slimmer. Reservations are essential.

## Ksar Es Saoussan

*3 Derb El Messaoudyenne, off rue des Ksour (044 44 06 32).* **Open** 8pm-1am Mon-Sat. **Average** *Prix fixe* 350dh/450dh/550dh. **Credit** MC, V. **Alcohol served**. **Map** p252/254 B5.

Yet another historic-house/fixed-menu combination, but one possessed of a peculiar old-world charm. The tone's set by the elderly French gent who greets guests with an invitation to ascend to the roof for the fine view of the Koutoubia. Then back down to be seated in silk-cushioned corners with gentle piano concertos filling the space where other diners' conversation would be (the number of covers barely reaches double figures). African giants in uniform take the orders from a choice of four set dinners; all but the most ravenous should be satisfied by the three-course 'petit' option (350dh), which comes with aperitif, a half-bottle of wine and bottled water.

**Eat, Drink, Shop**

**Comptoir**
*Darna*

PARIS - MARRAKECH

**RESTAURANT - BOUTIQUE**
Av. Echouhada Hivernage, Marrakech, Maroc
Tél.: (212) 44 43 77 02/10/044 43 56 35 - Fax : (212) 44 44 77 47/44 43 11 53
E-mail : comptoirdarna@menara.ma - Site Web : ilove-marrakesh.com/lecomptoir.html

### Maison Arabe

*1 Derb Assehbe, Bab Doukkala (044 38 70 10).*
**Open** 7-11pm daily. **Average** *Prix fixe* 350dh
(drinks not included). **Credit** MC, V. **Alcohol
served. Map** p252 A4.

Other than the address, the house restaurant of the
hotel of the same name (*see p43*) has no connection
to the original and legendary Maison Arabe. But the
food's commendable and the surroundings are beautiful – a grand dining room under a brilliant blue-
hued Persian-style ceiling with heavily draped
tables generously spaced and discreetly attended by
liveried staff. It feels more like an exclusive private
club than a restaurant. It's a *prix fixe* menu but there
are choices between some wonderful tajines (including the excellent lamb and pear) and several kinds
of couscous. Afterwards, take tea or coffee out in the
charming little candlelit courtyard with trompe l'oeil
façade. Reservations are recommended.

### Marrakchi

*52 rue des Banques, Jemaa El Fna (044 44 33 77/
www.lemarrakchi.com).* **Open** 11.30am-1pm daily.
**Average** 160dh-250dh. **Credit** MC, V. **Alcohol
served. Map** p252/254 C5.

There are two huge pluses to this place: one's the
location, on the edge of Jemaa El Fna, which is laid
out panoramically beyond the wrap-around windows. The second is that it serves Moroccan food à
la carte – although you can go down the set-menu
route if you wish (250dh or 350dh meals). Skip the
claustrophobic first-floor salon with its heavy Fès
tiling and continue up to a top-floor dining room
made luscious with dusky-pink tablecloths, maroon
tableware and a billowing ceiling of swagged black
material. The lighting is dim and the black-clad staff
charming. The menu holds no surprises (tajines and
couscous at around 100dh-140dh) but the food is
good, and there's a short list of local wines.

### Restaurant Toubkal

*48 Jemaa El Fna (044 44 22 62).* **Open** 7am-11pm
daily. **Average** 25dh-45dh. **No credit cards.
Map** p254 C6.

Big with backpackers from the budget hostels off
nearby Riad Zitoun El Kedim, but also popular with
Marrakchis, this is the next to last stop on the restaurant chain, just above eating al fresco at the food
stalls on Jemaa El Fna. The Toubkal does some of
the cheapest tajines around (25dh); couscous dishes
are 18dh-30dh and brochettes, chicken and lamb
served with fries are all around 25dh.The premises
are as basic as it gets, with plastic furniture and plastic tablecloths, but the wildlife is real. Chiller cabinets at the rear sell basic grocery-style provisions
including yoghurt, packets of biscuits, cheese, chocolate and juice for takeouts.

### Tobsil

*22 Derb Abdellah Ben Hessaien, Bab Ksour (044 44
40 52).* **Open** 7.30-11pm Mon, Wed-Sun. **Average**
*Prix fixe* 580dh dinner. **Credit** MC, V. **Alcohol
served. Map** p252/254 B5.

Considered by some to be Marrakech's premier
Moroccan restaurant, Tobsil offers a lesson in local
gastronomy. There is no menu. On being led by a
uniformed flunkey to the door (the place is otherwise
impossible to enter), diners are greeted by owner
Christine Rio then seated either downstairs in the
courtyard or upstairs in the galleries. And so the
endurance test begins. Aperitifs (included in the
price of the meal, as is the wine) are rapidly followed
by a swarm of small vegetarian meze dishes. Then
comes a pigeon pastilla, followed by a tajine, then a
couscous dish, and finally fruit and tea or coffee
accompanied by cakes or pastries. It's all delicious
but by about the pastilla stage you begin to feel like
an overstuffed boa constrictor. Reservations (and a
doggy bag) are recommended.

## International

### Casa Lalla

*16 Derb Jamaa, off Riad Zitoun El Kedim (044 42
97 57/www.casalalla.com).* **Open** 7-11pm Tue-Sun.
**Average** *Prix fixe* 350dh. **Credit** MC, V. **Alcohol
served. Map** p254 C6.

Richard Neat is an extraordinary chef. That's not
just our opinion: he was awarded two Michelin stars
for his first restaurant Pied-à-Terre in London and
a further star for his Neat Restaurant in Cannes.
Even more extraordinary is that he's now in
Marrakech running a guesthouse (*see p47*). He cooks
six nights a week preparing a set six-course menu
of the most exquisite creations. It's impossible to
define the cooking, except as a fantastic fusion of
French, Mediterranean and Moroccan. So briouettes
are filled with oyster, the pastilla substitutes cab-
bage leaf for pastry, the ingredients of a tajine might
be quail and dates and couscous is a dessert, mound-
ed in a little pyramid and soaked in a jus de passion
fruit. Presentation is stunning, with each dish a
miniature work of art. Neat attends each table to
explain what you're about to eat. However, this is
not a restaurant as such; Neat cooks primarily for
guests of his riad and only a limited number of
places are available for non-residents. We recommend booking well in advance because a meal here
may turn out to be a highlight of your trip.

### Foundouk

*55 rue du Souk des Fassi, Kat Bennahïd (044 37
81 90).* **Open** noon-4pm, 7pm-midnight Tue-Sun.
**Average** 200dh-250dh. **Credit** MC, V. **Alcohol
served. Map** p253 D4.

The rutted trench of a street that leads to this restaurant appears so unpromising that many probably
turn back. Those who locate the two lanterns mark-
ing the door enter to a gorgeous courtyard space
with creamy leather seating around a flower-filled
sunken water tray. A massive spindly chandelier
hangs above, looking like something from one of
Tim Burton's skewed fantasies. Softly glowing side
rooms are filled with plush sofas and armchairs: one
holds a shimmering bar. There's more dining space

**Eat, Drink, Shop**

Pizza with Koutoubia at the **Pizzeria Venezia**. *See p106.*

# Square meals

As the sun sets on central Jemaa El Fna, the stew of musicians, snake charmers, dancers, dentists and herbalists shift their pitches to accommodate the early evening arrival of massed butane gas canisters, trestle tables and tilly lamps. With well-practised efficiency, it takes only an hour to set up 100 food stalls in tightly drawn rows, with benches for diners, strings of lights overhead and masses of food banked up in the middle. Stallholders fire up the griddles and the smoke drifts and curls to create a hazy pall over what must be one of the world's biggest open-air eateries.

Most stalls specialise in one particular dish, and between them they offer a great survey of Moroccan soul food. Several places do good business in ladled bowls of *harira* (a thick soup of lamb, lentils and chickpeas flavoured with herbs and vegetables). Similarly popular are standbys of grilled *brochettes* (kebab), *kefta* (minced, spiced lamb) and *merguez* (spicy sausage; stall No.31 apparently sells the best in all Morocco). Families perch on benches around stalls selling boiled sheep heads, scooping out the jellyish gloop inside with small plastic forks. Elsewhere are deep-fried fish and eels, bowls of chickpeas drizzled with oil, and mashed potato sandwiches, while a row of stalls along the south side have great mounds of snails, cooked in a broth flavoured with thyme, pepper and lemon. Humblest of the lot is the stallholder selling nothing more than hard-boiled eggs.

Menus and prices hang above some of the stalls, but not everywhere. It's easy enough to just point, and prices are so low that they're hardly worth worrying about. Etiquette is basic: walk around, see something you like, squeeze in between fellow diners. Discs of bread serve instead of cutlery. For the thirsty, orange juice is fetched from one of the many juice stalls that ring the perimeter of the square.

The food is fresh and prepared in front of the waiting diners, so you can actually see the cooking process. Few germs will survive the charcoal grilling or boiling oil; plates and dishes are a different matter. The single same bucket of water is used to wash up all night, so play safe with your stomach and ask for the food to be served up on paper.

**Eat, Drink, Shop**

At nightfall **Jemaa El Fna** becomes one vast open-air eatery.

Sophisticated French cooking practised on hapless crustacea at **Pavillion**. *See p106.*

upstairs at candlelit tables ranged around a gallery open to the sky. The food (French-Moroccan) is hit and miss; a *filet de boeuf* was excellent, an aubergine salad inedible. Play safe, order the simple stuff, and leave experimentation to the barstaff, who know what they're about when it comes to mixed drinks, ideally sipped on the roof terrace beneath the stars.

### Jardins de la Koutoubia
*26 rue de la Koutoubia (044 38 88 00).* **Open** 12.30-4pm, 7.30-10.30pm daily. **Average** 200dh. **Credit** MC, V. **Alcohol served**. **Map** p252/254 B5.
The poolside grill at this recently built five-star hotel (*see p41*), just a few minutes' walk from the Jemaa El Fna, is a fine spot for a peaceful lunch serenaded by birdsong. The setting is a spacious central court with trees and shrubbery flanking the rectangle of blue water, around which a few residents will probably be reclining on sunbeds. Choose from a simple but intelligent menu of salads, hearty sandwiches and dependable standards such as chicken with pasta (100dh) or a mixed grill (145dh).

### Narwama
*30 rue de la Koutoubia (044 44 08 44).* **Open** 8pm-12.30am daily. **Average** 160dh-200dh. **Credit** MC, V. **Alcohol served**. **Map** p252/254 B5.
Opened in early 2005, Narwama is the city's first proper Thai restaurant (if you don't count the pricey, out-of-town affair at the Amanjena). The setting is

Grilled meats and a garden party setting at the **Rôtisserie de la Paix**. *See p109.*

the vast central courtyard of a palatial 19th-century residence tucked down an alley behind the Jardins de la Koutoubia hotel. It's an enormous space that, with its plastic-sheeted roof and potted palms and other trees, feels like a dimly lit conservatory. Some intimacy is offered in a smaller rear room with the most fantastic old painted ceilings and a couple of even more private curtained *diwans*. The kitchen doesn't quite have the courage of its convictions and the Thai dishes (prepared by a chef imported from Bangkok) are supplemented by a miscellany of Moroccan and international standards. Avoid the desserts. If it's not in operation, ask a waitress to turn on the fire-shooting, water-spewing feature at the centre of the room.

## Pavillion

*Derb Zaouia, Bab Doukkala (044 38 70 40).* **Open** 7.30pm-midnight Mon, Wed-Sun. **Average** 200dh-300dh. **Credit** AmEx, MC, V. **Alcohol served.** **Map** p252 A4.
The setting is superlative: the courtyard of a splendid old house where tables are squeezed under the spreading boughs of a massive tree. Several small salons provide for more intimate dining. In typical French fashion, the day's menu is scrawled out on a white board presented by the waiter. Offerings change regularly but expect the likes of *agneau*, *canard* and *lapin*, all exquisitely presented with seasonal veg and rich wine sauces. The staff can be supercilious, but otherwise this is a classy affair. The restaurant is a little difficult to find, but if you can locate the alley with Maison Arabe (which is well signposted), then Pavillion is 100 metres north, hidden down the next alley but one. Reservations are recommended.

## Pizzeria Venezia

*279 avenue Mohammed V (044 44 00 81).* **Open** noon-3pm, 6pm-midnight daily. **Average** 80dh-120dh. **Credit** MC, V. **Map** p252/254 B5.
It's worth eating at the Venezia at least once, if only for the view: it occupies a rooftop terrace opposite the Koutoubia minaret and overlooking Mohammed V with its shoals of darting mopeds. Although it's only a pizzeria, general manager Ahmed Bennani is fussy about the quality and freshness of ingredients, so the wood-oven cooked pizzas (45dh-60dh) are as good as it gets this side of the Med. The menu also stretches to salads (30dh-45dh) and meat dishes, including a good fillet steak in a green peppercorn sauce (70dh). On Friday and Saturday there's a self-service buffet (120dh) with an enormous choice including vegetable dishes and puddings. Although no alcohol is served you are allowed to BYO.

## Terrasses de l'Alhambra

*Jemaa El Fna (no phone).* **Open** 8am-11pm daily. **Average** 50dh-100dh. **No credit cards.** **Map** p252/254 C5.
A clean, smart, French-run café-restaurant on the east side of the main square (across from the landmark Café de France). The ground floor and patio is a café for drinks and ice-cream; the first floor with terrace is for diners; the top-floor terrace is for drinks (non-alcoholic). The menu is brief – salads, pizzas and pasta (all around the 50dh mark), plus a few desserts, ice cream and milkshakes – but the food is good. If you're new to Marrakech, it's somewhere you can eat and feel confident that your stomach will hold up. Settle in air-con comfort indoors or slow roast in the open air overlooking the madness of Jemaa El Fna.

## Trois Palmiers

*Mamounia Hotel, avenue Bab Jedid (044 38 86 00).*
**Open** 12.30-3pm daily. **Buffet** 490dh. **Credit**
AmEx, MC, V. **Alcohol served. Map** p254 A6.

There are five restaurants at the Mamounia but the poolside lunch buffet is the only thing we'd recommend. For starters there's a huge salad bar, with plenty of fish and cold meats to supplement the assortment of vegetables and dressings. Hot food comes in form of various tajines (try the meatballs and eggs) and a *couscous de légumes* (the only hot vegetarian option). Afterwards there's a choice of fruit, pastries and ice cream. This cornucopia is usually consumed by the pool underneath big sun umbrellas but moves indoors to a comfortable salon when the weather is inclement – but we'd recommend simply eating somewhere else on days when it's not warm enough. We'd also recommend bringing an appetite, as it's hardly the cheapest lunch in town (although the the the quality is excellent). Otherwise it's a nice spot to linger over a newspaper from the hotel bookshop and you can walk it all off afterwards with a stroll around the splendid gardens. Drinks are charged extra.

## Guéliz

## Moroccan

### El Fassia

*232 avenue Mohammed V (044 43 40 60).* **Open**
noon-2.30pm, 7.30-11pm daily. **Average** 120dh-
180dh. **Credit** AmEx, MC, V. **Map** p256 C3.

One of the few posh Moroccan restaurants in town that allow diners to order à la carte, El Fassia is also unique in being run by a women's co-operative – the chefs, waiting staff and management are all female.

We'd recommend skipping starters (mainly pastillas), not because they're not good (they are), but because the main courses are so huge. Choose from ten tajines or three types of couscous (all around 100dh) – mostly meaty (chicken, lamb or rabbit), although there are a couple of vegetarian options. The décor's a bit drab, service can be grumpy and there's no alcohol, but who cares when the food's this good? El Fassia is on the main avenue halfway between the Medina and Guéliz proper.

## International

### Bagatelle

*101 rue Yougoslavie (044 43 02 74).* **Open** noon-
2pm, 7-11pm Mon, Tue, Thur-Sun. **Average** 120dh-
150dh. **Credit** MC, V. **Alcohol served.**
**Map** p256 A2.

In business since 1949, Bagatelle is a charming relic of the last days of French rule. There's a spacious salon indoors but the place to be is the open-air patio, with shade provided by vine-trailed trellising that for part of the year bows under the weight of clustered grapes. The menu is old-school bistro: salads (35dh-50dh) and standard entrecôtes, escalopes and fillets (70dh-85dh), veal, kidneys and calf's liver. These are supplemented by a few Moroccan dishes and a typed page of daily specials. Waiters wear black bow ties and waistcoats; a sound system wafts smoky-voiced *chanson*. The place is particularly popular with lunching mademoiselles on time out from raiding the nearby boutiques, examining purchases over oysters and a bottle of Gris Guerrouane.

### Bar L'Escale

*rue de Mauritanie (044 43 34 47).* **Open** 11am-
10.30pm daily. **Average** 50dh-70dh. **No credit**
**cards. Alcohol served. Map** p256 B2.

# The Moroccan (lack of a) menu

Moroccan cuisine is practical and unfussy. Dishes have evolved from Persia via the Arabs, from Andalucía with the returning Moors and from the colonial French – but the overriding principle is to throw all the ingredients into a dish and then leave it to cook slowly.

Prime exhibit is the national dish of tajine. It's essentially a slow-cooked stew of meat (usually lamb or chicken) and vegetables, with olives, tangy preserved lemon, almonds or prunes employed for flavouring. The name describes both the food and the pot it's cooked in – a shallow earthenware dish with a conical lid that traps the rising steam and stops the stew from drying out.

The other defining local staple is couscous, which is again the name of the basic ingredient (coarse-ground semolina flour) and of the dish; the slow-cooked grains are topped with a rich meat or vegetable stew, not unlike that of a tajine. It's a full meal, not a side dish.

Don't expect a menu in most traditional Moroccan restaurants (including **Dar Yacout**, *see p99*; **Ksar Es Saoussan**, *see p99*, and **Tobsil**, *see p101*). Once customers are seated, the food simply arrives. First thing will be a selection of small hot and cold dishes, called *salade marocaine*, actually carrots, peppers, aubergine, tomatoes and the like, each prepared differently, as well as diced sheep brains and chopped liver. Next, *briouettes* – little envelopes of paper-thin *ouarka* (filo) pastry wrapped around ground meat, rice or cheese and deep fried. Next, *pastilla* (or *b'stilla*), which is *ouarka* pastry filled with shredded pigeon or chicken, almonds, boiled egg and

spices, baked then dusted with cinnamon and powdered sugar. Next, a tajine of lamb or chicken. Following that, a couscous of chicken or lamb. Next, dessert of flaky pastry drizzled with honey and piled with fruit. Next, indigestion and the beginnings of a long-term aversion to all foodstuffs delivered in pottery dishes with conical lids.

All the above is delivered with Moroccan wine and finished off with mint tea and, gawd help us, more pastries.

To be frank, many liken the set-menu dining experience to being a duck on a foie gras farm. That a great portion of the excessive mounds of food is inevitably sent back to the kitchen almost untouched seems supremely wasteful as well as offering the diner poor value for money. Uneaten food is distributed to the poor but perhaps you might appreciate being able to make your own choices as to how you dispense your charity.

À la carte Moroccan menus are available in only a few blessed places, notably **El Fassia** (*see p107*) in Guéliz and **Marrakchi** (*see p101*) on Jemaa El Fna.

It's primarily a bar (*see p151*), but L'Escale's also a good place for a quick cheap lunch – unless you're a vegetarian. The humble house special is grilled chicken, leg (*la cuisse*) or breast (*le blanc*), which comes with a tomato and onion salsa and a basket of bread for mopping-up. The spicy merguez sausages are also good. There's a back-room specifically for dining but prime seating is at one of the half-dozen sun-shaded tables out on the pavement.

## Catanzaro
*42 rue Tarek Ibn Ziad (044 43 37 31)*. **Open** noon-2.30pm, 7.30-11pm Mon-Sat. **Average** 80dh-120dh. **Credit** MC, V. **Alcohol served**. **Map** p256 B2.
It's a simple, rustic-styled neighbourhood French-run Italian (red-checked tablecloths, faux-woodbeam ceiling) with a homely air and reliable cooking, but Catanzaro is probably the most popular eatery in town. White-hatted chefs work an open kitchen with

a big wood-fired oven turning out excellent thin-crust pizzas (average 45dh-60dh). Alternatives include various grills and steaks (75dh-80dh), with a good selection of salads and a good choice of wine by the bottle or half-bottle. The dessert list includes a tiptop crème brûlée. Customers all seem to be regulars – most are greeted by name as they arrive – and, although the place seats 60 or more, reservations are recommended in the evenings. It's easy to find: one street back from avenue Mohammed V, behind the site of the old Marché Central.

### Jacaranda

*32 boulevard Mohammed Zerktouni (044 44 72 15/www.lejacaranda.ma)*. **Open** noon-3pm, 6.30-11pm daily. **Average** 200dh-300dh. **Credit** MC, V. **Alcohol served**. **Map** p256 A2.

With large picture windows looking on the traffic tango of place Abdel Moumen, Jacaranda's the place for an urban dining experience. Inside it's hardly less busy: a crush of furniture, chintzy table settings and assorted paintings spill down from the mezzanine gallery cluttering all available wall space. But it's friendly and comfortable. The kitchen specialises in *cuisine française* with plenty of *viande* and *poisson*, but it's hardly haute cuisine and as such a bit overpriced with entrées at 70dh-95dh and mains at 110dh-150dh. However, decent value is offered by a lunchtime two-course *menu rapide* at 85dh or the *menu tourisme*, three courses for 105dh. In the evenings there's a *menu du marché* for 180dh. In addition to beer and wine, the tiny bar counter stretches to aperitifs and a small selection of cocktails. Chin chin.

### Kechmara

*3 rue de la Liberté (044 42 25 32)*. **Open** 7am-midnight Mon-Sat. **Average** 80dh-120dh. **Credit** MC, V. **Alcohol served**. **Map** p256 B2.

New in 2005, Kechmara is a hip young café-bar-restaurant. All white and clean-lined with chrome fittings and white moulded plastic chairs, the look is what would be called retro in Notting Hill or the East Village but given that the style never happened here first time around it's probably just 'moderne'. Lunch and dinner are a *prix fixe* continental menu (80dh/100dh/120dh); choice is limited (soup, salads, meat in sauces, grills and desserts) but the food is generally excellent and well presented. Absolutely nothing for vegetarians, however. The drinks menu includes *bière pression* at a reasonable 25dh and a good line-up of cocktails to be drunk at the bar counter or, better still, up on the fine first-floor terrace – which makes Kechmara one of the few places in Marrakech where you can legitimately booze al fresco. The black logo'd T-shirts sported by the staff are offered for sale on the menu. And the name? It's mara-kech reversed.

### Lolo Quoi

*82 avenue Hassan II (072 56 98 64)*. **Open** 7pm-1am daily. **Average** 120dh-160dh. **Credit** MC, V. **Alcohol served**. **Map** p256 B3.

Currently and deservedly the hottest spot in town. Twin to a well-established restaurant in Lyon, Lolo Quoi is stylish, sexy and appealingly quirky. The interior is all black, minimalist and barely lit by angled spots, with a long bar counter where those who neglected to book must languish for a goodly while. The crowd is predominantly young, Moroccan and monied, and the atmosphere is buzzing. The brief but satisfying menu offers crostini and salads, pasta, carpaccio and steak; the pasta, in particular, is superb (and well priced at 65dh-75dh), cooked al dente and inventive with the ingredients – chopped walnuts and pine nuts in the quattro formaggi, for example. Desserts are rich and heavy things like biscuity tiramasu and profiteroles with chocolate sauce spooned out of a pan.

### Pizzeria Niagra

*31 Centre Commercial El Nakhil, route de Targa (044 44 97 75)*. **Open** 12.15-2.15pm, 7.15-11pm Tue-Sun. **Average** 60dh-130dh. **Credit** MC, V (over 150dh only). **Alcohol served**. **Map** p256 A1.

One of three adjacent pizza joints five minutes' walk north of central Guéliz on the road out to the French Lycée, and easily the best (although neighbouring Pizzeria Exocet shades it in the name stakes). An excellent menu of far more than just pizza (pasta, escalopes, steaks, fillets and 14 different salads) at cheap prices ensures that the place is packed most every lunch and dinner – the latter often quite boozy given that beer and wine are sold at almost supermarket prices. With pink and chintzy decor, it's far from being an event restaurant, but if you lived in Marrakech then Niagra would probably become a much loved local.

### Rôtisserie de la Paix

*68 rue Yougoslavie (044 43 31 18)*. **Open** noon-3pm, 6.30-11pm daily. **Average** 100dh-150dh. **Credit** AmEx, MC, V. **Alcohol served**. **Map** p256 B2.

Flaming for decades, the 'peaceful rôtisserie' is a large garden restaurant with seating among palms and bushy vegetation. Simple and unpretentious, it's utterly lovely whether lunching under blue skies (shaded by red umbrellas) or dining after sundown when the trees twinkle with fairy lights. (In winter, dining is inside by a crackling log fire.) Most of the menu comes from the charcoal grill (kebabs, lamb chops, chicken and own-made merguez sausage; average prices 55dh-85dh) but there are also delicacies such as quail, and a selection of seafood. We recommend the warm chicken liver salad, listed on the menu as a starter but easily a meal in itself and a bargain at 65dh.

### Salam Bombay

*1 avenue Mohammed VI (044 43 70 83)*. **Open** noon-2.30pm, 7pm-12.30am daily. **Average** 200dh-250dh. **Credit** DC, MC, V. **Alcohol served**. **Map** p250 A2.

Not only is this Marrakech's first Indian restaurant, it's also the first in Morocco, set up by four guys from Madras who already have a successful Indian

# CAFE ARABE
## café restaurant

Restaurant of Italian and Moroccan
*"Haute cuisine"* in the Medina

184, rue el Mouassine - Médina - Marrakech - Maroc - Tél.: 00212 (0)44 42 97 28 - Fax : 00212 (0)44 42 97 25
e-mail : info@cafearabe.com   web site : www.cafearabe.com

restaurant in Toulouse. They've adapted to local sensibilities by going over the top with the design – it's all very big, very ornate and very pink and there's a row of painted elephant heads studding the road-side wall. The serving girls wear shimmery *kurta*s and *bindi*s dot their foreheads but they're Moroccan and the biryani is served in a tangier clay pot. The Rajasthani chefs have also been careful to tone down the spicing to the extent that anyone familiar with Indian food as eaten in India (or even the UK) is liable to find their curries and masalas (all 140dh-190dh) a little bland. The menu is heaven for vegetarians, though.

### Trattoria de Giancarlo
*179 rue Mohammed El Bekal (044 43 26 41/ www.latrattoriamarrakech.com).* **Open** 7.30-11.30pm daily. **Average** 200dh-300dh. **Credit** AmEx, MC, V. **Alcohol served**. **Map** p256 A2.
La Trattoria remains possibly Marrakech's finest Italian restaurant, serving superb food in the most enchanting of surroundings. The Felliniesque interiors (lush, occasionally lurid and more than a little louche) are by local legend Bill Willis (*see p32*) and are a delight, but the best tables are those overhung by oversized greenery out on the tiled garden terrace beside the large luminous pool. In the evening the place is lit by lanterns and candles to ridiculously romantic effect. While the menu is hardly extensive, it holds plenty of appeal (a variety of salads, several vegetarian pastas, meat and seafood dishes). Service is excellent going on obsequious: 'Would sir like his beer with a head or without?.' Reservations are recommended.

## Hivernage

### International

#### Alizia
*Corner of rue Ahmed Chouhada Chawki (044 43 83 60).* **Open** noon-2.30pm, 7-11pm daily. **Average** 120dh-180dh. **Credit** MC, V. **Alcohol served**. **Map** p256 C4.
Presided over by Madame Rachida, who learned her English in Bayswater, this is an intimate, relaxed and well-established Italian-flavoured venture that's popular with the old-school expatriate crowd. In addition to the expected pizzas (50dh), pastas (60dh-80dh), fillets and steaks (around the 100dh-120dh mark) also serves some wonderful fish dishes (100dh-130dh). How about a starter salad of small red mullet fillets flamed in balsamic vinegar, followed by fillet of John Dory in a prawn bisque sauce? The choice is extensive. Or ask about the special of the day – a roll of plaice stuffed with salmon and spinach on a recent visit. The dessert selection is one of the best in town and there's a very decent wine list too. Although the pitch is upscale, prices are reasonable and the atmosphere relaxed, especially if the weather is warm enough to sit in the bougainvillaea-draped garden.

#### Comptoir
*avenue Echouada (044 43 77 02).* **Open** 4pm-1am Mon-Thur, Sun; 4pm-2am Fri, Sat. **Average** 180dh-300dh. **Credit** MC, V. **Alcohol served**. **Map** p256 C4.
Inevitably Comptoir's exotic-East-meets-moneyed-West style has become diluted by overexposure. What began as a hangout for hipsters, fashionistas and models now seems to cater largely for coach parties from Club Med. The menu is divided between *saveurs d'ici* (Moroccan) and *saveurs d'ailleurs* (French), a smart move to satisfy both the visitor fresh off the plane and those who've already done one tajine too many. Food quality varies wildly, though. What's constant is an ebullient party atmosphere, aided by a four-piece of elderly fez-wearing musicians and brought to a raucous climax each Friday and Saturday evening with the arrival of a troupe of belly dancers. Audience participation is encouraged; you have been warned. *See also p153.*

## Palmeraie

It's a long way to travel for lunch unless you're actually staying out here or have an ulterior motive; for instance, L'Abyssin is attached to Palais Rhoul, popular for its fantastic hammam (*see p163*). Meanwhile, the food at Sunset Club is secondary to its swimming pools.

### International

#### L'Abyssin
*Palais Rhoul, route de Fès, Dar Tounsi (044 32 85 84/www.palaisrhoul.com).* **Open** 8-11pm Tue; noon-3.30pm, 8-11pm Wed-Sun. **Average** 120dh-180dh. **Credit** MC, V. **Alcohol served**.
Garden restaurant of the Palais Rhoul, a surreal retro-modern villa on the edge of the Palmeraie, L'Abyssin is no more than a series of gauzy, open-fronted white pavilions set around a central slate basin. It's all very low slung, with white sofas, lounging platforms and plump cushions. White-costumed staff waft across green lawns under brilliant blue skies. It's like some cultish retreat for the fabulously rich and misguided. The handwritten chalkboard menu is French (and in French) but it stretches to include tajines, pasta and a 'maison burger'. Food is priced a lot more reasonably than the drinks – a glass of cranberry juice cost us almost the same as a penne carbonara.

#### Sunset Club
*Royal Golf Palace, Circuit de la Palmeraie (044 36 87 27/www.sunset.ma).* **Open** 10.30am-7pm daily. **Average** 80dh-120dh. **Credit** AmEx, MC, V. **Alcohol served**.
On the grounds of the Royal Golf Palace but independently managed, the Sunset is totally Miami. It's a series of gorgeous aqua-blue swimming pools surrounded by sun-shaded seating. Further back from the water are numerous massive loungers like four-

**Eat, Drink, Shop**

**Marrakchi**. *See p101*.

# Marrakech without meat

Moroccan cuisine may be justly celebrated but the vegetarian visitor will find little to get excited about. While all around, others are licking their lips over a lemony chicken tajine or an elaborate pigeon pastilla, the non-carnivore will be making do with yet another processed cheese omelette or toying with one more drab mountain of *couscous de légumes*.

It's a frustrating thing. There is no shortage of fine ingredients. Markets are piled high with vegetables so fresh they still have a little loam attached. Spices are plentiful and various. There is also no problem with cooking methods. Tajines and couscous, soups and pastilla – it's a simple matter to make vegetarian versions of any of these things. All that's lacking is imagination.

Moroccans find vegetarianism puzzling. Here, proper hospitality means serving up a tajine with a good big hunk of meat. The idea of deliberately going without is quite alien and vegetables are mostly viewed as mere accompaniments to the main event. Thus the tendency in less sophisticated restaurants to conjure up vegetarian cuisine by simply taking the lamb off the top of the couscous or fishing the beef out of the tagine.

A simple salad of tomato and onion, finely chopped, often features as a starter in Moroccan restaurants. This is just as well, because the apparently vegetarian harira, a

spicy broth made from chickpeas and lentils, most often contains a bit of mutton or chicken and has almost certainly been made with meat stock. But look out for *salade marocaine*: a selection of small, single-vegetable dishes, each spiced and cooked separately, served together as a starter. When done well this can be quite delicious – and, if you ignore the dish of diced sheep's brains, it's the only naturally vegetarian thing in the standard Moroccan repertoire.

The cooks employed in many *maisons d'hôtes* will rise to the challenge if vegetarian food is requested in advance. If you're lucky you might get spinach briouettes or a vegetarian pastilla – and after a few too many omelettes this can be akin to a religious experience. But otherwise it's down to seeking out infidel food. French cuisine is worse than useless, but Italian restaurants can usually deliver something that doesn't involve meat; try **Aliza** (*p111*), **Catanzaro** (*p108*), **Lolo Quoi** (*p109*) or **Trattoria de Giancarlo** (*p111*). You'll also dine well at **Salam Bombay** (*p109*), and the kitchen can usually rustle up something edible at **Fondouk** (*p101*). There is now supposed to be a vegetarian restaurant at **Riad Eclectica** (044 44 16 10), but at the time of writing it had yet to fully open because of problems securing the necessary licences.

**Eat, Drink, Shop**

poster beds, and a host of plushly sofa'd little enclaves. There's an Indonesian-ornamented bar/servery and a swim-up bar at the centre of the largest pool. Lunch is served from a menu of salads (delivered in immense bowls), room service staples (cheeseburger, club sandwich) and meat grills (lamb chops, *brochettes de poulet*). Bring your swimsuit for a post-prandial splash about before taking to a recliner with a cocktail. It's an excellent place to spend a whole afternoon and kids love it. There is a 200dh entry fee to cover pool use but some riads have an arrangement whereby their guests get in free: ask. At night the place morphs into a full-on, loved-up nightclub: *see p154*.

## Further afield

The vast complex housing the Pacha nightclub (*see p154*) also includes two restaurants: **Jana** (Moroccan) and **Crystal** (international). There's also a Thai restaurant set to open in summer 2005 as part of the Sugar Factory complex, which lies less than a mile from Pacha.

## International

### Bô-Zin

*Km3.5, route de l'Ourika, Douar Lahma (044 38 80 12/www.bo-zin.com).* **Open** 8pm-1am daily.
**Average** 200dh-260dh. **Credit** AmEx, MC, V.
**Alcohol served**.

It's a way out of town (a 15-minute taxi ride from the Medina; 100dh each way) but we feel Bô-Zin is worth travelling for. It's a smart and stylish international restaurant of the kind that people dress up for (when the waitstaff are as good-looking as they are here then customers are obliged to make an effort). There are several sprawling rooms, each filled with a variety of bars, fireplaces, potted plants and heavy drapes. The place everyone wants to be, however, is the glorious and spacious rear garden. The menu is brief but wide-ranging, taking in Moroccan, Thai and an international miscellany. If the food doesn't quite live up to the surrounds, it's still a cut above most of the competition. The music can be good, too, depending on the DJ, but is sometimes loud enough to render conversation difficult.

### The Thai Restaurant

*Amanjena, route de Ouarzazate, km12*
*(044 40 33 53).* **Open** 11.30am-3.30pm, 8-10.30pm
daily. **Average** 300dh-400dh. **Credit** AmEx, MC, V.
**Alcohol served.**

The ultra-exclusive Amanjena resort (*see p61*) has
two formal dining options: the sublime onyx-
columned 'Moroccan', which is beautiful but serves
nothing that can't be had at plenty of other restaurants, and this prosaically named place, a venue for
which wealthy Marrakchis climb into their 4x4s and
drive for top-rank Thai food. The chef is formerly of
the highly regarded Celadon restaurant in Bangkok
and under his direction the kitchen turns out raved-
over flavours featuring the likes of fried fish salad
or green duck curry. Dishes are 200dh-300dh –
pricey, but you're paying for the regal 'Aman experience'. Although the restaurant's open for lunch, the
complex is at its best when illuminated by flicker-
ing torchlight at night.

# Cafés

Thanks to the French, Marrakech has a legacy
of continental-style places where you are likely
to find croissants and pastries, as well as the
ubiquitous oversweetened green mint tea and
thick gritty coffee. They open early for
breakfast and tend to close early too.

## Medina

### Café de France

*Jemaa El Fna (no phone).* **Open** 6am-11pm daily.
**No credit cards. Map** p252/254 C5.

The most famous of Marrakech cafés is these days
distinctly grotty but boasts a prime location and terrace fronting right on the main square. No one seems
to know exactly how old the place is but it crops up
as a landmark in Peter Mayne's *A Year in
Marrakech*, written in the early 1950s. It remains a
prime meeting place for both travellers and for locals
with business in the Medina: assorted Morocco
guidebooks and copies of the day's Arabic-language
press are present in about equal numbers. Neither
category is favoured and prices are posted ensuring
fair trade for all.

### Pâtisserie des Princes

*32 rue Bab Agnaou (044 44 30 33).* **Open** 5am-
11.30pm daily. **No credit cards. Map** p254 C6.

A weak-kneed wobble (the heat! the heat!) from
Jemaa El Fna, des Princes offers gloriously icy air
conditioning in a dim coldstore of a back room.
Sounds gloomy but we guarantee, the hotel swimming pool aside, there's no better retreat on a sun-
hammered afternoon. Front of house is taken up by
glass display cabinets filled with excellent cakes and
pastries to be accommpanied by cappuccino (10dh),
English tea (10dh), orange juice (8dh) or shakes
(18dh). There's another large salon upstairs.

**Sunset Club**. *See p111.*

**Eat, Drink, Shop**

## Guéliz

### Amandine

*177 rue Mohammed El Bekal (044 44 96 12).* **Open** 6am-11pm daily. **No credit cards. Map** p256 A1.
Amandine comes in two parts: there's the smart pâtisserie with a long glass display cabinet layered with continental-style cakes and pastries and a few chairs and tables in front; or next door there's a proper café space with a high bar counter, fewer cakes and far more atmosphere. Both spaces are air-conditioned but we prefer the café, where efficient table service provides the usual coffees and (mint) teas, plus hot savouries and things like croissants and French toast.

### Boule de Neige

*Corner of rue Yougoslavie, off place Abdel Moumen, (044 44 60 44).* **Open** 5am-11pm daily. **No credit cards. Map** p256 A2.
Don't come particularly for the coffee or food, but do come for a look. The setting's a large room coloured a fetching mint green and pink, with tables laid out canteen style. There's a food counter at one end with things shiny, gelatinous and best left well alone. There's also an extensive breakfast menu but it only baffles the staff if you attempt to order from it. Instead, just nip next door to the Pâtisserie Hilton and bring something back – this is permitted, even encouraged. Then settle in and watch the almost sitcom-like spectacle of staff chasing cats chasing other cats dodging men eyeing single girls… Huge fun.

### Café les Négociants

*place Abdel Moumen, avenue Mohammed V (044 43 57 82).* **Open** 6am-11pm daily. **No credit cards. Map** p256 B2.
Far classier than the endearingly sleazy Café Atlas, which it faces across the road, Les Négociants is a Parisian boulevard-style café with acres of rattan seating and round glass-topped tables crowded under a green-and-white striped pavement awning. We like it for breakfast: café au lait, orange juice and croissants, plus the papers from the international newsagent across the road.

## Hivernage

### Table du Marché

*Corner of avenue Echouda & rue du Temple (044 42 12 12).* **Open** 7am-11pm daily. **Credit** MC, V. **Map** p256 C4.
Attached to the Hivernage Hotel & Spa, this is a good new French-style pâtisserie and café with outdoor patio seating. The view isn't up to much – it's of the massed balconies of the Sofitel opposite – but the wickerwork furniture is attractive and maroon canopies offer shade from the sun (there are just a few seats in the air-conditioned interior). The tarts, croissants and breads are excellent, coffee comes is coffee flavoured (which isn't always the case in Marrakech), and there are sandwiches and panini (40dh). While it's off-route for most visitors, the local middle classes have taken to the place, driving over to exit with a baguette tucked under one arm.

# Kitchen breaks

Just can't get enough of those tajines? Then sign up for lessons in how to make your own. **Maison Arabe** (*see p43*) offers cooking workshops held in a purpose-built teaching kitchen in a small villa in verdant surrounds on the edge of town. Each session is preceded by a brief introduction to Moroccan cuisine and a gathering of herbs and spices from the garden. Participants lunch beneath olive trees on the meal they've prepared. **Jnane Tamsna** (*see p59*) and **Kasbah Agafay** (*see p62*) also offer similar; call for details.

Various riads and *maisons d'hôtes* also welcome guests into the kitchen. At **Riad Enija** (*see p43*) and **Riad Ifoulki** (*see p49*) guests are invited to accompany the cooks out on shopping expeditions to the local produce market and then join in preparation of the evening's meal. Ursula at Enija has also written her own Moroccan cookbook.

UK-based Rhode School of Cuisine constructs whole holidays around the kitchen.

Its courses, held at a luxury Palmeraie villa called Dar Liqama ('House of Green Mint'), run for a whole week, although daily lessons last only about two hours – the rest of the time is spent making forays into the souk for ingredients, or snoozing off the food with poolside lounging.

### Maison Arabe

*1 Derb Assehbe, Bab Doukkala (044 38 70 10/www.lamaisonarabe.com).* Workshops are held on demand for a minimum of two people (charged at 1,600dh per person), a maximum of eight (500dh per person).

### Rhode School of Cuisine

*Hambledon House, Vann Lane, Hambledon, Surrey, GU8 4HW, England (01252 790 222/ www.rhodeschoolofcuisine.com).* Courses are held February and March, October and November. Prices per person per week – including accommodation, food, tours and classes but not flights – start at £1,165.

# Shops & Services

Don't shop for bargains, shop for fun.

Founded at the confluence of ancient trade routes – first point of arrival for goods from across the Sahara, last place to stock up when heading in the opposite direction – Marrakech has always been, in some sense, about shopping. The trade in ostrich feathers may no longer be brisk and there aren't any slaves on sale these days, but shopping remains way up there on the Marrakech list of things to do. Rightly so, for to avoid the haggle and hustle of the souks, or to peer at all the products of artisanal Marrakech merely as if they were exhibits in a museum, would be to miss out on the city's central activity and liveliest culture.

And, hey, this is a great place to shop. There is both beautiful and bizarre stuff to be looked at and maybe lugged away. The souks are commerce at its most intoxicating – a riot of strong colours, seductive shapes and rampant exoticism. The first impulse is to embark on a mass shop for a Moroccan makeover back home. Fine, but be aware that back in drizzly northern Europe those bright oranges and reds just look garish, the brass lanterns are the height of tack and the curly yellow slippers, well, best just hide them at the back of the wardrobe, eh?

Still, the artisans of Marrakech do their best to knock out things that might prise open Western wallets and there is always interesting stuff to be found. Good buys include fashion accessories, fabrics, spices, natural oils and pottery. But there's also plenty of fun to be had in considering a few less conventional purchases. A mother-of-pearl inlaid dowry chest? A pair of shoulder-high brass candlesticks? Obscure musical instruments? Magic supplies? Mummified baby alligator? Above all else, shopping in Marrakech can be a hoot – and you wouldn't be human if you didn't go home with a few utterly unnecessary items.

### SHOPPING THE SOUKS

The vast bazaar that spreads north of Jemaa El Fna is actually a coalescence of different markets, most specialising in one kind of item (for map, *see p73*). If you have a particular thing in mind, head for the section that specialises in it. General handicrafts and bric-a-brac emporia are scattered everywhere, but particularly on the two main souk streets of rue Mouassine and rue Semarine. An intrepid spirit brings its rewards as the closer you remain to the Jemaa El Fna, the higher the prices.

Eat, Drink, Shop

Akkal. *See p132.*

...s in the wall with
...act business. It's
...purposefully, avoid eye
...n deaf to overtures of 'Just
...d 'I give you Asda price!' Any
...r sign of fatigue will be punished
...tent offers of tea and assistance.
...bate rages on the issue of guides. Yes,
they can zero in on the shops selling the items
that you're looking for, and yes, they can haggle
on your behalf, but wherever they lead it ends
in a commission and that goes on your bill.

### BEYOND THE SOUKS
Some of the best shopping lies outside the
Medina, up in the *nouvelle ville* of Guéliz. On
and around avenue Mohammed V are plenty
of smart and sophisticated little boutiques
stocking exclusive designer items and one-offs
superior in style and quality to anything found
in the souks – and without the hassle of hard
sell, haggling and yet more mint tea.

Committed shoppers might ride out to the
**Quartier Industriel** at Sidi Ghanem (taxi
up the Casablanca road, left just before the
McDonald's on to the route de Safi, left again
opposite the mosque); it's about eight
kilometres (five miles) north of town and, as
the name suggests, not somewhere you head
for the scenery. This is the warehousing belt
and it's home to several fine factory
showrooms including those of **Akkal** (*see
p132*) for pottery and tableware and **Amira**
(*see p127*) for candles. If you take a taxi out
here then you will have to ask the driver to
wait, otherwise you'll never get back to town;
50dh for an hour is a fair price.

### OPENING HOURS
Just as prices are highly elastic, so are hours of
business. We've done our best to extract from
recalcitrant shop owners the times they're
likely to be open and trading, but it's all a bit
*inshallah* (God willing). A chance meeting with
a colleague in the street and the *fermé* sign can
stay in place all morning. As a rule of thumb,
the working day stretches from around 9am to
7pm with a break of a couple of hours for
lunch and a snooze. Shops in the souk will
often close on the Muslim holy day of Friday,
at least for the morning; shops in Guéliz take
Sunday off. Some places take both. During
Ramadan (for dates, *see p234*) it's even more
unpredictable, but there's a general shift for
businesses to open and close later.

### PAYMENT
Generally speaking, it's dirhams only. Some
shops are authorised to take euros, pounds
sterling or US dollars, particularly the more
heavily touristed places. But this won't be self-
evident and the only way to find out is by
asking. Many shops purport to take credit
cards, but actually would much rather not and
will press for cash. Payment by plastic also
often incurs a five per cent surcharge (to cover
processing costs). If you find yourself short
of cash, shops are often prepared to deliver
to your hotel and accept payment on receipt.

Note that there are no added taxes and hence
nothing to be claimed back.

### BRINGING IT ON HOME
Lots of shops offer a shipping service for
foreign visitors. Beware. Tales of goods last
seen somewhere in Marrakech are legion.
Unless it's a container load, the best advice
is to take charge yourself of transporting
purchases home. The most straightforward
option is to bite the bullet and pay the excess
baggage fee. On British Airways this is about
100dh per kilogram (32 ounces). **Worldsoft** is
a reliable *transitaire* in Daoudiate; it charges
around 15dh per kilo to London, plus 800dh per
shipment to cover paperwork. Alternatively, go
to the main post office on place du 16 Novembre
in Guéliz, *see p234*.

There is a levy of between five and 15 per
cent payable on anything above the 2,300dh
duty-free customs allowance.

### Worldsoft
*26 avenue Allal El Fassi, Daoudiate (044 31 05 55).*
**Open** 8.30am-12.30pm, 2.30-6.30pm Mon-Fri; 8.30am-
12.30pm Sat. **No credit cards. Map** p250 C1.

## One-stop shopping
In addition to places listed below there's a small
Western-style supermarket in Guéliz on avenue
Abdelkarim El Khattabi just south the junction
with avenue Mohammed V.

### Aswak Assalam
*avenue du 11 Janvier, Bab Doukkala (044 43 10 04).*
**Open** 8am-10pm daily. **Credit** MC, V. **Map** p256 C2.
Across from the *gare routière* at Bab Doukkala,
this decent-sized *supermarché* offers the closest
good grocery shopping to the Medina. There's no
booze though (the owner's a religious man). It has
less choice than Marjane (*see below*) and it's prici-
er, but it's also a lot more convenient for anyone
without a car.

### Marjane
*route de Casablanca, Semlalia (044 31 37 24).*
**Open** 9am-10pm daily. **Credit** MC, V.
How did Marrakech manage before Marjane? This
massive *hypermarché* is the utimate shopping destination for the city's middle and upper classes. It
combines a supermarket (food and plentiful booze,
clothes, household items, electronics, white goods,
CDs, computers) with a Kodak Express Lab,

McDonald's, Lacoste, Yves Rocher and Caterpillar franchises, plus banks, Méditel and Maroc Télécom, and a pharmacy. It's about 8km (five miles) north of town; a *petit taxi* will get you out here for around 30dh each way.

## Antiques

Antique is a manufactured style here, and few things in Marrakech are as old as they would first appear. Plus, fraud is widespread. Buy it because you like it, and if one day you discover it really was as old as the vendor said it was then that's an added bonus.

### Amazonite

*94 boulevard El Mansour Eddahbi, Guéliz (044 44 99 26).* **Open** 9.30am-1pm, 3.30-7.30pm Mon-Sat. **Credit** AmEx, MC, V. **Map** p256 B2.
Probably the only shop in town where you have to ring a doorbell to enter. It's a cramped three-storey repository of all manner of objets d'art, top quality Berber jewellery, early 20th-century oil paintings (displayed in the basement), a stunning collection of ancient silk carpets, plus miscellaneous ethnic trappings, including old marriage belts. A place for serious buyers in search of rare finds.

### El Badii

*54 boulevard Moulay Rachid, Guéliz (044 43 16 93).* **Open** 9am-7pm daily. **Credit** AmEx, MC, V. **Map** p256 A2.
Two floors of museum-quality antiques, hand-picked by owners Najat Aboufikr and his wife, featuring a dazzling array of gold and silver jewellery, unusual lamps, carved Berber doors, ornate mirrors and a huge choice of carpets. Pride of house are ancient ceramics from Fès in traditional yellow and cobalt blue. They display photos of Brad Pitt, Tom Cruise and Hillary Clinton browsing here, but the fixed prices and warm welcome are for everyone.

### Bazaar Ikhouan

*15 Marché Sidi Ishak, off rue Sidi Ishak, Medina (044 44 36 16).* **Open** 10am-7pm daily. **Credit** AmEx, MC, V. **Map** p73.

Just how antique most of these pieces are is open to debate – antiquity is in the eye of the beholder. Anyway, curious excavators can sift through piles of tarnished jewellery, dull-bladed daggers, trays and teapots, greening brass lanterns, fancy-headed walking sticks, silver Koranic carry-cases, gunpowder flasks and ivory-handled muskets. Owner Khalid is a real charmer and speaks fluent English.

### De Velasco

*4 rue le Verdoyant, avenue Hassan II, Guéliz (044 43 03 27).* **Open** 9am-1pm, 3-8pm daily. **Credit** AmEx, MC, V. **Map** p256 B3.
Adolfo de Velasco was a kaftan designer and colourful raconteur who until recently held court in a Mamounia boutique, fitting splendid one-off kaftans to royals and flogging a few *objets* on the side. Now Adolfo has gone to the great salon in the sky and the shop still bearing his name has gone to Guéliz. There's still a rack of kaftans in the back, but mostly it's an ornate orientalist clutter of outsize vases, lacquer cabinets, silver rhinos, chaises longues, paintings of souks, ceramic leopards and the occasional mounted pair of tusks – everything you might need to furnish a camp fantasia of the colonial era. It's pricey stuff and not much fun to browse; charmless staff pursue in packs.

### Moha

*73 Laksour Sabet Graoua, Mouassine, Medina (044 44 37 81).* **Open** 9am-8pm daily. **No credit cards.** **Map** p73.
One of several *objets d'art* shops around Mouassine, this place offers a good selection of choice, if not always particularly old, doors, large vases, armoires and chests. Moha himself speaks English and will happily hold court in his modest showroom and serve mint tea while discussing purchases. He also has a second shop nearby.

### L'Orientaliste

*11 & 15 rue de la Liberté, Guéliz (044 43 40 74).* **Open** 9am-12.30pm, 3-7.30pm Mon-Sat; 10am-12.30pm Sun. **Credit** MC, V. **Map** p256 B2.
Both a small street-front boutique and a huge basement space hidden round the corner. The former is stuffed with piles of inexpensive items – Fès

# The hassle of haggling

It's a drag, but when shopping in the souk haggling is expected, even demanded. There are no hard and fast rules as to how to do it, but when you've spotted something you want it's smart to do a little scouting around and get a few quotes on the same or similar item at other stores before making your play.

Don't feel you need to go through the whole silly charade of offer and counter-offer like in some B-movie dialogue; simply expressing

interest then walking away on being told the price is usually enough to bring about some fairly radical discounting.

Otherwise, to avoid having to haggle, try shopping at either the **Centre Artisanal** or **Ensemble Artisanal** (for both, see p120), both of which display fixed prices, or at the boutiques in Guéliz – where you might still be paying over the top but at least the onus isn't on you to do anything about it.

ceramics, filigree metal containers, painted tea glasses, scented candles and perfume bottles, some filled with essences. The latter is crammed with pricey antique furniture, early 20th-century Moroccan paintings and engravings, and leather-bound notebooks with original watercolours.

## La Porte d'Orient

*6 boulevard El Mansour Eddahbi, Guéliz (044 43 89 67).* **Open** 9am-7.30pm Mon-Sat. **Credit** AmEx, MC, V. **Map** p256 A2.

The most mind-blowing of shopping experiences occurs when a door at the rear of this modest shop is opened to a back room, which then gives on to a space of warehouse proportions. The enormous room is loaded with an impressive panoply of Berber jewellery, ancient carved doors of fantastic size and patterning from Fès and Meknès, irridescent lanterns, beautiful glass cases of illuminated manuscripts, gilded lion thrones. The only thing you won't find is too many bargains. English is spoken.

## Tinmel

*38 rue Ibn Aicha, Guéliz (044 43 22 71).* **Open** 9am-7.30pm Mon-Sat. **Credit** AmEx, MC, V. **Map** p256 A2.

A highly browseable mini-museum of Islamic art with a staggering variety of antiques: aged silver swords, Touareg earrings and pendants, 18-carat-gold jewellery from the early 20th century, colossal bronze lanterns that once adorned palaces, decorative oil jars, mirrors with cedar and camel-bone frames, silk-embroidered camel-skin bags, and a variety of marble fountains. And don't miss the exquisitely crafted backgammon tables displayed upstairs.

## Arts & handicrafts

Almost every store in the souk is a handicrafts store of some description, but for anyone pushed for time, the two artisanals are good one-stop options. For other stores selling similar, *see p127* **Home accessories**.

## Centre Artisanal

*7 Derb Baissi Kasbah, off rue de Kasbah, Medina (044 38 18 53).* **Open** 8.30am-8pm daily. **Credit** AmEx, MC, V. **Map** p254 B8.

Don't let the humble entrance fool you – this is the closest thing to a department store in Marrakech, albeit a department store selling nothing but handicrafts. It's the ultimate souvenir store, with everything from trad clothing (*babouches, jellabas*, kaftans) to jewellery to home furnishings to carpets. Prices are fixed at slightly above what you would pay in the souk, but this at least does away with the tiresome process of haggling. The stalker-like behaviour and rudeness of the sales assistants can irritate.

## Ensemble Artisanal

*avenue Mohammed V, Medina (044 38 67 58).* **Open** 8.30am-7.30pm daily. **Credit** AmEx, MC, V. **Map** p252/254 A5.

Second major tourist stop after photo ops at the Koutoubia, the EA is another state-sponsored crafts mini-mall like the Centre Artisanal described above – but far more popular because of its central location. All the artisans selling within are purportedly here by royal appointment, selected as the best in their field (a licence therefore to charge higher prices, which are completely non-negotiable). Expect everything from fine embroidered table linen (first floor at the back) to jewellery, clothing, lamps and even knock-off European handbags.

## Carpets

For an idea of where to shop for carpets and how much to pay *see p122* **The souk for dummies**.

## L'Art de Goulimine

*25 Souk des Tapis, Medina (044 44 02 22).* **Open** 9am-6.30pm daily. **Credit** AmEx, MC, V. **Map** p73.

For something a little different, Rabia and Ahmed are two young dealers specialising in Rhamana carpets from the plains north of Marrakech. They have a small showroom displaying choice pieces downstairs from the main sales space, where you'll find plenty of all the more usual carpet types at competitive prices.

## Bazaar du Sud

*117 Souk des Tapis, Medina (044 44 30 04).* **Open** 9am-7pm daily. **Credit** AmEx, MC, V. **Map** p73.

This place has possibly the largest selection of carpets in the souk, covering all regions and styles, new and old. The owners say they have 17 buyers out at any one time scouring the country for the finest examples. Although considerable effort goes into supplying collectors and dealers worldwide, sales staff are just as happy to entertain the novice. Prices range from 2,000dh to 350,000dh. Ask for Ismail, who speaks perfect English.

## Bazaar les Palmiers

*145 Souk Dakkakine, Medina (044 44 46 29).* **Open** 9am-7pm Mon-Thur, Sat, Sun. **Credit** AmEx, MC, V. **Map** p73.

Hamid is a fourth-generation carpet dealer. His passion is carpets from the High Atlas, characterised by their beautiful colouring. His pieces take in the old and not-so-old, with prices starting at an affordable 100dh (although all that gets you is a cushion). He speaks English and is happy to expound on his favourite subject over a glass of mint tea.

## Tapis Akhnif

*6 rue Mouassine, Medina (044 42 60 96).* **Open** 9am-8pm daily. **Credit** MC, V. **Map** p73.

A small family business (run by a father and his two sons), Akhnif offers plenty of choice including carpets, raffia and wool rugs, pillow cases and pouffes without any sales hassle. Prices are fair and there's good *café au lait* on request. Ask for Moubarek, who speaks English.

Ask to see the blue one at the bottom on the right: the **Bazaar du Sud**. *See p120.*

## Fashion

A word of warning: what wears well in Marrakech will not necessarily have the same glamour in inner London or downtown NYC. Kaftans suit souks not subways. Accessories are another matter, and there are some fun things to be found.

### Akbar Delights

*45 place Bab Fteuh, Medina (071 66 13 07).* **Open** 10am-1pm, 3-9pm Tue-Sun. **Credit** V. **Map** p73.

A very upmarket boutique specialising in luxury clothing and textiles from Kashmir (with a few odd items from Uzbekistan). These include embroidered tops and dresses, cotton robes, silk shawls and scarves, and shimmery, golden shoulder bags. The only made-in-Morocco items are some extraordinary brocaded *babouches*, which sell for a suitably extraordinary 1,320dh.

### L'Art de la Couture

*42-44 rue Rahba El Biadyne (044 44 04 87/mobile 061 34 40 26).* **Open** 9am-1pm, 3.30-7.30pm daily. **Credit** AmEx, MC, V. **Map** p73.

It looks nothing from the outside – nor within for that matter – but this tiny shop sells wonderful classic coats and jackets for men and women, and has made to order for the queen. Cuts are simple, with embroidered details in subtle colours. The best garments are made from B'zou wools, a fabric speciality of a small mountain town. Prices start at 1,000dh and custom orders take two weeks (shipping overseas is available). Coming from Derb Dabbachi, look for a modest light-pine frontage on the right with an AmEx sticker on the glass.

### Beldi

*9-11 Soukiat Laksour, Bab Fteuh, Medina (044 44 10 76).* **Open** 9.30am-1pm, 3.30-8pm daily. **Credit** MC, V. **Map** p73.

Toufik studied fashion in Germany and, now back in Marrakech, he and brother Abdelhafid have transformed the family tailoring business into maybe the most talked-about boutique in town. They do both men's and women's ranges in the most beautiful colours and fabrics, fashioned with flair and an eye to Western tastes. Beautiful velvet coats lined with silk start at around 1,600dh; men's shirts in fine linen at about 400dh. Collections change seasonally.

### Eva/Adam

*144 Souk El Hanna, Medina (044 44 39 69).* **Open** 10am-12.30pm, 3.30-6.30pm Mon-Thur, Sat, Sun. **Credit** AmEx, MC, V. **Map** p73.

No high fashion or class cuts, just practical and genuinely comfortable warm weather clothes in neutral colours. Lots of cottons and lightweight wools. Everything is very loose fitting yet elegant. It's the kind of stuff you might actually wear on a day-to-day basis, and prices are reasonable enough. To find it, walk north up Souk El Attarin just past the entrance to the mosque (to your left), look to the right for the word 'Lacoste' painted on a whitewashed arch: Eva/Adam is the first on the right, with barely more than a door as shop frontage.

### Au Fil d'Or

*10 Souk Semmarine, Medina (044 44 59 19).* **Open** 9am-1pm, 2.30-7.30pm Mon-Thur, Sat, Sun; 9am-1pm Fri. **Credit** AmEx, MC, V. **Map** p73.

It's near indistinguishable from the multitude of small stores around, but Au Fil d'Or is worth honing in on for the finest quality *babouches* and wool

# The souk for dummies

Like Mambo shirts in Sydney, Turkish Delight in Istanbul and amoebic dysentery in Delhi, every city has that something that you just have to pick up before you leave. Marrakech has numerous must-buys. Here's our checklist of the standard purchases:

## Argan oil

Morocco's famed argan oil (rich in vitamin E and essential fatty acids it lowers cholesterol levels, unblocks arteries, relieves rheumatic joint pain, reduces scars and wrinkles, whitens your smile, makes you horny and pays off your mortgage – so they say) is available at countless 'Berber pharmacies' (herbal shops) in the souk. This stuff is okay as a massage oil but should not be ingested. It's likely to have been cut with some other inferior oil, like cooking oil. For argan oil to use as a food dressing you need to go to a reputable outlet (*see below*). You might pay a little more at these places but you can be sure of the provenance and quality of the product.

The average price for argan oil in Marrakech is around 150dh a litre, but you can pay more for fancy packaging. You'll find it cheaper if you're going to Essaouira or Taroudant.

● The quality stuff is available at **Marjane** (*see p118*), **Scènes de Lin** (*see p128*) and at **Naturelle d'Argane** (5 rue Sourya, 044 44 87 61) by the former Marché Central in Guéliz.

## Babouches

There's no departure tax at Marrakech airport, but in order to leave every traveller has to present a newly purchased pair of canary-yellow *babouche*. Why else would so many shops in the souk sell them?

*Babouche*-buying is not as straightforward as it seems. The slippers come in leather, nubuck, suede or sabra (which looks like silk but is actually a kind of viscose). The sole will be leather, plastic or rubber and can be sewn on (good) or glued (not good). Yellow is the traditional Moroccan fave but *babouche* come in all colours as well as round-toed or pointy, with or without sequins, embroidered or not furry or stripey – you name it, someone does it.

Prices vary but expect to pay around 50dh for fake leather babouche with glued soles and around 150dh for the all-leather, stitched-sole variety.

● Available from just about everywhere but the obvious place to go is the **Souk des Babouches** (*see* map p73).

## Carpets

There's one simple rule when it comes to carpets: buy it because you like it, not because you've been told it's worth money. They were probably lying: very few carpets are antique. And ignore claims that a carpet is made of cactus silk. It's most likely not because genuine cactus silk carpets cost ten times as much as normal ones. What they call cactus silk is usually viscose.

When you see a carpet that you like, bear in mind that you are unlikely to find its double in another shop as most are unique. And don't be afraid of not buying after having a guy unfurl two dozen specimens for you: it's his job and anyway carpets have to be unrolled now and then to let them breath a little.

Carpets come in three standard sizes with standard prices, although there are modifying factors of age, quality and type. As a rule of thumb, something one metre by 1.5 metres should cost around 1,500dh; a carpet 1.5 metres by 2.5 metres will go for around 2,500dh; and a rug two metres by three will set you back somewhere around 4,500dh-5,000dh.

● The main places to buy carpets are along rue Mouassine (try **Tapis Akhnif**, *see p120*) and rue Semarine and in the Souk des Tapis off the Rahba Kedima, which is where you'll find **L'Art de Goulimine** (*see p120*) and **Bazaar du Sud** (*see p120*). In Guéliz, **El Badii** (*see p119*) carries an extensive stock of carpets in its basement showroom.

## Ceramics

The local style is plain terracotta glazed in bright colours. As an alternative to the standard hard enamel finish (done here with startling colours), there's also *tadelakt* effect, which is smooth and satiny to the touch with more subdued tones of mustardy yellows, minty greens and burgundy.

Price for the standard enamel finish start at around 30dh (ashtrays and bowls) up to 200dh for large fruit platters. Tadelakt-style pottery is slightly more expensive, ranging from 50dh for a candleholder up to 400dh for a tablelamp.

● Available everywhere but particularly in and around the Souk des Teinturiers (try **Création Chez Abdel**, *see p132*) and along the lower part of rue Mouassine (notably **Caverne d'Ali Baba**, *see p132*). For superior quality visit **Akkal** (*see p132*). The cheapest option is to shop at the sprawling, open-air **pottery market** just outside the south-eastern Medina gate of Bab Ghemat (map p255 F6).

## Lanterns

Styles range ones inspired in mosques including tall goatskin. The which is ofte

increases with the addition of glass, patterned or plain (the latter is known as Iraki glass, and is more expensive than the patterened sort because it's better quality). Brass and copper are a bit more expensive but lanterns made of these materials are generally better finished, harder wearing and are more easily integrated into a modern interior.

Prices range from 30dh to 250dh for tin, and from 100dh to 400dh for copper and brass.

● Available in the **Souk des Ferroniers** or the **Souk des Dinandiers** (for both, *see* map p73) and at **Founoun Marrakech** (*see p128*).

## Leather bags

Marrakech is good for quality leather, much of which ends up being fashioned into shoulder bags and travel luggage. But be careful: some of the work is shoddy and you can end up with a bag that leaves its contents stinking like a cowshed or transfers its colour to your skirt or trousers (rub the bag with a wet tissue before buying).

Also popular are vintage shoulder bags, often decorated with aged metal coins and copper discs. These sell for between 200dh and 400dh, or you can get modern copies for less.

Contemporary handbags go for anywhere from 150dh to 300dhs, while travel luggage starts at around 400dh and up to 800dh, depending on the size.

● Available from the northern end of the **Souk El Kebir** (*see* map p73) in the alleys of the Kissaria or, for something more modern and stylish try **Miloud El Jouli** (*see p125*) or take a taxi up to Guéliz and the **Galerie Birkemeyer** (*see p127*) or **Place Vendome** (*see p127*).

*jellabas*, plus fantastic own-label hand-stitched shirts (400dh) in gorgeous deep hues, and finely braided silk-lined jackets (2,200dh) – just the thing should one be invited to the palace. Note that the bulk of the stock is kept in the cellar-like space downstairs, accessed via a trapdoor behind the counter. Watch your head (and your spending).

### Intensité Nomade
*139 avenue Mohammed V, Guéliz (044 43 13 33).*
**Open** 9am-12.30pm, 3-7.30pm Mon-Sat. **Credit** AmEx, MC, V. **Map** p256 B2.
IN features owner-designer Frédérique Birkemeyer's own chic 'nomad' line of colourful kaftans, suede skirts, comfy raffia slippers, men's cotton shirts, leather jackets and a host of relatively inexpensive accessories. Pickings are mixed but the place draws a glitzy local clientele, poking around the racks for casual prêt à porter.

### Kulchi
*1 rue des Ksour, Bab Laksour, Medina (044 42 91 77).* **Open** 9.30am-1pm, 3.30-7pm Mon-Sat.
**No credit cards. Map** p252/254 B5.
Florence Taranne's small boutique stocks a quirky hand-picked collection of boho Moro chic, including leather shopping bags with *khamsa* ('hand') motif, lovely ruffly silk dresses and chiffon blouses in flowery prints by Spanish designer Lola, T-shirts by Hassan Hajjaj, Zina-label plastic shopping bags with brightly coloured flower designs imprinted on them and delicate jewellery, including rose petals laminated as earrings. It's pricey, at around 1,200dh-1,600dh for a silk/chiffon blouse, although you can find the odd bargain kaftan for 65dh or less. Our biggest beef is that most of the clothes are too small around the bust and would suit only Kate Moss or Sienna Miller – both of whom have been seen here.

### La Maison du Kaftan Marocain
*65 rue Sidi El Yamami, Medina (044 44 10 51).*
**Open** 9am-7.30pm daily. **Credit** AmEx, MC, V.
**Map** p73.
La Maison may have the unloved, run-down look of a charity store, but it also has the widest selection of Moroccan clothing for men, women and children in the souk, housed in what sustained exploration reveals to be a vast mausoleum of a place. Stock ranges from *pantalon turque* (traditional men's trousers) to beautiful velvet jackets and vintage kaftans that go for 20,000dh. Scouts for international fashion houses often drop by placing orders and looking for inspiration.

### Marrakech Maille Sarl
*69 boulevard El Mansour Eddahbi, Guéliz (044 43 95 85).* **Open** 8am-1pm, 3-7pm Mon-Sat. **No credit cards. Map** p256 B2.
A well-kept secret amongst Moroccan royalty, and the chic wives of diplomats, this small and unprepossessing boutique contains some very wearable clothes which will also make that all-important transition home to a colder climate. In winter, the owner and designer Khadija Daaraoui stocks lovely

woollen shawls and scarves, quality wool and mohair suits and *jellabas* in natural fibres. And in summer, lightweight cotton T-shirts in all colours (think John Smedley) and cotton and linen skirts, trouser suits and kaftans. Classic.

### Mia Zia
*Quartier Industriel Sidi Ghanem No.322, route de Safi (044 33 59 38/www.miazia.com).* **Open** 8am-6pm Mon-Fri; 8am-5pm Sat. **Credit** MC, V.
Fashion designer Valerie Barkowski has ultra-chic shops in Paris, Marseille, Geneva and Saint-Barth; in Marrakech her stripy socks, stripy *babouches* and stripy jumpers, crisp white cotton bed linen with embroidered borders and plush fringed towels are displayed and sold out of the Akkal pottery showroom (*see p132*). Prices are roughly 30 per cent less than you pay in Europe, with some slight seconds selling at 50 per cent less.

### Miloud El Jouli
*6-8 Souk Smat El Marga, off Souk El Kebir, Medina (044 42 67 16).* **Open** 9am-7.30pm daily. **Credit** MC, V. **Map** p73.
Join buyers from boutiques in Chelsea and New York's Upper East Side rifling through patterned *babouches*, vibrantly coloured shirts and blouses in Indian silks, silk and dyed-leather sequinned handbags, beaded belts with heavy silver buckles and *jellabas*. Some of this stuff is Miloud's own design, some of it is cleverly crafted local copy, as in the Hermes sandals that fill one shelf. Prices are less than you'd pay back home but not that much less. Souk Smat El Marga is in the Kissaria, the third narrow alley from the northernmost end of Souk El Kebir.

## Fashion accessories

For bags and belts and the like try **Kulchi** (*see above*) and **Miloud El Jouli** (*see above*); for scarves, shawls and souped-up *babouches* visit **Akbar Delights** (*see p121*).

## Jewellery

Most of the jewellery for sale in Marrakech is ethnic in either inspiration or origin. Favoured materials are silver, amber and beads, and pieces tend towards the heavy and chunky.

### Bazaar Atlas
*129 boulevard Mohammed V, Guéliz (044 43 27 16).*
**Open** 9.30am-1pm, 3.30-7.30pm Mon-Sat; 9.30am-1pm Sun. **Credit** MC, V. **Map** p256 B2.
A small but eye-catching boutique in central Guéliz (opposite the Marché Central) – one room lined with floor-to-ceiling cabinets filled with jewellery: antique, antique-styled, ethnic (Berber and Touareg) and modern. In among it all is also a smattering of odd gift items including ceramics and everything from tiny silver pill boxes to sculpted gazelle-horn and camel-bone ink wells and letter openers. The owner speaks fluent English.

**Eat, Drink, Shop**

## Bellawi

*Kessariat Lossta No.56, off Souk El Attarin, Medina (044 44 01 07).* **Open** 9am-7pm Mon-Thur, Sat, Sun. **No credit cards. Map** p73.

Abdelatif, whose closet-like jewellery store this is, is brother to the famed 'Mustapha Blaoui' (*see p128*). Here, there's just about room for Abdelatif, his workbench and one customer. The walls are hung with beads clustered like bunches of berry fruits, along with a fine selection of traditional Moroccan-style silver bangles and necklaces, and rings set with semiprecious stones. The shop is along the same narrow passage as Eva/Adam (*see p121*); no sign in English but just ask for Abdelatif – eveyone knows him, he's been here over 40 years.

## Boutique Bel Hadj

*22-23 Fundouk Ourzazi, place Bab Fteuh, Medina (044 44 12 58).* **Open** 9am-8pm daily. **Credit** AmEx, MC, V. **Map** p73.

The landmark Café Argana on Jemaa El Fna occupies the south-west corner of an old *fundouk* (merchants' inn); walk right round the corner and into place Bab Fteuh and you'll find Mohammed Bari's shop, which is piled high with a mad assortment of bits and pieces of jewellery, old and new. The range and quality are impressive, the prices are fair and Mohammed will never knowingly try to foist off the newly made as antique.

## Micheline Perrin

*Mamounia Hotel, avenue Bab Jedid, Medina (044 38 86 00/mobile 061 61 82 15).* **Open** 10am-1pm, 4-8pm daily. **Credit** AmEx, MC, V. **Map** p254 A6.

Perrin is one of the old guard who blew into Marrakech during its glamorous 1970s heyday. Her jewellery shop is in the little forecourt kiosk around which the Mamounia driveway arcs. She sells self-designed enamelled pieces that are a fusion of Moroccan and Indian stylings, as well as lots of one-of-a-kind necklaces strung from old and new precious stones.

## El Yed Gallery

*66 Fhal Chidmi, rue Mouassine, Medina (044 44 29 95).* **Open** 9.30am-12.30pm, 1.30-6.30pm Mon-Sat. **Credit** AmEx, MC, V. **Map** p73.

Opposite the side of the Mouassine Mosque, El Yed is a real collectors' haunt, specialising in beautiful antique Moroccan jewellery and pottery. Much of it comes from the deep south and it's not for the delicate of frame – bracelets look like great silver sprockets and the favoured stone is amber by the hunk. The owner speaks English and is highly knowledgeable about his stock, and happy to discuss details and provenance, but probably less willing to talk prices, which are fixed and expensive.

# Leather

For more on buying leather bags in Marrakech, *see p122* **The souk for dummies**.

## Chez Said

*51 Souk Chkairia, Medina (044 39 09 31).* **Open** 9.30am-7.30pm daily. **No credit cards. Map** p73.

Said does fashionable leather bags decorated with coins or beads, or with just a simple metal disc on the front. Designs come in both modern and vintage styles. The leather is either *au natural* or dyed; when the latter, colouring is properly fixed and doesn't come off on your skirt. Said speaks English, and also sells his bags in bulk to certain well-known stores in the UK.

Scènes de Lin. *See p128.*

### Galerie Birkemeyer
*169 rue Mohammed El Bekal, Guéliz (044 44 69 63).*
**Open** 8.30am-12.30pm, 3-7.30pm Mon-Sat; 9am-
12.30pm Sun. **Credit** AmEx, MC, V. **Map** p256 A2.
A long-established haunt for leather goods from
handbags and luggage, to shoes, jackets, coats and
skirts, with a sportswear section of international
designer labels. The sales assistants aren't particularly helpful and founder Ms Birkemeyer no longer
has anything to do with the place (she now owns
Intensité Nomade, *see p125*), but you still might
stumble across a bargain, such as a beautifully crafted purse for 600dh.

### Place Vendome
*141 avenue Mohammed V, Guéliz (044 43 52 63).*
**Open** 9am-12.30pm, 3.30-7.30pm Mon-Sat. **Credit**
AmEx, MC, V. **Map** p256 B2.
Owner Claude Amzallag is known for his custom-
designed buttery leather and suede jackets, and
sleek line of handbags and wallets, which come in
every colour from forest green to hot pink. The suede
shirts for men and stylish luggage are also big hits
with the fortysomething crowd.

## Shoes

### Atika
*35 rue de la Liberté, Guéliz (044 43 64 09).* **Open**
8.30am-12.30pm, 3-7.30pm Mon-Sat. **Credit** MC, V.
**Map** p256 B2.
This is where well-heeled residents and enlightened
tourists flock for stylish and affordable men's and
women's ranges – everything from classic loafers
and spiky black pumps to natural leather sandals
and stylish beige canvas mules. Prices start at 300dh
and rarely go beyond 750dh. It also carries children's
shoes and a small selection of handbags. There's a
second branch a few hundred metres south at 212
avenue Mohammed V.

### Cordonnerie Errafia
*Riad Zitoun El Jedid, Medina (mobile 062 77 83 47).*
**Open** 9am-1pm, 3-9pm daily. **No credit cards**.
**Map** p255 D6.
In a little workshop opposite the Préfecture de la
Medina, artisan Ahmed cobbles together classic
loafers out of rafia for gents, with more extrava-
gantly coloured and cut stylings for women. Given
three or four days, he can also make to order.

## Florists

There's a corner given over to florists at the
**Marché Central**, wherever that may be by the
time you read this (*see p131* **To market, to
market**), and an excellent flowerseller at the
**Mamounia** (*see p42*).

### Vita
*58 boulevard El Mansour Eddahbi, Guéliz (044 43
04 90).* **Open** 8.30am-12.30pm, 3-7.30pm Mon-Sat;
9am-1pm Sun. **No credit cards**. **Map** p256 A2.

A Western-style florist-garden ce
stock of cut flowers and ready-n
also does delivery (local and Inte
potted plants, seeds and compost.

## Food & drink

The greatest range of food and drink is found at
**Aswak Assalam** and **Marjane** (for both, *see
p118*). For fresh fruit and veg there's the Marché
Couvert and Mellah market in the Medina, and
the Marché Central in Guéliz: *see p131* **To
market, to market.**

### Entrepôt Alimentaire
*117 avenue Mohammed V, Guéliz (044 43 00 67).*
**Open** 8am-noon, 3-10pm Mon-Sat; 8am-noon Sun.
**No credit cards**. **Map** p256 B2.
A dusty little place that appears disorganised, but it
does have one of the best selections of wine (Moroccan
and French) in town. If you can't see it, ask.

### Jeff de Bruges
*17 rue de la Liberté, Guéliz (044 43 02 49).*
**Open** 9am-1pm, 3.30-8pm Mon-Sat. **Credit** MC, V.
**Map** p256 B2.
Not real Belgian chcocolates but still the best
chocolates in Marrakech. They make a great gift if
you're invited to dinner at a local home (Moroccans
are notoriously sweet-toothed), but don't expect a
share because they'll be hoarded away for later.
There's also a branch at Marjane (*see p118*).

### Yacout Services
*2 rue Yakoub El Marini, Guéliz (044 43 19 41).*
**Open** 8am-9pm daily. **No credit cards**.
**Map** p256 B3.
Just south of place du 16 Novembre and not far from
the church, Yacout is a fantastically well-stocked
minimarket with a basement store devoted to booze
– local and imported wines, beer and spirits. Plus,
next door is a shop that does own-made pasta.

## Home accessories

By which we mean crystal, china and pottery,
furnishings and drapes, lanterns and candles,
gee-gaws and knick-knacks. In this city of a
1,001 interior designers, 'home accessories' is
just about the biggest business in town.

### Amira
*Quartier Industriel Sidi Ghanem No.344, route de
Safi (044 33 62 47/www.amirabougies.com).* **Open**
9am-1pm, 2.30-6pm Mon-Sat. **Credit** MC, V.
Candles are a core standard of magical Moroccan
nights, and the best are made by Amira, run by
Rodolphe and Geraldine from Brittany. They come
in all kinds of shapes and colours: giant orange or
purple cubes, candles that can also be used as vases,
knee-high stripy cylinders and candles within candles. Amira also has simple contemporary bases to
complement the wax. Selected pieces can be bought

other outlets around town, but for the full range you need to head out to the showroom in the Sidi Ghanem industrial zone: for directions *see p118*.

## Cherkaoui

*120-122 rue Mouassine, Medina (044 42 68 17).* **Open** 8.30am-7.30pm daily. **Credit** AmEx, MC, V. **Map** p73.

Opposite the Mouassine fountain, a glittering Aladdin's cave full of everything imaginable for home decoration Moroccan style (except carpets). The proprietors, one local (Jaoud) and one German (Matthias), use their own local artisans, working in various media including wood, leather, metal and clay, to supply the store. Customers include the famed restaurant Dar Yacout and the Hotel les Jardins de la Koutoubia. Any piece can be made up in eight weeks and shipping can be arranged.

## Founoun Marrakech

*28 Souk des Teinturiers, Medina (044 42 62 03).* **Open** 10am-7pm daily. **No credit cards. Map** p73.

This is the place if you want a lantern (*founoun*) of quality. At first glance it's tiny, but walk through to the glittering back room to find an impressive choice of truly beautiful things. Rachid El Himel, the owner, is both helpful and charming; ask nicely and he'll take you through to the workshop in which a team of men and young boys hammer and cut at sheets of copper fashioning the goods to fill the shop. To find it, walk east past the Mouassine fountain, then through the arch, and it's the first lantern shop on the left.

## Kifkif

*8 rue des Ksour, Bab Laksour, Medina (061 08 20 41).* **Open** 9.30am-1.30pm, 2.30-7.30pm daily. **No credit cards. Map** p252/254 B5.

A quality knick-knack shop, with an eclectic array of goods, including unique bangles, belts, earrings and other accessories, little towelling dressing gowns for kids, embroidered napkin sets and own-designed glasses, electric lights, vases and table decorations. Stephanie is the owner, and everything is made in Morocco, bar a few imports. Some things are too expensive, like the set of Momo's *Arabesque* CDs at 350dh (buy the bootleg in Jemaa El Fna), but others like the charming white cotton baby romper suits at 100dh a throw, or the attractive beaded cigarette lighter covers for tabletops are worth buying.

## Lun'art Gallery

*24 rue Moulay Ali, Guéliz (044 44 72 66).* **Open** 9am-12.30pm, 3.30-8pm Mon-Sat. **Credit** AmEx, MC, V. **Map** p256 A2.

Eclecticism reigns supreme at this rather odd gallery and Moro curio shop. It has a garden space show-casing wrought-iron garden furniture and heavy mosaic tables, while indoors is a grab bag of mod-ern paintings by Moroccan artists, traditional pot-tery, *tadelakt* lamps, bric-a-brac and the odd curveball such as cinema costume accessories (for example, neckties left over from the filming of Scorcese's *Kundun*). Prices are reasonable.

## La Medina

*Quartier Industriel Sidi Ghanem No.24, route de Safi (044 33 61 32/www.la-medina.fr).* **Open** 8.30am-12.30pm, 2.30-6.30pm Mon-Sat. **No credit cards.**

A show space for the creations of metalworker Bernard Schmidt, who produces iron chandeliers, metal-framed mirrors, lamps, chairs and other assorted wonderful items. Also here are blown-glass pieces by his wife Myriam Roland-Gosselin (*see p131*) and copies of furniture and table accessories designed by Thierry Isnardon for his super-stylish restaurant Foundouk. In addition, there's a wide selection of non-Foundouk ceramics and *artisanat* that Isnardon has designed for wholesale distribu-tion to shops and boutiques throughout Europe. For directions to the Quartier Industriel, see *p118*.

## Mustapha Blaoui

*142-144 Bab Doukkala, Medina (044 38 52 40).* **Open** 9am-8pm daily. **Credit** AmEx, MC, V. **Map** p252 B4.

This is the classiest, most beloved 'best of Morocco' depot in town. It's a warehouse of a place crammed, racked, stacked and piled with floor-to-ceiling irresistibles – lanterns, dishes, pots, bowls, candlesticks, chandeliers, chests, tables and chairs... If Mustapha doesn't have it, then you don't need it. He supplied almost all the furnish-ings for the Villa des Orangers. Even people who don't own a hotel will find it almost impossible to visit here and not fill a container lorry. Added to which, Mustapha's a real sweetheart, his staff are ultra-helpful and shipping here is a cinch.

## Scènes de Lin

*70 rue de la Liberté, Guéliz (044 43 61 08).* **Open** 9.30am-12.30pm, 3.30-7.30pm Mon-Sat. **Credit** MC, V. **Map** p256 B2.

A chic fabric store that specialises in linens, and also offers a huge range of brilliant hues in striped woven cloth or delicate pastel organdie. Any combo can be ordered for custom-made curtains, tablecloths or place settings. There's plenty of other top quality stuff besides, including luxuri-ous fringed hammam towels, cushions with Fès embroidery, natural essential oils (including argan oil) and unusual contemporary lamps. Downstairs is a small selection of Moroccan couture.

---

# Furniture

For something in a traditional vein pay a visit to **Mustapha Blaoui** (*see above*); for something a little more unique look at the work of Thierry Isnardon at **La Medina** (*see above*).

## Ministerio del Gusto

*22 Derb Azouz El Mouassine, off rue Sidi El Yamami, Medina (044 42 64 55).* **Open** 9.30am-noon, 4-7pm Mon-Sat. **Credit** MC, V. **Map** p73.

The Ministero is HQ to ex-*Vogue Italia* fashion edi-tor Alessandra Lippini and her business partner Fabrizio Bizzarri. It's a surreal space – a sort of

Founoun Marrakech.
*See p128.*

الصناعة التقليدية

**Bab Ftouh**

*Artisant Marocain*

**Glamorous Interiors for Glamorous People !**

Avenue Prince My. Abdellah
Sidi Abbad
Marrakech
Tel: +212 44 31 04 85
Mobile: +212 (0) 612 42944
Fax: +212 44 44 55 04
Email: artbabftouh@iam.net.ma

We are the largest producers and wholesalers in Marrakech of Moroccan handi-crafts for interior decoration. Our 2000 square metre gallery offers a vast range of antique and reproduction furniture, including tables, chairs, cabinets, screens, shelving, mirrors, ceramics, lighting and carpets, both traditional and modern, free car service on demand by calling mobilephone. Contact name is Jalil

# To market, to market

The greater part of the Marrakech Medina is one vast market or bazaar, but away from the main lanes of the souk are several other areas of concentrated open-air commerce.

Down in the old Jewish quarter of the Mellah there's the **Bab Es Salam market** (*map p255 D7*) one block east of the place des Ferblantiers. It's very much a local affair with traders selling predominantly fruit and vegetables, herbs and spices. Few tourists venture around here. Nearby, on the south side of avenue Houman El Fetouaki is the **Marché Couvert** (*map p255 C7*), again a working market supplying fresh produce, meat and fish to the kitchens of the homes of the southern Medina.

At the opposite extreme, in all senses, is the **Souk El Khemis** (*map p253 D2*). At the northern end of the Old City, just inside the Bab El Khemis gate, it's as much rubbish dump as market. A last chance saloon for manufactured goods, stalls here can be no more than a blanket spread with a pitiful heap of cast-offs – single shoes, a box of rusted

bicycle gears, a bag of unravelled audio cassettes. But it's also a legendary treasure trove of architectural salvage. Palmeraie villas have been kitted out at the Souk El Khemis, and when the Mamounia underwent its last refit, the discarded sinks, fittings and even carpets all turned up here.

The **Marché Central** (*map p256 B2*) in Guéliz was set to move in summer 2005 from its old plot on avenue Mohammed V to a site just east of place du 16 Novembre. It used to be the place where the city's expats would come to buy fruit and veg, meat and fish, cheese and wine, Cheerios and Frosties, but nobody knows in quite what form it will be reincarnated.

A kilometre north-east, just off avenue Yacoub El Mansour and in the neighbourhood of the Majorelle Gardens, is the city's **Wholesale Market** (*map p256 C1*). Operating from seven to ten each morning, it's where farmers from outlying villages bring crates of oranges and tomatoes, baskets of dates and grapes.

Gaudi goes Mali with a side trip to Mexico. As well as filling the role of informal social centre for friends and assorted fashionistas and creatives blowing through town, the two floors of Del Gusto also act as a sometime gallery (*see p144*) and showcase for funky 'found' objects (sourced from house clearances) such as African-inspired furniture, chairs by Eames and Bernini glassware.

## Glassware

### Myriam Roland-Gosselin

*6 route de l'Aeroport (044 36 19 88).* **Open** by appointment only. **No credit cards**.

Roland-Gosselin has a studio in a tranquil garden just off the airport road where she makes delicate hand-blown glass objects for the home. Her collection, exhibited in an adjacent showroom, consists of vases, tumblers, bowls, bells, wine glasses, candle holders and small lamps. Her colour schemes range from neutral to warm ambers and oranges that bring to mind fiery Moroccan sunsets. Purchases are packaged in her lovely signature boxes. Her work is also exhibited and sold at La Medina (*see p128*).

## Metalwork

### Artisanat Berbère

*33 Souk El Attarin, Medina (044 44 38 78).* **Open** 9am-8pm daily. **Credit** MC, V. **Map** p73.

A charmingly dusty old place filled with heaps of largely useless items fashioned from brass, copper, pewter and other pliable metals. Lots of trays, pots and lamps, plus ancient flat irons and giant sculpted animals. And you've got to love a place that promises on its business card 'small margin profit'.

### Dinanderie

*6-46 Fundouk My Mamoun, Mellah (044 38 49 09).* **Open** 8am-8pm Mon-Sat. **Credit** MC, V. **Map** p255 D7.

Moulay Youssef is one of the country's handful of elite artisans. If you need something extravagant wrought from metal – and if you have the money – then Moulay is your man. The bulk of his work is made to order, but adjacent to his workspace is also a crowded gallery of smaller pieces. A little difficult to find, the Dinanderie atelier fills an alley immediately west of the small rose garden across from the place des Ferblantiers.

### Mohammed Ouledhachmi

*34 Souk El Hararin Kedima, Medina (066 64 41 05).* **Open** 9am-6pm Mon-Thur, Sat, Sun. **No credit cards**. **Map** p73.

Mohammed does copper. Copper trays, copper pots, copper kettles, copper you-name-it. Some of the pieces are new, but the bulk of the stock is aged. Mohammed sometimes has pieces by well-known metalsmiths whose work is prized by collectors. To find him, head north up Souk El Attarin and take the second right after passing the entrance to the mosque on the left.

## Yahya Creation

*49 passage Ghandouri, off rue de Yougoslavie, Guéliz (044 42 27 76/www.yahyacreation.com).* **Open** 10am-12.30pm, 2.30-7pm Mon-Sat. **Credit** MC, V. **Map** p256 A2.

Yahya Rouach's mother is English and Christian, his father is a Jew from Meknès, and he's a Muslim convert brought up in the UK and now resident in Marrakech. He designs extraordinary items, such as lanterns, torches and screens, all of finely crafted metals. His pieces are completely unique, often stunning one-offs. Most of them are big too: conversation pieces for a chic sheikh's Dubai penthouse. Prices range from 150dh to 150,000dh. This arcade outlet is a showroom rather than a shop, where customers drop in to place commissions, joining a client list that includes Harrods and Neiman Marcus.

## Pottery

For general information on buying pottery, *see p122* **The souk for dummies**.

### Akkal

*Quartier Industriel Sidi Ghanem No.322, route de Safi (044 33 59 38).* **Open** 8am-6pm Mon-Fri; 8am-5pm Sat. **Credit** MC, V.

The Akkal pottery factory does Conran-worthy modern takes on classic Moroccan shapes (tajines to tea glasses) and pick 'n' mix dinnerware, all in fantastically rich colours. The pottery looks great on the shelves but it's not quite as dishwasher-proof as Akkal claims. The factory showroom also sells Mia Zia (*see p125*), as well as jewellery, handicrafts and furniture by a wide and varied assortment of other local designers. It is one of the best stores in town. Overseas shipping can be organised.

### Caverne d'Ali Baba

*17A Fhal Chidmi, Mouassine, Medina (044 44 21 48).* **Open** 9am-8pm daily. **Credit** MC, V. **Map** p73.

Ali Baba's an Akkal imitator, but a good one. This huge shop is stocked with an incredible array of everything from egg cups to lamp bases in all imaginable colours. In fact, just about any pottery trend that has hit the Medina will very quickly be copied and put on sale here. Especially attractive are the *tadelakt*-finish items, which have an almost soft leather-like appearance.

### Création Chez Abdel

*17 Souk des Teinturiers, Medina (044 42 75 17).* **Open** 9am-9pm daily. **No credit cards. Map** p73.

Another good outlet for *tadelakt* pottery. This is a small shop packed from floor to ceiling with simple shapes in rich, luminous colours. There are great bowls and lamps, but also lighter and more portable items such as candlesticks and ashtrays. Quality is excellent and prices are reasonable. There's no name on the shop so it can be difficult to spot – walk east past the Mouassine fountain and there's a sharp right, then a left, then Abdel's is the pine-framed door on the right.

### Chez Aloui

*52 rue des Ksour, Mouassine, Medina (062 08 48 71).* **Open** 9am-8pm daily. **No credit cards. Map** p73.

A great place for ceramics in a variety of styles including Berber (which looks very African, with strong, simple shapes) and both old and new pieces from Safi, one of Morocco's main pottery-producing centres. Our favourites are the traditional green ceramics from Tamegroute near Zagora. The green glaze never seems to come out quite the same so each piece is almost unique, and some of the plates and bowls are marked with a spiral motif, the Berber circle of life.

## Textiles

### Art Ouarzazate

*15 rue Rahba Kedima, Medina (067 35 21 24).* **Open** 10am-6.30pm daily. **Credit** MC, V. **Map** p73.

A small sparsely stocked shop, but with an interesting stock, including beautiful throws handwoven from agave fibres. Colours are jewel-like and prices pretty reasonable. There are also old kaftans and *jellabas*, and *babouches* made of silk (about 200dh a pair). Mohammed speaks English and you can accept his offer of tea, without feeling cornered into buying.

### Chez Brahim

*101 Rahba Lakdima, Medina (044 44 01 10).* **Open** 9.30am-6.30pm daily. **Credit** AmEx, MC, V. **Map** p73.

Brahim offers an overwhelming selection of fabulous Moroccan textiles. His collection covers all regions and styles. Many of his textiles are old and it is hard to find things like his elsewhere. Chez Brahim is like going to a museum where everything is for sale. Prices are steep, but these are collectors' pieces.

### Chez Moulay Youssef

*Souk El Kchachbia, off rue El Hadadine, Medina (044 44 34 01).* **Open** 10am-8pm daily. **No credit cards. Map** p73.

One of our favourite shops in the souk, Moulay Youssef does beautiful richly coloured and stripy bedspreads in sabra, cotton or raffia. There are also homeware items such as jewellery boxes, napkin rings and pillow cases, plus fashion accessories like belts and hand-embroidered bags. It isn't the easiest place to find, but if you can locate the general neighbourhood just ask – everybody knows Moulay Youssef.

# Leisure

## Bookshops

Marrakech is not a literary city and reading matter in any language is scarce, though particularly so in English. That could be about

The **pottery market** at Bab Ghemat, source of the cheapest earthenware. *See p123.*

to change because as we went to press we received word of a new English-language bookshop and café to open in Guéliz on rue Tarek Ibn Ziad, close by the restaurant Catanzaro. Otherwise, beyond the places listed below, the **Musée de Marrakech** (*see p75*) and the **Mamounia** (*see p42*) both have bookshops but they're both very poor.

### ACR Libraire d'Art

*Immobelier Tayeb, 55 boulevard Mohammed Zerktouni, Guéliz (044 44 67 92).* **Open** 9am-12.30pm, 3-7pm Mon-Sat. **Credit** MC, V. **Map** p256 B2.
ACR is a French publishing house notable for its lavish art books. The company is seemingly dedicated to photographing every last mud brick and orange blossom in Marrakech and publishing the results in a series of coffee-table volumes. Get them all here, along with other (non-ACR) titles on the art and architecture of Morocco and the Islamic world, guides, cookery books and art cards. What little English-language stock the shop used to have seems to have disappeared.

### Librairie Chatr

*23 avenue Mohammed V, Guéliz (044 44 79 97).* **Open** 8am-1pm, 3-8pm Mon-Sat. **Credit** MC, V. **Map** p256 A2.
These days it's mainly a stationers, the long bar counter perpetually swamped by short-trousered fiends in search of marker pens and notebooks, but there is a large back room where a heavy patina of dust fogs the titles of what's mainly Arabic and French stock. A single shelf represents the English-language world and most of what it contains is heavier on pictures than words.

### Maktabet El Chab

*rue Mouassine, Medina (044 44 34 17).* **Open** 8.30am-8.30pm daily. **No credit cards**. **Map** p73.
Aka the 'FNAC Berbère' bookshop, this corner kiosk claims to be 'La première librairie à Marrakech', founded in 1941. Stock is pitifully limited but full marks for perseverance.

## Music

There are stalls selling cassettes and CDs among those of the juice sellers on the Jemaa El Fna. There are others in the southernmost crook of the souk – turn into the passage that runs west from the Terrasses de l'Alhambra as if heading towards the egg market, then turn first left.

Stock doesn't vary much, so choose one where you feel comfortable about hanging around and listening to a few things. It may all seem impenetrable at first but stallholders will be happy to play whatever ignites your curiosity. Good buys include percussive bellydance music, live gnawa recordings from the Festival d'Essaouira, Algerian rai and Tuareg blues from the Sahara.

Most of this stuff is pirated so prices are low. You shouldn't pay more than 20dh-30dh per CD. One stall on the west side of rue Bab Agnaou has a posted fixed price of 15dh.

## Newsagents

The two best newstands are both on avenue Mohammed V in Guéliz: one on the corner of rue de Mauritanie and the other two blocks north

Rahal Herbes.

beside the tourist office, just off place Abdel Moumen. There's also a decent newstand outside the Hotel CTM on Jemaa El Fna.

## Services

### Beauty & hair salons

Suntan lotion is available at pharmacies (*see below*), but the choice is better at **Marjane** (*see p118*).

#### Salon Jacques Dessange
*Sofitel Marrakech, rue Harroun Errachid, Hivernage (044 43 34 95).* **Open** 10am-8pm daily. **Credit** MC, V. **Map** p256 C5.
A French hairdresser, formerly at the Meridien, with a growing reputation among the moneyed set.

#### L'Univers de la Femme
*22 rue Bab Agnaou, Medina (044 44 12 96).* **Open** 9am-1pm, 3-8pm Tue-Sun. **Credit** MC, V. **Map** p254 C6.
All beauty treatments are available here, and the well-trained assistants know how to look after you.

The pleasant surroundings are perfect for pampering at affordable prices.

#### Yves Rocher
*13 rue de la Liberté, Guéliz (044 44 82 62).* **Open** 9am-1pm, 3-7pm Mon-Sat. **No credit cards**. **Map** p256 B2.
The French beauty chain has several sites, but the rue de la Liberté branch is the easiest to find. All offer moderately priced beauty products as well as manicures, pedicures, facials and epilation.

### Herbalists

For an explanation of what a dried lizard can do for you, *see p79* **Jinn and tonics**.

#### Rahal Herbes
*43-7 Rahba Kedima, Medina (044 44 00 60).* **Open** 9am-8pm daily. **No credit cards**. **Map** p73.
The west side of Rahba Kedima is lined with herbalists and 'black magic' stores; we recommend Rahal for owner Abdeljabbar's fluency in English and his wickedly dry sense of humour.

### Pharmacies

#### Pharmacie Centrale
*166 avenue Mohammed V, corner of rue de la Liberté, Guéliz (044 43 01 58).* **Open** 8.30am-12.30pm, 3.30-7.30pm Mon-Thur; 8.30am-noon, 3.30-7.30pm Fri; 8.30am-1pm, 3.30-7.30pm Sat. **Credit** MC, V. **Map** p256 B2.
The most conveniently central pharmacy in the New City. On the door is a list of the city pharmacies which are on 24-hour duty that particular week.

#### Pharmacie du Progrès
*Jemaa El Fna, Medina (044 44 25 63).* **Open** 8.15am-12.30pm, 2.15-6.30pm daily. **No credit cards**. **Map** p73.
An excellent pharmacy with knowledgeable, qualified staff, who will advise you on minor ailments and suggest medication. English is spoken.

### Photography

There's also a Kodak Express lab at the *hypermarché* **Marjane** (*see p118*).

#### Ikram Photo Lab
*Centre Kawkab, 3 rue Imam Chafii, Guéliz (044 44 74 94).* **Open** 9am-noon, 3-9pm Mon-Sat. **Credit** MC, V. **Map** p256 B3.
A smart and modern Fuji lab near the Jnane El Harti for 24-hour print processing, plus slide and video.

#### Wrédé
*142 avenue Mohammed V, Guéliz (044 43 57 39).* **Open** 8.30am-12.30pm, 2.45-7.30pm Mon-Sat. **Credit** MC, V. **Map** p256 B2.
Staff are friendly and the quality of processing is fine. Slide film is sent to Casablanca and returns in three days. Some English is spoken.

Eat, Drink, Shop

# Arts & Entertainment

| | |
|---|---|
| **Children** | **136** |
| **Film** | **139** |
| **Galleries** | **142** |
| **Music** | **145** |
| **Nightlife** | **148** |
| **Sport & Fitness** | **156** |

**Features**

| | |
|---|---|
| The joy of sets | 140 |
| Maroc 'n' roll | 147 |
| The disreputable business | |
|   of beer-drinking | 149 |
| Gay Marrakech | 152 |
| Lions of the Atlas | 158 |
| Greening the desert | 161 |

# Children

Snakes and monkeys on the square, chameleons for sale in the souk – how could kids not love Marrakech?

In many ways Marrakech is not a child-friendly place. There's next to nothing in the way of kiddie entertainments, children's clothes shops and toy shops are almost non existent and the concept of children's menus or highchairs in restaurants is unknown.

However, children are also universally adored in Marrakech. It's not unusual for a businessman talking on a mobile phone to stop to smile at a cute kid. There may even be overzealous kissing and hugging of your baby. People generally tend to be very tolerant of other people's kids and unruly behaviour that in other countries would inspire stern looks is here more likely to inspire indulgent cooing.

Moroccan families tend to be large and entertainment comes in the form of brothers, sisters, myriad cousins and neighbours' children. They're allowed the freedom to play in the street. The risks of scrapes and bumps aside, Marrakech is extremely safe, particularly the Medina, which is largely traffic-free. There are few crimes against kids and no parent has any cause to fear when their children are out of sight. It's all reminiscent of the childhoods remembered by your gran and grandad – 'We just had a stick and a tin can in our day and it would keep us happy for hours.' And in Marrakech it does.

For many families the hottest outing is to Marjane (see p118), the hypermarket, where kids can gaze wide-eyed at the shelves of toys. Likewise, petrol stations are a popular place to take little boys (really), and anything with a playground such as the McDonald's (see p138) is swamped when school's out.

## SIGHTSEEING

Sightseeing with very young children is difficult, particularly in the Medina. The heat can be hard on kids, especially in summer months when temperatures can reach over 40°C (104°F). Avoid the middle of the day when the sun is at its strongest. Be sure to take the usual precautions: light, loose cotton clothes, sun hats, high-factor sun cream and plenty of fluids.

Apart from cafés, there are few parks or other places to take a break from walking and amenities such as toilets and washrooms are scarce. It's worth making use of toilets in hotels and restaurants wherever possible. And carry toilet roll just in case.

Avoid unpurified water (bottled mineral water is widely available), stay away from uncooked food, such as salads, and be sure to peel or wash fruit and veg. Diarrhoea and stomach complaints are common in Morocco and children are even more susceptible than adults. Pack some rehydration sachets just in case.

## ACCOMMODATION

If you decide to come to Marrakech with your children, the first thing you need to decide is where you want to stay. Although riads are the height of fashion, they are not well suited to children. They tend to be quiet intimate spaces, very peaceful, with all rooms arranged off a central courtyard with no activities or places to play – fine if you have a quiet, well-behaved child, but a potential nightmare otherwise. In this respect it's worth noting that **Riad Ifoulki** (see p49) is arranged in such a way that certain parts can be separated off by doors behind which families can have their own courtyard and rooms.

The alternative is to go for one of the larger five-star-style hotels (see p57 **The chain gang**) in the Hivernage district. Otherwise, particularly recommended for kids is the **Coralia Club Palmariva**, one of the few hotels in the city that claims specifically to cater for children. The hotel complex is huge, so much so that rollerblades are handed out to help get around. Facilities include the Baboo Kids Village, a playgroup and activity centre for four to 12-year-olds that is open seven days a week. Most of the activities of the hotel are included in the price and include golf, archery and canoeing. There's also the nearby **Palmeraie Golf Palace**, another large resort complex with heaps of activities, including a kiddies' adventure playground, horse and pony stables and camel rides. Both the Palmariva and Golf Palace are out in the Palmeraie some distance north of the Medina, involving lots of taxiing around, which could be an issue.

The majority of hotels will not charge for children under the age of two. Between two and 12 years, so long as the room is being shared with parents, children are commonly charged around 50 per cent of adult rates.

Note that budget hotels are unlikely to have adequate bathroom facilities for small children – they are often communal.

Entertainment for kids in Marrakech comes mostly in the form of other kids.

### Coralia Club Palmariva

*route de Fès, km6 (044 32 90 36).* **Rates** 580dh per person per day (half board); 50% discount under-12s. **Credit** AmEx, MC, V.

### Palmeraie Golf Palace

*Palmeraie Golf Palace Hotel & Resort, Palmeraie (044 30 10 10/fax 044 30 63 66/www.pgp.co.ma/ golfpalace@pgp.ma).* **Rates** from 3,200dh double; free under-4s. **Credit** AmEx, MC, V.

### TRANSPORT

If you decide to rent a car for a day trip or even plan to do some exploring by taxi, do not expect child seats. You could bring your own; there is a type that is attachable to the seat belts. The spectacular panoramas out of the car window – especially in the south – should be enough to keep the little ones interested, but it's worth bringing something to keep them entertained on long journeys. Make sure you have enough water and food as shops may be few and far between on the open road.

### BABYSITTING

Most riads and hotels can provide babysitters upon request. Most won't speak English but the language of play is universal.

## Activities

There's not a great deal specifically for children to do in Marrakech. Attempts have been made at creating kids' attractions but they haven't worked. In 2002 a children's activity park opened just across from the airport with mini golf, a pool with slides and various rides. It closed in under eight months. Work began on a much vaunted safari park, Bab Africa, but that was abandoned. Currently there is a waterslide park being built on the route d'Ourika, but it remains to be seen if it will ever be completed and if it is, whether it will do business. Most locals can't afford this kind of luxury entertainment.

Never mind, most kids will be just as taken by the unfamiliar sights, sounds and smells as their parents are. It's not as if Marrakech has any shortage of visual stimulation. For a wonderful take on Marrakech from a child's view read Esther Freud's *Hideous Kinky*.

### Carriage rides

*place de Foucault, Medina.* **Map** p68.
A ride in a brightly painted horse-drawn carriage (*calèche*) is great fun. They seat around four and can be hired for a circuit of the walls, which is a pretty

ride, or taken even further afield up and through the Palmeraie. The wall circuit will probably take an hour or more; the Palmeraie run two or three hours. The rate is officially 80dh an hour but be prepared to negotiate down from 100dh or so. Note that the rate is per carriage not per person. Pick them up on the north side of place de Foucault, midway between the Koutoubia Mosque and Jemaa El Fna.

## Jemaa El Fna

Map p68.

Children love the Jemaa El Fna. During the day there are dancing monkeys and snake charmers, while the water carriers with their bright red outfits can easily be mistaken for clowns. At night food stalls are set up, displaying all kinds of strange things to eat and there are acrobats, fire-eaters and magicians.

## Kawkab Jeu

*1 rue Imam Chafii, Kawkab Centre, Hivernage (044 43 89 29).* **Open** 8.30am-10pm daily. **No credit cards.** Map p256 B3.

Next door to the Royal Tennis Club, Kawkab Jeu is a coffeeshop (big on crêpes and fancy ice-creams) with both an indoor play area for the really little 'uns, plus an outdoor playground with swings, slides, climbing frames and so on. For young teens there's also table football, table tennis and video games.

## Tansift Garden

*Circuit de la Palmeraie (044 30 87 86).* **Open** 10am-3pm, 5.30-10pm daily. **Credit** MC, V.

Just off the main road that winds through the Palmerie, the Tansift Garden is a combination of playground and coffeeshop. Plastic tables are set up among the palm trees where children can run and play and scream their lungs out bothering no one. There are also slides, swings, monkey bars and camel rides in the parking lot.

## Parks & outdoor spaces

There are several parks and gardens around town (*see pp90-4*) but they're going to be of limited interest to most children. The exception is possibly the **Menara Gardens**, which has a big water-filled basin at its centre, home to huge and greedy fish. Children can buy bags of bread from a kiosk and feed them. The **Jnane El Harti** (*see p88*), a landscaped park in Guéliz, has a children's play area with sandpits, climbing frames and a big blue dinosaur.

## Menara Gardens

*avenue de la Menara, Hivernage (no phone).* **Open** 5am-6.30pm daily. **Admission** free; picnic pavilion 15dh. Map p251 A5.

## Sports & leisure

The range of distractions increases with the age of your children. If they're able to swing a club or stay astride, then the **Royal Golf Club** has a

kids' club every Wednesday and Saturday and the **Palmeraie Golf Palace** has a weekly pony club. The Golf Palace also has a **bowling alley**, which is open 4.30pm-1am daily and is accessible to non-residents.

For a day rate of 100dh-250dh per person, including lunch, **Club Med** will bus you to its site in the Palmeraie for pool access and a full range of sporting activities. **Le Relais du Lac**, which is based a half-hour south of the city, offers something similar; a driver will pick you up in Marrakech and drive you down there for a day of darts, canoeing, pedal boats, donkey rides, biking, volleyball and badminton with lunch included. Little children might enjoy it too, as it's a lakeside site with mountain views, and ducks and geese wandering freely. The price is 450dh per person (under-12s half-price).

## Club Med

*place de Foucault, Medina (044 44 40 16).* **Credit** AmEx, MC, V. **Pool admission** 250dh; 12-17s 150dh; 4-11s 100dh. **Credit** MC, V. Map p252 & p254 B5.

## Palmeraie Golf Palace

*Palmeraie Golf Palace Hotel & Resort, Palmeraie (044 30 10 10/fax 044 30 63 66/www.pgp.co.ma/ golfpalace@pgp.ma).* **Credit** AmEx, MC, V.

## Le Relais du Lac

*barrage de Lalla Takerkoust (mobile 061 24 24 54/ 061 18 74 72).* **No credit cards.**

## Royal Golf Club

*Ancienne route de Ouarzazate, km2 (044 40 98 28).* **Open** *Summer* sunrise-sunset daily. *Winter* 9am-2.30pm daily. **Credit** MC, V.

## Restaurants

Shame on us for promoting it, but the kids do love **McDonald's**. Marrakech has three: one up by the Marjane hypermarket, a few minutes' drive north of town on the Casablanca road, one at Marjane itself, and the other in central Guéliz on place du 16 Novembre. **Catanzaro** (*see p108*) is the sole restaurant, so far as we know, that has a children's menu.

## Shopping

For nappies and baby food you'll have to make the trek to **Marjane** (*see p118*), as most small grocery stores don't stock them. UHT and powdered milk, however, are easily available. For clothing try **Jacadi** on avenue Mohammed V in Guéliz. For toyshops, again, hit Marjane or there's **La Drogerie** (163 avenue Mohammed V, 044 43 07 27) in Guéliz, and, just round the corner, **Articles pour le Bébé** (68 rue de la Liberté, 044 43 12 00) specialises in baby needs.

# Film

Casablanca may mean Morocco in Hollywood folklore, but Marrakech is the focal point of North Africa's growing film industry.

The indelible image of Morocco in the movies is always going to be conjured by the name 'Casablanca', no matter that Rick's Café never existed, and Bogart and Bergman never left the Warner Bros backlot in Burbank.

If you're looking for traces of the real Morocco on screen, it comes in many guises – in recent years it's become the exotic backdrop of choice for foreign filmmakers, standing in for Tibet in Martin Scorsese's *Kundun*, Somalia in Ridley Scott's *Black Hawk Down* and Ethiopia in Renny Harlin's 2004 *Exorcist: The Beginning*. It was a generic North Africa for Matthew McConaughey and Penelope Cruz in *Sahara*, for Jean-Claude Van Damme in *Legionnaire* and for Ridley Scott's *Gladiator*, sections of which were shot at the Atlas Studios in Ouarzazate, the pre-desert town that's home to Morocco's biggest film facilities.

The country's tradition of religious tolerance has made it a popular substitute for the Holy Land: Ben Kingsley was a cable TV Moses, Willem Dafoe was Jesus here in Scorsese's *The Last Temptation of Christ* and Ridley Scott blew into town yet again for his Crusader epic *Kingdom of Heaven*. Closer to geographical authenticity – and probably the most evocative representation of the landscape's mysterious charms – Bernardo Bertolucci adapted Paul Bowles's *The Sheltering Sky*, filming in the author's old stomping ground Tangier as well as south in the Sahara – and Gillies Mackinnon brought Esther Freud's *Hideous Kinky* to the screen, easily the sparkiest Western take on Marrakech and the Moroccans.

## SWORDS AND SANDALS

The $457-million, multiple-Oscar-winning success of *Gladiator* has transformed the prospects for the local industry, inspiring the biggest new wave of 'sword and sandal' epics since the 1960s. Wolfgang Petersen's Trojan War epic *Troy*, with Brad Pitt as Achilles, was all set to shoot in Morocco until jitters over US action in Iraq caused the producers to relocate to Mexico. But Oliver Stone came with *Alexander* and Ridley Scott returned with *Kingdom of Heaven*.

Appearing as a guest of honour at the 2004 Film Festival Stone took to the stage to announce: 'Without Morocco there would be no film. It is the place where East meets West.' He went on to elaborate the more prosaic reason that Morocco is so attractive to foreign filmmakers: cost. 'We tried to make the film in Hollywood. But when we factored in all the unit costs in California we were way over budget. In Morocco we could run 500 to 2,000 extras a day. It's not possible to do this kind of movie in America.' In America, an extra earns $100 a day. In Morocco it's $15.

It's not just the financial savings either. Morocco has varied and versatile scenery. Since David Lean filmed much of *Lawrence of Arabia* around Ouarzazate, many other directors have used Morocco's diversity of desert landscapes. And for *Alexander*, Oliver Stone used Essaouira for Greece, shot the Atlas Mountains to double as the Hindu Kush and used a flat plain outside of Marrakech for his battle scenes. All this and around 300 clear sunny days per year.

And what's good for Hollywood is also good for Morocco. A major production such as *Alexander* brings an investment in the region of $60 million for Morocco. Up to perhaps 10,000 people get work as extras and crew, drivers and technicians. Not to mention the £30,000 leading man Colin Farrell is supposed to have clocked up at the bar of Marrakech's Le Meridien.

Enlightened government policies regarding foreign filmmaking in Morocco also boost the indigenous film sector. To receive a production licence, at least one producer must be Morocco-based. In addition, ten per cent of all domestic cinema box office is directed to funding Moroccan movies, of which there are usually between ten and 12 a year. Nevertheless, the industry faces grave problems. In a country of about 150 cinemas, Moroccan films can rarely hope to pay for themselves. Nor does it help that the local Arabic dialect is not widely understood beyond Morocco and Algeria. In any case, many Moroccan films are French co-productions and are often in French. Not surprisingly, emigration to Europe is a common theme (see 2001's *Au-delà de Gibraltar*, for example), though raucous comedies and historical romances are also popular. Few of these films have excited international attention, although the engaging neo-realist fable *Ali Zaoua: Prince de la Rue* (directed by Nabil Ayouch, 2000) was distributed across Europe.

Despite the government encouraging Western filmmakers to come to Morocco and throwing its support behind the local industry, it is Bollywood films that local audiences want to see. Bollywood legends Amitabh Bachan and Shah Rukh Khan are the biggest film stars in the country. In 2004, the Film Festival contained a restrospective of Indian movies and in 2005 Marrakech will play host to a major Bollywood awards ceremony.

## Cinemas

Marrakech has no more than a half-a-dozen or so city-centre cinemas, with just a handful more dotted around the outskirts. Movie programming tends to a mix of Hollywood blockbusters, Bollywood, martial arts pictures and mainstream French releases. This is a francophone country with Arabic subtitling,

Arts & Entertainment

# The joy of sets

Superbly stocked with mountains, coast, desert and sun, southern Morocco stands in for an assortment of historical locations, including just occasionally itself:

● **Alexander** (2004) Essaouira goes Greek and the High Atlas becomes the Hindu Kush for Oliver Stone's awkward epic.
● **Gladiator** (2000) Russell Crowe is sold into slavery at the kasbah of Ait Benhaddou (*see p204*) near Ouarzazate.
● **Hideous Kinky** (1998) A *fundouk* in Mouassine (*see p77*) is a hotel and the Ben Youssef Medersa (*see p75*) is a Sufic retreat.
● **Kingdom of Heaven** (2005) Ridley Scott made 12th-century Jerusalem out of 21st-century Essaouira.
● **Kundun** (1997) When Scorsese finished his life of the 14th Dalai Lama he left part of the set behind at what's now the Kasbah Toubkal (*see p197*) and some more of it further south at Ouarzazate's Atlas Corporation Studios (*see p206*).
● **The Man Who Knew Too Much** (1955) Doris Day and James Stewart appear in scenes in the Jemaa El Fna and Mamounia hotel (*see p42*).
● **The Man Who Would Be King** (1975) Michael Caine and Sean Connery set off to conquer mythical Kafiristan – ably played by the Atlas Mountains.
● **The Mummy** (1999) Doubling as Cairo, rue Bab Doukkala (*see p80*) was the location for a car chase in Stephen Sommers' action-adventure.
● **Othello** (1952) Orson Welles brought the Moor back to Morocco, opening on the Essaouira ramparts and setting Rodrigo's murder in a local hammam (*see p184* **The Moor the merrier**).

Janes Stewart is *The Man Who Knew Too Much.*

so unless you speak French you're fuqued. Screenings are typically three times daily at 3pm, 7pm and 9pm.

In addition to the cinemas listed below (the pick of a poor crop) films are also shown roughly twice a week at the **Institut Français** (Route de Targa, Jebel Guéliz, 044 44 69 30, 20dh), an adequate venue with a more eclectic programming remit.

### Cinéma le Colisée

*boulevard Mohammed Zerktouni, Guéliz (044 44 88 93).* **Tickets** 15dh, 25dh Mon; 25dh, 35dh Tue-Sun. **No credit cards. Map** p256 A2.

This place trumpets itself as 'the best cinema in Morocco' and it's certainly the best in Marrakech – a comfortable, modern, good-sized venue with excellent sightlines and relatively plush with it.

### Cinéma Rif

*Daoudiate (044 30 31 46).* **Tickets** 15dh. **No credit cards. Map** p251 D1.

A barn-like Moorish movie palace, again with a balcony, red carpets on the steps and (sometimes) tea in the forecourt.

### Saada

*Quartier Hay Hassani, Douar Laasker (044 34 70 28).* **Tickets** 15dh. **No credit cards**.

An auditorium in 1950s style, again with carpets and tea, in a dusty neighbourhood square off the Essaouira road past the railway station.

## International Film Festival

The first Marrakech International Film Festival had the misfortune to kick off in 2001 – within days of 11 September. Nevertheless, the fallout from that day has subsequently lent focus and definition to an ambitious, multifaceted festival ideally placed between East and West. Sponsored by His Majesty King Mohammed VI – a film buff, apparently – and presided over by the powerful UniFrance chief Daniel Toscan du Plantier (and paid for entirely by commercial interests in France and Morocco), the festival, which will celebrate its fourth anniversary in 2005, has been able to attract a good deal of star-power and (consequently) media attention: Francis Ford Coppola, Martin Scorcese and Sean Connery have all made the trip, and Catherine Deneuve, Emmanuelle Béart and Charles Aznavour have all weighed in for the former colonial power.

The *raison d'être* of the event is to encourage international filmmakers to come to Morocco to shoot, a job which it does very well. Hence, actual film screenings and competition take second place to the lavish parties thrown every night by lead sponsors aiming to match the King's dinner that annually opens the event. The 12-film competition that forms the centrepiece of the screening programme is composed almost entirely of movies from other festivals, many of them already awarded prizes. Instead much of the excitement comes from the festival's screening venues, which include the Jemaa El Fna and the grand ruins of the Badii Palace. Tickets are available for almost all films on a first-come-first-served basis from the cinema box offices; the parties, however, are closed affairs.

In 2004 the festival took place in December to avoid the holy month of Ramadan, but plans are afoot for a new November date in 2005.

# Galleries

Art follows money, and Marrakech is beckoning.

Islam's aversion to representational forms has historically channelled artistic impulses into decorative work rather than fine art. This is as true in Morocco as it is everywhere in the Muslim world. And what goes for Morocco goes double for artisanal Marrakech, where the primacy of crafts over arts has only been encouraged by the city's dialogue with Western style and decor. Still, there are artists here, both Moroccans and foreigners, and galleries where their work may be exhibited. But there's no Marrakech school or style, and little sense of a coherent scene.

## ADVENTURING ORIENTALISTS

Not until European painters began coming to North Africa in the 19th century was Morocco first captured on canvas. Adventuring artists were captivated by the clear light and rich colours. It also helped that pictures of fearsome desert warriors and dusky harem girls sold well back home. The work produced by **Eugène Delacroix** on a visit to Morocco and Algeria in 1823 diverted French painters from the traditional pilgrimage to Italy and set them scurrying all over North Africa instead. 'I am like a man dreaming,' wrote Delacroix, 'and who sees things he is afraid will escape him.' He captured what he could on 80 canvases with North African themes, defining the style that became known as Orientalism.

Orientalism is today widely derided for treating its subjects as colourful curiosities, but it motivated **Henri Matisse** to settle in Tangier for a productive stint, now regarded as the culmination of his Fauve period. Matisse protégé **Raoul Dufy** travelled to Marrakech and painted the typically cartoony *Couscous Served at the Residence of the Pasha*, but few other painters made it this far south.

The notable exception is **Jacques Majorelle**, a tuberculosis sufferer who came on the advice of his doctor. He settled here in 1923, building a villa and later adding the gardens that perpetuate his name. Majorelle's work still falls under the heading Orientalist but is redeemed by his apparent empathy with his subjects; that and a superbly graphic sense of line and colour. Some of Majorelle's most striking works were posters to promote exotic Maroc. He's also noted for his attachment to a particularly intense shade of cobalt that now goes by the name 'Majorelle Blue'.

## INDEPENDENT ABSTRACTIONISTS

It was only after independence in 1956 that Moroccan artists began to emerge with their own styles, mostly abstract, naïve or calligraphic, and mostly in the north and on the coast. Many were trained at the fine arts school in Tetouan, founded in 1945. Tangier used to have cash and international connections, and still has Morocco's only contemporary art museum. Nearby Asilah hosts an annual art festival, hitting its 27th edition in August 2005 with three weeks of exhibitions and workshops.

But one of the key figures of Moroccan modernism, **Farid Belkahia**, is a Marrakchi. Born in 1934, he works with Berber symbols (spirals, hands) and traditional materials (sheepskin, pigments) and still lives in Marrakech. If Belkahia is the city's fine-art founding father, **Mohammed Melehi** is its current power, less important as a painter of gaudy abstracts than as president of Morocco's oldest artists' association and co-founder of the Asilah festival. Although Asilah-born, he too now lives in Marrakech.

The wealthy of Casablanca and Rabat increasingly have second homes in Marrakech. Foreign art buffs pass through waving wallets; some stay and set up house. Marrakchis themselves are getting richer. Art follows money, and Marrakech is beckoning.

## SCENE NOT HEARD

At first glance, the Marrakech art scene doesn't seem to have moved on much since Matisse. There aren't many galleries, and those that do exist are filled with hazy Orientalist daubings of kasbah sunsets and veiled women. This is a result of the Marrakchi artistan mentality: whatever sells, be it lanterns or slippers or paintings, should be knocked out in the appropriate style.

But there are plenty of artists living and working here. Apart from Belkahia and Melehi, there's writer and painter **Mahi Binebine**, back in his home town after decades abroad. The sadness of his pieces – constricted, tormented faces and figures – is said to be inspired by the 20-year imprisonment of his brother for his part in a 1970s coup. Other Marrakech artists to look out for include Pop painter **Hassan Hajjaj**, photographer **Hicham Benouhoud** and calligraphy painter **Nouredine Chater**.

Art vies for attention with the architecture at **Dar Cherifa**. *See p144.*

Apart from galleries, there are other moves to anchor art in the area. **Labied Miloud**, a local painter of the Belkahia generation whose canvases remind of Paul Klee, has been setting up a foundation in the village of Mejjat, near Amizmiz. It's not finished yet, but there is meant to be a gallery, rooms that artists can rent, and a common studio. Younger abstract painter **Mohammed Morabiti** (044 48 40 02,

061 19 58 59) has been working on a similar but more ambitious centre. This one is some 28 kilometres (17 miles) out of Marrakech on the Asni road, at a place called El Maquam near Tahanaout. With a proposed bookshop, restaurant and gallery as well as studio space and rooms for artists, it officially opened in December 2004, although as we went to press the road to the centre wasn't even finished yet.

The opening of Les Atlassides in April 2004 has added some much-needed gravity to the scene. Most Marrakech galleries are uninspiring, full of Orientalist tat that might as well be selling in Woolworth's. Apart from places listed below, the restaurant **Jacaranda** (*see p109*) and the boutique **Lun'art Gallery** (*see p128*) both have small selections of modern Moroccan art for sale. The **Musée de Marrakech** (*see p75*) hosts regularly changing temporary exhibitions and there's a permanent display of work by Jacques Majorelle at the **Museum of Islamic Art** (*see p92*) in the Majorelle Gardens.

## Les Atlassides

*22 boulevard Yacoub El Marini, Guéliz (044 43 79 93/ http://almanar.ifrance.com).* **Open** 8am-12.30pm, 3-8pm Mon-Sat. **No credit cards. Map** p256 B3.
A beautiful big space for a serious commercial gallery and bookshop. The division between main space and mezzanine allows ample room for two shows at once. That means changing exhibitions downstairs, while upstairs is a selection of work from the impressive crew of Moroccan heavy-weights that the gallery represents. These include Farid Belkahia, Tibari Kantour, Mohammed Melehi, Mahi Binebine and the late Mohammed Kacimi. Les Atlassides was launched in April 2004 by local entrepreneurs in conjunction with Franco-German gallerists Christine and Alain Gorius, who formerly ran the Al Manar gallery in Casablanca and still run a publishing imprint of the same name in Paris.

## Dar Cherifa

*8 Derb Charfa Lakbir, Mouassine, Medina (044 42 64 63/www.marrakech-riads.net).* **Open** 9am-7pm daily. **No credit cards. Map** p73 & p252 C4.
This gorgeous townhouse is the Medina's premier exhibition space. Parts of the building date back to the 16th century and it has been lovingly restored by owner Abdelatif Ben Abdellah, who's taken great pains to expose the carved beams and stucco work while leaving walls and floors bare and free of distraction. Regular exhibitions lean towards resident foreign artists, but there have also recently been shows by Moroccan artists Hassan Hajjaj and Milaudi Nouiga. Openings often feature performances by gnawa or Sufi musicians. The space also includes a small library, tea and coffee are served, and there's a light lunch menu (50dh-120dh) from noon to 4pm daily.

## Galerie Bleue

*119 avenue Mohammed V, Guéliz (044 42 00 80).* **Open** 10am-1pm, 4-8pm Tue-Sun. **Credit** MC, V. **Map** p256 A2.
Handsome but low-key space on the main boulevard of Guéliz, just around the corner from the tourist office, devoted to solo shows by contemporary French and Moroccan artists. When we last looked in there were colourful but claustrophobic neo-Orientalist canvases by French painter Véronique Engels. There's also a small mezzanine space carrying a grab-bag selection of canvases.

## Marrakech Arts Gallery

*60 boulevard El Mansour Eddahbi, Guéliz (044 43 93 41/www.art-gallery-marrakech.com).* **Open** 9am-1pm, 3-7.30pm Mon-Thur, Sat; 9am-noon, 3-7.30pm Fri; 9.30am-1pm Sun. **Credit** MC, V. **Map** p256 A2.
More art shop than art gallery, this small space in central Guéliz is simply crammed with paintings. They crowd the walls like posters in a teenage bedroom and are stacked in piles according to price. Despite the quantity there's precious little of interest, but if you're looking for a job lot of small, cheap canvases with Moroccan subjects to decorate the walls of your budget hotel, then this is the place to find them.

## Matisse Art Gallery

*61 rue Yougoslavie, No.43 passage Ghandouri, Guéliz (044 44 83 26/www.matisse-art-gallery.com).* **Open** 9am-1pm, 3.30-8pm Mon-Sat. **Credit** MC, V. **Map** p256 A2.
A decent space devoted to solo shows by young Moroccan artists such as calligraphy painters Nouredine Chater and Nouredine Daifellah, expressionist Said Lahssini and figurative painter Driss Jebrane. They have also exhibited more established names such as Mohammed Melehi and Hassan El Glaoui (the late son of the former 'Lord of the Atlas' was devoted to painting horses). Upstairs, they also have some vintage Orientalist canvases. In autumn 2005 young gallerists Nabil El Mallouki and Youssef Falaky also intend to open a new space at the Complex Atlas Golf Cherifa, four kilometres (2.5 miles) out of town on the route du Barrage.

## Ministerio del Gusto

*22 Derb Azouz El Mouassine, off rue Sidi El Yamami, Mouassine, Medina (044 42 64 55).* **Open** 9am-noon, 4-7pm Mon-Sat. **Credit** MC, V. **Map** p73.
Showroom for the design talents and eclectic tastes of owners Alessandra Lippini and Fabrizio Bizzarri, this eccentric space also hosts occasional exhibitions and after these are over continues stocking work by the artists they like. These include Essaouira-based English artist Micol, American photographer Martin HM Schreiber, Italian multimediaist Maurizio Vetrugno, Indonesian painter Ribka and Marrakchi Pop artist Hassan Hajjaj.

## La Qoubba Galerie D'Art

*91 Souk Talaa, off place Ben Youssef, Medina (044 38 05 15/www.art-gallery-marrakech.com).* **Open** 9am-1pm, 2.30-6.30pm daily. **Credit** MC, V. **Map** p253 D4.
Around the corner from the Koubba El Badiyin and almost opposite the Musée de Marrakech, La Qoubba has both solo and group exhibitions of local artists. It's fairly predictable stuff, though a thorough search of the gallery's two floors stands a chance of turning up something interesting.

Arts & Entertainment

# Music

The world's oldest rock 'n' roll band but no venues to play.

Music on Jemaa El Fna.

'The most important single element of Morocco's folk culture is its music,' wrote author and composer Paul Bowles. He would have known. The long-time Tangier resident toured the country in the late 1950s with a tape recorder and a commission from the US Library of Congress, aiming to capture examples of music it seemed then might soon die out.

Selections from Bowles recordings were released as an album (*Music of Morocco*) in 1972 and the Library of Congress still holds the tape archive, but rumours of the death of Moroccan music proved to be somewhat exaggerated. There's still Berber music and Arab music, Jewish music and the music of the descendants of slaves, music to accompany dance and music that goes with story-telling, music for harvest festivals and music for circumcision rituals, classical music rooted in medieval Andalucia and pop music that belongs to the urbanised Arab cultures of today. In short, music in Morocco is as varied and resilient as its people. The only thing lacking is any way to hear it.

Musicians perform in private homes, at ceremonies, marriages, funerals, religious events and festivals. Only rarely do they play as any kind of accessible concert. There's no performance tradition in the Western sense, and not much of a music industry either.

## THE WORLD'S OLDEST BAND

With its own instruments and tunings, its own rhythms and sounds, Berber music (called *grika* – 'improvisation') is entirely different from Arabic music. It's rootsy, rural stuff traditionally performed at community celebrations, especially harvest and religious festivals. The sound is heavily percussive, with harsh shrieks from the *ghaita* – an instrument related to the oboe. The music is composed of several fairly simple parts, intricately woven together and extended into performances that can last for days, with musicians taking breaks as others step in to replace them. The ritualised formula has changed little over the centuries.

Prime exponents of *grika* – and one of Morocco's better known exports – are the **Master Musicians of Jajouka**, described by William Burroughs as 'the world's oldest rock 'n' roll band'. According to their website, the musicians – from the village of Jajouka in the foothills of the Rif – have been passing their tunes and traditions from father to son for 4,000 years. Prior to French rule, they were court musicians to seven sultans. Now they play with the Rolling Stones (*see p147* **Maroc 'n' roll**).

## TRANCE TRADITION

If Berber music comes across as elemental, bordering on mystical, it's got nothing on *gnawa* (also spelled gnaoua).

The name refers both to the music and its practitioners. The gnawa trace their ancestry back to sub-Saharan Africa – 'gnawa' may derive from the same root as Ghana or Guinea – whence they were dragged to Morocco as slaves. To reflect their difficult history, the gnawa claim spiritual descent from Bilal, the Ethiopian slave who suffered much before becoming the Prophet's first *muezzin*.

Gnawa communities are concentrated mostly in the southern, less Europeanised parts of the country – notably Marrakech and Essaouira. A strong oral tradition has kept alive the culture of their ancestors, and gnawa is the best-preserved manifestation of the black African aesthetic within Morocco.

At its simplest, gnawa is just drum and bass. The *gimbri*, a long-necked lute, is the main component, combining a fat acoustic bass sound with a metallic rattle. Accompaniment is provided by the insistent clatter of chunky iron castanets called *karakeb*. Bigger ensembles add drums, call-and-response vocals, and lots of dancing. It's repetitive, hypnotic stuff built around looping riffs.

At their most authentic, gnawa performances are part of all-night healing rituals involving trance and possession. Different powers in the gnawa spirit world are denoted by different colours (seven in all), and the different colours by different music. At a *leila* (from the Arabic word for 'night'), as one of these rituals is called, the musicians will play until they figure out which colour is dominating the proceedings or needs to be exorcised.

Back in the mundane world, gnawa lyrics are riddled with references to the pain of slavery and exile, the turmoil of dislocation. In this sense gnawa is similar to both blues and reggae, speaking the universal language of suffering. But it also has much in common with European trance or techno, in which music ceases to have a beginning, middle or end and instead becomes a single, enveloping continuum of sound and rhythm.

## GLOBAL GNAWA

Although marginal in Moroccan society, gnawa has made an impact on both the local and global music scenes – particularly since the Festival d'Essaouira (*see p181*) gave it an annual focus and international respect. A

music of loops, spaces and extended durations, gnawa lends itself easily to fusion experiments and collaborations. Perhaps too easily. Most gnawa encounters with the wider world of music are little more than boring old jazzers soloing over the rhythms.

Still, attempts to merge gnawa with other musics have been going on since the 1970s. The torch was lit by a Casablancan group called **Nass El Ghiwane**. They were a long-haired five-piece who played traditional instruments and fused gnawa with elements of popular Egyptian and Lebanese song. That and a political edge gave them Bob Marley-like status across North Africa. The band leader died in a plane crash in the 1980s, but two of the group play on under the original name.

Gnawan fusionist **Hassan Hakmoun** cut his teeth playing around Jemaa El Fna before moving to New York in the mid 1980s, where he made the impressive *Gift of the Gnawa* (1991), featuring legendary trumpeter Don Cherry and Richard Horowitz, an avant-garde musician and composer (contributor to the soundtrack for Bertolucci's *The Sheltering Sky*), and some-time resident of Marrakech.

Gnawa fusion also made radical moves forward with **Aisha Kandisha's Jarring Effects**, who pioneered Arabic techno across several albums – although their momentum has slowed since founding member Habib El Malak left the band to become a politician in Marrakech. Paris-based **Gnawa Diffusion** blend gnawa with ragga and reggae. In the UK, three-piece **Momo** peddle their version of gnawan 'dar' (house) to a clubbing crowd, while DJ **U-Cef** mixes samples of Moroccan music with just about anything.

Back in Morocco there is little market for anything too edgy. Home-grown innovations are social than musical. Recent years have seen the emergence of women's gnawa. The most high-profile exponents are **B'net Marrakech** (Women of Marrakech), a group of five taboo-breaking women (gnawa has always been a male preserve) who do weddings, births – and international world music festivals. Their debut CD *Chamaa* included songs about love, demonic possession and the national football team.

## MASTERS AT WORK

Where to see music in Marrakech? The short answer is, 'nowhere'. Or almost nowhere. There's a near total absence of concert halls and live music clubs. The **Musica Bar** (*see p153*), **VIP Room** (*see p155*) and **Montecristo** (*see p152*) all feature live bands, but in the first two that means the Arab equivalent of cheesy cabaret and in the latter lots of boring French jazzers. Jemaa El Fna is filled with musicians,

# Maroc 'n' roll

Long before the words 'world' and 'music' were first linked as a marketing term, Morocco had some of the only ethnic music that attracted any sort of Western attention. Proximity to Europe was part of it, as was its key role as 'alternative' destination in the wake of Burroughs and the Beats. It was Burroughs friend and collaborator Brion Gysin who turned doomed Brian Jones on to the Master Musicians of Jajouka (*see p145*). In 1969 Jones recorded an album with the Master Musicians: *Brian Jones Presents the Pipes of Pan at Jajouka,* released posthumously in 1971. The remaining Stones would work with them again on 'Continental Drift' for 1989's *Steel Wheels* album.

Other musicians followed. The Beatles holidayed in Marrakech, inspiring Lennon to write a song called 'The Road to Marrakech':

On the road to Marrakech
I was dreaming more or less
And the dream I had was true
Yes the dream I had was true

It never made a Beatles album so he changed the words and it became 'Jealous Guy'.

Cat Stevens came, discovered Islam, and changed his name to Yusuf Islam. Jimi Hendrix passed through Essaouira in summer 1969, though the story that he was inspired to write 'Castles Made of Sand' is nonsense (*see p174*). Led Zeppelin were enthralled enough by their 1970 visit that when Robert Plant and Jimmy Page reunited in 1994 they made Morocco their base, recording the *No Quarter* album with local musicians and filming a video on Jemaa El Fna.

Robert Plant has never lost his passion for Moroccan music. 'I have a great lust for Berber music from Morocco and Algeria,' he says. 'It seems to be the most wailing, plaintive, untouched music I've ever heard. I don't know what the fuck it's all about. But it's stirring, primal stuff. It's not affected by any outside trend. And the songs haven't changed for hundreds of years.'

Jazz musicians, too, have looked to North Africa for inspiration. African-American pianist Randy Weston settled in Tangier in 1968 and has since recorded many albums with Moroccan musicians. Saxophonist Pharoah Sanders collaborated with gnawa master Mohammed Ginia on an album called *The Trance of the Seven Colours*.

In the 1990s a new wave of Westerners swept into the country. The prolific Bill Laswell recorded several Moroccan albums, including one with the Master Musicians of Jajouka. Anglo-Indian percussionist and producer Talvin Singh followed in 2000 with yet another Master Musicians collaboration, this one attempting to fuse Berber beats with underground dance rhythms.

More recently, Blur spent a month recording 2003's *Think Tank* in Marrakech. While Damon Albarn stressed that they were not trying to make 'a world music album', he added: 'Marrakech and its music definitely have an effect on you.'

Or, as Crosby, Stills and Nash so memorably put it on 1969's 'Marrakesh Express': 'Whoopa, hey mesa, hooba huffa, hey mesha goosh goosh.'

solo and in groups, but these are just street buskers. The costumed gnawa playing in restaurants are usually a cut above, but this is still not the real deal.

According to **Brahim El Belkani**, respectable gnawa musicians just don't do that sort of stuff. El Belkani is a *maalim*, or master, one of only eight such gnawa dignitaries in Marrakech. He's scornful of playing for 'tips' and makes his living as a butcher. But he's not above turning out for international festivals or visiting stars. On his music room wall there are photos of Brahim with Dizzy Gillespie, Page and Plant, Carlos Santana.

Chances of witnessing such masters at work occur only at major cultural jamborees or occasional exhibition openings (check what's happening at **Dar Cherifa**, *see p144*).

## FESTIVALS

There are no music festivals in Marrakech, but over on the coast there's the **Festival d'Essaouira** (*see p181*). Launched in 1998 and staged each June, this is a free and freewheeling four-day event. Essaouira fills up with around 200,000 spectators and attracts musicians from all over the world to become one great big jammed-up jam session. There's more jazz than trance, but it's the only event at which all the masters come out to play. For details visit the festival website (www.festival-gnaoua.co.ma).

Essaouira also hosts the **Festival des Andalousies Atlantiques** in autumn, which focuses on arabo-andalucian music and flamenco (www.festivaldesandalousies.com), and the **Printemps des Alizés** classical music festival each spring.

# Nightlife

Prepare for an entertaining rag-bag of piano bars, pick-up joints, seedy locals, daft discos and one brand-new mega-club.

Marrakech's nightlife scene hovers on the verge of cataclysmic change. But then again nothing might happen. The opening of the enormous 3,000-capacity club Pacha (*see p154*) on the outskirts of town represents nightlife ambition on a scale Morocco has never seen before, but traditionally drinking and clubbing has been a fairly low-key pastime. This is, after all, an Islamic society.

The Koran cautions against substances that cloud the mind, a much debated injunction that has traditionally been interpreted to mean 'lay off the booze'. But the reality is that attitudes towards drink remain much more ambiguous. For instance, Morocco has prohibitions against alcohol (including, notably, that it shouldn't be drunk in public) but not against its production or sale. Which is handy when it's the authorities who produce over half of the country's booze. Sales of beer, wine and spirits generate several millions of dirhams annually in profit for the largely state-owned alcohol industry.

Generally speaking, Moroccans aren't fussed about alcohol; they might not drink that much themselves but they aren't overly censorious of others who do. Anyway, the comparative expense of wines and spirits means that consumption is largely limited to the moneyed – and more liberal – upper-middle classes and confined to pricey restaurants. The few local bars that there are typically draw their custom from the seamier side of life (*see p149* **The disreputable business of beer-drinking**).

Until very recently it has been down to tourists and the expat community to float Marrakech nightlife: almost all the clubs are attached to hotels, while the most popular independent bars (including Bodega, Comptoir and Montecristo) are all foreign owned.

But change beckons with the arrival of Pacha, as in the international DJ club Pacha, with its long-standing venues in Ibiza, London, Madrid and now Marrakech. The Marrakech version, which stands several miles south of

Arts & Entertainment

**Bodega.** *See p151.*

# The disreputable business of beer-drinking

Weary of tourist-tailored places, keen to find a truly Moroccan experience, or simply in need of a cold, uncomplicated beer, many are drawn in search of a local bar.

The first problem is finding one. There aren't many, they don't advertise, and they are often tucked in obscure sidestreets. (In Marrakech that means on and around the northern end of rue Mohammed El Bekal in Guéliz, in the vicinity of the Cinema La Colisée.) Even up close, there's nothing to see from outside. Windows will be opaque and the entrance kinked so you can't peer within. This is as much to shield the clientele from prying gazes as it is to protect the passer-by from depravity. But most of all it's so everyone can pretend that nothing as disreputable as beer-drinking is really going on.

Don't be deterred by the unwelcoming exterior but expect few frills within. Basic furniture. Even more basic toilets. Nothing on sale but beer, except maybe a dusty bottle of Ricard behind the bar somewhere. A couple of old posters on peeling walls. Uncollected empties crowding unwiped tabletops. Lots of drunken guys in jellabas. And no women, unless they're whores or tourists.

Nobody will mind you wandering in. Though there can be a disconcerting lack of middle ground between everyone studiously ignoring you, and everyone trying to buy you a beer. Some places are raucous and jostly; others are quiet and concentrated. But either way, people are mostly too busy drowning their sorrows to bother about bothering you.

Two things shape the atmosphere. The first is a sense of camaraderie. The business of beer-drinking is the province of defiant reprobates, united in their shared sense of marginality. The second is a sense of enormous frustration – with sex, with poverty, with whatever. These places are all about getting drunk enough to forget about it, and they teeter on a manic edge, feeling like they might kick off at any moment. But they can also have an almost joyful, all-in-this-together kind of quality.

Moroccan bars don't all double as hooker hangouts, but many in Marrakech do. It obviously makes sense to the authorities for the disreputable business of prostitution to cohabit with the disreputable business of beer-drinking, the better to keep an eye on it all. Non-Moroccan women, accompanied by men, will be left alone but may still feel uncomfortable. The whores in these places are mostly ageing and sad, but they can be as cheerful as the next guy once they've got enough beer inside them.

town, has been opened not by a foreigner but by a young Moroccan businessman. Clubbers now flock down from Casablanca for weekend sessions and other Pachas in Spain, the UK and elsewhere will be chartering flights for party weekends in the Pink City.

The club only started operating in February 2005 but if – and it is a big *if* – it takes off then the city is looking at an influx of several hundred clubbers each weekend. Marrakech as the new Ibiza? Hardly, but you can't expect to massively increase the number of revellers in town without it having a knock-on effect.

Beware the holy month of Ramadan when all bars other than those in hotels close for the duration: for dates *see p234* **Islamic holidays**.

### WHAT MARRAKECH IS DRINKING

Beer comes in both local (Flag and Flag Spéciale brewed in Tangier, Stork from Fès, and Casablanca, 'the legendary beer from the legendary city') and foreign brands (usually Heineken). Chilled, the local stuff is perfectly drinkable and sells by the bottle for anything from 12dh to 70dh.

Local wines are drinkable if undistinguished. Reds predominate and the best are Cabernet du Président or Domaine de Sahari. The best white is probably Sémillant or Coquillages. Local rosés can be good on a hot day; try the Gris Guerrouane.

Cocktails are only just beginning to make an appearance and should be ordered with care – you may think it impossible to screw up a G&T but, believe us, it can and will be done.

## Bars

### Medina

The sale of alcohol in the Medina with its seven saintly shrines is heavily restricted. It's practically impossible to get a licence. A few restaurants have persevered and are able to

The **Churchill Piano Bar**: you hum it, he'll play it.

offer beer and wine to diners, but bars are an absolute no-no, except in the 'international zones' that are hotels.

### Alanbar
*47 rue Jebel Lakhdar, Bab Laksour (044 38 07 63).* **Open** 8pm-2am daily. **Credit** DC, MC, V. **Map** p252 B4.
Inspired by waning Parisian fashion haunt the Buddha Bar, Alanbar tops a grand flight of stairs with a glowing HR Geiger goddess. It also features a baronial fireplace, a grand piano in the corner and a basement palm-court dining area, all of which are rendered completely insignificant by the sheer scale of a place that has the ungainly size, atrium-style layout and acoustics of a shopping mall. You could march the entire population of Liechtenstein inside here and still feel agoraphobic. But it does boast maybe the best-stocked bar in town and you are always guaranteed to get a table (several if you like).

### Churchill Piano Bar
*Mamounia Hotel, avenue Bab Jedid (044 38 86 00/ www.mamounia.com).* **Open** 7pm-1am daily. **Credit** AmEx, MC, V. **Map** p254 A6.
So it's not original and much of the current decor dates from a 1986 refit, but for fans of bar culture – deco bar culture, no less – this one's a beaut. It's intimate and dark (leather padded walls!) and full of gleaming surfaces, not least the polished pride-of-place grand (hence the name) in its own sunken pit. A backlit painted-glass montage of jazz greats fills the wall behind like an altarpiece. Leather seats are in British racing green with brass go-faster stripes and there's a proper high bar counter complete with brass foot rail. It's a venue made for dry Martinis, but you could settle for a local beer at 50dh a pop. If you time it right (about 9.30ish most nights) you'll catch the resident pianist at the ivories. Requests to 'Play it again, Sam', will probably be treated with the disdain they deserve.

### Le Club
*Maison Arabe, 1 Derb Assehbe, Bab Doukkala (044 38 70 10/www.lamaisonarabe.com).* **Open** 3-11pm daily. **Credit** MC, V. **Map** p252 A4.
Le Club is a Moroccan take on the gentleman's lounge, with leather-panelled walls, club chairs, scatterings of tribal rugs, a fire in the hearth (very welcome in winter, let us tell you) and imposing big-game art (elephant in oils, a wood-carved African lady breast feeding). It could be the bar at the Swaziland Royal Links. If this sounds a bit hokey, it's actually very comfortable and further redeemed by a bar counter that's sized to mean business and that delivers better-than-competently mixed drinks (cocktails 70dh). Local and imported beer by the bottle is 40dh to 60dh.

### Grand Tazi
*Hotel Grand Tazi, corner of avenue El Mouahidine and rue Bab Agnaou (044 44 27 87).* **Open** 7-11pm daily. **No credit cards**. **Map** p254 C6.
The Tazi's a godsend – the only place in the central Medina where the weary and footsore can kick back with a cheap beer. There's no real bar as such, just a sofa space off to one side of the lobby (and a large empty room beyond that) where accommodating waiters will fetch a cold one for anybody who succeeds in snaring their attention. You don't have to be a resident, just not too fussy about the company you keep or addicted to quality furnishings. Fellow drinkers tend to be young locals in leather jackets and budget travellers swapping stories of loose bowels amid the dunes of Merzouga.

### Narwama
*30 rue de la Koutoubia (044 44 08 44).* **Open** 8pm-12.30am daily. **Credit** MC, V. **Map** p252/254 B5.
Narwama is primarily a restaurant (*see p105*), but pony-tailed proprietor and all-round nice guy Ali Bousfiha is intent on developing the front-of-house

bar as a stand-alone entity. At the moment the bar space acts as no more than a sort of antechamber to the dining room but the idea is to make it more comfortable with lounge seating. Until then, you are invited to prop up the bar counter with no obligation to eat. For many years Ali was a DJ in Milan, hence the agreeable lounge-core soundtrack.

### Piano Bar
*Hotel les Jardins de la Koutoubia, 26 rue de la Koutoubia (044 38 88 00).* **Open** 5pm-midnight daily. **Credit** AmEx, DC, MC, V. **Map** p252/p254 B5.
A small space in red and gold, the piano bar is just off the lobby of this conveniently located five-star – a mere stumble from the Jemaa El Fna. From 7pm to 11pm there is music, and the quality of your drinking experience will depend on how well you take to whoever is at the actual piano. We hated the player on our last visit, which was a shame because the bar is well stocked, the staff knows how to mix a cocktail and the counter is a fine place for perching. Drinks aren't cheap (50dh-100dh) but there's no dress code, and if the next pianist they book can't sing without tons of echo and a cheesy percussion track, you can always take your drink out to the poolside terrace and contemplate the sky instead of the cigar selection.

## Guéliz

The neighbourhood for vaguely-to-outright-disreputable local bars, most of which are a short falter from central place Abdel Moumen.

### Bar L'Escale
*rue de Mauritanie (044 43 34 47).* **Open** 11am-10.30pm daily. **No credit cards. Map** p256 B2.
The menu claims L'Escale opened in 1927; the window says '47. Either way, the customers look as if they've been settled in place since opening night. Most nurse slowly emptying bottles of Flag Spéciale (13dh), half an eye on the big, boxy wall-mounted TV, while engaging in sporadic chat with the red-jacketed, grey-haired old gent who patrols the big, bare paddock behind the high bar counter. Though all male – or perhaps because it *is* all male – Bar L'Escale is a totally non-threatening environment (although hygiene freaks might have a tough time of it). Beers can be taken out to the pavement tables and there's food in the form of grilled meats (*see p107*).

### Bodega
*23 rue de la Liberté (044 43 31 41).* **Open** 7pm-1am daily. **Credit** MC, V. **Map** p256 B2.
There are two defining characteristics of Bodega: very, very red and very, very loud. It's a Spanish-style tapas bar with stools up at the counter for boozers (local and imported beers, including *pression* at 25dh, wine and cocktails), tables and benches for diners (tapas, tablas and boccadillos, although the food is mediocre) and no space for dancing, which deters no one at all from trying, stomping on tables

and toes and elbowing earholes to the reckless encouragement of DJ-mixed Latino vibes and urban R&B. Add flashing lights and video screen for a fine time had by all or a splitting headache, depending on your age and outlook.

### Café Atlas
*place Abdel Moumen, avenue Mohammed V (044 44 88 88).* **Open** 8am-10pm daily. **Credit** MC, V. **Map** p256 A2.
You used to be able to take your beer at one of the outside tables but that is no longer the case. Otherwise, a reputation as a rendezvous for foreign gents and local gigolos does the place few favours, but obviously uninterested parties are left alone to contemplate the traffic free-for-all on place Abdel Moumen. A beer costs 13dh-20dh depending on the mood of the waiter, and patrons are also offered the chance to purchase anything from peanuts to lotto cards to carpets by itinerant salesmen. Leaving your cigs in view on the table invites a steady stream of supplicants, including those precisely groomed and scented boys in their snug-fitting white trousers.

### Chesterfield Pub
*Hotel Nassim, 1st floor, 115 avenue Mohammed V (044 44 64 01).* **Open** 9am-1am daily. **Credit** MC, V (min 200dh). **Map** p256 A2.
Also known as the 'Bar Anglais', but don't be fooled as there's nothing particularly English about this vertically challenged little first-floor hotel bar. A tiny lounge is cast in an eerie glow by a luminously underlit pool on the other side of a glass wall, while a larger back bar is an equally twilit gents' hangout, permanently heavy with a fug of cigarette smoke. Between is a polished mahogany counter area dispensing bottled and draught beers, spirits and cocktails at reasonable cost (*pression* 30dh). Best of all is the open-air, pool-side patio with its languid air and friendly waiter service – a popular Friday night meet-up venue for expats on the razz.

### Kechmara
*3 rue de la Liberté (044 42 25 32).* **Open** 7am-midnight Mon-Sat. **Credit** MC, V. **Map** p256 B2.
A café by day and restaurant by night, Kechmara (*see p109*) also functions perfectly well as a lively and convivial bar. There's a long bar counter to the right as you enter with a tap for *bière pression* (25dh), back shelves lined with spirits and bar stools for perching. The menu lists long drinks and cocktails but this is new ground for Morocco so we weren't that surprised when a gin and tonic arrived without the gin. Although it was too chilly for it to be open last time we visited, there is a fine, spacious roof terrace, where drinks are served.

### Le Lounge
*24 rue Yougoslavie (044 43 37 03).* **Open** 11am-midnight daily. **Credit** MC, V. **Map** p256 A2.
Just north of place Abdel Moumen at the top of the short stretch of pedestrianised street beside the petrol station, Le Lounge is a small bar-restaurant

# Gay Marrakech

Moroccan law is clear when it comes to homosexuality – it's forbidden, and the penalty for homosexual acts can be a prison sentence (for locals, that is; foreigners are left well alone). Despite this, sex among men is, and always has been, common, particularly given Moroccan society's strict separation of the sexes – no fraternising before marriage, the all-importance of a woman's virginity on the wedding night and so on. Things are getting ever more permissive, but male-on-male is still an expedient option. Besides, only the 'passive' partner has ever been considered un-macho.

Since inheriting international favoured status, Marrakech has taken up the reins from Tangier as Morocco's most gay-friendly city. Young colts are attracted from all over the country, eager for the freedom of playing away from home. There also remains the traditional heavy presence of old queens from Europe and America on tour in passionate pursuit of young delicacies, plus a newer, younger crowd of sophisticated weekend-away gays attracted by the glamour of Marrakech, staple of the fashion mags.

None of which amounts to any kind of gay community, but there is a lot of action going on. So much so that a single man walking alone might be approached at any time of day, and more especially at night. Male prostitutes are a slick and practised crowd (we wouldn't be surprised if they carry credit-card swipers), used to being spoiled by

wealthy Europeans eager to spend on sex (often disappointing, we hear, because of the Moroccans' insistence on only taking the 'active' role). Prime hangouts include the **Café Atlas** (see p151) in Guéliz, and several of the seedier nightclubs round place de la Liberté, notably **Diamant Noir** (see p154). Not every come-hither glance will be a rent boy, but being poor here ain't going to make you many new friends.

Avenue Mohammed V between place de la Liberté and the Koutoubia Mosque doubles as a cruising area after midnight, but again, it's a search for money rather than love that propels. Romantic souls head for avenue El Yarmouk and a bench beneath the Old City walls, haunt of men looking for a bit of companionship. The biggest gay pick-up joint of all, though, is Jemaa El Fna. Straight tourists pass through oblivious, but among the circled audiences crowding the entertainers there are plenty of locking eyes. Likely prospects are approached from behind and a hardened 'expression of interest' none too discreetly pushed against them.

Pick-up by internet is increasingly popular and facilitated by the proliferation of internet cafés. Local favourite is www.cybermen.com (Moroccan area code: mar). Cyber-contacts are quickly translated into mobile numbers and hence to meetings. Personal ads and responses also feature at www.kelma.org, which includes an online e-zine 'Kelmaghreb' focusing on gay issues in North Africa.

cherishable for its outdoor, booze-permitted terrace. It's even got a sofa set beneath a palm wound around with twinkly strip lights – you can fight with the street cats for possession. The drinks listed run to varieties of bottled beer plus cocktails and shooters: the 'bay cinquante-deux' (that's a B52 to you) is perfectly acceptable. If you're forced inside by the weather, the tiny mezzanine area is far more loungy and comfortable than the cold ground-floor salon.

### El Moualamid Bar

*Hotel El Moualamid, 6th floor, avenue Mohammed V (044 44 88 55).* **Open** 5pm-2am daily. **No credit cards. Map** p256 A2.

It has all the charm of a Mongolian bus station waiting room – with added drunkenness – but the beer is cheap and there are great views from the outdoor terrace (six floors up) south down Mohammed V to the Koutoubia minaret. A resident band with a frightening way with a synth brings the elderly boozy males to their unsteady feet, while the hard-

faced local 'ladies' patiently bide their time. On the right night it could pass for fun. To ascend to these tawdry heights, enter the uninviting corner bar just north of place Abdel Moumen and take the lift.

### Montecristo

*20 rue Ibn Aicha (044 43 90 31).* **Open** 8pm-2am daily. **Credit** AmEx, MC, V. **Map** p256 A2.

On the ground floor is the 'Bar African', a world music venue, where French musicians indulge in interminable twiddly solos. Upstairs is where a smart set of foxy chiquitas and macho hombres slink and strut to samba and salsa. Off to the side of the dancefloor is a small area of non-ergonomic seating, made all the more uncomfortable by the inevitable crush of bodies. For elbow room and aural respite head up to the cushion-strewn rooftop terrace, which is peaceful and pleasant until the drinks menu arrives and you note that a crappy little bottled beer goes for an outrageous 70dh (almost five of your English pounds).

## Musica Bar

*boulevard Mohammed Zerktouni (no phone).* **Open**
7pm-midnight daily. **No credit cards. Map** p256 B2.
Its gaping black hole of an entrance, signed with a
desultory scrawl of neon, looks as if it belongs on
the Reeperbahn or at least the darkest corner of
Soho. But the Musica Bar isn't as classy as that.
Enter – if you dare – into a huge tiled hall of swimming pool acoustics that nightly reverberates to the
mad cacophony of a five- or six-piece mini Arab
orchestra. Fuelled by cheap bottled beer, punters are
too far gone to dance but they bang their hands on
the tabletops and wail along with the chorus.
Downstairs is a nightclub of sorts that kicks off as
the bar closes, but we're not that brave.

## Samovar

*133 rue Mohammed El Bekal (no phone).* **Open** 7pm-
2am daily. **No credit cards. Map** p256 A2.
Possibly the most raucous saloon in town. Two
rooms heave with a crush of slurry young men in
cheap leather jackets, rambling old soaks and
'mature' prostitutes. Every table teeters beneath the
weight of squadrons of Stork empties. Body contact
is frequent, unavoidable and occasionally oppor-
tunistic. It's a place where 'too much to drink' is the
natural state of being and the underlying threat of
violence is periodically realised before being quickly smothered by laconic bar staff who calm the odd
alarmed foreigner with a resigned shrug. You don't
want to go to the toilets. Visit, if you will, and take a
walk on the Marrakech wild side, but don't come cry-
ing to us afterwards.

## La Strada

*90 rue Mohammed El Bekal (061 24 20 94).* **Open**
7pm-2am daily. **No credit cards. Map** p256 A2.
By day this is a local take on a pizza restaurant
(which means at least the tabletops and floor get a
wipe every now and again), but by night the oven
goes cold, the heavy drapes are drawn across the
windows and place settings are pushed aside to
accommodate steadily growing collections of empty
bottles. Upstairs is a small air-conditioned lounge
with cushioned seating, which is where the 'ladies'
hang out. We feel safer staying down on the ground
floor, watched over by a grimacing, bare-chested
Anthony Quinn in a large, framed film poster of
Fellini's *La Strada.*

# Hivernage

Purpose-built restaurant, bar and club the **Jad
Mahal** opened to much fanfare in 2003 on a site
just outside the city walls, 100 metres from the
Mamounia. On the few occasions we've stepped
inside its overblown spaces, we've been almost
the only folk present. Unsurprisingly, we've
also heard that it is in financial difficulties.
Otherwise, all the neighbourhood's big hotels
come complete with a couple or more bars – and
that's as much as we need to say about them.

## La Casa

*Hotel El Andalous, avenue Président Kennedy
(044 44 82 26/www.elandalous-marrakech.com).*
**Open** 8pm-2am daily. **Credit** MC, V. **Map** p256 B4.
A bar that thinks it's a club, La Casa mixes food,
music and dance to great effect. It *is* primarily a bar,
dominated by a huge central serving area, surrounded on all sides by table-led seating. Above the
counter hangs a giant rig of multicoloured lights fit
for a Pink Floyd gig. Much flashing and strobing
occurs in accompaniment to a heavy Arab/Latin
beats soundtrack. There's no dancefloor, but then
there's none needed, as everyone just lets go where
they are. About the stroke of midnight expect an
'impromptu' performance of dancing from the chefs
in the corner kitchen area. Berber columns cloaked
in purple drapes and characters from the ancient
Tifinagh alphabet highlit in ultraviolet add the
thinnest veneer of Moroccan theming.

## Comptoir

*avenue Echouada (044 43 77 02).* **Open** 4pm-1am
Mon-Thur, Sun; noon-1am Fri, Sat. **Credit** MC, V.
**Map** p256 C4.
Been-there-dahling Marrakchi socialites will tell you
that Comptoir is *sooo* over, but on the right night it's
still the best night in town. From the outside it's a
well-behaved little villa on a quiet residential street,
but inside the place buzzes with dressed-up diners
(*see p111*) on the ground floor, while upstairs is a
sizeable lounge filled each weekend night to within
a whisper of health and safety violations. The crowd
is a mix of good-looking locals, sharper expats and

Comptoir.

Arts & Entertainment

wide-eyed tourists delighted to have stumbled on the Marrakech they'd always heard about. Drinks are pricey and wine mark-ups hefty, but you were expecting that, weren't you?

## Clubs

Pacha and the Sunset Club aside, the scene is firmly stuck at disco – with nothing knowingly retro or ironic about it either. Expect a mix of jazzy Latino, Arab beats and the occasional descent into Euro cheese. Turn up before midnight and staff will outnumber customers – most of whom will also be 'working', if you know what we mean.

### Diamant Noir

*Hotel Marrakech, place de la Liberté, avenue Mohammed V, Guéliz (044 43 43 51).* **Open** 10pm-4am daily. **Admission** 80dh Mon-Thur, Sun; 100dh Fri, Sat (incl 1 drink). **No credit cards.** **Map** p256 C3.

Spurned by the smart set, Diamant Noir nevertheless remains popular with party boys and girls, and a smattering of expats, including the Euro queens. It's a non-judgemental crowd, making it something of a refuge for Moroccan gays. Scout out the talent going in from the vantage of the neighbouring house pizzeria before descending down and down to the sub-basement dancefloor (passing a couple of bar levels and pool area en route). Music is a better-than-average mix of Arabesque and electrobeats spun by competent DJs.

### New Feeling

*Palmeraie Golf Palace, Palmeraie (044 30 10 10).* **Open** 11pm-3.30am daily. **Admission** 100dh Mon-Thur, Sun; 150dh Fri, Sat (incl 1 drink). **Credit** MC, V.

New Feeling numbers local TV and movie stars among its habitués, and was once the haunt of the current king in his 'princely' days. A raised glass dance podium allows for maximum exhibitionism, while lesser stars twinkle on the polished steel dancefloor below. Weekends are so busy that it is virtually impossible to get a drink at the bar. Sit-outs are best spent on the smaller upper gallery, which is usually pleasantly empty. Be warned: taxis charge a minimum of 100dh each way to get out here from the Medina.

### Pacha

*boulevard Mohammed VI, Zone hôtelière de l'Aguedal (061 10 28 87/www.pachamarrakech.com).* **Open** 11.30pm-6.30am Mon-Sat. **Admission** 100dh Thur; 150dh Fri, Sat. **Credit** MC, V.

On the flat dusty plain that is the proposed new hotel zone Pacha stands alone like a sun-burnt Theban funerary temple. It's monolithically massive. Only a part of it is the club: the rest is a chill-out lounge (open 6pm-2am Mon-Sat), two restaurants (open for lunch and dinner) and a swimming pool with sunbathing terrace. The dancefloor and associated bars can accommodate up to 3,000 smiley souls and var-

ious areas can be closed off so that the space doesn't overwhelm lesser crowds earlier in the week. Guest DJs are flown in most weekends and names so far have included Eric Morillo, Danny Rampling and Lotte. Be warned: the place is around seven kilometres (four miles) south of town and getting there and back involves some serious taxi costs.

### Paradise Club

*Kempinski Mansour Eddahbi, avenue de France, Hivernage (044 33 91 00).* **Open** 10.30pm-4am daily. **Admission** 150dh (incl 1 drink). **Credit** MC, V. **Map** p256 A4.

Before Pacha the Paradise held the title of largest club in town. It always attracted a fairly sophisticated and moneyed crowd, which was predominantly Moroccan. A grand flight of luminous steps leads down to the main arena, where spacious enclaves of seating encircle the comparatively small – and hence crowded – dancefloor. An upper level is equally as vast with added distractions of pool and table football, as well as prime viewing of the impressive light show playing over assembled little disco-poppets below. Now that Pacha is here, however, who knows how Paradise will fare.

### Sunset Club

*Royal Golf Palace, Circuit de la Palmeraie (044 36 87 27/www.sunset.ma).* **Open** 7pm-2am daily. **Admission** 200dh. **Credit** MC, V.

Modelled on Miami's Nikki Beach Club, a beachfront bar and club where plastic-enhanced babes and hunks emerge dripping from the surf to collect chilled cocktails from the bar, the Sunset is easily the sexiest place to party in town. While there's no beach there is a series of beautiful swimming pools ringed by loungers and great big four posters tailor-made for group lounging. There's an Indonesian-ornamented bar and a swim-up bar at the centre of the largest pool. Guest DJs spin trance and house on twin Technics in a sweet little whitewashed DJ shack. At the time of writing the place was being used exclusively for private parties but by the time you read this it should be open nightly to all comers. *See also p111.*

### Théatro

*Hotel Es Saadi, avenue El Qadissia, Hivernage (044 44 88 11/www.essaadi.com).* **Admission** 150dh. **Open** 11.30pm-5am daily. **Credit** MC, V. **Map** p256 C5.

The last time the Hotel Es Saadi (*see p59*) was hip was when Cecil Beaton photographed Mick Jagger and Keith Richards beside the pool back in 1967. That has all changed with the opening of Théatro, a very cool and happening new nightclub occupying a former theatre in the hotel grounds. The stalls are now filled with sofa-and-table groupings (each and every one typically bearing a little 'reserved' ticket) while the balcony is tiered with throw cushions. A series of semi-private, gauze-veiled crash crèches fill the stage, while what was the orchestra pit houses a long curve of a bar well stocked with

The Abba look is in at **Théatro**. *See p154*.

chilled champagne and Red Bull. The sound system is thunderous and psychedelic cinema projections entertain the eye, just a pity no one thought to leave space for a dancefloor.

## VIP Room

*place de la Liberté, avenue Mohammed V, Guéliz (044 43 45 69)*. **Open** 9pm-4am daily. **Admission** 150dh (incl 1 drink). **Credit** MC, V. **Map** p256 C3.
This club was hailed as the Studio 54 of Marrakech when it opened several years ago. Ahem. It falls an abyss short of those ambitions, but that's not to say it isn't worth a visit. Flounce down the neon-striped tunnel to the upper-basement level where a jobbing Arabic orchestra saws away at Middle Eastern classics while local couples canoodle in the semi-gloom. Down again to the nightclub proper, with a circular dancefloor overhung by a sci-fi spider-like light rig. Equally alarming are the predatory, leather-clad local ladies, who between sultry demands of random men to 'light their cigarettes' (nervous males should not visit unaccompanied) shoot a mean game of pool.

## White Room

*Hotel Royal Mirage Deluxe, rue de Paris, Hivernage (060 59 55 40/www.whiteroomclub.com)*. **Open** 11.30pm-4am daily. **Admission** 100dh Mon-Thur, Sun; 150dh Fri, Sat. **Credit** MC, V. **Map** p256 C4.
The most recent entry to the city centre nightlife scene is a smart club/bar that offers exactly what it promises: it's a white room. Minimal going on bland any colour is left to the music, which is typically a mix of techno and Arabic dancefloor pleasers spun by house DJs and the occasional international guest act. Another thing that marginally sets the White Room apart is that its rather dashing bar serves an exemplary list of drinks. For serious clubbers who can't be bothered schlepping all the way out to Pacha, this is the default option.

# Sport & Fitness

Action gets largely sidelined in favour of physical pampering.

This is not a sporting city. Look past soccer and there's little else to see, except maybe some lone figures in numbered vests, single-mindedly pounding along an arcing stretch of pink gravel. The international success of athletes such as Said Aouita (former 1,500m, 2,000m, 3,000m and 5,000m record holder), Hicham El Guerrouj (five-times 1,500m world champion) and Abdelkader El Moaziz, London Marathon winner, has proved a national inspiration. Sweat-stained runners are a common sight on the wide road that rings the age-old walls of Marrakech Medina. The success of Moroccans in these track events is remarkable considering the lack of facilities at grass-roots level – which is also the reason why Moroccans have made little impact in the more technical (which is to say, more expensive) disciplines.

Instead, the development of the local sporting scene is led by foreign money – so, few municipal swimming pools or five-a-side football courts for the street kids, but loads of moneyed-up activities like golf and quad bikes. The other growth area – again, linked with an excess of money – is health, specifically spas. It's only logical when you consider that this is a city with a reputation for pandering to sensual indulgence.

## Spectator sports

Gates for league football games at El Harti Stadium are counted in the hundreds rather than thousands. The top local soccer team is **Kawkab** ('KAC'; *see p158* **Lions of the Atlas**). Second string to Kawkab are **Najm Sport Marrakech**, a second division semi-pro side in perpetual money trouble, whose players are forced to earn their keep elsewhere.

Marrakech also possesses **handball** and **basketball** teams, but interest is minimal at best, particularly since the local boys have dropped out of national competition.

The only other sport with any presence is athletics, with plenty of running clubs in town, whose members compete in local, regional and national competitions at all levels. However, the only real spectator sport element to this is the **Marrakech Marathon** held each January. The marathon starts and finishes on Jemaa El Fna and the route goes around the city walls and out through the Palmeraie. In 2005 runners numbered around 5,000, though as yet, it

attracts few foreign competitors other than the French. A half-marathon is also held on the same day over the same course. The date for 2006, which will be the marathon's 17th year, is Sunday 29 January; for further details see www.marathon-marrakech.com.

### Daoudiate Stadium

*Route les Philistines, off avenue Palestine, Hay Mohammadi, Daoudiate.*
An indoor stadium that's the venue of choice for all non-footballing sports events of any significance.

### El Harti Stadium

*Jnane El Harti, Guéliz (044 42 06 66).* **Map** p256 B3.
Home to the Kawkab and Najm football teams. It seats just 15,000 and facilities are a little sparse. Tickets are usually purchased on the day, but sometimes can be bought in advance for big games (against the top Casablanca teams for example).

## Active sports

In addition to the regular urban pastimes, sporting activity in Marrakech recieves a boost from the proximity of the Atlas Mountains. A day trip tramping around the Ourika Valley or, in season, up at the ski resort of Oukaimeden makes for a good day out.

### Climbing

The Todra Gorge (*see p211*) on the southern side of the Atlas Mountains is the best known and most widely climbed bit of Morocco, but there are also plenty of places to climb in the Marrakech region. Most of these sites are unknown and undeveloped.

#### High Country

*31 Bab Amadel, Amizmiz (044 33 21 82/www. highcountry.co.uk).* **Open** 8.30am-5pm Mon-Fri.
High Country is the only reputable locally based operator to offer rock climbing. It's a British- and American-run operation of around 15 years experience that sets up climbs for groups of four or more using sites deep in the Atlas Mountains.

### Golf

It's the most bizarre phenomenon – the push to market Marrakech as a golfers' paradise (*see p161* **Greening the desert**). At present there are three courses, all open to the public, though proof of handicap is required. October

The **Marrakech Marathon**. *See p156.*

# Lions of the Atlas

Stylish, image-conscious Marrakech can hardly be described as a hotbed of football, but the town has managed to maintain a top-flight club for many decades. Kawkab ('KAC Marrakech') last won the national championship (GNFE league) and cup (Coupe du Trône) in the early 1990s. Based at the sparse El Harti Stadium in Guéliz – and not tempted to move to the new sports complex being built on the outskirts of town – KAC's ambitions are as modest as their recent achievements. Football in Marrakech is a minor distraction. Elsewhere around the country, particularly in Casablanca and Rabat, it is a lifelong passion.

The Moroccans took to football in the early 1900s. The Spanish introduced the game to Ceuta and Ifni, the French to Fès, Tangier and Casablanca. Much like South America, boys of every age could be seen kicking a ball about in communal games in the streets and on the beach. A local league was set up in 1916, won by CA Casablanca, where the league headquarters were based. Casablanca soon became the powerbase for the Moroccan game. Fierce competition bred world-class players, who exported their talents to the professional game in France. The prime example was Casablanca-born Larbi Ben Barek, a virtuoso talent who became a hero at Olympique Marseille and went on to play many times for the French national team. Ben Barek was a figurehead for the burgeoning game in pre-independence Morocco.

Morocco were the first African nation to compete at a modern World Cup finals – 36 years after Egypt's one-game appearance in 1934. Having beaten major European teams in friendlies during the 1960s, the 'Lions of the Atlas' gave future semi-finalists West Germany – Beckenbauer, Seeler, Müller and all – a huge fright, only falling to a late goal to lose 2-1. A creditable 1-1 draw with Bulgaria saw the Moroccan amateurs leave Mexico with pride. Star of the side was Mohammedia striker Ahmed Faras, who would lead his country to their only African Nations Cup victory in 1976. By now the local game had garnered enough state funds and sponsorship to keep the likes of Faras at home, and the leading players could turn professional. The Lions qualified for three more finals, 1986, 1994 and 1998, and are leading their qualifying group for the World Cup 2006 tournament in Germany. Morocco missed out to South Africa for the right to host the following tournament in 2010, and no African nation is likely to stage the games for another 16 years at least.

to May is the best period – summer is too hot. Several tour companies specialise in Moroccan golf packages; typing 'golf' and 'Morocco' into a web search engine will provide names and phone numbers.

## Golf d'Amelkis

*Route de Ouarzazate, km12 (044 40 44 14).* **Open** *Summer* 7am-6.30pm daily. *Winter* 8am-2pm daily. **Rates** 18 holes 500dh; daily green fees 700dh; caddy fee 80dh for 18 holes. **Credit** MC, V.

The newest course in town: 18-hole, 72 par, designed by American Cabell B Robinson. It's around a ten-minute drive south from the Medina, with the über-expensive Amanjena resort as a neighbour – slice your drive and you could take out a celeb. There's a kasbah-styled clubhouse fit to grace any first-class course in California, with a well-stocked pro shop. Clubs are available for hire at 200dh.

## Palmeraie Golf Palace

*Palmeraie Golf Palace Hotel & Resort, Palmeraie (044 30 10 10/www.pgp.co.ma).* **Open** 7am-7pm daily. **Rates** 18 holes 450dh; daily green fees 600dh; caddy fee 80dh for 18 holes. **Credit** AmEx, MC, V.

Part of a massive Palmeraie resort complex (complete with swimming pools, a kiddies' playground, tennis and squash courts, stables and paddocks, and various other activities), this is an 18-hole, par 72 course designed by Robert Trent Jones in classical US style, with a Mauresque clubhouse, seven lakes and lots and lots of palms. Individual clubs to hire are 25dh, or 260dh for the full bag.

## Royal Golf Club

*Km2 ancienne route de Ouarzazate (044 40 98 28).* **Open** *Summer* 7am-7.30pm daily; *Winter* 7am-6pm daily. **Rates** daily green fees 400dh; caddy fee 80dh for 18 holes. **Credit** MC, V.

Built in the 1920s on the instructions of the despotic Thami El Glaoui, the Royal Golf has a down-at-heel post-colonial feel; fairways are tatty round the edges but some of the holes offer stirring views of the mountains to the south. Winston Churchill and Dwight D Eisenhower did the rounds here, and it remains a favourite with members of the Moroccan royal family. Required handicap for men is 32; for women 35. Caddies are mandatory. There's no clubhouse and only a limited selection of equipment is available for rent.

# Horse-riding

Marrakech has its horsey set, comprised of expats and moneyed locals. For the latter group, it's very much a status thing; the current king's aunt, Amina El Alawi, is the president of the Royal Association Equestre, and as such it enjoys powerful royal patronage. For visitors, a canter round the fields outside town makes for a fine release from Medina madness.

## L'Atlas à Cheval

*932 Résidence El Massar, route de Safi (044 33 55 57).* **Open** 8am-6pm daily, but phone ahead to book. **Rates** 600dh-900dh per person per half day. **No credit cards**.
Situated some 25 kilometres (15 miles) from Marrakech, this extremely professional operation has been around for nearly five years. They have a stable that can accommodate debutants as well as accomplished riders. The price includes pick-up from your hotel.

## Club Equestre de la Palmeraie

*Palmeraie Golf Palace Hotel & Resort, Palmeraie (044 36 87 93/www.pgp.co.ma).* **Open** *Winter* 8am-noon, 3-6pm daily. *Summer* 8-11am, 3-8pm daily (Wed & Sat afternoon reserved for club members). **Rates** *Horses* 150dh per hr; 800dh per day. *Ponies* 50dh per 15mins; 90dh per hr. **No credit cards**.
Part of the Palmeraie Golf Palace resort (*see also p158*), the Club Equestre has extensive stables with an adjacent training area for beginners. Experienced riders are led out into the groves of the Palmeraie to canter by local villages.

## Jebel Atlas

*Golf Palmier Club, Club Boulahrir, route de Fès, km8 (044 32 94 51/fax 044 32 94 54/www.golf palmier.ch).* **Open** 9am-6pm Tue-Sun. **Rates** 170dh per hr. **Credit** MC, V.
This beautifully constructed, Swiss-run site has a great atmosphere, and caters to all levels. After a session in the saddle, head to the relaxing clubhouse. Accommodation is available at the club, as well as swimming, mini-golf and tennis facilities.

## Royal Club Equestre de Marrakech

*Route d'Amizmiz, km4 (044 38 18 49).* **Open** 8am-noon, 2-6pm Tue-Sun. **Rates** *Horses* 150dh per hr. *Ponies* 15dh per 15mins. **No credit cards**.
Trainers are often ex-national equestrian competitors and this well-run, state-owned establishment has a wonderfully relaxed atmosphere. Longer group trips don't have fixed prices or times, so it's best to call beforehand.

# Karting & quads

Why Marrakech is such a magnet for karting and quad operators is a mystery (too much silly money floating around, perhaps?), but their numbers continue to grow steadily. Quad novices receive a short training session before being allowed to roam wild.

## Atlas Karting

*Route de Safi (061 23 76 87).* **Open** 8am-7pm daily. **Rates** *Karts* 100dh 10mins; 250dh 30mins; 300dh 40mins; 450dh 1hr. *Quads* 340dh as passenger, 500dh as pilot 90mins. **No credit cards**.

Hoof on sand action at the **Palmeriae Golf Palace** stables. *See p158.*

Owned and run by a French karting pro, this is a fully competitive course, challenging and fun to drive. It's the venue for an annual 24-hour marathon and is on the European Karting competitive circuit. The company also has quad bikes and offers a full-day adventure package comprising half a day on the karts and half on the quads for 1,900dh, hotel pick up included. We should think so.

### Nakhil Quad
*Route de Palmeraie (061 15 99 10).* **Open** 9am-noon, 2-5pm daily. **Rates** 500dh for 2hrs pilot; 340dh passenger. **No credit cards**.
Tucked away behind the Coralia Club hotel, Nakhil was the first with quads in Marrakech. However, it hasn't invested in updating and the machines are a little old and not as well maintained as they could be. Great location, though, allowing for fantastic rides through the Palmeraie and its villages.

## Microlights & hot-air balloons

### ULM
*Km 22, route de Tahanahout (071 66 13 50, www.ulm-maroc.com).* **Operating** by appointment only. **Rates** 750dh for 15 mins, 2,520dh per hr. **No credit cards**.
Two French pilots have wangled the necessary flight authorisation and since January 2005 have been taking passengers up and over the Pink City. They have also teamed up with fellow air enthusiasts to offer all-day packages that include microlight flights, hang gliding and hot-air ballooning; rates start at 2,000dh per person.

## Skiing
Oukaimeden *(see p202)*, 70 kilometres (43 miles) south of Marrakech, boasts a number of chair lifts and ski runs. Skiing season is usually from December through to the beginning of March. You'll have to negotiate the hire of a taxi for the day, as it is almost impossible to find a return ride down from the resort.

## Swimming
Fewer hotels than might be expected have pools, thanks to the space restrictions of the Medina. Those places that do, zealously enforce a guests-only policy. Exceptions are few: the **Palmeraie Golf Palace** (Circuit de la Palmeraie, 044 30 10 10 ext 2973, pool open 9am-7pm daily) charges 200dh for day use but you must call in advance; the **Sofitel** *(see p57* **The chain gang**; pool open 8.30am-6.30pm daily) charges 300dh, which includes lunch. **Hotel El Andalous** (avenue du Président Kennedy, 044 44 82 26, pool open 8.30am-6.30pm daily) charges 150dh including lunch, which is served from noon to 2pm, and the

**Jardins de la Koutoubia** *(see p41)* charges 150dh by reservation only, but if the hotel is busy the pool is closed to non guests.
A new alternative to the hotels are the club/restaurants with pools *(see below)* out of town. You get relative peace, greenery, good food and a swim; the only drawback is that you need your own transport.
Forget municpal pools in the Medina; there are only three, which most of the time are reserved exclusively for local swimming clubs. At other times they're filled with horny little boys who'd be highly amused at a foreigner in their midst and would wet themselves at the sight of a woman in a swimsuit.

### Beldi Country Club
*Km6 route de Barrage (044 44 42 21).* **Open** 10am-6pm daily. **Pool access** 200dh per person, 320dh per couple. **No credit cards**.
Rambling gardens and lots of private spaces, with a wonderful large pool. Lunch is served for an additional 220dh.

### L'Oliveraie de Marigha
*route d'Amizmiz (044 48 42 81).* **Open** 10am-6pm daily. **Pool access** 160dh per person. **Credit** MC, V.
A 300 sq m pool one hour's drive from Marrakech in the heart of an old olive grove. The cover charge includes lunch, but not drinks.

## Tennis
Most of the large hotels have tennis courts but, as with their swimming pools, use tends to be restricted to guests only. One exception is the Palmeraie Golf Palace (see the Golf section for details), where both squash and tennis courts are for hire to the general public at 100dh per person per hour.

### Royal Tennis Club de Marrakech
*rue Oued El Makhazine, Jnane El Harti, Guéliz (044 43 19 02).* **Open** 7am-8pm daily. **Rates** 100dh per hr. **No credit cards**. **Map** p252 B3.
As much social club as sports centre, this is where Marrakech's well-heeled families meet to gossip and model all-whites. There are only six courts and the place is popular, so reservations are essential.

## Health & fitness
Weightlifting and bodybuilding are beloved of Moroccan men across all income brackets and social groups (check the number of magazines on the newsstands devoted to ballooning musculature). Cheaper gyms and fitness centres tend to be dominated by men, and women will certainly not feel comfortable. Most of the larger hotels *(see p57* **The chain gang**) offer gym access to non residents for around 180dh-200dh per hour.

# Greening the desert

In a region where average temperatures for most of the year are a grass-withering 25˚C-38˚C (77˚F -100˚F), where precipitation is minimal and water resources are at a premium, covering great swathes of land with high-maintenance turf seems more than slightly mad. But it is madness with method.

Tourism is one of Morocco's few major industries and, after beaches, scenery and history, nothing attracts high-rolling, big-spending foreign visitors like golf.

Morocco's previous monarch, King Hassan II, also happened to be a golfing fanatic. He played as often as the royal schedule allowed and employed a squadron of caddies, one of whom was responsible for gripping the royal cigarette with a pair of silver tongs while the king swung.

Although not a natural player, the king's scores were improved with help from American pro instructors (notably Claude Harmon, father of Claude Harmon Jr, teacher of Tiger Woods) and also by the fact that kings are not obliged to play from bad lies or out of sand traps.

Building golf courses became an important part of the royal vision for the modernisation of the country. Prime showpiece is the Dar Es Salam Royal Golf Club in Rabat, which is also the venue each November for the annual King Hassan II Trophy, famous in sportswriting circles for its lavish junkets.

Marrakech benefits from any and all pro-am tournaments (including the Open du Maroc held every April) because although the comps tee off far to the north, plenty of the players also take the opportunity to indulge in a little golfing tourism down south. That's not to mention the jet-set European golfers who flit down to these balmy climes when winter rain puts a halt to their game at home.

The main course in Marrakech is the Amelkis, a rolling landscape of baize-like greenery, studded with palm groves – and real desert sandtraps – and fringed by sumptuous Moorish fantasy villas. For rich Marrakchis a house overlooking the greens is the ultimate in one-upmanship. Property options are soon to widen too, with a further 18 holes to be added at Amelkis and two completely new courses on the city fringes.

## Gyms/fitness centres

There are probably over 100 small- to medium-sized gyms in Marrakech. Every area of the city has one. They all have equipment for weight training and possibly some of the following: boxing, judo, karate and taekwondo. Entry is typically by monthly subscription, which on average is around 150dh. Day rates are uncommon, but we bet you can get in on payment of a nominal fee.

### Kawkab Sportif du Marrakech

*Battement Lahbess, Bab Doukkala, Medina (044 43 31 33).* **Open** 6am-10pm daily. **Rates** 270dh-300dh per mth. **No credit cards. Map** p252 A3.

### Nakhil Gym

*75 rue Ibn Aicha, Guéliz (044 43 92 90).* **Open** 8am-10pm daily. **Rates** 270dh-300dh per mth. **No credit cards. Map** p256 A2.

This place also offers aerobics classes for women three days a week.

## Hammams

Anyone who's visited the bathhouses of Turkey or Syria is in for a big disappointment. The public hammams of Marrakech are a pedestrian lot. But if they're lacking in architectural finery, they are rich in social significance – and they do a good job of getting a body clean.

The advent of internal plumbing for all has meant that hammam-going is no longer the popular ritual it used to be, but many who live in the Medina will still go at least once a week to meet friends and gossip. For the uninitiated, entering a hammam for the first time can be a baffling experience. After paying (prices are set by the state at 7dh for men, 7.50dh for women), leave your clothes (and a little *baksheesh*) with the attendant. Men keep on their shorts, women go naked (all hammams are single sex). There are three rooms: one cool, one hot, one very hot (although for some of the poorer hammams read cold, cool, tepid). The idea is to spend as long as you can in the hottest room then retreat to the less-hot place and douse yourself with water. In public hammams there's usually a 'trainer' who, for an additional fee, delivers a massage. Bring your own towels etc.

It's increasingly common for hotels to include a hammam as part of the facilities, and these are now some of the best in town (although without the social opportunities). Use tends to be restricted to guests only, but exceptions are **Maison Arabe**, **Bains de Marrakech** (*see p164*) and **Palais Rhoul**.

### Hammam El Bacha

*20 rue Fatima Zohra, Medina (no phone).* **Open** *Men* 7am-1pm daily. *Women* 1-9pm daily. **Rates** 7dh men; 7.50dh women; massage 50dh. **No credit cards. Map** p252 B4.
Probably the best-known hammam in town, thanks to its past role as local soak for the servants and staff of the Dar El Bacha opposite. It boasts impressive dimensions and a 6m (20ft) high cupola, but it's very badly maintained – we wouldn't necessarily count on coming out any cleaner than you went in.

### Hammam El Grmai

*Bab Aylen, Medina (no phone).* **Open** *Men* 7am-1pm daily. *Women* 1-9pm daily. **Rates** 7dh men; 7.50dh women; massage 50dh. **No credit cards. Map** p253 F5.
This place has the old-fashioned basin from which you collect water to wash in a bowl (modern hammams have taps). In the changing areas the floor is covered with *hsira* mats made of grass or palm leaves; interiors throughout are done out in *tadelakt*. Unlike modern hammams at which you pay on entry, here you pay as you leave.

### Hammam Menara

*Quartier Essaada, Medina (no phone).* **Open** *Men* 10am-9pm Tue, Thur, Sat. *Women* 10am-9pm Mon, Wed, Fri, Sun. **Rates** 60dh; massage 60dh. **No credit cards**.
The Menara is the first of a new breed of high-end 'luxury' hammams aimed at the local market. It's beautifully done with individual *vasques* with marble stools (so you don't have to sit on the floor), and the scrubdown with the *kissa* (loofah mitten) takes

place on a slab. There's a pleasant salon in which to relax afterwards. It's located out beyond the Menara Gardens but most taxi drivers know how to find it.

### Maison Arabe

*1 Derb Assehbe, Bab Doukkala (044 38 70 10/ fax 044 38 72 21/www.lamaisonarabe.com).* **Open** by appointment only. **Credit** MC, V. **Map** p252 A4.
The ultimate in self-indulgence – a hammam with rubdown (*gommage*) administered by a vicious pro, followed by an all-over body treatment (350dh). Another package includes the most thorough of massages (650dh).

### Palais Rhoul

*route de Fès, Palmeraie (044 32 94 94/www.palais rhoul.com).* **Open** by appointment only. **Rates** 400dh. **Credit** MC, V.
The Palais Rhoul is one of those ridiculously opulent and exclusive Palmeraie villas, which exist outside the credit limit of most ordinary human beings. It is possible to breathe in its rarefied air, though, by booking a visit to the hammam. It's the most beautiful setting in which most of us are ever likely to voluntarily sweat buckets. Best of all is the massage, administered by Abdelkhader, whose manipulation of joints is so vigorous that victims are reduced to jelly. Slither into the cool basin afterwards to be revived with fresh mint tea. It's the best pampering money can buy – but don't forget to factor in the cost of getting out to the Palmeraie and back.

## Massage

Almost all riads offer massage on request, but it's not always any good. Sometimes it seems like no more than an experiment to see how much oil the masseur can get your skin to absorb. As with most things in Marrakech, quality comes at a price. Massage is also an integral part of the hammam (*see p161*) and spa (*see p164*) experience and, for our money, the best massage by far is offered at the Palais Rhoul (*see above*).

### Pia Westh

*Villa Vanille dour Bellaguid, Sidi Brahim, route de Palmeraie (063 72 79 77/scoubia@menara.ma).* **By appointment only. Prices** 450dh-550dh per session. **Credit** V.
Westh has been trained by Axelsons in Stockholm and specialises in *tuinia*, which is a medicinal massage with a 2,000-year history in China of efficacy against a range of ailments from chronic pain to allergies. Tuina works by addressing the *qi*, or internal energy, of the patient to balance their overall state of health. Westh has also recently completed a diploma in Swedish massage.

### Rene Bales

*(067 04 79 70).* **By appointment only. Prices** 450dh. **No credit cards**.

Hands-on action at the
**Maison Arabe** hammam.
*See p162.*

Rene was trained in the US and does superb Swedish massage. If you want deep touch this is it. Rene also does teaches massage. Book well in advance.

## Spas

Not too long ago rituals of relaxation and well-being in Marrakech started and ended with readings from the Koran. That's history. Spas and associated treatments are becoming big news. However, it's still early days and the scene is very undeveloped. Everybody tends to do the same few body masks and facials, along with massage and a session in the hammam. As yet there seems to be nobody with any kind of interesting signature treatments. Proper training is also lacking – and it really is off putting to receive a *gommage* delivered by an assistant with body odour problems.

The bar may shortly be raised: **Timalizen** is a project in the Ourika Valley slated to open in January 2006, which involves a full spa with trained European staff. Meanwhile, Richard Branson's **Kasbah Tamadot** (*see p198*) is also investing heavily in staff. The spa future in Marrakech, it seems, is out of town.

### Bains de Marrakech

*Riad Mehdi, 2 Derb Sidi, Bab Agnaou, Medina (044 38 47 13).* **Open** 9am-1pm, 3-8pm daily. **Prices** treatments from 110dh-400dh; day packages 540dh. **Credit** MC, V. **Map** p254 B8.
Attached to the *maison d'hôte* Riad Mehdi, which is just inside the Bab Agnaou, is this extensive spa complex occupying several rooms and a courtyard of an old Medina house. Treatments include all manner of baths – with essential oils, algae, refreshing mint and orange blossom milk – as well as various massages (Moroccan, Californian, relaxing, medical). It's one of the only places in town that does a shiatsu massage. All the reports we've heard have been very positive, and it's good value too.

### Hotel Hivernage & Spa

*angle avenue Echouhada & rue des Temples, Hivernage (044 42 41 00/www.hivernage-hotel.com).* **Open** 9am-10pm daily. **Prices** treatments from 150dh-750dh; day packages 1,500dh. **Credit** AmEx, MC, V. **Map** p256 C4.
The Hotel Hivernage is a smart, mid-range new build just a few minutes walk from the Bab Jedid and Mamounia. It has a dedicated spa with a separate section for men and women, both kitted out with state-of-the-art equipment. Staff are notably smiley and welcoming and most of them speak English. It's a great place to come as a couple.

### L'Oriental Spa

*Hotel Es Saadi, avenue El Qadissia, Hivernage (044 44 88 11/www.essaadi.com).* **Open** 9.30am-12.30pm, 2.30-7.30pm daily. **Prices** treatments from 250dh; day packages from 1,300dh. **Credit** AmEx, MC, V. **Map** p256 C5.

The Hotel Es Saadi (*see p59*) is a long-standing and much-appreciated Marrakech fixture. A recent extension and facelift has added this spa. It looks stunning and the premises are spacious, but more money has been spent on decor than staff training. In addition, the fact that it closes in the middle of the day is a pain, with day-customers ejected and told to come back in a couple of hours.

### Secrets de Marrakech

*62 rue de la Liberte, Guéliz (044 43 48 48).* **Open** 10am-8.30pm Mon-Sat. **Prices** treatments from 400dh; day packages from 650dh. **No credit cards. Map** p256 B2.
The newest day spa to open at the time of writing and a rarity in that it is not attached to a hotel. It's a small establishment and more personal than other spas, but it also offers correspondingly fewer treatments. The eyecatcher is a 'Better than Botox' facial (650dh), which beautician Laurence swears leaves you looking like you've been on holiday for two weeks. A light menu of salads and fruit salads is served on the terrace.

### Sofitel Marrakech

*rue Harroun Errachid, Hivernage (044 42 56 00, www.sofitel.com).* **Open** 9am-9.30pm daily. **Prices** treatments 500dh-1,000dh; day packages from 2,000dh. **Credit** AmEx, MC, V. **Map** p256 C5.
The Sofitel group has the most experience of any of the spa operators in town, so it's no surprise that this is the number one spa in Marrakech. Staff are well trained (diploma-holders, the lot) and thoroughly professional, and facilities and treatments are world class and cleverly grouped in a series of appealing packages: the 'stress package', the 'beauty package' etc. It's essential to book well in advance, and weekends are reserved exclusively for hotel guests.

### Sultana

*Rue de la Kasbah, Kasbah (044 38 80 08/lasultana marrakech.com).* **Open** 10am-8pm daily. **Prices** treatments from 300dh; day packages from 850dh. **Credit** AmEx, MC, V. **Map** p254 B8.
The Sultana (*see p45*) is a new five star in the Medina; its spa section opened in December 2004. This is the option for those looking for small and intimate. It's a lovely little complex with a grotto-like feel. We love the free Jacuzzi that comes with all treatments, but the limit of a strict one complimentary tea per customer – even if you've booked hours of treatments – seems bafflingly mean.

## Yoga

### Olivier Lefebvre

*063 54 40 59.* **By appointment only. Prices** 450dh-550dh per session.
Olivier has been teaching yoga for eight years. He offers individual sessions in his studio for 450dh per lesson (these usually last from one and a half to two hours) or will visit your hotel for 550dh bringing mats with him. Book well in advance.

# Essaouira

| Essaouira | 166 |

**Features**

| Moga-ouira? | 169 |
| Wind City Afrika | 177 |
| The Festival d'Essaouira | 181 |
| The Moor the merrier | 184 |

**Maps**

| Essaouira | 172 |

# Essaouira

Morocco's age-old Atlantic port mixes mystical gnawa traditions, hippy myths, surf hangouts and a thriving filmic history with sardines.

There's a point on the road from Marrakech, about 120 kilometres (70 miles) towards Essaouira, where the buildings stop being pink and green and switch to blue and white – the colours of earth and vegetation displaced by the colours of sea and sky. This elemental reorientation is matched by a change in climate. Where Marrakech is hot and arid, Essaouira is subject to winds that keep at bay the searing temperatures of the interior.

Southern Morocco's most favoured coastal town – and the one most easily reached from Marrakech – offers both a contrast and an escape. It's around three hours away by bus, quicker by car or taxi, and, while just about doable as a day trip, is also the only other settlement in the region where travellers tend to linger. Out on a limb from the country's rail network and until recently with no airport of its own (it now has a small one with few flights), Essaouira has managed to retain a laid-back timelessness rarely felt in the seething streets of Marrakech. It's a relaxing place, and a charming one too. Sandy-coloured ramparts shelter a clean and bright Medina built around French piazzas, carved archways and whitewashed avenues and alleys.

Over the past decade, Essaouira has become known as a centre of arts, crafts and music, attracting visitors to its galleries and workshops and hosting an assortment of annual festivals. Apart from the well-known gnawa festival in June, there is also a festival of flamenco and Arabo-Andalucian music in the autumn (www.festivaldesandalousies.com) and a classical music festival each spring. The fishing port, overlooked by grand fortifications, provides a constant source of supplies for local restaurants, while the wide, sandy beaches to the south, combined with high winds of up to 40 knots (46mph), have put Essaouira on the international windsurfing map.

It's also probably the best place to be in Morocco during Ramadan. Cafés and most restaurants remain open through the day, unlike in the bulk of Moroccan towns, and the atmosphere in the evening is crowded but calm as the locals come out after the *iftar* to meet up in the streets and cafés. The town can also claim to be one of the cleanest and freshest in Morocco, with no vehicles in the Medina,

regular street sweeping, and the Alizés winds keeping the temperature to an equable average of 22°C (72°F).

## THE PERNICIOUS WEED

In 1878 British consul Charles Payton observed of the locals that 'they are a tough and hardy race these Moorish fishermen, bronzed and leathery of skin, sinewy of limb and yet not too fond of hard work… they would rather smoke the pernicious hasheesh in a foul and froway den of the back slums of the Moorish quarter than live out on the rippling sea.'

Today the Westerners arriving in ever-increasing numbers envy the Souiris's ability to be comfortable doing nothing, even when not smoking the pernicious weed. This relaxed attitude is just as well. Despite the town's recent popularity, all the renovations taking place (of the Medina's 16,000 houses, over 1,000 are owned by Europeans) and the fact that Essaouira has been named a World Heritage Site by UNESCO, there is high unemployment and considerable poverty. Factories lie empty in the industrial quarter north of the Medina, the once thriving port no longer provides a living and the foreigner-driven upswing in property prices is pushing the poorest Souiris out to the city limits.

The population knows that it is now largely dependent on tourism and this reinforces its instinctive tolerance – only occasionally tested by behaviour considered inappropriate in a Muslim country.

## History

Essaouira has attracted travellers since the seventh century BC when the Phoenicians established their furthest outpost in Africa on one of its offshore islands. During the first century BC, King Juba II extracted purple dye from Essaouira's murex shells for the Romans. The dyeworks were on what are still known as the Îles Purpuraires. In the 15th century, the Portuguese occupied Mogador, as it was then called, and built fortifications around the harbour. The town was one of their more important bases until they abandoned it in 1541. Sir Francis Drake ate his Christmas lunch on the Île de Mogador in 1577.

In 1765 the local ruler, Sultan Sidi Mohammed Ben Abdellah, captured a French vessel and hired one of its passengers – French architect Théodore Cornut – to redesign the place. The sultan wanted a fortified southern base to counter trouble from the port of Agadir to the south, which was threatening revolt at the time, but also an open city for foreign traders. A grid street layout was drawn up and the sultan shipped in black slaves from the Sudanese empire to begin building what was to become the most important port on the North African coast. The gnawa brotherhood of mystic musicians (*see p146*) first set foot on Moroccan soil as part of the shackled workforce. With the work completed, Mogador became Essaouira (*see p169* **Moga-ouira?**).

A sizeable Jewish community was welcomed, numbering around 9,000 at its peak, and British and European merchants were drawn by protected trade status and a harbour free from customs duties. For a long time, Essaouira was the only Moroccan port on the Atlantic coast that was open to European trade, and it prospered greatly until the French arrived in 1912. It is said that Marshall Lyautey visited Essaouira on a Saturday when the Jewish community was at prayer, took one look at the deserted streets, and decided to make Casablanca the principal Moroccan port. Trade began slipping away. The town slipped into further decline with the departure of all but a handful of the Jewish community following independence in 1956.

### HIPPY TRIPS

Orson Welles stayed here for a time, shooting part of his *Othello*: *see p184* **The Moor the merrier**. In the late 1960s Essaouira and the neighbouring village of Diabat were inked on the hippy map. Jimi Hendrix famously passed through: *see p174*. So, it is said, did Tennessee

**Place Moulay Hassan.** *See p169.*

The fishing fleet moored in Essaouira's harbour.

Williams, Margaret Trudeau and Cat Stevens, who, now Yusuf Islam, still returns each summer to stay at the Hotel des Îles. The influence of the hippies lingers on in the town's school of naïve painters and in its several annual music festivals.

## Sightseeing

As in Marrakech, Essaouira offers next to nothing in the way of formal sightseeing, of monuments and museums. The Medina itself is one big sight, with highlights including the ramparts, the souks and the Mellah. You can march from one end to the other in ten minutes, but a more leisurely exploration can take days. The port is a separate entity, worth its own stroll. Connecting the two is the place Moulay Hassan, the town's social nexus, which you'll pass through a dozen times a day.

Arriving from Marrakech, you'll most likely enter the Medina through the arch of **Bab Sbaâ**, one of five gates. The useless tourist information office is on the left of avenue du Caire; the police further down on the opposite side. The few cross streets around here also contain several hotels, galleries and restaurants and a rowdy Moroccan bar, but it's a strangely detached part of town, cut off from both the Kasbah area and the rest of the Medina.

The narrow, shady avenue du Caire intersects the broad, open **avenue Oqba Ibn Nafia**, spine of the Medina. Left, this leads out to the port. Right, it dips under an arch, changes its name to **avenue de l'Istiqlal**, and becomes Essaouira's main commercial thoroughfare. Opposite avenue du Caire, the arch in the wall leads into the Kasbah district and, bearing left, to the place Moulay Hassan.

### PLACE MOULAY HASSAN & THE PORT

Connecting the Medina to the port, place Moulay Hassan is Essaouira's social centre. You can sit at any of the cafés and watch the theatre of the town unfolding. Early in the morning, fishermen pass by on their way to work, and the first wave of itinerant musicians and shoe-shine boys appears. (The latter can become quite insistent. Though it's easy to become exasperated the tenth time they suggest polishing your sandals, bear in mind that these kids are often the sole earner in their families.) By 10am or 11am the café tables have begun their secondary function – as al fresco offices from which most Souiris conduct business at some time or another. Purveyors of sunglasses, watches and carpets sweep from table to table, only occasionally selling something. By now tourists have started to appear, buying day-old newspapers from **Jack's Kiosk** (*see p185*).

Apart from the cafés at street level, place Moulay Hassan is also overlooked by the balconies of **Beau Rivage** (*see p175*), one of the better budget hotels, and the terrace of **Taros** (*see p184*), a multi-purpose venue in prime position above the corner with rue de la Skala. The occasional gust of Pink Floyd or Bob Marley across the square reminds of the town's formative late 1960s/early '70s, and the occasional old hippy can be spotted among the passers-by. Back in the day they used to congregate nearby at what was then known as the Hippy Café and is now the hotel **Riad El Madina** (*see p179*).

The entrance to Taros, just a few yards off the square down rue de la Skala, stands among a clutch of interesting shops. **Galerie Aida** (*see p185*) stocks second-hand *objets d'art* and books; **Bazaar Mehdi** (*see p185*) is the place for rugs and carpets.

# Moga-ouira?

The original name was Mogador. Or so the town was called when the Portuguese occupied it in the 16th century. Mogador is said to be a corruption of the Berber word *amegdul*, which means 'well-protected'. Or so it's said by some, anyway. Others claim it refers to the Koubba of Sidi Mgdoul, a landmark used for navigating safe passage into the bay. Still others cling to the improbable legend that the town's patron saint was a Scot called McDougal, shipwrecked in the 14th century. This ranks with the local myth that Disraeli was born here, or that Jimi Hendrix paid anything more than a fleeting visit.

Whatever Mogador meant, it stopped being that and started being Essaouira after Theodore Cornut redesigned the place in the 18th century. Alas, no one knows what Essaouira means either. Some say 'little picture'. Others say 'fortified place' or 'fortress protected by ramparts'. Some hedge their bets with 'little ramparts'. Others go out on a limb with 'ocean rose'. And there are those who will tell you it means 'well drawn', as in the words uttered by the sultan in 1764 when presented with Cornut's rectilinear town plans.

Anyway, Essaouira it was until the French arrived in 1912. Then it became Mogador again – until independence in 1956, when it once more became Essaouira. And there the matter rests.

The **port** is worth a walk at any time of day, but is most interesting in the late afternoon when the fishing fleet rolls back into the harbour. Essaouira is Morocco's third largest fishing port after Agadir and Safi. The catch is auctioned between 3pm and 5pm at the market hall just outside the port gates, and fresh fish are grilled and served up at stalls (*see p182*) on the port side of place Moulay Hassan.

## SKALA DE LA VILLE

The narrow **rue de la Skala** leads along the inside of the sea wall. It's also possible to get this way by ducking through the spooky tunnel-like alley that leads off place Moulay Hassan by the Café de France. The entrance to **Dar Loulema** (*see p176*) can be found in this gloomy area, the dark heart of the Kasbah.

Rue de la Skala leads to the **Skala de la Ville**, where you walk on top of the ramparts. There is one ramp up to the top near the junction with rue Ibn Rochd at the southern end, and another near the junction with rue Derb Laâlouj at the northern end. Locals gather up here to watch the sunset and lovers cuddle in the crenellations, where ancient cannon offer places to perch. At the far end is the tower of the **North Bastion**, the top of which offers good views across the Mellah and the Kasbah.

You may recognise this place as the location for the opening of Orson Welles's *Othello*. The town is proud of the association and has named a small square after the filmmaker (*see p184* **The Moor the merrier**). Since then many other movies have been shot in and around Essaouira, most recently Oliver Stone's *Alexander the Great* and Ridley Scott's *Kingdom of Heaven*.

Painters lay out their work for sale on and around the ramparts. Artisans sculpting thuya – a local hardwood with a smell like peppery cedar – have their workshops in the arches below and here you can find all manner of carvings and marquetry.

From near the North Bastion, rue Derb Laâlouj leads back into the heart of the Medina, past a variety of handicraft and antique shops, a handful of restaurants including the excellent **Silvestro** (*see p183*), and Essaouira's lone museum, the **Musée des Arts et Traditions Populaires**: *see below.*

At one time Essaouira was known as the Sanhedrin (Jewish cultural centre) of North Africa As recently as the 1950s the city still claimed 32 official synagogues. One of the remaining functioning examples remains at 2 derb Ziry Ben Atiyah, which is the last lane on the right off rue Derb Laâlouj before it intersects with avenue Sidi Mohammed Ben Abdellah. The synagogue was founded by British merchants from Manchester; at the height of Essaouira's importance this section of the Kasbah was the location of various consulates and administrative buildings.

Skala de la Ville.

## Musée des Arts et Traditions Populaires

*7 Derb Laâlouj (044 47 23 00).* **Open** 8.30am-noon, 2.30-6pm Mon, Wed, Thur, Sat, Sun; 8.30-11.30am, 3-6.30pm Fri. **Admission** 10dh.

Also known as the Museum of Sidi Mohammed Ben Abdellah, this renovated 19th-century mansion, used as the town hall during the Protectorate, hosts a reasonably interesting collection of weapons, woodwork and carpetry. There are also gnawa costumes and musical instruments and a collection of pictures of old Essaouira.

### THE MELLAH

British merchants outnumbered other nationalities during the 19th century to the extent that 80 per cent of the town's trade was with Britain and sterling was the favoured currency. Muslims were not permitted to conduct financial transactions, so the sultan brought in Jews from all over the kingdom who by 1900 outnumbered the locals. All but the wealthiest lived in the Mellah district between the North Bastion and Bab Doukkala, an area that has been neglected since most of the Jews emigrated to Israel in the 1950s and 1960s.

The Mellah can be found by following the alleys just inside the ramparts beyond the Skala de la Ville – turn down rue Touahen off rue Derb Laâlouj, passing **Dar Adul** (*see p176*) – or by following avenue Sidi Mohammed Ben Abdellah. When the shops and business start

to peter out, the Mellah begins. These days its alleys are grubby and dilapidated; some houses look ready to fall down. It was always a gloomy quarter. Until the end of the 19th century it was even locked up at night. The family of Leslie Hore-Belisha, British Minister of War in 1939 and inventor of the belisha beacon, lived at 56 rue de Mellah. These days there remain maybe two dozen Jews in Essaouira, some still distilling fiery *eau de vie de figues*, but they don't necessarily live around here.

At the northern end of the Mellah is **Bab Doukkala**. Just outside of the gate is the **Consul's cemetery**, another reminder of the town's cosmopolitan past. It's crammed with the graves of British officials from the days when Mogador had as many links with Manchester as with Rabat. Over the road, tombstones are packed tightly together in the old **Jewish cemetery**, where graves are reputed to be five layers deep.

### THE SOUKS

Leading south from Bab Doukkala, avenue Zerktouni is a busy commercial street of butchers and vegetable stalls. The narrow lanes of the Chabanat district on the eastern side are full of tiny workshops and these lanes are worth a wander.

In the centre of the Medina, the **souks** are in cloistered arcades ranged around the intersection of avenue Mohamme Zerktouni and

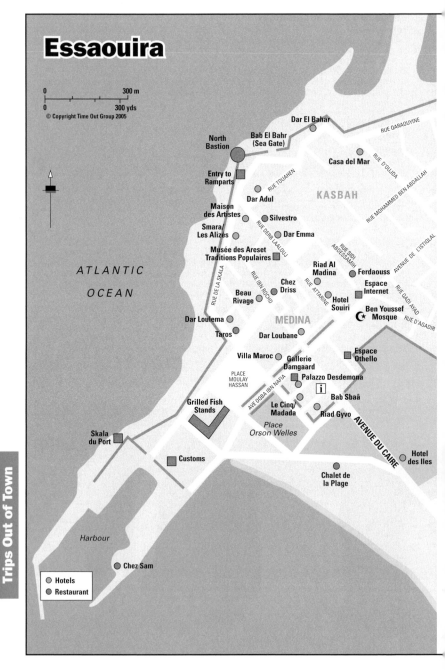

# Essaouira

0 — 300 m
0 — 300 yds
© Copyright Time Out Group 2005

Dar El Bahar

RUE QARAOUYINE

Bab El Bahr
(Sea Gate)

North
Bastion

Casa del Mar

RUE D'OUJDA

Entry to
Ramparts

RUE TOUAHEN

KASBAH

RUE MOHAMMED BEN ABDALLAH

Dar Adul

Maison
des Artistes

Silvestro

RUE DERB LAALOUJ

Smara/
Les Alizes

Dar Emma

RUE SIDI ABDESSAMIH

AVENUE DE L'ISTIQLAL

Musée des Arts et
Traditions Populaires

Riad Al
Madina

Ferdaouss

Espace
Internet

RUE QADI AYAD

RUE DE LA SKALA

Chez
Driss

RUE IBN ROCHD

RUE ATTARINE

Beau
Rivage

Hotel
Souiri

Ben Youssef
Mosque

RUE D'AGADIR

ATLANTIC
OCEAN

Dar Loulema

MEDINA

Taros

Dar Loubane

Villa Maroc

Gallerie
Damgaard

Espace
Othello

PLACE
MOULAY
HASSAN

AVE OQBA IBN NAFIA

Palazzo Desdemona

Grilled Fish
Stands

Le Cinq/
Madada

Bab Sbaâ

Riad Gyvo

AVENUE DU CAIRE

Place
Orson Welles

Skala
du Port

Hotel
des Iles

Customs

Chalet de
la Plage

Harbour

Chez Sam

○ Hotels
● Restaurant

Trips Out of Town

To Safi ↗

AVE 2 MARS

RUE QARAOUYINE

MELLAH

Bab Doukkala

ZERKTOUNI

AVENUE MOHAMMED

RUE DE BAGDAD

Dar Beida

BOULEVARD MOULAY YOUSSEF

RUE CHBANAT

S o u k s

☪ Mosque

RUE IBN KHALDOUN

BOUAKHIR

Jewellery
Souks

AVENUE MOHAMMED EL OQOURI

RUE DE TIRAQ

Lalla Mira

RUE D'AGADIR

L'Heure Bleue

Bab
Marrakech

Ficus
Remarquable

ENSEMBLE
ARTISANAL

South
Bastion

Supratours
Kiosk

AVENUE LALLA AICHA

✉

Catholic
Church
✚

RUE LADUDAS

BLVD MOHAMMED V

AVE EL MOUKADUAMA

Camping

Côté Plage    To Marrakech, Agadir

avenue Mohammed El Qouri, another busy
street leading at right-angles towards Bab
Marrakech and the hotel **L'Heure Bleue**
(*see p177*). First on the left as you come under
the arch from avenue Zerktouni is the **grain
market**. Slaves were auctioned here until the
early 20th century. Now there is an assortment
of small shops, including **Chez Aicha** (*see
p185*). The next cloistered square along, the
**Joutiya**, comes to life between 4pm and 5pm
for a daily auction. The auctioneers walk in a
circle holding up old alarm clocks, fishing reels,
slippers, transistor radios – like a demented
Moroccan version of 'The Generation Game'.

On the other side of the avenue, the **fish
and spice souk** is lively and interesting, but
beware of unscrupulous stallholders, expert
at the hard sell. It is here that Souiri women
come to buy chameleons, hedgehogs and
various weird and wonderful plants for use
in sorcery and magic.

Beyond this point, avenue Zerktouni turns
into avenue de l'Istiqlal. The **jewellery souk**
is on the left, curling around the outside of the
mosque. It's a surprisingly quiet corner where
it's possible to browse in peace. Avenue de
l'Istiqlal offers Essaouira's most upmarket
stretch of shopping. **Trésor** (*see p186*) and
**Mogador Music** (*see p185*) are along here,
as is cybercafé Éspace Internet. Turn down
rue Malek Ben Morhal to find the traditional
pharmacy, Azurette.

After the arched Kasbah gate, avenue de
l'Istiqlal changes names again, becoming
avenue Oqba Ibn Nafia. We are now back in
the neighbourhood around Bab Sbaâ. **Galerie
Damgaard** (*see p187*), a commercial gallery
that has nurtured Essaouira's naïve school of
painters, can be found on this stretch.

## THE BEACHES & DIABAT
Essaouira has wonderful beaches, but the
north-westerly winds, known as the Alizés,
make it cold for swimming. It's ideal for
windsurfing, though. To the north of town,
the **Plage de Safi** can be dangerous when
it's blowing, but is nice when it's warm and
is usually less crowded than the main beach.

The main beach stretches for miles to the
south, backed by dunes once the town peters
out. Closer to the Medina it's the venue for
football. There's always a game going on
and at weekends there are several played
simultaneously, their kick-offs timed by the
tides. You'll also find guys with camels, or they
will find you, insistently offering rides. It can be
fun to trek around the bay to the ruined old fort
of **Borj El Berod**, but wait until you find a
camel guy you feel comfortable with, and
agree a firm price before setting off.

Trips Out of Town

It is said that Jimi Hendrix was inspired to write 'Castles Made of Sand' by the picturesque Borj El Berod ruins. This seems plausible, but is nonsense. Hendrix visited in July 1969; 'Castles Made of Sand' was recorded in October 1967. It is also said that Hendrix spent time in **Diabat**, the small village south and a little inland from here, through the scrubby dunes. This too is nonsense. The village was certainly a hangout for hippies, but Hendrix was never among them; he stayed only a short while in Essaouira's Hotel des Îles. Still, Diabat is a friendly place and the oyster tagine at the **Café Hendrix** is excellent.

## Where to stay

There's no shortage of accommodation in Essaouira, but it's still wise to book in advance if you've got your heart set on a particular guesthouse, and essential to secure anything at all over Christmas or Easter and during the gnawa festival in late June. Happily, there are rooms to suit all budgets and there's no such thing as a bad location – most places are just a few minutes' walk from the central place Moulay Hassan and the fishing port.

As in the Marrakech Medina, small *maisons d'hôtes* have proliferated in the last few years. Old Essaouira houses wind around open courtyards and tend to be smaller and less fussy than their Marrakchi equivalents. Most rooms in such places overlook the inner patio, but Essaouira also boasts rooms with ocean glimpses and roof terraces affording cinematic vistas of sea and sky. On the other hand, terrace breakfasts can be prey to high winds, and some houses on the ocean side fight a running battle with damp. This is a town where you will be glad of a log fire in winter.

Football on the beach kicks off as soon as the tide goes out.

There is self-contained accommodation, too. Apartments of one sort or another can be found via Hotel Smara (*see p177*), Jack's Kiosk (*see p185*), Dar El Bahar (*see below*) and Riad Gyvo (*see p179*).

For something a bit special, consider **Dar Beida** ('the White House'). Deep in a corner of the Medina, a twist or two off the tourist trail, this is a wonderful 200-year-old house owned by English couple Emma Wilson and Graham Carter. They've renovated and furnished with a playful good taste, mixing Moroccan materials and flea-market finds with imported antiques and a retro vibe. The result manages to be both idiosyncratically stylish and unpretentiously comfortable. It can sleep four couples, has two bathrooms, two roof terraces, a lounge, a small library, open fires and a well-equipped kitchen, and comes with two amiable grey cats for £300 per person per week.

Emma Wilson also owns less luxurious but more affordable **Dar Emma**. This small 19th-century house in an alley off rue Derb Laâlouj has a kitchen, two double bedrooms off the narrow central stairwell, and a roof terrace. The whole place can be rented for £600 a week. Both houses can be booked through www.castlesinthesand.com or by calling 067 96 53 86 in Morocco or 07768 352 190 in the UK.

### Beau Rivage
*14 place Moulay Hassan (044 47 59 25/ www.essaouiranet.com/beaurivage).* **Rates** 250dh single; 350dh double; 500dh suite. **Credit** MC, V.
The pick of the inexpensive options, Beau Rivage has been operating above the Café Opera on the Medina's main square since 1939 – and was renovated in 2002. There are 15 bedrooms and six suites. All are clean, colourful and bright and have toilets and showers en suite. Rooms on the second floor also have balconies overlooking the square. The location can be noisy but is as central as it gets and, though still offering big views from the roof terrace, is cosier and more sheltered than those places overlooking the ramparts. Breakfast is an extra 20dh, but it's just as easy to nip downstairs for croissants from Chez Driss and a coffee at one of the tables on the square. **Hotel services** *Restaurant.*

### Casa Del Mar
*35 rue d'Oujda (044 47 50 91/mobile 068 94 38 39/www.lacasa-delmar.com).* **Rates** 600dh-750dh double. **No credit cards**.
This house on the ocean side of the Mellah is in a rough and ready part of town but feels cool and sophisticated within. It's owned by Mallorcans and the four rooms are named after Balearics – light and bright Ibiza was our favourite. Friendly staff have a sense of humour and can rustle up some English, Spanish or German as well as French. The terrace affords interesting views of the run-down former Jewish quarter and Essaouira's 'industrial zone' along the coast, but be warned that this can be an insanely windy corner of the Medina. Still, the rooms face inwards and the big living room on the ground floor, where dinner can also be served (150dh per person), is as calm, cool and sheltered as can be. **Hotel services** *Parking.*

### Dar El Bahar
*1 rue Touahen (044 47 68 31/www.daralbahar.com).* **Rates** 450dh-500dh double; 600dh-700dh triple; 1,500dh apartment (sleeps two). **No credit cards**.
'The House by the Sea' is right on the northern ramparts, with waves crashing on the rocks below – there's no place in town quite as close to the ocean. The French-Dutch couple who own the place have decorated their nine rooms in clean, bold colours, bright fabrics and local naïve art. Not all of them have sea views and they're not the biggest lodgings in town but even the non-view ones are nice enough and more economically priced. The big roof terrace affords breakfast with a tang of sea spray.

Trips Out of Town

Essaouiran institution **Taros**. *See p183.*

## Dar Adul

*63 rue Touahen (071 52 02 21/fax 044 47 3910/*
*www.dar-adul.com).* **Rates** 450dh single; 550dh-
750dh double. **No credit cards**.

Houses on the ocean side of the Medina need a lot of
maintenance if they're not to fall into decline in the
wind and damp, so it was good to see the five bedrooms of this French-owned former notary's house
being renovated on our last visit. The shared sitting
room with open fire remains its comfortable self and
they've also added – the first such in Essaouira – a
skylight that closes off the atrium in inclement conditions. There are excellent views from the roof terrace, where breakfast is served when it's not too
windy, but the rooms all face inwards.
**Room services** *Heating.*

## Dar Loulema

*2 rue Souss (044 47 53 46/mobile 061 24 76 61/*
*www.darloulema.com).* **Rates** 750dh-1,300dh double.
**Credit** AmEx, MC, V.

A serious and straight-faced sort of place at the
Kasbah end of the Medina, just behind the Taros
café, which the terrace overlooks. It's a nice old
house, more generously proportioned than many of
its competitors. There are seven double rooms and
three 'mini-suites' (essentially just larger double
rooms). They're mostly named, and vaguely themed,
after Moroccan cities, so 'Essaouira' is blue and
white and 'Marrakech' is pink. The most expensive
room, 'Zagora', is up on the terrace, has a bathtub as
well as shower, and a bed that can be curtained off

from the lounging area. Breakfast can be served in
your room, on the lower of the two terraces, in the
patio, by the central fountain, in one of the living
rooms with open fires – just about anywhere, really. They'll also make dinner at 180dh per person.
**Room services** *Heating.*

## Dar Mimosas

*Route d'Agadir (044 47 59 34/fax 44 78 52 74/*
*www.skara-bee.com/~moa/darmimosas).* **Rates**
3,800dh-5,900dh suite. **Credit** MC, V.

On the right-hand side of the Agadir road about a
kilometre after it forks away from the route back to
Marrakech, this is a walled compound of peace and
luxury around the bay from Essaouira proper. Four
suites and four villas are scattered in beautiful
Italianate gardens. Two of the suites have their own
gardens; the other two have terraces with views of
the sea – 15 minutes' walk away across scrubby
dunes. The villas have one or two bedrooms, sitting-
rooms, well-equipped kitchens, two bathrooms each
and walled gardens with fountains. All of the lodgings have log fires. You need never see another guest
if you don't feel sociable, but it would be a shame to
miss out on the gorgeous swimming pool, tiled in
blue and white. The main house, coloured a brilliant
terracotta, has dining rooms, TV room, a terrace, a
well-stocked bar and the apartment of Morocco-born
French owner Philippe Cachet. Service is nicely
pitched between attentive and discreet and the food
is excellent – they bake their own bread for breakfast and offer honey from their own hives. Ridley

Scott, Orlando Bloom, Pet Shop Boys and the King of Morocco have been among the guests since it opened in September 2000.
**Hotel services** *Bar. Gym. Internet. Pool (outdoor). TV: satellite.* **Room services** *Airconditioning. CD player. Fridge. Safe.*

### L'Heure Bleue

*2 rue Ibn Batouta (044 78 34 34/www.heure-bleue.com).* **Rates** 2,200dh double; 3,300dh-3,900dh suite. **Credit** AmEx, MC, V.

This new upmarket renovation of what was once a private mansion offers 16 rooms and 19 suites around a spacious, leafy courtyard as well as the Medina's only lift ascending to the Medina's only rooftop pool. The standard rooms (all on the first floor) are spacious and in 'African' style – black marble, dark wood, zebra-patterned upholstery. Suites on the second floor, which get more light and seem better value, also come in Portuguese (blue and white), British colonial (19th-century engravings) and 'eastern' (gold and burgundy) flavours. The British colonial theme, further reflected in a 'club-room' bar with big armchairs and mounted animal heads, seems particularly pretentious and daft.

**Hotel services** *Bar. Billiard room. Hammam. Pool (outdoor). Restaurant. Screening room. Solarium.* **Room services** *Airconditioning. DVD. Heating. Internet. Minibar. Safe. Telephone. Television.*

### Hotel Smara

*26 rue de la Skala (044 47 56 55/mobile 061 08 62 62).* **Rates** 96dh-156dh double; 210dh quadruple. **No credit cards.**

Upstairs from Les Alizés Mogador (*see p182*), simple rooms with bed, sink and table, overlooking the ramparts and ocean or (at the cheaper rate) not. There are shared toilets and showers on every floor. Breakfast is an extra 14dh, or 18dh if you want juice. It's all very basic and the staff are a bit brusque, but you can't argue with the prices. They also have apartments in the Medina.

### Hotel Souiri

*37 rue Attarine (044 47 53 39).* **Rates** 95dh-220dh single; 150dh-310dh double; 225dh-375dh triple; 375dh-450dh quadruple; 600dh apartment. **Credit** MC, V.

The budget option when the Beau Rivage (*see p175*) or Hotel Smara (*see above*) are full has a central location but no sea views. There are 39 cool and colour-

# Wind City Afrika

With frequent high winds between March and September, Essaouira is Morocco's capital of windsurfing and has begun to market itself as such under the rubric 'Wind City Afrika'. Known as the Alizés, the north-westerly winds really are strong, however: wetsuits and sturdy sails are necessary. In winter, surfers can also be found on the town's broad and sandy beaches.

A 20-minute walk along the sea front (or short cab ride from Bab Smaâ), **Ocean Vagabond** is the best place to hire equipment and receive instruction for surfing, windsurfing and kite-surfing. It's also a good beach café for breakfasts, salads and pizzas with the sun on your face and your toes in the sand.

Many windsurfers, particularly those sweeping in for a weekend from Marrakech or Casablanca, prefer to stay in the neighbouring village of Diabat rather than Essaouira. The **Auberge Tangaro** (044 78 47 84), between the Diabat turn-off and the village itself, is popular, and there is a cheap campsite next door. The sea is a half-hour hike away, however, and staying here would be difficult without your own transport.

There is more hardcore windsurfing at **Sidi Kaouki**, 25 kilometres (15.5 miles) to the south of Essaouira, where a broad beach stretches for miles. The small village here is

also popular with non-surfers in search of peace and quiet. There are several hotels, including the **Auberge de la Plage** (044 47 66 00, aubplage@aim.net.ma) which also has horses and can arrange trekking. The No.5 bus runs regularly to Sidi Kaouki from outside Bab Doukkala. It's also possible to get here via grand taxi.

### Ocean Vagabond

*boulevard Mohammed V (061 13 56 44/ www.oceanvagabond.com).* **Open** 8am-6pm daily. **No credit cards.**

Friendly French and Moroccan team offers instruction and provides all the equipment you need for surfing (150dh per hour), windsurfing (250dh per hour) and kite-surfing (300dh per hour). It's also a good beach café.

### No Work Team

*7 rue Houman El Fatouaki (044 47 52 72/ mobile 061 34 73 07).* **Open** 9am-8.30pm daily. **No credit cards.**

Only distantly related to shops of the same name in Puerto Ventura and Tarifa, No Work Team caters for the windsurfing community with brand-name gear for all eventualities. And there's enough business to keep two branches going within a couple of hundred yards of each other.

**Trips Out of Town**

ful rooms, of which 24 have bathrooms en suite. The apartment sounds like good value but we didn't get to see it. Nice stained glass throughout.

## Lalla Mira

*14 rue d'Algerie (044 47 50 46/fax 044 47 58 50/www.lallamira.ma).* **Rates** 246dh-526dh single; 412dh-652dh double; 752dh suite. **Credit** MC, V.
Named after Essaouira's oldest public hammam, now part of the establishment, this is a 13-room German-owned 'bio-hotel' in a peaceful part of the Medina. Guests can use the hammam for free, and like the under-floor heating, it's solar-powered. The rooms have allergy-free furnishings and the organic restaurant (open to non-residents) has both vegetarian (90dh) and carnivorous (120dh) menus, using ingredients from the hotel's own farm. Rooms are tasteful and cosy and come in three sizes. Some have the beds up on mezzanines. If we have one criticism it's that the restaurant is a bit poky and airless. But if it's mid-priced organic 'well-being' you're after, there's no better option in town. Around 90 per cent of the guests are from Britain, we're told. Breakfast is buffet and costs 60dh.
**Hotel services** *Hammam. Internet. Restaurant. Safe.* **Room services** *Heating. Telephone. TV.*

## Madada

*5 rue Youssef El Fassi (044 47 55 12/ www.madada.com).* **Rates** 1,000dh-1,200dh double; 1,500dh suite. **Credit** MC, V.
At the south-west corner of the Medina, this newest addition to Essaouira's *maisons d'hôtes* scene is a stylish six-room affair that, refreshingly, doesn't work too hard at looking 'Moroccan'. Upstairs from and owned by the same people as Le Cinq restaurant (*see p182*), the accents are mostly Parisian rather than Souiri. The four rooms on the first floor have their own crenellated terraces overlooking the town and the port, but these are separated from each other only by wrought-iron fences and lack a feeling of privacy. Two of the rooms are on the roof, where breakfast is also served, and there's a panoramic view of the whole bay from a small upper level.
**Room services** *Airconditioning. Heating.*

## Maison des Artistes

*19 rue Derb Laâlouj (044 47 57 99/mobIle 062 60 54 38/www.lamaisondesartistes.com).* **Rates** 500dh-950dh double; 1,200dh-1,450dh suite. **Credit** MC, V.
A characterful French-run guesthouse making the most of its oceanfront location and the slightly eccentric taste of its original owners. It has six com-

**Villa Maroc.** *See p181.*

fortable rooms, three overlooking the sea, three facing on to the patio, all furnished differently and some boasting some intriguingly odd pieces. The suite is splendid, overlooking the ocean on three sides and lording it over the roof terrace like the bridge of a ship. It's pretty exposed, however, and can get a bit rattly in high winds. La Maison seems to be a home from home for an assortment of young and vaguely arty French folks, and whether you'll like it here depends greatly on whether you get on with the crowd. Manager Cyril is also proud of his 'Judeo-Berber' kitchen and lunch or dinner (150dh per person, non-residents 200dh, booking necessary) can be served on the terrace with an ocean view.

**Hotel services** *Cook. Internet (wi-fi enabled).*

## Palazzo Desdemona

*12-14 rue Youssef El Fassi (044 47 22 27).*
**Rates** 500dh-700dh double; 900dh-1,300dh suite.
**Credit** AmEx, MC, V.
A big, rambling place overlooking the main avenue de l'Istiqlal, the Desdemona has a huge lounge and breakfast area on the ground floor, and seven rooms with four-poster beds above. It's clean and spacious and efficiently run but these days feels a bit tired and lacking in that extra something special. The large suite, complete with dining table and open fire, looks good, but there's no view and some of the rooms are gloomy.

## Riad El Madina

*9 rue Attarine (044 47 59 07/www.riadalmadina.com).*
**Rates** 432dh single; 664dh double; 864dh-1,764dh suite; 192dh extra bed. **Credit** MC, V.
Once the location of the Hippy Café, this is now a rather lackadaisical mid-price hotel. The beautiful courtyard is one of the nicest breakfast spots in town, but the rooms which all overlook it, though decorated with colourful materials, tend to be poky and dark. No sea views, either, but the location is central enough.

**Hotel services** *TV room.*

## Riad Gyvo

*5 rue Mohammed Ben Messaoud (044 47 51 02/ www.riadgyvo.com).* **Rates** 900dh-1,000dh double; 1,250dh apartment. **Credit** MC, V.
This big 200-year-old house in the corner of town by Bab Sbaâ is handy for arrivals or departures, but it's the space rather than the location that is the real draw. Many Essaouira guesthouses can feel a bit poky, but the three studios, two apartments and one

Avenue de l'Istiqlal.

terrace room ranged around the big central court-yard are all truly spacious, and all but one have their own kitchenettes. The apartments are particularly grand, and can sleep up to four, with a 200dh supplement per person beyond double occupancy (60dh for under-10s). The ground-floor rooms are a bit dark but there are sunbeds and genuinely panoramic views up on the roof terrace, where breakfast (60dh) can be served.

**Hotel services** *Internet. Parking.* **Room services** *Heating. Kitchenette. TV.*

### Villa Maroc

*10 rue Abdellah Ben Yassine (044 47 61 47/ www.villa-maroc.com).* **Rates** 850dh-1,050dh double; 1,250dh-1,500dh suite. **Credit** MC, V.

The first boutique hotel in Morocco when it opened in 1990, Villa Maroc is now a mature establishment well-known and confident enough to publish its own cookbook. It's nicely located just inside the walls of the Kasbah quarter, its roof terraces overlooking the square and the fishing port. Twenty rooms and suites are nicely furnished and arranged around an intriguing warren of open terraces, narrow staircases and small, secluded spaces – the result of knocking together four old merchants' houses. Some rooms are a bit cramped and gloomy, and the suites are built around a central patio, so you can hear what's happening on the next floor. But the place is in a continual process of renovation and no two rooms are alike. The latest addition is an 'oriental spa' with a beautiful small hammam for individuals or pairs, and a variety of massage and beauty treatments – also open to non-residents (basic hammam and massage, 500dh). Dinner is 180dh and the food is good here, served in one of several small salons and using ingredients from the owners' own farm. Non-residents are welcome, but must order by 5pm.

**Hotel services** *Bar. Hammam. Restaurant. Shop.* **Room services** *Heating.*

## Restaurants

Undoubtedly the best budget lunch in Essaouira is fresh fish charcoal-grilled and eaten in the open on the quayside. Well, almost on the quayside. Some tidying-up initiative has moved the dozen or so stalls away from the waterfront so that they now cluster less romantically, and in uniform blue and white, in an L-shaped row on the port side of place Moulay Hassan. There is also now a list of fixed prices posted on a signboard (it's at the end furthest away from the water and includes a number for complaints: 044 78 40 33), so there's

# The Festival d'Essaouira

It's been described as the world's best jam session. Every June, around 200,000 people arrive for the Festival d'Essaouira, four days and nights of gnawa and world music. Among them are musicians from Europe, the USA and other parts of Africa, and members of the gnawa brotherhood from all over Morocco. There's a main stage outside Bab Marrakech, a secondary stage in place Moulay Hassan, and smaller events dotted about the Medina. The whole place turns into one big party, like a Moroccan Notting Hill Carnival, or a Mogador Love Parade.

The gnawa (or gnaoua) are descendants of slaves from sub-Saharan Africa, now constituted as a itinerant brotherhood of healers and mystics. Their music is rooted in trance and possession rituals, where spirits are represented by colours and colours are represented by music. It's compellingly rhythmic stuff. Played on bass drums, clattering iron castanets and a sort of bass lute called a *guimbri*. However, the gnawa aren't really professional performing musicians in the western sense and the Festival d'Essaouira is the one place where they all come out to play in public.

That public numbered around 20,000 for the first festival in 1998. These days there are ten times as many, mostly young Moroccan men, but also several thousand foreign visitors and the occasional world music celebrity (both Paul Simon and Damon Albarn have been in the audience). Past guest performers have included Archie Shepp, Joe Zawinul, Ali Farka Toure, Oumou Sangaré and the Wailers. But the real stars of the show are gnawa masters such as Mohammed Ginia, H'Mida Boussou and Hamid El Kasri.

If there's a downside, it's that French organisers tend to invite too many bland Francophone artists and boring old jazzers. Still, 200,000 festival-goers can't be wrong and the event has had a positive effect for both Essaouira and the gnawa. Once looked down upon and regarded with suspicion, they are now celebrated as a cultural treasure and given the nod from on high – the king's closest advisor, André Azoulay, is a regular festival attendee.

For more on the musical traditions of the gnawa *see p146*. For the latest festival news visit www.festival-gnaoua.co.ma.

**Trips Out of Town**

no longer any pressing need to agree a firm price when ordering. Some of the stallholders can get a little too insistent when trying to usher you into their joint, but this shouldn't deter you from comparing places and the iced catch on display before settling and snacking. Your choice will be sprinkled with salt, grilled on the spot and served on a plastic plate with a slice of lemon and half a baguette. We favour **Ali's stall** at No.33, Les Bretons du Sud (067 19 42 34). Prices range from 10dh for eight sardines to 350dh-400dh per kilo of lobster, calling in between at calimari, sole, shrimp, bass, red mullet, urchin and crab. A 60dh menu includes a salad and a selection.

Beyond the delights of fresh fish, Essaouira is no citadel of gastronomy. In fact, the poor selection of restaurants is Essaouira's biggest disappointment. Still, good dinners can be tracked down in all price ranges, though you'll probably have to book or queue for a table in the best of the cheaper places.

In addition to restaurants listed here, dinner is also served to non-residents in most hotels and many guesthouses. Worth noting are **Villa Maroc** (*see p181*), **Lalla Mira** (*see p178*) and the **Maison des Artistes** (*see p178*). Villa Maroc has an assortment of secluded salons for dining, and will cater confidently for vegetarians if informed in advance. Lalla Mira has an organic restaurant with two menus, one vegetarian (90dh). And the Maison des Artistes has a fantastic roof terrace for moonlit dining on nights when it's not too windy. The **Ocean Vagabond** café (*see p177* **Wind City Afrika**) is a good spot for a laid-back lunch followed by a deckchair doze.

### Les Alizés Mogador

*26 rue de la Skala (044 47 68 19).* **Open** *Lunch* 1st service noon; 2nd service 1.30pm. *Dinner* 1st service 7.30pm; 2nd service 9.30pm. **Menu** 85dh. **No credit cards**.
Opposite the wood workshops under the ramparts, and thus sheltered from the winds that lend the restaurant its name, this is a spot justly popular for its stone-arched interior, its friendly, candlelit atmosphere and above all for hearty portions of good and reasonably priced Moroccan home-cooking from a set menu. Expect to wait for a table sometimes – especially when it's feeding time for backpackers from the Hotel Smara upstairs.

### Chalet de la Plage

*1 boulevard Mohammed V (044 47 59 72).* **Open** noon-2.30pm, 6.30-10pm daily. **Average** 150dh; menus 120dh, 220dh. **Credit** AmEx, MC, V.
Built in 1893 entirely out of wood, this Essaouira beachside institution – just outside the Medina, opposite place Orson Welles – has been a restaurant ever since. Good fish dishes are the highlight of a solid, unfussy menu, there's beer and a small wine

list, and the overall vibe is friendly and efficient. It's at its best for lunch, when the terrace affords a tremendous panorama of the bay, from the guys touting camel rides and the kids playing football in the foreground to the ruins of the Borj El Berod on the headland.

### Chez Sam

*Port de Pêche (044 47 62 38).* **Open** noon-3pm, 7-10pm daily. **Average** 200dh; menus 80dh, 200dh. **Credit** MC, V.
Right by the harbour, the building is a waterside wooden shack, designed like a ship, cramped and full of clutter. But the staff seem to know what they're doing, you can peer out of portholes to see fishing boats bringing in the catch, and this is a no-nonsense kind of place where you'll always get something edible even if you rarely get anything exceptional. The average price will drop markedly if you shun the shellfish.

### Le Cinq

*7 rue Youssef El Fassi (044 78 47 26).* **Open** noon-midnight Mon, Sun; 4pm-midnight Wed-Sat. **Average** 160dh. **No credit cards**.
Some Souiris are snooty about this recent (June 2004) arrival, seeing it as 'too Marrakech' in style. In fact the style (by the same designers as the Madada restaurant upstairs, *see p178*) is more Parisian than Marrakchi, and we liked the giant lampshades every bit as much as we liked Anne-Marie Teilloh's 'Atlantic' kitchen – essentially French with Spanish and Moroccan influences.

### Côté Plage

*boulevard Mohammed V (044 47 90 00).* **Open** noon-3pm, 7-10.30pm daily. **Average** 280dh. **Credit** AmEx, MC, V.
On the promenade opposite the Sofitel, by which it is owned and operated, this is a good spot for mildly upmarket beachside lunches and interminable menu descriptions, both epitomised by the likes of Duo de Melon du Pays au Jambon Cru de Parme et Pain Tomate or Escabêche d'Ombrine et Saumon Frais aux Épices de la Médina et Herbes Fraîches de l'Atlas, Toast Chaud. It's about a ten-minute stroll from the Medina. Barbecue on Sundays.

### Dar Loubane

*24 rue de Rif (044 47 62 96).* **Open** noon-2pm, 7-10pm daily. **Average** 120dh. **Credit** MC, V.
Strange place on the ground-floor patio of an old mansion. The decor is unconsciously eccentric – weird knick-knacks and nasty ornaments – but the French-Moroccan dining is ordinary. Their gnawa music Saturday nights are very popular, and for these we'd advise reservations.

### Ferdaouss

*27 rue Abdessalam Lebadi (044 47 36 55).* **Open** 7-11pm daily. **Menu** 85dh. **No credit cards**.
Cute and cosy place where the kitchen is bossed by a former chef from the Villa Maroc (*see p181*) and traditional Moroccan food is served with an imagi-

native twist at prices so reasonable that you usually need to book a couple of days in advance. It's quite a way down an alley off rue Sidi Mohammed Ben Abdellah in the central Medina, from which it is signposted.

## Silvestro

*70 rue Derb Laâlouj (044 47 35 35).* **Open** 11am-3pm, 7.30-11pm daily. **Average** 130dh. **No credit cards**.

This is a cool and unpretentious first-floor Italian restaurant – run by Italians – with an open kitchen, an espresso machine and a basic but sensible menu of antipasta, pasta and pizza. The food's all very well prepared and served with a smile. Wash it down with something from their short but reassuring list of Italian wines.

## Taros

*place Moulay Hassan (044 47 64 07).* **Average** 250dh. **Open** 11am-4pm, 6pm-midnight daily. **Credit** MC, V.

Perched above the town's main square on a corner overlooking the sea, Taros is a multi-purpose venue in a prime location. It has a first-floor salon and library, where you can drink tea and read quietly in the afternoons or have a beer and hear live music on Thursday through Saturday nights. Then there's a cocktail bar on the fine roof terrace (mojitos, margaritas, caipirinhas and such like: 70dh) with tables and bar stools. Food is served in either area, and the menu offers a modest vegetarian selection as well as the best steaks in town (120dh). An art gallery and small shop round off the complex. A much loved Essaouiran institution.

The town's 15th-century sea walls provide perfect perching for gulls.

## Cafes & bars

The cafés of place Moulay Hassan are much of a muchness, serving the same coffee, tea and soft drinks at outdoor tables, though **Café de France** has an interestingly dated interior. **Taros** (*see above*) is as much a café as anything else and the only place where you can get a drink without a meal, apart from at the Moroccan bars, Le Trou and Bar (*see below*).

### Chez Driss

*10 rue El Hajali (044 47 57 93).* **Open** 7am-10pm daily. **No credit cards**.
The pâtisserie at the end of place Moulay Hassan, founded in 1925, serves a mouth-watering selection of croissants, tarts and cakes at prices everyone can afford. You can eat them with coffee here in the small, sheltered courtyard, or take them to one of the cafés with tables on the square (waiters are quite happy for you to consume food from off premises).

### Bar

*boulevard Mohammed V (no phone).* **Open** 9am-8pm daily. **No credit cards**.
Attached to the beachfront restaurant Chalet de la Plage (*see p182*) on the side furthest from the port, and accessed by a discreet entrance signed only with the single word 'Bar', this is a no-frills drinking den where Moroccans gather over cold bottles of Flag Spéciale (12dh) on either a small terrace overlooking the sands or sheltered indoors in the cosy saloon. It's a friendly place and locals are welcoming of unfamiliar foreign faces.

### Gelateria Dolce Freddo

*25 place Moulay Hassan (063 57 19 28).* **Open** 7.30am-10pm daily. **No credit cards**.
A prime location around the corner and facing across the open part of the town's main square. The Italian coffee here is a welcome change from the French-Moroccan varieties at the other cafés. A selection of garish ice-creams also helps to keep the outdoor tables full.

# The Moor the merrier

In June 1949, Orson Welles arrived in what was then Mogador to film his *Othello*. It didn't look good. 'I got a telegram that [the Italian backers] had gone bankrupt... Sixty people! No costumes, no money, no return tickets, nothing!' It was just one more problem in an interrupted four-year filming process in a variety of locations – with Welles regularly flying off to borrow money or act in other people's films to finance his own. But as it turned out, in Essaouira Welles experienced 'one of the happiest times I'd ever known'.

Souiris pitched in as extras, each receiving two dirhams a day, plus bread and a tin of sardines. Welles strode about on the ramparts, caped and in blackface as the jealous Moor. At some point, he lost his false nose. No chance of finding a new nose in Essaouira, so he shot the rest of his scenes without one. But Othello appearing sometimes big nosed and sometimes not was the least of the movie's inconsistencies. There were, for example, at least four different Desdemonas.

Welles' ingenuity rose to the challenges. The lack of costumes, for example, inspired the most legendary scene: the murder of Rodrigo in a steamy hammam, actors clad only in towels. After shooting it, Welles was delirious, walking through the streets in his nightgown. 'It was heavenly! I was convinced I was going to die. The wind blew all the time which seemed to me associated with my

death... and I was absolutely, serenely prepared never to leave Mogador.' His words echo those of his character, which might also have been uttered about Essaouira: 'May the winds blow till they have waken'd death.'

It needed further ingenuity in the edit to deal with a disparate assortment of shooting styles and locations, with different actors playing the same parts, and sometimes no actors at all. The result was eventually shown at Cannes in 1952. A fascinating film despite dodgy dubbing and a terrible soundtrack, it bagged a Palme d'Or but only received a limited US release. For decades the original negative was lost. In the early 1990s it turned up in a New Jersey warehouse and the film was wonderfully restored, along with its reputation.

In 1992, *Othello* was screened in Essaouira to an audience including King Mohammed VI (then Crown Prince). As part of the event, the small park-like area outside the Medina's south-west corner was officially named 'place Orson Welles'. The Prince also unveiled a memorial by local craftsman Samir Mustapha that is curiously unrecognisable as either Welles or Othello.

At the nearby Hotel des Îles, which is where Welles stayed for eight months, there are additional memorials: an Orson Welles Suite ossified in the early 1950s, and an Orson Welles cocktail bar stocked with photos and assorted memorabilia.

## Le Trou

*rue Mohammed El Ayachi (no phone).* **Open** 11am-
11.30pm. **No credit cards**.
At the cul-de-sac opposite and beyond the restaurant El Yacoute, the entrance to 'the hole' is obvious
at night, with a small barrow selling cigarettes and
snacks outside, and a beery glow from within. It's a
disreputable sort of place, full of fishermen in
*jellaba*s drinking Stork beer at 12dh a bottle, with a
drunken hubbub and the occasional row. Walls
brightened by a few still lifes and basketball posters
narrow to a locked door which once opened into the
Hotel Mechouar.

# Shopping

Essaouira is a good place for shopping. It
lacks the quantity of Marrakech, but has
pretty much all the variety, plus its own local
specialities, such as argan oil and products
sculpted from thuya wood. The spice souk
is hassly but elsewhere you're mostly left to
browse in peace and there are some interesting
individual shops.

## Afalkay Art

*9 place Moulay Hassan (044 47 60 89).* **Open** 9am-
8pm. **Credit** AmEx, MC, V.
The one-stop shop for all your Essaouiran woodcraft
needs. Searching the wood workshops under the
ramparts might turn up the odd different item, but
pretty much anything they can make out of fragrant
thuya wood – from tiny inlaid boxes to hefty treasure chests, toy camels to bathroom cabinets – can
be found somewhere in this big barn of a place opposite the cafés of place Moulay Hassan. Staff speak
English and are used to shipping larger items.

## Azurrette

*12 rue Malek Ben Morhal (044 47 41 53).* **Open**
9.30am-8pm daily. **No credit cards**.
At some remove from the hassle and hustle of the
spice souk, this traditional Moroccan pharmacy has
the largest herb and spice selection in the Medina
and also offers perfumes, pigments, remedies,
incense and essential oils. The big, cool space is lined
with shelves of common condiments, exotic ingredients, mysterious herbs and colourful powders, all
stored in glass jars or baskets. English is spoken by
amiable young owner Ahmed, who'll happily
explain what's what.

## Bazaar Mehdi

*5 rue de la Skala (044 47 59 81).* **Open** 9am-8pm
daily. **Credit** AmEx, MC, V.
As good a place as any to buy a Moroccan carpet.
It's not a stock to match the big dealers of
Marrakech, but there are literally heaps of rugs, with
floorspace to lay them out and nimble helpers to
unfurl them. Owner Mustapha is a good sort, speaks
excellent English, and will provide detailed biogra-
phies of each carpet. Don't expect any bargains,
though. If nothing here takes your fancy, there are

other carpet shops further up rue de la Skala, and
Mustapha's brother has a smaller shop, the Galerie
Jama, at 22 rue Ibn Rochd.

## Chez Aicha

*116 place aux Grains (044 47 43 35).* **Open** 9am-
8pm daily. **Credit** MC, V.
Moroccan ceramics can be much of a muchness –
and much Essaouiran pottery is poorly glazed and
chips easily. Aicha Hemmou's stock is a cut above.
It's mostly Berber pottery, made near Marrakech.
Some of the designs are a bit fussy, but others are
clean-lined in warm, solid colours. There's also a bit
of glassware and argan oil in gift bottles.

## Chez Boujmaa

*1 avenue Allal Ben Abdellah (044 47 56 58).* **Open**
8am-midnight daily. **No credit cards**.
Expats call this small, central grocery 'Fortnum &
Mason's'. It's the place to find English teas and biscuits, Italian pasta and parma ham, French cheeses
and tinned haricots. And at the basic deli counter
they'll make up a sandwich to your specifications.

## Galerie Aida

*2 rue de la Skala (044 47 62 90).* **Open** 10am-1pm,
3-8pm daily. **Credit** AmEx, MC, V.
A big place filled to bursting with an intriguing
selection of old jewellery, paintings, glassware,
crockery and other Moroccan antiques, plus a small
but interesting (and pricey) selection of second-hand
books. Nice stuff throughout, but no bargains.

## Hassan Fakir

*181 Souk Laghzel (070 23 00 17).* **Open** 9am-8pm
daily. **No credit cards**.
Second on the right among the row of *babouche*
stalls as you turn into the fish and spice souk from
rue El Fachtaly, Hassan sells all the (un)usual
Moroccan slippers and sandals and, usefully, he
speaks decent English.

## Jack's Kiosk

*1 place Moulay Hassan (044 47 55 38).* **Open**
9.30am-10.30pm daily. **No credit cards**.
In a key location on the square, Jack's is where to
find day-old international newspapers and other foreign periodicals, plus a small selection of new and
second-hand English, French, German and Spanish
books – mostly guides and bestsellers. Jack also
rents sea-view apartments by the ramparts.

## Mogador Music

*52 avenue de l'Istiqlal (070 72 57 79).* **Open** 10am-
10pm daily. **No credit cards**.
Gnawa, arabo-andalusian, grika, bellydance, rai,
desert blues – Mogador Music is well stocked with
all varieties of North African and West Saharan
music on CD and cassette. If you can't find it here
you probably won't find it anywhere: owners
Youssef and Azza know their stuff and distribute to
all the other music shops.
**Other locations:** 1 place Chefchaouen (061 72
83 62).

The reason Essaouira is windy and damp.

## Riri d'Arabie

*66 rue Boutouil (044 47 45 15).* **Open** 10am-7pm daily. **No credit cards**.

French exile Richard Brecquehais accumulates a variety of intriguing bric-a-brac, some of which he sells on as *objets trouvés*, some of which he polishes up or arranges in his own eccentric way, matching pictures to frames or ornaments to shelving units. The result is a small curiosity shop of old postcards, framed mirrors, ancient signs, out-of-date toys and a scatter-brained sense of comedy.

## Trésor

*57 avenue de l'Istiqlal (064 84 17 73).* **Open** 9am-8.30pm daily. **Credit** AmEx, MC, V.

On the Medina's main avenue, jeweller Khalid Hasnaoui speaks good English and offers a more discerning selection than that found in the stalls of the nearby jewellers' souk. It's a mixture of Berber, Arab, Tuareg and other pieces – some old, some new, and some new but using old designs. Look out for work in the local filigree style, made by Essaouiran Jews.

## Galleries

The naïve school of painting for which Essaouira has become famous began in the 1950s with the mystical painting and sculpture of local artist Boujemaâ Lakhdar (1941-1989). During the 1960s, hippies painted psychedelic murals wherever they found an available wall (none have survived) and this undoubtedly encouraged the Souiris to pick up their brushes and experiment with colour. **Galerie Damgaard** (*see p187*) is the place to see the most serious results, but you'll find paintings and sculpture on sale all over town – sometimes alongside handicrafts, sometimes in tiny artists' studios-cum-shops that turn up even in obscure corners of the Medina.

Outside of the galleries, we particularly like the quirky assemblages of French artist Anne Marie Duprés (070 40 47 62), who constructs intriguing boxed scenarios out of old postcards, product packaging, plastic toys, pieces of fabric and other found objects. Call to visit and see her pieces, priced 600dh-3,000dh. There are also usually one or two on sale at **Riri d'Arabie** (*see above*), a funny little place which itself inhabits a very Essaouiran overlap between bric-a-brac and art.

On place Moulay Hassan, look out for young local artist Mustapha Elharchi (066 92 68 88). Confined to a wheelchair, he holds the paintbrush in his mouth to produce small abstract watercolours. He's usually at work near the basketball hoop and you can buy his unframed naïve miniatures, fresh from the easel, for just 20dh each.

## Espace Othello

*9 rue Mohammed Layachi (044 47 50 95).* **Open** 9am-7pm daily. **Credit** AmEx, MC, V.

The extremely mixed bag of work by artists from Essaouira and beyond includes some small pieces as well as large paintings and sculptures. There's some interesting stuff in here, but you might have

to poke around a bit to find it. The gallery's architecture is a worth a look in its own right. It's behind the Hotel Sahara.

### Galerie Damgaard

*avenue Oqba Ibn Nafiaa (044 78 44 46).* **Open** 9am-1pm, 3-7pm daily. **Credit** AmEx, MC, V.
Essaouira's only serious commercial gallery. Frédéric Damgaard has helped develop the work of around 20 local artists. It's bright and colourful, almost hallucinogenic work, heavy with folk symbolism and much of it rendered with pointillist techniques. Gnawa artist Mohammed Tabal is the star of the show, with his 'paintings of ideas' inspired by the gnawa trance universe of colour-coded spirits and his younger wanderings as an itinerant drummer. We also like the paint-splattered wooden furniture sculptures of Saïd Ouarzaz and the dreamlike canvases of Abdelkader Bentajar.

## Getting there

### By bus

Supratours (044 43 55 25) run a bus service from their depot next door to Marrakech railway station; departures for Essaouira are at 8.30am, 11am and 7pm every day. It's wise to buy tickets (one-way 55dh) the day before as the bus fills up for the three-and-a-half-hour journey. In Essaouira buses arrive and leave (at 6am, noon and 4pm) from the south side of the big square outside Bab Marrakech, where tickets are sold at a kiosk (044 47 53 17) next to the Telecom building.

### By taxi

Shared grand taxis from Marrakech (80dh per person) leave from Bab Doukkala. Coming back, they leave from outside Essaouira's *gare routière*. You can also hire your own taxi for around 700dh. From Essaouira, we'd recommend Taxi Mustapha (061 20 71 68).

### By air

Royal Air Maroc runs Monday and Friday flights from Casablanca to the tiny Aéroport de Mogador. Air Horizons (www.airhorizons.com) run a Thursday flight from Paris. At press time, the Atlas Blue (www.atlas-blue.com) had announced it was also starting a weekly Paris flight from July 2005, and there were rumours they'd be starting a London service.

## Resources

### Internet

**Espace Internet Café** *5 avenue de l'Istiqlal (044 47 50 65).* **Open** 24 hours daily. **No credit cards**.

### Police

*avenue du Caire (emergencies 19).*

### Post Office

*Avenue El Moqaoumah.* **Open** 8.30am-12.15pm, 2.30-6.30pm Mon-Thur; 8.30-11.30am, 3-6.30pm Fri; 8.30-11.30am Sat.

### Tourist Information

**Syndicat d'Initiative** *10 rue du Caire (044 78 35 32).* Open 9am-noon, 3-6.30pm Mon-Fri.

**Trips Out of Town**

# The High Atlas & Sahara

Getting Started                          190
Tiz-n-Test to Taroudant                  196
The Ourika Valley                        201
Tiz-n-Tichka to
  Ouarzazate                             203
The Dadès Valley
  & the Gorges                           208
The Tafilelt & Merzouga                  213
The Drâa Valley                          218

## Features

The best…                                190
Day trips                                191
Park your ass                            194
Argan oil                                199
Glaoua power                             206
Family silver                            211
Berber dictionary                        212
Getting the hump                         220

## Maps

The High Atlas & Sahara                  192

# Getting Started

It's a one-hour drive to the mountains, six to the edge of the desert.

Throughout its history, Marrakech has stood on the border between the governable plains and coast of the North and West, and the unruly mountains and desert of the South and East. Hardly any Europeans had ventured into the High Atlas or journeyed through the Moroccan Sahara before the French Foreign Legion built roads and garrisons in the 1920s and '30s. To ascend into the dramatic mountain valleys and pass through the lush oases of the South is still somehow to pass into another world. Even if you're never off the mobile phone network and stay only in tasteful riads, the desert can still be a raw and salutary experience, and the Atlas sometimes might as well be Tibet. Coming back, tired and dusty, from the point where civilisation peters out into the desert sands, along with all the roads and rivers, makes Marrakech seem like New York City.

The landscape might be wild and often seemingly inhospitable but in most places people are unbelievably friendly. They're also unbelievably poor, and often the former is a result of the latter – they're happy to make contact with you in case it leads to a money-making transaction. But then, if it doesn't, they're happy to talk to you anyway. Most Moroccans love to laugh and many are incorrigibly curious about the world you come

**The best...**

**Sand dune sunrise**
Merzouga. *See p216.*

**Brooding kasbah**
Telouet. *See p204.*

**Mountain gorge**
Todra. *See p212.*

**Film location**
Aït Benhaddou. *See p205.*

**Palmeraie**
Amazrou. *See p219.*

**Mountain pass**
Tizi-n-Test. *See p200.*

**City walls**
Taroudant. *See p200.*

**Waterfalls**
Cascades d'Ouzoud. *See p191.*

**Camel trekking**
M'Hamid. *See p221.*

# Day trips

There are plenty of destinations within day-tripping distance of Marrakech. Along the routes covered in detail in other chapters, **Imlil** and **Tin Mal** on the Tizi-n-Test road (*see p196*), **Telouet** on the Tizi-n-Tichka road (*see p203*) and the whole of the **Ourika Valley** (*see p201*) can be done as day trips. Otherwise, there are decent excursions in two other directions – to the south-west, and to the east.

## Route d'Amizmiz

Leave Marrakech as if heading for the Tizi-n-Test, and then fork right soon after the Royal Club Equestre. After a further 15 minutes' drive is the turning for **Tamesloht**, home of a potters' co-operative. The village also boasts ancient olive oil presses with gigantic grindstones until recently driven by mules – decommissioned when the villagers were given modern machinery. They are located 'derrière la commune'. There's also a rambling kasbah still partially occupied by descendants of the village founders, and next to it a Shrine of Moulay Abdellah with a minaret that appears to be toppling under the weight of an enormous storks' nest. Visitors can drop by the offices of the Association Tamesloht (place Sour Souika) for additional information and directions.

South of Tamesloht, the fertile landscape becomes a brilliant patchwork of greenery. Visible to the left is **Kasbah Oumnast**, a location for Scorsese's *The Last Temptation of Christ* and Gillies MacKinnon's *Hideous Kinky*. A little *baksheesh* can probably persuade the guardian to show you around.

Eight kilometres (five miles) further south, the road swings on to a perilously narrow-looking bridge over the Oued N'fis before looping around to hug the shore of the **Barrage Lalla Takerkost**, a sizeable reservoir with the mountains as backdrop. There are several restaurants and campsites in the area, the best of which is the **Relais du Lac** (061 24 24 54/061 18 74 72). It has a grassy garden beside the water's edge, where tajine and couscous are served al fresco for about 80dh per head.

The road ends at **Amizmiz** (pronounced 'Amsmiz'), 55 kilometres (34 miles) south-west of Marrakech. The town has a dilapidated kasbah and a former mellah, as well as a Thursday market that's one of the biggest in the region (*see p194* **Park your ass**). There are regular bus and *grand taxis* between Marrakech (from Bab Er Rob) and Amizmiz. The journey takes just over an hour.

## Cascades d'Ouzoud

The route de Fès runs east out of Marrakech. After ten kilometres (six miles) there's a right-hand turn on to the road for Demnate and Azilal. After 40 kilometres (24 miles) skirting the foothills of the Atlas, look for a right turn down to the village of Timinoutine, which is on the edge of the Lac des Aït Aadel. Also known as the **Barrage Moulay Youssef**, this is another large reservoir with a High Atlas backdrop. The scenery is gorgeous and it's a popular picnic spot for Marrakchis.

At Demnate, a side road runs south to **Imi-n-Ifri**, which scores with a natural rock bridge, a slippery grotto and fossilised dinosaur footprints. East from Demnate on the way to Azilal is a signposted turn-off north for the **Cascades d'Ouzoud**: the biggest waterfall in Morocco, it plunges 110 metres in three tiers down to a picturesque pool overlooked by cafés. You arrive at the top, where people will want to 'guide' you down, though help isn't really necessary. By car it should take about two-and-a-half hours from Marrakech. For anyone who doesn't fancy going straight back, the **Riad Cascades d'Ouzoud** (023 45 96 58, www.ouzoud.com, 750dh double) is rustically tasteful. Two buses a day run from Marrakech to Azilal, and from here you can hire a *grand taxi* for the 20-minute backtrack to the falls. Make that trip on a Thursday to coincide with Azilal's weekly market (*see p194* **Park your ass**).

from and the life you lead – as alien to them as theirs is to you. It's depressing to see children begging, though, and everywhere you'll run into kids trying to scam a dirham or two, sometimes very ingeniously. If you want to give them something useful rather than money or 'bonbons', take a few ballpoint pens. Kids are always asking for 'un stylo'.

## Where to go

South of Marrakech, there are two main passes over the High Atlas. The **Tizi-n-Test** (*see p196*), to the south-west, runs up past the 12th-century mosque of Tin Mal, snakes over the spectacular pass, and hairpins down to the Sous Valley and the pre-Saharan town of

Taroundant. The **Tizi-n-Tichka** (*see p203*) to the south-east runs over the mountains near the kasbah of Telouet, and then down to Ouarzazate and the edge of the Sahara. In between the two, another road follows the **Ourika Valley** (*see p201*) into the High Atlas as far as the village of Setti Fatma and its waterfalls. This is the easiest trip from Marrakech and it's a popular day-excursion for visitors and locals alike, especially in winter when snowfall brings a surge of activity to the ski resort of Oukaimeden.

Ouarzazate is basically the gateway to the Moroccan Sahara, and here it's possible either to head further south down the palmeraie of the **Drâa Valley** (*see p218*) until both road and river peter out at M'Hamid, or bear east along the rugged **Dadès Valley** (*see p208*), taking in the Dadès and Todra gorges. Further east lies the great **Tafilelt Oasis** and the dunes of **Merzouga** (*see p213*), which can be reached from either the Drâa or Dadès valleys.

Whichever route takes your fancy, there are basically two kinds of country south of Marrakech: the colourful mountains of the High Atlas, and the stony plains and lush oases of the Moroccan Sahara.

## The High Atlas

There are some serious peaks in the Atlas. At 4,167 metres (13,667 feet), Jebel Toubkal is North Africa's highest mountain. But you needn't be a climber to enjoy the landscape and various valley roads take you into – and over – some of the most interesting areas.

Rugged and remote, throughout history the Atlas has been home to an assortment of Berber tribes, and every now and then one of them has come galloping down to conquer the rest of the country and establish a new dynasty. These tribes were never really conquered by anyone, and their traditions are very different from those of urban Moroccans. The women, for example, wear headscarves but are never veiled and wear clothes in bright, clashing patterns. They seem to do all the work: you see them carrying huge bales of brushwood on their backs while the men sit around smoking and talking.

They live in villages up on the valley sides looking on clear streams, rugged skyscapes, wriggling roads and verdant valley floors. In spring, like the clothes of the women, it's all one big patchwork of colour.

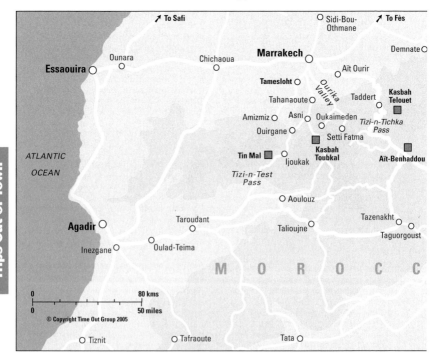

## The Sahara

Strictly speaking, the area south of the Atlas is the pre-Sahara, rather than the full-blown desert itself, but the aridity is palpable the minute you cross the watershed, and the pattern of lush oases separated by barren stretches of stony plain begins just beyond the town of Ouarzazate.

An oasis basically means a palmeraie – densely cultivated land, anchored by palm trees, with other crops grown beneath. In the palmeraies you'll also find *ksours* (fortified tribal villages) and *kasbahs* (fortified family mansions) made out of *pisé* mud and straw. Most of these aren't anywhere near as old as they look (feudal days ended less than a century ago) and they decay fairly quickly once abandoned, melting back into the landscape. The great oases, however, have been inhabited for centuries, if not millennia.

There are both Berber and Arab settlements in the Sahara, and at the far end of the road also Tuaregs and Saharwis, though not everyone wearing a blue robe and burnoose is really a 'blue man' of the desert. Many dress that way just to help sell their souvenirs or camel treks.

While the areas covered in the following chapters are mostly a kind of Saraha Touristique, the desert can still be dangerous and should be treated with respect. Don't venture off the road unless you know where you're going.

## When to go

The best time to visit any of these places is in the spring (mid March to May), when all is lush and the almond trees are in bloom. October and November are also fine temperature wise, but you don't get the greenery. Forget the Sahara between June and September: it's unbearably hot and there are sandstorms. In winter the nights can be cold but the days are clear and bright and not too hot. The Atlas is wonderful in the summer, however: Marrakchis scoot up there just to escape from the heat of the city, and you may well want to follow their example. There is sometimes snow in winter, and even skiing between February and April at Oukaimeden (*see p202*). Bad weather will occasionally close both the Tizi-n-Tichka and the Tizi-n-Test, and in winter it's best to check the situation before setting out.

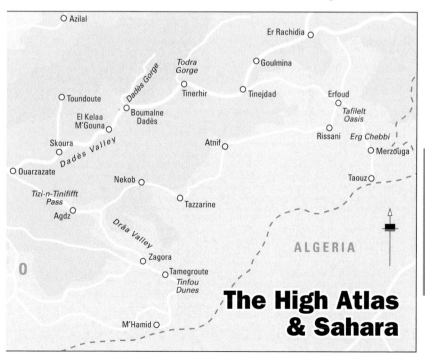

**The High Atlas & Sahara**

## Where to stay

Most hotels are pretty basic, but there are exceptions, and riad culture is beginning to seep south from Marrakech. Most places will try to sell you half-board – room plus dinner – and in most places this makes sense. Apart from in Ouarzazate (and that's not exactly a gourmet paradise), there are almost no decent restaurants anywhere outside of the hotels. Even most hotels only serve the same old couscous and tajines, which are the only things anyone knows how to cook. There are upmarket exceptions, such as **Riad Maria** (*see p216*) near Merzouga and **Chez Pierre** (*see p211*) in the Dadès Gorge, both with good restaurants open to non-residents (though Riad Maria needs a little advance warning). But expect to return sick to death of Moroccan food.

## Getting around

It's possible to reach most places mentioned in these chapters by bus, but it would be an exhausting and dispiriting experience to hop around that way, with lots of long waits, inconvenient connections, dawn starts and cramped journeys. We'd recommend it only if you've got one particular destination in mind and intend to go there, hang around for a while, and then return.

The *grand taxi* network is a little more flexible, and the shared ones aren't much more expensive than buses, but they're often just as cramped (it's usual to pack in six people before setting off) and it still involves a lot of waiting around. You can get to everywhere on the main roads this way, and also to a lot of places off them by hiring your own. Make sure the price is clearly agreed beforehand.

But the best way to explore is by renting both car and driver. Car hire isn't exactly cheap: 350dh-500dh per day for a Fiat Uno, depending on the season; about 600dh per day for something with air-conditioning; and 1,200dh per day upwards for a 4x4. Drivers are more affordable relative to Europe or America, adding about 300dh per day to the deal. Most car-hire companies can sort out a driver who knows the routes much better than you ever will, so why not enjoy the scenery while someone else deals with all those mountain hairpins, desert tracks and donkey carts?

A 4x4 is great for exploring remote mountain valleys and the more deserted bits of desert, but unless otherwise stated, everywhere we write

# Park your ass

Most towns and villages in the Atlas have some kind of weekly market. People ride in from the surrounding hills on bikes and donkeys, as much for the buzz and gossip as for the buying and selling. The typical market spreads over a couple of roadside fields, or occupies some dusty, dedicated area on the edge of a settlement. And one of the first things you'll notice is the donkey park, where the beasts are tethered in rows.

Here you can also buy a donkey, or trade an old one in part exchange. (Some are sold to the zoo in Rabat, where they're rewarded for a patient, long-suffering life by being fed to the lions and tigers.)

At the market's heart will be stalls and groundsheet pitches of agricultural produce. But all the best fruit and veg goes straight to the cities and what's left at these markets is bruised, bargain-basement stuff. There will also be sellers of groceries and cigarettes, cheap clothing, cassettes (music and Islamic sermons) and farming implements, plus a few people touting souvenirs and trinkets – and looking to latch on to someone like you. Sheep and cattle will be auctioned off to one

side. Tajines will be cooking somewhere. There's typically also a row of busy Berber barbers, each cropping hair in their own makeshift cubicle. Sometimes there are dentists, too.

Interesting though these markets are, the people attending are dirt poor, and if you visit we recommend leaving the flash camera gear and expensive shades back at the hotel. Not that they're liable to get stolen, but you might feel a little self-conscious about such ostentatious displays of wealth.

Within day-tripping distance of Marrakech, markets are held on the following days:
● Monday: **Dar Caid Ourika** near Aghmat (*see p201*) in the Ourika Valley.
● Tuesday: **Amizmiz** (*see p191*) and **Tahanaoute** (*see p196*).
● Thursday: **Ouirgane** (*see p198*); **Setti Fatma** (*see p202*) and **Touama** (32km/ 20 miles east on the Tizi-n-Tichka road).
● Friday: **Aghmat** (*see p201*); and **Tamesloht** (*see p191*).
● Saturday: **Asni** (*see p196*)
● Sunday: **Chichaoua** (52km/32 miles east of Marrakech on the Essaouira road).

Southern Morocco staples: 4x4s and 'blue men' (who may not be blue men at all).

about can be reached by Fiat Uno. Filling stations are infrequent so top up whenever possible. Pack a torch and some toilet paper. For more details on car rental, including contacts, *see p225*.

## Specialist tours

Independent travel in southern Morocco is manageable and inexpensive, but if time is short, or if you have a specific holiday interest, such as trekking, safari, cycling or cooking (for which also *see p116* **Kitchen breaks**), or you're just looking for something different it can be worth enlisting the help of the experts.

For more options on places to stay take a look at **www.travelintelligence.com**, which provides honest reviews of dozens of select hotels scattered throughout the Atlas and pre-Sahara, and offers a booking service.

### Best of Morocco

*Seend Park, Seend, Wiltshire SN12 6NZ (01380 828 533/www.morocco-travel.com).*
A leading tour operator with over 30 years as a Morocco specialist, with all the in-depth knowledge that suggests. Tours are tailor-made to suit individual needs, including flights, transfers, hotels and travel, but must be a minimum of four nights. Activities on offer include cooking, trekking, skiing and camel trekking. Recommended.

### Destination Evasion

*Villa El Borj, rue Khalid Ben Oualid, Guéliz (044 44 73 75/www.destination-evasion.com).*
Based in Marrakech but with years of experience in southern Morocco, Pierre Yves Marais and Beatrix Maximo specialise in organising trips into and over the Atlas. They work with lots of other small operators to provide whatever clients want, from yoga sessions in secluded valleys to ballooning over the dunes. They cater for groups from two to 200.

# Tizi-n-Test to Taroudant

There's not much to see in Taroudant but the getting there is just splendid.

The road to Taroudant heads directly south out of Marrakech, winds over the Tizi-n-Test pass, and snakes down to the Sous valley. It then cruises due east through argan country into Taroudant – a total distance of 223 kilometres (138 miles).

That's about a five-hour drive. If getting to Taroudant is what it's all about then it's easier to take what looks on the map like a longer route – the highway west from Marrakech to Chichaoua and then south over the Tizi Maachou with all the Agadir traffic. But to go that way would be to miss out on one of the most spectacular drives in North Africa.

About 100 kilometres (62 miles) or two hours' leisurely drive from Marrakech, Tin Mal is also doable as a day trip. On the way, Moulay Brahim (see below) sports a shrine to Moulay Brahim, Asni (see below) hosts a Saturday morning souk, and Ourigane (see p198) offers a couple of good hotels and some fine dining. An alternative trip is to bear left at Asni up to Imlil and maybe have an overnight stay at the Kasbah du Toubkal (see below).

Heading towards the Tizi-n-Test, after Tin Mal there's not much but the road itself – but hey, what a road!

It's a tricky one, though, for drivers without much experience of mountains. Originally built by the French in 1928, it's well surfaced and contoured, but loops and twists like a sack of serpents and in places is treacherously narrow. The stretch after the pass hairpins around blind corners all the way down on to the plain, and it's only half as wide again as your car. The Gorges of Moulay Brahim below Asni are another stretch that demands a little respect. You wouldn't want to come off this road, for precisely the same topographical reasons that make it so worth driving in the first place.

All this makes it sound more dangerous than it is. There isn't too much traffic and frankly, stuck among all the trucks, we find the Agadir road much more scary as well as much less interesting.

Snow sometimes closes the Tizi-n-Test in winter. There's a sign on the way out of Marrakech that warns if the pass isn't open, and another one just after Tahanaoute.

Buses that run all the way to Taroudant via the Tizi-n-Test tend to leave Marrakech very early in the morning (5am or 6am) and take 7-8

hours. If you're heading for one of the classier hotels in these parts, such as the Kasbah du Toubkal or the Gazelle d'Or, they can arrange a car to collect you from Marrakech.

## Moulay Brahim & Asni

It's a boring administrative sort of town but **Tahanaoute** is the only feature of note on the plain between Marrakech and the mountains. After it, though, the road gets picturesque, winding uphill through the Gorges of Moulay Brahim. Drive carefully.

**Moulay Brahim** also has a village named after him, which is off up to the right just before Asni, and in the middle of the village he has a green-roofed shrine – entry forbidden to non-Muslims. Nearby stalls sell charms, incense, nougat, chameleons and other esoteric supplies. Moulay Brahim is said to sort out female fertility problems, if asked nicely. This is a popular summer day-trip destination for Marrakchi families and it can get quite bustly in a bank holiday sort of way.

**Asni** is a few kilometres beyond the gorges. Its approach is lined with poplar and willow trees. The lively Saturday souk draws people from all over the area and it's worth a look if you're here on the day, but expect hassle from trinket-sellers. The village is bigger than it first appears, with clumps of houses dotted about the valley. But there's nothing else to see here.

Beyond Asni the road continues up towards Ourigane and Tin Mal; see p198. The road for Imlil forks off to the left.

## Imlil & Kasbah du Toubkal

The road to Imlil hugs the side of a broad valley, its bottom a wide bed of shale. Not far out of Asni, surrounded by high walls and cypresses, is the restored **Kasbah Tamandot** (see p198), part of Richard Branson's portfolio of Virgin hotels. Further up the valley, across on the far side and perched above green pastoral enclosures and walnut groves, is the hilltop hamlet of **Aksar Soual**, also known locally as 'Clintonville'. In 1999 the place was descended on by a fleet of big black SUVs with accompanying helicopter support. It was Hillary, visiting her niece who lives up here and is married to a local Berber guide.

At the head of the valley the road comes to a halt at **Imlil**, a small village that serves as the centre for trekking in the region, lying, as it does, at the foot of **Jebel Toubkal**, which at 4,167 metres (13,667 feet) is North Africa's highest peak. Guides can be hired at the Bureau des Guides in the centre of the village. There are also several small café/restaurants and basic budget accommodation. But the place to stay around here is Kasbah du Toubkal.

### Kasbah du Toubkal

*Kasbah Toubkal, BP31, Imlil, Asni (044 48 56 11/ fax 044 48 56 36/www.kasbahdutoubkal.com).* **Rates** dorm 300dh; double 1,200dh-1,700dh; suite 2,500dh-4,000dh. **Credit** MC, V.

A stunning restoration of an abandoned kasbah by two English brothers and their local Moroccan partner, Toubkal is one of the most atmospheric places to stay in southern Morocco. Guests are transported up from Imlil by mule (an adventure in itself) and enter the compound beside a tower constructed for the filming of Scorsese's *Kundun*. Key scenes were shot here and some of the abandoned props remain, notably a Tibetan prayer wheel. Rooms range from 'mountain hut' dorms to a split-level, glass-walled suite that's like a Bond villain's shag pad. The views from the various terraces are breathtaking, with Jebel Toubkal rising up sheer behind. The kasbah is also doable as a daytrip from Marrakech (850dh per person): at 9am a car picks you up in the city, ferries you up here for a Berber lunch and a spot of walking, then returns you by 6pm. One other plus: the kasbah is a flagship for sustainable tourism and works closely with the local community.

**Hotel services** *Bicycles. Car hire (4X4). Conference facilities. Cook. Garden. Hammam. Library. Mountain guides. Mules. Trekking.*

**Kasbah Tamandot**. *See p198.*

Tin Mal.

## Kasbah Tamandot

*BP67, Asni (044 36 82 00/fax 044 36 82 11/*
*www.virgin.com/kasbah).* **Rates** *6 Jan-28 Feb,*
*July, Aug* 2,700dh-4,500dh suite. *Mar-June, 1 Sept-*
*5 Jan* 3,150dh-4,850dh. **Credit** AmEx, MC, V.
Built in the 1920s as the residence of the *caid* of the
valley, the kasbah was bought in 1989 by Italian-
American antiques dealer Luciano Tempo. He
rebuilt extensively and so it isn't necessarily the
fault of the Virgin hotel group that the property feels
like a Disneyfied version of a Moorish palace.
Tempo is also responsible for many of the tasteless
fittings and furnishings, left behind as a job lot when
Richard Branson bought the kasbah in 2000. On the
plus side, the setting is spectacular, there are four
hectares of landscaped gardens including orchards,
and the Berber staff are completely charming. Also,
the place is undeniably luxurious. If you can't afford
to stay here then consider visiting for lunch prepared
by an extremely talented South African chef and
taken on one of the many rooftop terraces.
**Hotel services** *Car parking. Hammam. Library.*
*Mountain guides. Restaurant. Sauna. Swimming*
*pools (one indoor, one outdoor). Tennis courts.*
*Trekking. TV room.* **Room services** *Air-*
*conditioning. Heating. Minibar. Safe.*

## Ouirgane

Ouirgane ('weer-gan') at first seems like the
tiniest place, consisting of little more than its
two well-known hotels – La Roseraie and the
Au Sanglier Qui Fume – on either side of the
Oued Nifis. But after a while you realise that the
houses are hidden in forest and scattered up the
valley sides, safe from occasional flash flooding.
It's a pretty location, in a basin surrounded by
wooded mountains, with glimpses of Toubkal
towering highest of all. There's a Jewish hamlet
(deserted) nearby to the south-east, and a
primitive salt factory (operational) back down
the main road a little and off to the west. You'll

need a guide to find either of them. It's also
the most comfortable base from which to do
Tin Mal, though if you don't have your own
transport this will involve commandeering a
taxi for a few hours. But Ouirgane is a place for
chilling rather than sightseeing, with a little
light walking on the side. It's also a good lunch
stop, as both the hotels have decent restaurants.
   **La Roseraie** (044 43 91 28, bookings@
laroseraie.com; from 2,200dh a double) is a
peaceful place set among rose gardens and
groves of lime and lemon. It has two
restaurants, indoor and outdoor pools, a
hammam, a tennis court, and facilities for
hunting, shooting and riding. More basic
and perhaps better value, the **Sanglier
Qui Fume** (044 48 57 07, fax 044 48 57 09,
www.ausanglierquifume.com; 600dh-800dh
half-board for two) is a friendly French-run inn,
opened in 1945, that has 22 cabin-style rooms
and suites with log fires, an outdoor pool, a
convivial bar and a restaurant serving good
French country cooking. They also rent out
mountain bikes.

## Tin Mal

Beyond Ouirgane, it all begins to feel rockier
and more remote. The twisting road climbs
high up the valley sides, with riverside
cultivation glowing green far below while flat-
roofed Berber villages blend into the stony
background above the fertile stretches.
   The village of **Ijoujak** has several basic
cafés, some of which also offer rooms. Just
after it, on the right, is the kasbah of **Talaat-
n-Yacoub**. This, and the other kasbahs that
crown strategic heights in the area, were all
fortresses of the Goundafi tribe, who ran the
Tizi-n-Test until 'pacified' by the French.
Though they look ancient, the kasbahs mostly

date from the late 19th and early 20th centuries – a reminder that the feudal era is still a living memory around here.

About three kilometres past the kasbah, a track to the right leads down and across the river to **Tin Mal**. The ancient mosque, built in 1153, stands above the undistinguished modern village. Soon after you arrive, someone will appear with a key to let you in.

How much more remote must this valley have been in the early 12th century? Yet back then it became the spiritual heart of the Almohad empire. Around 1120 one Ibn Toumart arrived after much wandering to make a pest of himself in Marrakech with criticism of the ruling Almoravids. He was banished and retreated up here to seek the support of local tribes for his militant version of Islam. In 1125 he established his capital at Tin Mal, creating a sort of Moroccan Lhasa – a fortified religious community run with a pitiless, puritanical discipline. He and his supporters called themselves El Muwahhidoun ('unitarians') – and hence their European name, the Almohads.

Ibn Toumart died in 1130 but his right-hand man, Abdel Moumen, kept up his work. Tin Mal proved a good base, as the Almoravids' strength was in cavalry, and horses couldn't get up here. In 1144 Abdel Moumen laid siege to Marrakech and went on to conquer the rest of Morocco, most of North Africa and much of Spain. Back here, in 1153, they used some of the loot to build the mosque that stands today. It was modelled after that of Tata, near Fès, and in turn provided the prototype for the Koutoubia in Marrakech, almost certainly built by the same craftsmen.

Tin Mal was a monument to Ibn Toumart and his doctrines. It also accommodated his tomb and that of other Almohad leaders. When the dynasty fell in the mid 13th century, Tin Mal was their last line of defence. It was taken by the Merenids in 1276, but even after that remained a place a pilgrimage. When the French turned up centuries later, the crumbling remnants of the mosque were home to a strange cult that worshipped the Stone of Sidi Wegweg.

Restoration had to wait until the 1990s, and has proceeded with funds raised in Morocco. There is no roof but the framework of sandy-coloured transverse arches is complete, offering receding perspectives of light and shade. For the non-Muslim visitor it's a rare chance to see inside a Moroccan mosque, but note that the minaret is almost never above the mirhab, as it is here. Normally it's over on the north wall, rather than the one facing east towards Mecca; no one knows why it's any different at Tin Mal.

# Argan oil

Goats clambering about in argan trees is part of the tourist mythology of south-western Morocco. The strangest thing is, you might even see it – and you certainly won't see it anywhere else. Round here grow the only argan trees in the world. A botanical relic from a remote, more tropical time, the argan is a fussy sort. The region where it consents to flourish – inland from the Atlantic coast between Essaouira and Sidi Ifni – has been declared a UNESCO Biosphere Reserve.

Spiny and knotted, argan trees look similar to olive trees. Like olive trees, they also bear a fruit from which oil can be extracted. And this is where the goats come in. Some are allowed to graze in the trees, others are fed the fruits after they've been harvested in May or June. The goat's digestive system is how the tough, elastic fruit is stripped from the useful but recalcitrant nut. Yes, the nuts are collected from goat droppings. They are then split, toasted, pulped, pressed – and it takes 30kg of them to make just one litre of argan oil. Translated into goat dung this just doesn't bear thinking about.

After all that, you'd better believe the product is highly prized. Berbers have long used the orange-brown oil to help heal scars and ease rheumatic pain. Rich in vitamin E, it's good for the skin and has become a staple of Moroccan massage and beauty treatments. You can also get argan soap.

Modern research has pronounced the efficacy of argan oil in reducing cholesterol and countering arteriosclerosis. Taken internally it also proves to be very tasty indeed – sweet and rich, great on its own for drizzlings or bread-dunking. Useful as conversation piece as well as exotic ingredient, it's the perfect gift for a foodie friend. But argan's no bargain: expect to pay around 150dh per litre; *see p122* **The souk for dummies**.

Resourceful locals have also found one other use for the argan tree. In areas where tourists might wander by, kids hover near specimens with grazing goats. When the cameras come out, the kids demand a few dirhams – or they'll knock all the goats from the branches.

The snaking **Tiz-n-Test** pass.

The precise future of the site is uncertain. Maybe it will become a museum, maybe a mosque, maybe some combination of the two and maybe it will stay exactly as it is – on our recent visit we noticed nothing different from when we last stopped by in 2001. The roofless structure is currently used for prayers on Friday, which is the one day you can't visit. Tip the attendant with the key, who might point out the owl's nest, high overhead among the stalactite vaulting. But there isn't so much as a postcard on sale, and absolutely no information about anything.

## The Tizi-n-Test

The pass (2,092 metres) is about 40 kilometres (25 miles) beyond Ijoujak. The final stretch is beautiful as the road curls up to the heights, and then suddenly reveals the most amazing view across the plain of the Sous to the south. There's a small café on the pass where you can stop and enjoy the panorama, as well as the view back towards Toubkal.

On the other side, the road loses height recklessly, descending 1,600 metres in little over 30 kilometres (18 miles). The twists and loops aren't too dangerous, but this is not a stretch to hurry. Take your time and enjoy the views that continue to present themselves until shortly before the road joins the P32, the main east–west route across southern Morocco, for the final run across the prosperous farmland of the Sous valley and into Taroudant.

## Taroudant

Enclosed by reddish ramparts, with a backdrop of the High Atlas, commanding the trade routes across a plain, kitted out with souks – Taroudant is often considered to be a kind of junior Marrakech. It has its pretensions. For a couple of decades in the early 16th century it was the Saadian capital. They, and the gold they hauled up through the Sahara, built the well-preserved *pisé* walls which remain the town's most prominent feature. Later the Roudanis, as the inhabitants are called, joined a rebellion against Moulay Ismail. In 1787 Ismail took the town, destroyed the Saadian palaces, slaughtered the locals, and brought in a whole new Berber population from the Rif.

He left behind his own fortress – what is now the kasbah, one of the town's poorest and most crowded quarters – and the walls. A ride around their crenellated five-kilometre (three-mile) circumference – either on a horse-drawn *calèche* (from outside the Hotel Palais Salam, about 50dh per hour) or by bicycle (there's a little place on avenue Mohammed V, just east of place Assareg, that rents them for 10dh per hour) – is just about Taroudant's only standard tourist activity. On the way, you can look at the foul-smelling tanneries, on the western side, outside Bab Targhount.

There are two souks: the **Marché Berbère**, where the locals buy groceries; and the **Arab Souk**, more focused on traditional crafts. Local guides may show you an ancient fundouk 'used in the French film *Ali Baba*' (we've never heard of it either) or lead you to one of the local sculptors who work with limestone. It's also a good place to buy Berber jewellery.

The Arab Souk is west of **place Assareg**, the town's main square. Settling at one of its cafés and watching the laid-back daily life of this modest pre-Saharan market town, you realise that really it's nothing much like Marrakech at all.

### WHERE TO STAY

The **Hotel Palais Salam** (048 85 25 01, fax 048 85 25 54, pasalam@agadirnet.net.ma, from 1,250dh a double) is in a 19th-century palace, built into the ramparts of the Kasbah quarter, that was formerly the governor's residence. It's certainly the best hotel in town, has three restaurants and is the only place to get a beer, but it's a little cheesy in places – there's piped music by a swimming pool shaped like a Moroccan horseshoe arch.

A couple of kilometres out of town is the **Gazelle d'Or** (048 85 20 39, fax 048 85 26 54, www.gazelledor.com, from 2,250dh per person half board). It was built in 1961 as a Belgian baron's hunting lodge and has been a hotel since 1972. There are 30 grand bungalows set in enormous grounds, with tennis, croquet, a pool and its own organic farm. Exorbitant rates include dinner at what is considered one of the finest restaurants in Morocco (jacket required).

Taroudant's best budget beds are at the **Hotel Taroudant** (place Assareg, 048 85 24 16, 500dh double), a fading institution with a flavour of French colonial times.

# The Ourika Valley

It doesn't go anywhere, but it's Marrakech's favourite day out.

The vehicle park at the **Tnine de l'Ourika** weekly market.

Ourika is a spectacular cut deep into the High Atlas and an easy way to get a taste of mountain air. It's not a pass – the road stops at Setti Fatma, 63 kilometres (39 miles) from Marrakech – and unless you're interested in skiing or trekking it's more of a day trip than a fully fledged excursion. Marrakchis nip up here for a break from oppressive summer heat. But there are places to stay if you want to experience the peace of the valley after the daytime traffic has all gone home. And at the far end of the turn-off to Oukaimeden there is Morocco's best skiing.

Buses and *grand taxis* leave from outside Marrakech's Bab Er Rob. Make sure you're getting one that goes all the way to Setti Fatma, as most of the local traffic heads only as far as the larger village of Arhbalou, 24 kilometres (15 miles) short. The journey takes about two hours. Buses head to Oukaimeden in winter. If you want to go there at another time of year and don't have your own transport, you'll have to charter a taxi from Marrakech, although it might also be possible to find one in Arhbalou.

## To Arhbalou

The route d'Ourika begins at the fountain roundabout of Bab Jedid, by the Mamounia Hotel. The road follows that stretch of the walls which encloses the Agdal Gardens before crossing 34 kilometres (21 miles) of monotonous agricultural flatland.

There are two possible side excursions. **Aghmat** was the first Almoravid capital of the region. It is now a small village among olive groves and plant nurseries, and has a 1960s mausoleum dedicated to Youssef Ibn Tachfine, founder of Marrakech. The other is **Tnine de l'Ourika**, which has a Monday souk.

Beyond here, Berber villages cling to steep valley sides, camouflaged against a red-earth backdrop that forms a brilliant contrast with the deep, luminous greens of the valley floor and cultivated terraces. Terracotta pottery, made from this local earth, is on sale at stalls all along the road, sometimes shaped as a wild boar, a local speciality.

Prickly native plant life.

reached by footbridges made of bundled branches (tourists pick their way across these with trepidation; locals spring over them like mountain goats) – are a number of small tajine and brochette joints. Concealed behind these cafés is a steep side valley, and a climb up it will bring you to the first of the seven cascades. It's quite a strenuous scramble, over big river boulders and up a cliff or two. Anyone will point (or lead) the way, and there's a basic café at the foot of the first waterfall where you can rest with a cool drink. The other six are a more serious climb.

There is some rudimentary accommodation. **La Perle d'Ourika** (061 56 73 29, 120dh double), south of the main village, is friendly and about as stylish as it gets up here. The **Hotel Asgaour** (066 41 64 19, 70dh-150dh double) in the village proper has 20 basic rooms, some with shower, overlooking the river.

There's nothing much at Arhbalou, except for the turn-off to Oukaimeden (*see below*). On the stretch beyond it, there are a few decent hotels which also double as lunch spots, notably the French-owned **Auberge le Maquis** (044 48 45 31, www.le-maquis.com), just before the roadside settlement of Oulmès (no relation to the fizzy water), and **Ramuntcho** (044 44 45 21), which has a wonderful terrace and a salon de thé perfect for an after-lunch nap.

## Setti Fatma

After a final gorge-like stretch, with cafés and houses along the opposite bank reached by perilous-looking rope bridges, the road peters out at Setti Fatma. The village is nothing special – lots of cafés and souvenir shops, with satellite dishes on breeze-block houses – but the setting is wonderful, ringed by mountains with lots of streams and grassy terraces. If you arrive in mid August there's a big four-day *moussem* that's both religious occasion and sociable fair. The village also has a bureau de guides (near the Hotel Asgaour) where you can arrange an assortment of treks and hikes.

The shortest and simplest hike is the **Walk of the Seven Waterfalls**. On the other side of the river from the main body of the village –

## Oukaimeden

The road up here hairpins all the way from the valley, though in a fairly gentle fashion, rising eventually to 2,650m. This is Morocco's best ski resort, though conditions are unreliable. The season runs from December to May but snow is most likely to be found between February and April. Casablancans scurry down here at the first hint of it. These are not slopes for beginners – the snow is often icy and the runs are steep – but anyone can go up the ski lift, once the highest in the world and still, at 3,273 metres, the highest in Africa. It's not always in operation, though. Ski equipment can be hired at any of several shops and hotels.

The area's other attraction is the **prehistoric rock carvings** – of animals, weapons, battle scenes, and symbols with forgotten meanings – that can be found nearby with the help of a guide. Look for the book *Gravures Rupestres du Haut Atlas* by Susan Searight and Danièle Hourbette, which might be on sale at the CAF Réfuge or in Marrakech.

The **CAF Réfuge** (044 31 90 36, www.cafmaroc.co.ma, 130dh double) has both dorm beds and private rooms, and is a good place to find guides and check out trekking possibilities. The **Hotel de L'Angour** (044 31 90 05, 340dh half-board) has a decent bar and restaurant, clean rooms and hot showers.

In summer, the area below the village becomes what is known as an alpine prairie. The pastures are opened on 10 August, and after that become crowded with Berber tents and livestock, each tribe sticking to its own, traditional area. Compared to the ski resort, it's a scene not just from another season, but from another age.

# Tizi-n-Tichka to Ouarzazate

Over the High Atlas for the 'Gateway to the Sahara' – and its pharaonic monuments.

Running south-east out of Marrakech the P31 courses across the plain, then cuts into the High Atlas to snake spectacularly over the range's loftiest pass – the Tizi-n-Tichka. It then descends into the arid pre-Sahara and down to Ouarzazate, rightly considered to be the gateway to the desert, as well as being the centre of Morocco's film industry. Along the way, there are interesting side trips to the kasbahs of Telouet and Aït Benhaddou.

It's only 196 kilometres (122 miles) to Ouarzazate, and it's a decent road, originally built by the French Foreign Legion in 1931 and recently improved. But the mountains demand respect so leave a good four hours for the journey – longer if you stop at Telouet or Aït Benhaddou. And if you're not in a hurry, there are places to stay on the way.

There are several Ouarzazate buses daily from Marrakech's *gare routière*. Journey time is about four hours. One bus a day leaves Bab Ghemat (*see* map p255 F6) in Marrakech for Telouet in the early afternoon; the return journey is at 7am, but to reach Aït Benhaddou by public transport it's necessary to go to Ouarzazate and then backtrack.

## The Tizi-n-Tichka

About 50 kilometres (31 miles) south-east of Marrakech, the road begins to climb into the mountains. It's a spine-tingling journey, each bend revealing a new panorama. On the way

up, the fertile slopes are shrouded in forest or terraced for cultivation, and Berber villages can be seen clinging to vertiginous gradients. The mountains here are full of semi-precious stones and roadside sellers angle melon-sized geodes, broken in half, to show you the glittering light reflected by the red or green crystals within. A closer look reveals that some have been painted to appear more vivid for the passing motorist.

There are various places to take a breather. About 15 kilometres (nine miles) before the pass, the village of **Taddert** is the busiest halt. It's divided into two parts; the higher of the two has a better choice of cafés, some of which overlook the valley below. A barrier is lowered here when the pass is closed, and this is where the snow plough is garaged.

Beyond Taddert it's all much more barren and the road gets quite hairy in places – looping and twisting and running along the knife's edge of exposed ridges. Small shops selling minerals and fossils are perched in some seemingly impossible places. There's a point where you can stop and look back down over the hairpins you have just ascended.

The pass, at 2,260 metres (7,415 feet), is reached with little fanfare. There are a couple of masts and a few more stalls selling rocks. Beyond it there's an immediate and dramatic change to a more arid landscape, leaving little doubt that the desert is where you're headed. The turn-off to Telouet is just a few kilometres further on the left.

Ruined roadside kasbah.

Ait Benhaddou. *See p205.*

## Telouet

The village and kasbah of Telouet are a 21-kilometre (13 mile) detour deep into the remote heart of the mountains. Scattered settlements hang between barren peaks and luminous green valleys. In spring there is almond blossom everywhere. Kestrels and vultures weave in the blue skies above. The village of Telouet is tiny, dominated, as is the whole valley, by the slowly crumbling kasbah of the Glaoui clan.

For centuries, before the French built the Tichka road, this was the southern side of the main pass over the High Atlas. In the late 19th century, control of that pass was in the hands of the Glaoui clan – one of three tribes that dominated the ungovernable south of Morocco. After coming to national prominence following their assistance to Sultan Moulay Hassan in 1893, the Glaoua greatly expanded this kasbah, which remained their stronghold and last line of defence. However, while Thami El Glaoui (*see p206* **Glaoua power**), as ruler of Marrakech, ran the South on behalf of the Protectorate, the kasbah passed into control of his obstinately anti-French in-law Hammou. This was enough to stall French 'pacification' of the South until the 1930s, and they built the Tichka road, following a much trickier route, simply to avoid the fortress. It was abandoned upon Thami El Glaoui's death, in 1956. There have been several failed attempts to rescue the kasbah – all foiled by complicated inheritance

laws, which mean the site is jointly owned by all the descendants of the Glaoui whose myriad permissions would need to be sought before any transfer of ownership could be made.

The **kasbah** is reached by following the road around the edge of the village. Entry is by donation (maybe 10dh-20dh) and someone will appear with a bunch of keys to let you in and show you around. After lying empty for half a century, much of the fortress is in advanced disrepair and out of bounds for safety reasons. The main thing to see is the reception hall, built in 1942 and, alongside the ornately traditional decoration in cedarwood, stucco and mosaic, equipped with sockets for electric appliances – odd, among such apparently medieval surrounds. At the end of the hall is a delicate iron window grille that frames a commanding view of the valley below. You can also climb up steep, dark stairs to a terrace that offers a sense of the whole picturesquely decaying structure, its towers inhabited only by storks.

### WHERE TO STAY & EAT

Right by the kasbah, the pocket-sized **Lion d'Or** (044 88 85 07, 150dh double) has a handful of basic rooms. The **Auberge Restaurant Telouet** (044 89 07 17, www.telouet.com, 200dh-260dh double), which overlooks the kasbah from further back down the road, is marginally more sophisticated, and has a Berber-tented dining area (menus 60dh-80dh) across the road.

But if you want to overnight or linger in these parts, by far the nicest place is **Irocha** (067 73 70 02, www.irocha.com, 650dh double incl dinner). This small *maison d'hôte* is in a quiet spot, perched above the P31 (from which it's well signposted) at Tisselday, half way between the Telouet turn-off and Aït Benhaddou. The simple rooms, all but two surrounding a quiet courtyard, have tasteful touches, nice rugs and en suite showers. There's also a terrace overlooking the green valley floor and a dining room with generous windows, some interesting old books, and a few decent CDs. It's a friendly place and we hear the food is good too.

## Aït Benhaddou

If you have a 4X4 and about seven hours to spare, it's possible to go from Telouet to Aït Benhaddou via Anmiter (last stop for buses) and 36 kilometres (22 miles) of rough piste down what used to be the main route through this area. Sticking with the main P31, the turn-off for Aït Benhaddou is 11 kilometres (seven miles) south of the hamlet of Amerzgane (itself 50 kilometres south of the turn-off for Telouet). If you're already exhausted from your trip over the pass, it may make more sense to do Aït Benhaddou as a backtracking day trip from Ouarzazte (24 kilometres, or 14 miles, south), or as a last sight on the way back to Marrakech.

Whichever, it shouldn't be missed. The fortified village and cluster of kasbahs is one of the most striking and best preserved in southern Morocco, appearing to tumble down a slope above the Oued Mellah. It's also probably the most famous, used as a location in David Lean's *Lawrence of Arabia*, Robert Aldrich's *Sodom and Gomorrah*, Franco Zeffirelli's *Jesus of Nazareth* and Ridley Scott's *Gladiator*. But the film and tourist industries have only slowed Aït Benhaddou's decline from the importance it formerly had for its position on the old Saharan caravan route. The population is dwindling and the village is now under UNESCO protection.

The road brings you to the far side of the river, where there is a cluster of hotels, cafés and souvenir shops. In spring it can be necessary to paddle (or occasionally wade) through water across the ford. Locals will inevitably appear to guide you over the stepping stones or through the passages and stairways of the village. The owner of the principal kasbah, said to be 400 years old though no one really knows how long Aït Benhaddou has been here, charges 5dh to let you see the view from his terrace. The ancient fortified granary at the top of the complex is also worth the uphill clamber.

There's another intact kasbah 10 kilometres (six miles) up the road at Tamdaght. It's not as beguiling as Aït Benhaddou, but then it's not as full of tourists either. Beyond there you need a 4X4 to follow the piste up to Telouet.

### WHERE TO STAY & EAT
The cluster of business on the other side of the river testify to the importance of Aït Benhaddou on the tourist route, if no longer on the trade route. There isn't much reason to hang about but if you do want to stay then the **Hotel la Kasbah** (044 89 03 02, 200dh-500dh double incl breakfast) has a pool, a hammam (50dh) and, in some of the more expensive rooms, air-conditioning. Across the road, the **Auberge El Ouidane** is now an annexe of la Kasbah, where you can lunch on a roof terrace with a view across the river. Even if you don't have time to visit Aït Benhaddou proper, it's worthwhile pausing up here. Try the spicy Berber omelette.

## Ouarzazate

Pronounced 'wa-zar-zat', this doggedly unpicturesque town sits in prime position where the Dades and Drâa valleys fork off from the High Atlas route, and where the route de Taroudant winds in from the west.

It was founded by the French in 1928 as a regional capital and Foreign Legion outpost and still retains both a garrison and a drably functional air, with concrete buildings all along avenue Mohammed V, its one main street. Film industry folk like Ouarzazate for its five-star facilities and backpackers are increasingly drawn by the range of activity tourism on offer, but few others will find much cause to linger. On the other hand, its size and strategic position as gateway to the Sahara means that if travelling in the South you're almost bound to end up spending a night here sooner or later.

The mid 18th-century **Taouirt Kasbah** (8am-6pm daily, admission 10dh), at the eastern end of town, is Ouarzazate's one historical sight and the only thing remaining from before the Protectorate. During the 1930s, when the Glaoua were at their prime, this was one of the largest kasbahs in the area, housing lots of the clan's lesser known members, plus hundreds of servants and slaves. These days much is ruined, although some is being restored under UNESCO auspices. A big section is still inhabited. The part that faces the main road has been maintained, and this is what gets shown to visitors – the principal courtyard, the former harem, and a few other rooms around a central airwell. Some of the town's poorest inhabitants live in the area behind it, and here you can wander freely if you don't mind being hassled for dirhams or acquiring a small entourage of would-be guides.

Opposite the kasbah entrance is the **Ensemble Artisanal** (open 9am-noon, 2.30-6pm daily), a cluster of stalls and shops selling fixed-price arts and crafts, such as pottery, stone carvings, woollen carpets and jewellery.

**Tiffoultoute** (open 8am-7pm) is another Glaoui kasbah, just outside town on the by-pass (head back towards Marrakech, then turn left at the roundabout). Well preserved and dramatically located between the river and a *palmeraie*, these days it offers a restaurant and accommodation for tour groups.

The other face of Ouarzazate is its connection to the film industry, which dates back to David Lean shooting some of *Lawrence of Arabia* around here. Bertolucci's *The Sheltering Sky*,

Martin Scorsese's *Kundun*, the French production of *Asterix & Obélix Mission Cleopatra* and Ridley Scott's *Gladiator* have been among the other films to make use of the area's good light, cheap labour and variety of mountain and desert locations. But it's a up-and-down business disrupted by relations between the US and the Islamic world. Wolfgang Petersen's *Troy* was going to shoot here, for example, but relocated to Mexico because of the Iraq invasion.

The **Atlas Corporation Studios** (044 88 21 66, www.atlasstudios.com, open 8am-6pm daily, admission 30dh), seven kilometres (four miles) west of town, were built in the early 1980s to provide some infrastructure for the industry. The studios can be toured when there's no filming, which is most of the time. You can look at the Tibetan monastery built for *Kundun*, a

# Glaoua power

When the French first encountered Thami El Glaoui in the early 20th century, he was little more than an uncouth tribal warlord with a mountain base in Telouet. Installing him as boss of Marrakech in 1912, the French seemed to take the view that he might be a ruthless despot, but at least he was their ruthless despot.

European society took a similar tack. Although at first he didn't speak a word of French, within 20 years 'the Glaoui' had become one of the most fashionable names to drop, imbued with all the mystique and exoticism of an Indian maharajah. While his political enemies rotted in dungeons below the opulent Dar El Bacha, and his nephew-in-law Hammou ran Telouet as if medieval was going out of style, the Glaoui threw sumptuous banquets and lavished gifts on international guests – maybe a diamond ring, maybe a cute Berber boy or girl. While his subjects went hungry, the Glaoui diverted water from farmland to maintain an 18-hole golf course.

Europeans were less appalled by the Glaoui's excesses than they were suckered by his immaculate manners, generosity and *bons mots*. At one famous dinner party, the Glaoui overheard a young Parisian woman – who thought he understood no French – call him a pig, but admit to coveting his emerald ring. At the end of the meal, the Glaoui pulled her aside and said, in immaculate French, 'Madame, a stone like this emerald was

never made for a pig like me. Permit me to offer it to you'. His comment on the French war minister, Daladier, was often quoted: 'He is like a dog without a tail – there is no way to tell what he is thinking.'

His refined exterior hid a voracious sexual appetite. His enormous harem – 96 women at his brother Madani's death in 1918, from whose harem he poached a further 54 – wasn't distraction enough and he put great effort into the pursuit of European women. A network of talent scouts scoured Morocco for likely conquests. White-skinned *belles* would be invited by aides to tour the palace. If they took his fancy, the Glaoui would make a 'surprise' appearance and invite them to dinner – and further seductions. But as sophisticated as he made himself out to be, he was not always hip to European sexual practices. Once he threw a woman out of his bedroom in horror, screaming, 'She tried to eat me!'

Up in Telouet, Hammou's idea of a party was different. In 1931, three years before his death, he threw a huge banquet for Moroccan and French dignitaries. The guests were alarmed at the sound of fusillade after fusillade being fired outside. The kasbah had been surrounded by several thousand of Hammou's mounted warriors, and as the 'folkloric' demonstration began, he announced that he would like to see all Frenchmen in the country dead. Thami must have been mortified.

fighter plane made for *Jewel of the Nile*, a fake medina alley and Egyptian temple sets from the Asterix movie. It all has a run-down air. There's another studio complex a little further out of town, but this one is closed to the public.

### WHERE TO STAY

Ouarzazate has hotels for all budgets but a preponderance of four- and five-star places geared to the package tourist. **Dar Daif** (3km off the Zagora road, 044 85 42 32, fax 044 85 40 75, www.dardaif.ma, 830dh double incl dinner) is one of the few *maisons d'hôtes*. It's in a converted kasbah on the tatty outskirts, with 12 rooms and a 'typical Sahara' theme that seems a bit prissy after a spell in the actual desert. Still, the hammam is welcome and there's also a pool. No alcohol, though, and beware of stubbing your toe on the tiled bed bases, same colour and material as the surrounding floors.

The 234-room **Berbère Palace** (Quartier Mansour Eddahbi, 044 88 31 05, fax 044 88 30 71, mberpala@iam.net, 1,800dh-3,200dh double, breakfast 130dh) is our pick of the three big five-stars, with air-conditioned bungalows, a big pool, hammam, jacuzzi, tennis courts and even a small football pitch. The **Riad Salam** (avenue Mohammed V, 044 88 33 35, fax 044 88 27 66, www.salamhotelmaroc.com, 450dh-700dh double, breakfast 70dh) is comfortable with rooms in two price brackets. The same chain also has a branch at the film studios (Oscar Salam, 044 88 22 12, fax 044, 88 21 80, 450dh double, breakfast 70dh). The **Hotel Bab Sahara** (place El Mouahidine, 044 88 47 22, 130dh double) offers basic budget beds on a busy central square; it's also local HQ for the US Peace Corps.

### WHERE TO EAT & DRINK

Ouarzazate's relatively cosmopolitan dining doesn't seem much on the way out from Marrakech, but feels like heaven on the way back from too much couscous in the Sahara. **Chez Dimitri** (22 avenue Mohammed V, 044 88 73 46, average 150dh) is a Ouarzazate institution, founded in 1928 and serving French, Italian and Greek dishes as well as Moroccan. The new **Relais Saint Exupéry** (13 boulevard Moulay Abdellah, 044 88 77 79, average 250dh) offers upmarket French dining in aviation-themed surrounds. **Pizzeria Venezia** (avenue Moulay Rachid, 044 88 24 58, average 70dh-100dh) has decent pizzas and the next-door **Obélix** (044 88 71 17, average 120dh) serves Moroccan and international dishes in an atmosphere of high kitsch, with props from *The Mummy* and *Gladiator*. The nearby **Datte d'Or** (044 88 71 17, menus 90dh-110dh) is cosy and has reasonable set menus.

**Atlas Corporation Studios**. *See p206.*

# The Dadès Valley & the Gorges

The long run east to Er Rachidia is enlivened by gorgeous gorges, birding opportunities and some strange collectives.

Stretching east from Ouarzazate, the Dadès Valley runs between the High Atlas to the north and the bare, jagged formations of the Jebel Sarho to the south. It's sometimes referred to as the Valley of the Kasbahs, which is appropriate enough – there are dozens of them – even if the title could equally well apply to the Drâa Valley south of Ouarzazate. Anyway, just about every valley around here is supposed to be the Valley of Something Or Other.

The Dadès is also the most barren of the southern valleys, but the juxtaposition with such rugged surrounds just makes the oases seem all the more beautiful. North of the main road, from Boumalne du Dadès and Tinerhir respectively, are the gorges of Dadès and Todra, dramatic cuts into the Atlas that are well worth detouring for.

Skoura, which is at the westernmost end of the Dadès Valley can be done in a day trip from Ouarzazate. The Dadès Gorge, too. But trying to pack in the Todra Gorge as well is pushing it. There's decent accommodation along the route, and all this can be done with overnight stops on the way to the Tafilelt (*see p213*).

Infrequent buses run along the main road and *grand taxis* shuttle between the bigger towns. If you don't have your own transport and want to visit the gorges, you can commandeer taxis at Boumalne or Tinerhir, and hotels can also arrange transport. But this is an area where it really does make sense to have a 4x4 to explore a little of the Atlas beyond the various valleys or gorges, or to detour into the strange, sculpted landscapes of the Jebel Sarho.

## Skoura

About 40 kilometres (25 miles) east of Ouarzazate, Skoura is a big oasis but a small settlement. The main road bypasses what there is of the town centre – just one street with a few basic shops, a couple of down-at-heel cafés and signs pointing to a women's goat's cheese cooperative. Most of the population is scattered about the extensive oasis, which is beautiful, and liberally sprinkled with kasbahs. If you

want to explore some of these, it's worth considering a guide for the day, most easily arranged through your hotel.

One of the kasbahs, on the far side of the oued from the road, to the west of the centre behind Kasbah Ben Moro (see below), is the famous **Amridil** (open dawn-sunset daily, admission 10dh) which features on both the 50-dirham note and on the packaging (they proudly display an example) of Marrakesh Orange Juice. Built by a Middle Atlas tribe in the 17th century, it's now slowly being restored with local labour and foreign donations. Resident guide Aziz Sadikln brings everything to life with humour as he shows you around. Aziz can also do a tour of the oasis; call him on 064 91 45 53.

Another dramatic old kasbah, **Dar Aït Sidi El Mati**, is ten minutes' walk to the south-west of Amridil. And if you're still not kasbah'd out after that there are plenty of others, including ones you can stay in.

The road that heads north out of Skoura up to the village of **Toundoute** is a beautiful drive through what's known locally as the Vallée des Amandes (Valley of the Almonds).

### WHERE TO STAY AND EAT
**Kasbah Ben Moro** (044 85 21 16, hotelben moro@yahoo.fr, 650dh double) is on the Ouarzazate road, two kilometres (1.2 miles) before Skoura proper. It was founded by a Spanish exile in the 18th century and in 2000 turned into a modern 16-room hotel by a Spanish expat from Cadiz. The rooms are cosy but dark – but that's a kasbah for you. Breakfast is an extra 40dh and there's a 150dh lunch or dinner menu.

The stubbornly luxurious **Dar Ahlam** (044 85 22 39, www.lamaisondesreves.com, double 7,900dh) is the kasbah as designer labyrinth – the ground floor is a maze of corridors and salons – artfully exploited each evening. The gag is that you find your way from one of nine tasteful suites or three garden villas to the enormous lounge, then they escort you to where you'll eat dinner – somewhere different from the

Motion-sickness tablets are advisable for those with weak stomachs.

evening before, with different place settings, different food, different live music drifting from somewhere nearby. The kitchen is simply excellent, as it would have to be at these prices. Also thrown in is a gorgeous hammam, professional masseur, pool, three small libraries and use of a 4x4 and experienced guide (the price drops to 6,300 if you forgo the car and guide). The hotel makes its own luxurious soap and you can enjoy this in bathtubs big enough for two, or buy some to take home at their small but interesting shop.

The friendly, family-run **Gîte Tiriguioute** (044 85 20 68, bouarif_elhachmi@hotmail.com, 500dh double inc dinner), three kilometres (two miles) out of town, is the nearest thing to a budget option.

There isn't really anwhere to eat outside of the hotels, but if pushed then **Café Atlas** is probably the best place on the lone main street.

## El Kelaa M'Gouna

Fifty barren kilometres (30 miles) east of Skoura, oasis resumes at El Kelaa, which ribbons along the main road. It's famous for its rose products. All over the country, women rub rosewater into their face and hands, and most of it comes from here. It seems the most Moroccan of things, yet it was French perfumiers who, in the early 20th century, realise that round here were ideal growing conditions for the leafy rosa centifolia. You'd barely notice them among the palms when they're not blooming, but there are hundreds of thousands of rose bushes around here. The harvest is in May, towards the end of which there's a rose festival with dances, processions and lots of petal-throwing.

Essences are distilled at two factories and every other shop sells rose soap, rose skin cream, rose shampoo, rose shower gel and, of

Official camel stop.

course, rosewater. It's not otherwise a very interesting place, though there's also a dagger-making cooperative.

With a 4x4 you can drive north towards **Tourbist** through what's known, naturally, as the Vallée des Roses (Valley of the Roses). From here you can follow piste around to the top of the Dadès Gorge.

There's not much reason to linger around El Kelaa, but the old-school **Hotel les Roses** (044 83 63 36, fax 044 83 60 07, 320dh double) up by an old kasbah is a three-star with 102 rooms, good views, a pool, the town's only bar and a bit of faded grandeur.

## Dadès Gorge

Leaving El Kelaa and continuing east, ribbon development lines the road to Dadès for another 20 kilometres (12 miles) or so, with kasbahs left to crumble among new buildings that are made from concrete rather than *pisé*. There's not much of interest at the next major settlement, that of **Boumalne Dadès**, but it does mark the mouth of the Dadès Gorge.

The drive into the gorge is not for those of a nervous disposition. The road swoops and twists, climbing high up the steep valley sides through curvaceous formations of red rock and past clusters of kasbahs on rugged outcrops. The valley is at its most dramatic and gorge-like after the village of Aït Oudinar, about 27

kilometres (17 miles) along, where it turns into a deep, reddish canyon – though only for a couple of hundred yards.

It's a good road up to this point, but from here it gets more difficult. You'll need a 4x4 to proceed beyond Msemrir, but could then take the spectacular piste that runs east over the mountains to Aït Hani, whence you can come back down through Todra. This is also excellent hiking territory, and any can hotel can arrange guides and excursions.

Back on the main Dadès Valley road, just east of Boumalne Dadès is the turning for the **Vallée des Oiseaux** (Valley of the Birds), signposted to **Ikniouin**. Here amateur ornithologists can spot Houbara bustards, Egyptian vultures, eagle owls and bar-tailed desert larks.

### WHERE TO STAY AND EAT

Clambering up the steep valley side shortly before the canyon, **Chez Pierre** (044 83 02 67, chezpierre@menara.ma, 520dh double) is the most sophisticated option for either sleeping or eating. It's Belgian-run and has eight simple, spacious rooms, a small pool and a restaurant serving excellent food that includes vegetarian options. A little further up but still south of the canyon, **La Kasbah de la Vallée** (tel/fax 044 83 17 17, 400dh double) is big and friendly, with rooms in varying configurations, as well as a much-appreciated alcohol licence.

Just on the other (north) side of the canyon is the **Berbére de la Montagne** (044 83 02 28, 280dh-560dh double inc dinner), which has six rooms with showers and four without. All are well furnished.

Back down towards Boumalne, the **Kasbah Aït Arbi** (044 83 17 23, fax 044 83 01 31, 70dh-140dh double) in the hamlet of the same name is the star budget option. The cheaper rooms are on the roof with wonderful views, but the showers are two floors below (the other rooms have their own). There are also good trekking options at this lower end of the gorge.

Off to the left as the road east leaves Boumalne, **Le Soleil Bleu** (044 83 01 63, fax 044 83 03 94, www.soleilbleu.com, 200dh-250dh double) is a good, basic hotel overlooking the town. It's popular with birdwatchers, and the visitors' books record what they've spotted.

## Tinerhir

There's another desolate stretch beyond Boumalne, but after about 50km (30 miles) the road arrives in Tinerhir, the most interesting town on this road. The new part of it ribbons east and west along the road; the old part stretches out in huge kasbah-dotted palmeraies to the north and south. There's a pocket-sized Medina where you can find rug-weavers from the Aït Atta tribe at work on their looms. The carpets these women make are brilliantly coloured and of high quality, but you'll need an interpreter to negotiate as few speak anything but Berber. The main street is called the rue des Femmes because it mostly sells kaftans and suchlike. There are also lots of spice merchants. The small, gloomy Mellah on the far side of the Medina, closed off behind a big wooden door, is these days occupied by about 20 Berber families.

The modern part of town has all mod cons – post office, banks, cybercafés, and a small supermarket that sells beer, wine and spirits. It's on the south side of the main road, between Kasbah Lamrani and the old centre. Opposite Kasbah Lamrani is where you'll find Tinerhir's Monday souk.

### WHERE TO STAY AND EAT

**Kasbah Lamrani** (044 83 50 17, fax 044 83 50 27, www.kasbah-lamrani.com, 500dh double) has 22 rooms kitted with air-conditioning, heating, telephones, fridges, TVs and nice bathrooms. There's also a pool and three restaurants. It's all slightly Disneyfied, but that's common in mid-range places in these parts, and this hotel is very well-run. The **Hotel Todra** (avenue Hassan II, 044 83 42 49, fax 044 83 45 65, 150dh-250dh double) is well-placed for exploring the Medina, and is atmospherically old-school with lots of dark

# Family silver

In the southern oases, Berber women swathe themselves in metres of fine, black fabric and, no matter how menial their work, wear heavy and often beautiful silver jewellery. This has a different significance than in the West. Jewellery isn't just decoration, but a way of saving, an integral part of a family's capital. A piece or two might be sold off in times of drought, or to acquire animals or land. And thus women act as the family banker.

A woman's jewellery collection is begun in childhood, greatly increased at the time of her marriage, and added to whenever the men of the family have some spare money. Old pieces aren't prized. Berber women like to wear stuff that has been made for them personally, and inherited jewellery often goes back to the smith to be melted down and reworked. This is why you rarely see antiques, even though some techniques still used are ancient, dating back to Carthiginian times. And anyway, jewellery is bought and sold by weight, not workmanship. Also, in the past,

many of the jewellers were Jewish, and the traditions of craftmanship were broken with the exodus of the 1950s and 1960s. That and rising precious-metal prices means that newer work tends to be lighter and flashier, with less delicate effects.

Berbers prefer silver to gold, enriched with enamel, engraving or semi-precious stones with colour-coded symbolic significance. It's very different from the more delicate gold jewellery worn by the Arab women of urban Morocco. But while Berber women are often loaded with a remarkable quantity of necklaces and earrings, bracelets and rings, amulets and fibulas, the men wear very little. Just rings and, these days, maybe watches. Still, they traditionally wore ornate daggers; guns and powder flasks were often beautifully inlaid; and sometimes finely worked Koran cases were wound bound to turbans. You can see or buy versions of all these things in the jewellery souks and on souvenir stalls.

**Trips Out of Town**

# Berber dictionary

In any tourist economy, locals have their little jokes for the visitor. They're the common currency of cross-cultural exchange, designed to throw light upon their traditions, foster international understanding, affirm shared humanity through the precious gift of laughter – and sell you some useless damn thing you don't need. The gag in southern Morocco is to translate the function of everyday items into terms the foreigner will understand. Once you've wandered around a few souks and kasbahs, you'll have heard all these a dozen times. No harm, though, in being ahead of the game.

**Berber massage** Sex.
**Berber Mercedes** A donkey. See also Berber taxi.
**Berber pharmacy** A herbalist's shop; the place to buy Berber viagra.
**Berber taxi** A donkey. See also Berber Mercedes.
**Berber telephone** The narrow airwell that's an architectural feature in Berber kasbahs. Apart from admitting light and air to lower levels, these allow communication between different floors. 'Fatima! Where's the couscous?'
**Berber viagra** Ginseng. See also Berber pharmacy.
**Berber whisky** Mint tea. This is sometimes used with scarcely a hint of irony, as Moroccans credit their national hot beverage with powers that, to the foreigner, it simply does not seem to possess. 'I've drunk too much Berber whisky,' you may hear someone moan.

wooden panelling and heavy furniture. Go for the more expensive rooms as some of the cheaper ones don't have windows.

## Todra Gorge

The road up to Todra winds north around the edge of **Tinerhir**'s lush palmeraie. It reaches a couple of heights, from which there are good views back over the town. It also passes Tinerhir's football stadium, which is nothing more than a dusty flatland with goal-posts, but it draws large crowds on match days.

Once in the valley, the road runs along the bottom, never climbing the sides as the road does in Dadès. After about ten kilometres (six

miles) of palmeraie and campsites, the road fords the river and beyond this someone will usually be waiting to charge you 10dh to proceed. It's worth getting out and walking to enjoy the last, canyon-like stretch – it's not as narrow as at Dadès but it's much grander and more spectacular. Here the cliffs rise to about 300 metres, and provide a habitat for assorted birdlife, including a pair of Bonelli's eagles. There are two hotels here on the other side of a cold, clear stream, which is crossed by stepping stones, carefully placed just far enough apart that you might want to pay the boys who hang around to offer a helping hand in return for dirhams.

With a 4x4 it's possible to head on up beyond the gorge and follow the mountainous piste from Aït Hani to Msemrir, and then enter the Dadès Gorge from the north.

Going back down the road towards Tinerhir, notice the **Source des Poissons Sacrés**, a spring-fed pool full of 'sacred' fish, these days on the grounds of a rather tawdry campsite. We wouldn't recommend staying here, but you can go and have a look at the fish. According to local folklore, bathing in here on three successive Friday afternoons is reckoned to help women conceive.

Beyond Tinerhir the road continues to Er Rachidia. Long before then is **Tinejdad**, where you can follow signs to a small **Galerie d'Art** (in reality more of a museum, though they do exhibit some painters) and there's a turn-off to Erfoud and the Tafilelt (see p213), which takes you through towns and villages inhabited by members of the once widely feared Aït Atta tribe.

### WHERE TO STAY

This enclosed section of the gorge is an atmospheric place to stay the night, and feels quite remote despite being just 15 kilometres (nine miles) north of busy Tinerhir. At the bottom of the cliffs, next to each other on the side of the river, are two hotels: **Les Roches** (044 89 51 34, h-les-roches@hotmail.com, 400dh double inc dinner) and **Yasmina** (044 89 51 18, fax 044 89 50 75, www.todragorge.com, 360dh double inc dinner). Yasmina perhaps has the better restaurant, plus it has a tented 'Berber' dining area by the river, but there's honestly not a lot to choose between these places. Both are unremarkable buildings and, at the time of writing, neither have electricity most of the time, generators only being turned on in the evening (if you're staying up here, it's a good idea to bring a torch) – although a proper electrical supply is promised in summer 2005. Both places have gas heaters for cold winter nights.

# The Tafilelt & Merzouga

The locals no longer get rich on gold, ebony, ostrich feathers and slaves, but they can show you lots of sand.

Historically, the Tafilelt Oasis was the most important area south of the Atlas. Taroudant, Telouet and the Drâa Valley might all have had their moments, but the Tafilelt was where the medieval city of Sijilmassa once stood, nexus of desert trade routes, raking in gold from across the Sahara. It was the Talifelt that in 1893 sent Moulay Hassan and his tax-collecting expedition scurrying back over the Atlas with its tail between its legs, thus inadvertently hastening the end of independent Morocco and giving the Glaoui a leg-up to power. And it was from here that the Alaouites, three centuries ago, sallied forth to become the dynasty that still rules Morocco today.

You wouldn't guess any of this from a quick look at the area's two major modern-day settlements, bureaucratic Erfoud and impoverished Rissani. The area long ago stopped being on the way to somewhere and started being the end of the line. (The Algerian border isn't far away to either south or east.) But the Tafilelt does retain a kind of brooding quality, anchored in its decaying kasbahs, ancient palm groves and vague royal connections. This last has traditionally meant that it was a place to dispatch lesser or more

troublesome members of the ruling family to, out of sight and far from the country's centres of power.

Most travellers who get this far carry straight on through to Merzouga and the dunes of Erg Chebbi, which are one of the great sights of Morocco. This should be your plan too. But Rissani is worth some time either coming or going, and there is life to the south of Merzouga too.

You can get here by road from the Dadès Valley via the turn-off at Tinejdad (see p212). Buses run from Tinehrir (see p211) to Tinejdad, and from Tinejdad to Erfoud, but you'll not be able to do much around here without your own transport. Driving to or from the Drâa Valley there's a road that runs east–west through the empty quarter south of the Jebel Sarho, connecting with the Drâa Valley between Agdz and Zagora.

## Erfoud

Erfoud is a mostly French-built administrative town that also, on account of having the most mod cons within striking distance of the photogenic Merzouga dunes, has film business

Rissani.

connections. It's a desultory sort of place – a frontier town with a gridlike street pattern and ideas above its station. But it's where you'll find essential facilities such as banks and a pharmacy, and there's a Sunday souk and an October date festival.

The one unique local item is a kind of fossil-rich black marble. This is polished up and used for tabletops and bar counters. By another process, the stone is sculpted to bring the fossils into relief on everything from ashtrays to washbasins. The results are mostly quite kitsch, as can be seen at **Manar Marbre** (055 57 81 25, www.manarmarbre.com, 8am-noon, 2-6pm daily) a few hundred metres up the Tinehrir road. At the showroom here you can see or buy every imaginable kind of black marble item and look round the not very interesting factory.

Erfoud has a clutch of old-school four- and five-star hotels, suitable for housing film crews and correspondingly overpriced. The best is probably the **Hotel Salam** (055 57 66 65, fax 055 57 81 92, double 560dh), which has a pool, gardens, bar and sauna and is just about the first thing you'll see arriving from the Dadès – it's at the junction of Erfoud's main street and the road from Tinerhir. Six kilometres to the north of Erfoud is the Spanish-owned **Kasbah Xaluca** (055 57 84 50, fax 055 57 84 49, www.xaluca.com, 510dh double), a walled

enclosure around a central pool with a pizza restaurant. The rooms have air-conditioning and bathrooms with sculpted fossil fittings. DJs play nightly in the Tent Royale, and there's every kind of excursion, trek, rental, hike, adventure and experience on offer. It's the Tafilelt's stag-party destination.

## Rissani

Around 20 kilometres (12 miles) south of Erfoud, Rissani is a sprawling, untidy village with a small modern core and ksars and kasbahs scattered throughout its extensive palmeraie. This is the home town of the Alaouite dynasty, which started feeling expansive in the early 17th century and had taken power by 1664.

Before that it was the site of Sijilmassa, founded in the mid eighth century by Berber heretics. At the heart of such a fertile oasis, and at the nexus of trade routes connecting West Africa to Morocco and Europe – and Morocco to the rest of North Africa and the Middle East – Sijilmassa quickly became a great trading centre and dominated the South for five centuries. Huge caravans would set out from here heading first for the Saharan salt mines in what today is Mali, then to the Niger region, where salt was traded for gold, then back across the Sahara laden with gold, ebony, ostrich feathers and slaves. Meanwhile, coins from Sijilmassa have been found as far away as Akabar in Jordan.

The place was never the same after the Portuguese opened up maritime routes to sub-Saharan Africa, and Sijilmassa long ago sank back into the sands. Such ruins as there are can be found on the north side of Rissani, near the outlying hamlet of **El Mansouria**, where there's a gate known locally as the **Bab Errih**, which probably dates from the Merenid period. (You can ask for directions at the nearby Hotel Kasbah Asmaa, three kilometers – two miles – towards Erfoud.) The few other traces of Sijilmassa are only of academic interest – and archaeological excavations have long been under way. Some of the finds can be seen at the small museum of the **Centre d'Étude et de Recherches Alaouite** (open 8.30am-6.30pm Mon-Fri) on the north side of Rissani's main square. There are dusty pots, lots of information in French and, usefully, some large-scale maps of the area that will help in locating some of the features of interest. It's probably worth a look at those before setting off around Rissani's **Circuit Touristique**, a 21-kilometre (13 mile) loop around the ksours and kasbahs of the palmeraie.

The ancestors of the current ruling Alaouite dynasty settled in the region around the 13th century. Off the road running towards Merzouga, just after the village peters out, there are signposts to the **Mausoleum of Moulay Ali Cherif**, founder of the dynasty, who was buried here in 1640. It's a modern building, an older one having been destroyed by flash flooding in the mid 1950s, and entrance is of course forbidden to non-Muslims. Beyond it is a signposted turn on to the Circuit Touristique, where the first point of interest is the 19th-century **Ksar Akbar**, once used to house disgraced members of the Alaouite family. About two kilometres (one mile) further on is the grand **Ksar Ouled Abdelhalim**, built for Moulay Hassan's brother around the turn of the 20th century and touted as the 'Alhambra of the Tafilelt'. Its remains include imposing towers, cloistered courtyards and ornate gateways that do give a flavour of former grandeur. The whole circuit takes in a number of other kasbahs and ksours – some in an advanced state of erosion, others still housing a substantial part of Rissani's population.

Back downtown, Rissani has a lively and enjoyable souk on Sunday, Tuesday and Thursday, but once you've done the small museum there's not much else to see. It is also a notoriously hassly place, where locals will work a variety of schemes and scams to try and part you from your dirhams. The recent opening of a paved road to Merzouga has probably exacerbated the problem, as visitors

**Riad Maria**. *See p216.*

can now easily get to the dunes unaided, and Rissani can no longer make its living by offering excursions or escorting them there.

We wouldn't recommend staying in Rissani, but if you do, the **Hotel Kasbah Asmaa** (055 77 40 83, fax 055 57 54 94, 320dh double) is certainly the best place, just north of the village, with comfortable but unremarkable rooms, and a pool set among gardens. There aren't many eating options, though on market days you'll find a tajine or two on sale around the souk.

## Merzouga

Getting to Merzouga used to be half the fun. Or so old hands will tell you. Until recently the road ran out at Rissani and proceeding to Merzouga and the dunes of Erg Chebbi involved setting off across 30 kilometres (20 miles) of piste. Now there's good paved road as far as Merzouga village, and the stretch beyond that, to Taouz near the Algerian border, was scheduled for completion about the time this guide went to press. The only other option is to grab a *grand taxi*, but if you're heading to one of the better hotels and have no transport of your own, they'll probably send someone out to collect you.

There's nothing much at Merzouga itself but squat, flat-roofed houses, a few general stores, some extremely basic café-hotels, and a couple of carpet dealers. The real attraction here is the dunes looming over to the east of the road and to the north of the village. About 27 kilometres (17 miles) from north to south and eight kilometres (five miles) from east to west, **Erg Chebbi** is a huge, shifting expanse of pink sand that looks exactly how the desert always looks in the movies – probably because those movies were shot right here. But celluloid doesn't quite prepare you for the precise beauty of the sand, its contours and peaks picked out by shadow, its colours shifting from pink to gold against a backdrop of clear blue sky and particularly vivid at either dawn or sunset.

But it's not the world's quietest piece of desert. This area has long been a big tourist attraction. Around two dozen hotels nudge up to the western edge of the sands, and there are both tourists and locals running around on quads and motorbikes, as well as camel-trekking trains setting off to overnight at the small oasis that lies out of sight among the dunes. Such trips can be arranged at any of the hotels – indeed, by pretty much anyone you encounter.

Camels aren't the only wildlife. Birders may spot desert sparrows, fulvous babblers and blue-cheeked bee-eaters, but best of all is when there's been enough rainfall for a shallow seasonal lake to appear north-west of the village, which then attracts dozens of pink flamingos – a particularly exotic sight out here in the arid wilderness.

### WHERE TO STAY AND EAT

There are hotels dotted all along the western fringes of the dunes, and getting to the more northerly of these involves a further rattle across bumpy piste from the new road between Rissani and Merzouga. Individual establishments are well signposted. The only electricity comes from generators, so expect no power late at night or in the middle of the day.

All the hotels sell half-board, which makes sense around here as there aren't any restaurants. And if one of the main reasons to choose a hotel in these circumstances is the quality of the food, then **Riad Maria** (062 23 26 47, fax 055 57 73 03, www.riadmaria.com, 1,200dh-1,400dh double inc dinner, closed 10 June-10 Aug) wins by a mile. Maria Pesci is an Italian chef and gastronomy correspondent. Opening a top-notch gourmet *maison d'hôte* in this remote location has been a *Fitzcarraldo*-like enterprise for Maria and her husband Giuseppe, but they've done it, and 20 rooms furnished with nice touches, such as curtains and bedspreads of Indian silk, surround a pool with small bar. There's also a small hammam (150dh, massage 200dh extra) and a big dining room. The food is absolutely wonderful, sometimes Italian, more often Moroccan with a twist. Vegetarians may consider the Moroccan-Indian dishes sufficient reason in themselves to drive all the way from Marrakech. The desert sands begin outside the back of the hotel, and the two tasteful suites (2,800dh) have balconies from which to contemplate the contours of the sands.

Most else around here seems rather dull by comparison. If you want something cheaper and more typical, the **Auberge du Sud** (061 21 61 66, fax 055 57 86 31, www.aubergedusud.com, 300dh-440dh double inc dinner) is a good bet. The cheap rooms are comfortable without frills; and some thought has been put into the more expensive ones. All have showers. The hotel is so close to the dunes that sand is piling against the walls of the car park – though it's been left that way to look good for visitors rather than because it's out of control. The **Auberge Kasbah Derkaoua** (055 57 71 40, www.aubergederkaoua.com, 900dh double inc dinner, closed Jan, June, July), northernmost hotel along the fringes of the sand, has chalet accommodation and good French-Moroccan food. As near to Erfoud as to Merzouga, it's often also referred to as Chez Michel.

Keep walking east from **Merzouga** (*see p216*) and you eventually hit Egypt.

## South of Merzouga

The tarmac road from Rissani now continues
all the way to Taouz. About eight kilometres
(five miles) south of Merzouga is a gnawa
village called **Khamlia**, populated by the
Berber-speaking descendants of black African
slaves. The sun-blasted scattering of poor, flat-
roofed *pisé* houses feels like it could have been
lifted whole from the other side of the Sahara.
As with gnawa everywhere, music is one of the
locals' main pursuits and there are several
family bands here. You can sometimes find

them playing at the village's small cultural
centre, or you can locate the house of the family
Zaid on Khamlia's south-east side. Go in, say
hello, and settle on cushions in the room to the
left. Someone will bring you mint tea, and then
musicians in white robes will appear to play
and dance for you – drummers, castanet
players and a guy on a *gimbri*. It's excellent
entertainment. Tip them 50dh or buy their CD.

Sixteen kilometres (ten miles) further on,
past salt flats and (usually) dried lake beds,
is the village of **Taouz**. It's little more than a
military outpost by the Algerian border, but if
you like being stared at then this is the place.

Trips Out of Town

# The Drâa Valley

From Ouarzazate south to the road's end and a 52-day trek to Timbuktu.

The River Drâa begins where the Oued Dades, Oued Mellah and other streams come together at Ouarzazate, and theoretically it runs all the way to the Atlantic Ocean, some 750 kilometres (465 miles) distant. But the last time it actually managed that feat was in 1989. More usually, it vanishes into the sand near M'Hamid, the town that marks the end of the Drâa Valley route, some ten kilometres (six miles) short of the Algerian border.

Beyond M'Hamid, all travel is by camel, and you start measuring journeys in days, not hours. But before that, the Drâa Valley between Agdz and Zagora is a heartbreakingly beautiful drive through palm groves, kasbahs and geology in the raw.

Buses run south from Ouarzazate with reasonable frequency as far as Zagora, but from there onwards services are spotty. *Grand taxis* run between the bigger villages and are the best way of geeting around, but any kind of traffic gets sparse towards M'Hamid.

## Drâa Valley

The arid, stony plains south of Ouarzazate are breathtakingly bleak – flatlands of brown rubble as far as the eye can see. The road does get quite dramatic though as it winds up through the layered rock formations of the Jebel Sarho to the 1,600 metre (5,250 foot) Tizi-n-Tinififft pass.

On the other side of the pass, **Agdz** is a small market town with a few carpet shops and a Thursday souk. The **Hotel Kissane** (044 84 30 44, fax 044 84 32 59, 250dh double) has a decent restaurant and a pool. If you're not depending on public transport, there are a couple of nearby kasbahs worth looking at: the turn-off for **Tamnougalk** is on the left roughly six kilometres (four miles) past Agdz and the kasbah is down a further three kilometres of piste; the more palatial Glaoui kasbah of **Timiderte** is eight kilometres (five miles) further south.

Agdz is overlooked by the 1,500 metre (4,921 foot) **Jebel Kissane**, which looks like a single mountain until you draw abreast and realise it's actually one end of a long, brooding range. This is also where the Drâa Valley oasis begins. The next 100 kilometres (62 miles) is a long, verdant strip cut into the desert. Every last scrap of fertile land is planted to grow olives, lemons, oranges, almonds, cereals and, most of all, dates, which is the valley's principal crop. Dates like lots of water and are sweetest and plumpest where it is hottest. A Moroccan saying has it that date palms have 'their heads in fire and their feet in water'. Dense with such trees, the Drâa Valley produces some of the finest dates in North Africa. Local kids stand by the road trying to sell boxes of them to passing motorists.

Zagora. *See p219.*

Inter-oasis
transport.

The road runs along the edge of the fertile area. On the other side, where nothing will grow, there are dozens of red-ochre kasbahs and *ksours* – fortified Berber villages. The last stretch runs through the Jebel Azlag gorge before emerging on to the palm-filled plain that is the Zagora oasis.

## Zagora

Like Ouarzazate, present-day Zagora is a colonial creation, built by the French as a garrison and administrative centre. But the oasis has been inhabited for centuries, perhaps millennia. There's an 11th-century Almoravid fortress, built to guard the Sahara trade route, on top of Jebel Zagora at the end of town. And the Saadians would set out from around here at the beginning of the 16th century to conquer first Taroudant, then the rest of Morocco: *see p12* **History**.

This conquesting history is acknowledged in the town's famous sign that shows a camel train and the legend 'Timbuktu, 52 days'. It used to stand outside the Préfecture, where the road leaves habitation behind and strikes out for the desert. But the same tidying-up demon that has afflicted Marrakech's Jemaa El Fna and the Essaouira grilled fish stalls has removed the sign to a less prominent position and replaced the original with a more modern version. Mad, given that it's this inauspicious town's only landmark. Local souvenir merchants now sell versions of the old sign as paintings and plates.

The Préfecture is at one end of the long, dull main street, boulevard Mohammed V, and

pretty much anything you might want to find is along here: post office, banks, cafés, army barracks. There's a large souk on Wednesdays and Sundays, at which the biggest section is given over to dates, compressed and packed into plastic sacks. Common types include the small, black *bousthami* and the light, olive-coloured *bouzeki*. But the sweet *boufeggou* date, whose sugar content delays decomposition, is the most important. Highly nutritious and edible for up to four years if dried properly.

There's not much else going on in Zagora proper and it isn't the friendliest of towns. Expect a fair bit of hassle from locals in search of a buck. Over the river, the adjacent hamlet of **Amazrou** is more interesting. The palmeraie is wonderfully dense and lush, and crossed by paths which afford a good stroll. The nearby **Kasbah des Juifs** was, as its name suggests, built and formerly inhabited by Jews. They all left in the 1960s and local Berbers now make silver jewellery by old Jewish methods, using clay moulds. You can visit them at work making *fibulas*, brooches worn by Berber women (one below the right shoulder if not married, one below each shoulder if married or divorced). Any local will guide you round the kasbah, which has dark, underground passageways, hidden from the desert heat. It is still partially inhabited.

### WHERE TO STAY & EAT
**La Fibule du Drâa** (044 84 73 18, fax 044 84 72 71, fibule@menara.ma, 430dh double) is a small and friendly complex built around a pool on the edge of the Amazrou palmeraie. It has a basic but decent restaurant and a bar. Nearby,

# Getting the hump

Like mariachis with sombreros are to Mexico, or bicycles and windmills to the Netherlands, the image of the camel train – a chain of humped beasts, robed humans, palm trees, sand dunes – is graphic shorthand for the Saharan oases.

The camel isn't native to North Africa but, introduced from Asia at the time of the Arab conquest, its special properties were what made trans-Saharan trade routes possible. It thus anchored the existence of places like Zagora – as the famous 'Timbuktu 52 days' sign acknowledges.

Camels are remarkable. They can last five to seven days with little or no food or water and lose more than a quarter of their bodyweight without distress. When they do drink, they can slurp up over 20 gallons (91 litres) in ten minutes. And that's not all. They can carry loads of up to 900 pounds (407kg). Their hide provides tents for shelter. The meat is similar to veal, only tougher. Camel milk is more nutritious than cow's milk, and is both drunk fresh and made into cheese. Even camel dung is handy, as it can be used as a fuel without being dried.

But trans-Saharan trade is long gone. You sometimes see small camel trains moving stuff around within the bigger oases, and there are still some genuine nomads knocking about between the smaller ones, but the only volume item camels carry into the desert these days is tourists.

Camel-trekking boomed in the 1990s. So much so that extra camels were brought in from Mali. Maybe they brought in too many. Now camel-trekking seems to be a buyer's market, with every hotelier, guide, waiter and shopkeeper south of the Atlas trying to sell you some kind of hump-backed desert experience. In a place like M'Hamid, it seems like it's the biggest single contributor to the local economy.

Camel treks can be anything from a sandy sleepover to a fearsome 14-day lurch from M'Hamid to Merzouga. It can be fun to overnight in the dunes, at least – hear the desert silence, lie under the clearest night sky you've ever seen, and sway along on this strange beast imagining what it would be like to spend 52 days this way.

It costs around 300dh per person per day, with trimmings (music, food, bivouac) negotiable. Forget it between April and September, when the heat is just too intense. There are a variety of possible excursions from Zagora, M'Hamid or Merzouga and the trek organisers below have good reputations. They also do 4x4 excursions at around 1,200dh per day.

## Sahara Services

*Next to Restaurant Dune d'Or, M'Hamid (061 77 67 66/www.saharaservices.info).* **No credit cards.**
Abdelkhalek Benalila organises a variety of treks into the dunes around M'Hamid and can offer all-in deals that include transport to and from Marrakech, a night at the Dar Azawad (*see p222*) and camels out to Erg Chigaga and what they call the 'Sacred Oasis'.

## Caravane du Sud

*Amazrou (044 84 75 69, fax 044 84 74 97/ www.caravane-sud.com).* **No credit cards.**
Every imaginable kind of trek can be organised with this company, but it might be necessary to steer them away from tour group expectations. Not all their guides speak English so track down Ahmed (061 87 16 60).

among the palms (take the path along the irrigation canal), is the **Riad Lamane** (044 84 83 88, fax 044 84 83 89, www.riadlamane.com, 800dh double including dinner). As its name suggests, this is a *maison d'hôte* with just seven rooms. Decor verges on kitsch but proportions are gratifyingly grand. There's an indoor restaurant area or you can eat in the pretty garden, which is also equipped with a small swimming pool. The **Riad Salam** (boulevard Mohammed V, 044 84 74 00 fax 044 84 75 51, www.salamhotelmaroc.com, 545dh double) is on the way into town and has big air-conditioned rooms, some with TV, as well as a pool and two restaurants. It's an efficient sort of place, but a bit lacking in character. The hotels have the best restaurants.

## Tamegroute & Tinfou

Around 18 kilometres (11 miles) south of Zagora, the town of **Tamegroute** has long been an important religious centre. Its green-roofed *zaouia* (shrine) was founded in the 17th century and is headquarters of the Naciri Islamic brotherhood whose leaders, known as 'peacemakers of the desert' have traditionally been called upon to settle disputes between tribes or rival traders.

There's a *medersa* (Koranic school) along with the tomb of the Brotherhood's founder, a place of pilgrimage, but these are off-limits to non-Muslims. The main thing to see is the wonderful **library** (8am-3pm, 20dh donation), up a side street on the left of the main road. It was once much larger but there are still 4,000 volumes, carefully stored in glass-fronted cases, including an 11th-century gazelle-skin Koran as well as old books from as far afield as Egypt and Mali. The wizened librarian will sternly point out highlights: 'This Arab dictionary – Dictionary! History la ville de Fès – History! This Egyptian – Cairo! Cairo!!'

Back by the minaret, there's also a cloistered courtyard that acts as a sanctuary for the infirm or mentally ill. People huddle in blankets, waiting for miracles or donations, or just for the next square meal. Around the corner on the left as you head south is a clutch of **pottery shops** selling cups, plates and tajines in the distinctive green glaze native to Tamegroute. The same glaze is used for the green roof tiles on the nearby *zaouia*, as well as on mosques and royal buildings throughout Morocco.

About five kilometres (three miles) south of Tamegroute at a place called **Tinfou** is an isolated patch of sand dunes. It's only the size of a few football pitches, and you'll be sharing this Saharan experience with any number of tour groups, camel touts and kids trying to sell you animals made out of clay or palm leaves, but if you're not going all the way down to M'Hamid (*see below*) or across to Merzouga (*see p217*), this will be your only glimpse of desert sands.

There are a few hotels near the dunes. Our favourite is the eccentric and somewhat ramshackle **Repos du Sable** (044 84 85 66, 150dh double), owned by the widely exhibited naïve painter Fatima Hassan El Farouj. It has basic, clean, carpeted rooms, a hammam and a pool which was being renovated when we last looked in. There's also a resident barbary ape, who looks a bit cheesed off in his cage. The restaurant serves a 55dh menu.

## M'Hamid

Beyond Tamegroute the road narrows and runs through mostly arid landscape for the next 70 kilometres (42 miles), crossing the barren Jbel Bani before coming back into oasis country at Tagounite. Before M'Hamid it's

The dunes at **Tinfou**. *See p220.*

Dar Azawad.

worth stopping off to see the small, private **museum** (open 6am-10pm, admission 15dh) in Ouled Driss. Follow the 'Musée' sign from the main road and a guide will pick you up. It's a beautiful 17th-century Berber house, once owned by the village chief, containing an exhibit of costumes, jewellery and tools. Above all, it's a cool place to lay back with the mint tea you'll be offered. Be careful on the uneven stairs, though – this is ankle-twisting territory.

M'Hamid is a tiny town that really does feel like the end of the line, fighting a losing battle against the sand. The locals, many of whom are Saharwi rather than Berber, will stare like they've never seen a tourist before – although the entire town seems to be involved in the camel-trekking business (*see p220* **Getting the hump**). You'll be beating away touts from the various agencies and turning down special deals for bivouacs at the 'Sacred Oasis' as soon as you step out of the car.

If you're not getting on a camel and swaying off to the sands of **Chigaga**, there isn't a lot to do here, though the town is worth a stroll and a drive into the palmeraie is interesting. The Algerian border isn't far away and in the 1970s some of the outlying kasbahs were attacked and destroyed by Polisario guerillas. Half the locals wear robes of Tuareg blue (men) or desert black (women) and the futuristic new Maroc Telecom public phones look decidedly out of place among the tatty houses, sandy streets and shops selling chickens.

### WHERE TO STAY & EAT

Accommodation and dining in the town are basic, at best. The **Dunes d'Or** restaurant does simple meals (including some vegetarian choices) for 60dh, and has a couple of not very appealing rooms (but with shower) in the back charged at 70dh a double. The **Hotel Iriqui** (044 88 57 99, www.iriqui.com, 150dh double) is better, but not much.

The best place in the area is **Dar Azawad** (044 84 87 30, www.darazawad.com, 600dh-900dh double including dinner) a new French-owned *maison d'hôte* among the palms about four kilometres (2.5 miles) back towards Ouled Driss. In walled grounds there are nine cool and tasteful bungalow rooms furnished with Moroccan items and fabrics, as well as simpler, tented rooms at a cheaper rate. (The tented rooms don't have showers en suite, but each has its own shower in a shared facility.) There's also a pool, a dining room and a good kitchen. A poolside bar was under construction when we last visited, and we're told that a hammam is next on the list. The only problem is, you have to like dogs.

# Directory

| | |
|---|---|
| Getting Around | 224 |
| Resources A-Z | 227 |
| Vocabulary: French | 238 |
| Vocabulary: Arabic | 239 |
| Glossary | 240 |
| Further Reference | 241 |

## Features

| | |
|---|---|
| Travel advice | 227 |
| No hassle | 231 |
| Islamic holidays | 234 |
| Kif and majoun | 236 |
| Weather report | 237 |

# Directory

## Getting Around

### By air

Marrakech's international airport (Aéroport Marrakech Menara) is located just six kilometres (four miles) west of the city. From the airport forecourt to the city centre takes less than ten minutes by car. The airport information desk (9am-9pm daily) is in the check-in area. There are a couple of banks offering currency exchange in the arrivals hall, open 8am-6pm daily, as well as two ATMs. For flight information, call 044 44 78 65 or 044 44 79 10, but don't expect to learn anything of use.

Taxis wait outside the arrivals building. In a *petit taxi* (*see p225* **Taxis**) the official fare to anywhere in the Medina or Guéliz is 60dh (to the Palmeraie 120dh) but they'll usually demand more. Most taxi drivers picking up at the airport will accept dollars, euros or pounds at the equivalent dirham rate.

Most airlines have their offices in Casablanca.

### British Airways

*avenue des FAR, Casablanca (022 47 30 23)*. **Open** 8.30am-12.30pm, 2.30-6.30pm Mon-Sat. **Credit** AmEx, DC, MC, V.
Casablanca is the main British Airways office in Morocco and you must call here to confirm all flights. The sales-only agent in Marrakech is **Menara Tours**: 41 rue Yougoslavie, Guéliz (044 44 66 54, open 8.30am-12.30pm, 2.30-6.30pm Mon-Fri, map p256 A1).

### Royal Air Maroc (RAM)

*197 avenue Mohammed V, Guéliz (044 42 55 00)*. **Open** 8.30am-12.15pm, 2.30-7pm Mon-Fri. **Credit** AmEx, DC, MC, V. **Map** p256 B2.

There is a 24-hour call centre (090 00 08 00) for flight reconfirmation, flight information and reservations. RAM continually changes and cancels flights at short notice so reconfirming is a must.

### By rail

Trains are operated by the national railway company **ONCF** (044 44 77 68, www.oncf.org.ma). The railway station is on the western edge of Guéliz, on avenue Hassan II. Marrakech is the southernmost terminus of two lines, both of which pass through Casablanca and Rabat; some trains then continue north to Tangier, others north-east to Oujda on the Algerian border via Meknes and Fès. A swarm of taxis meets each incoming train; make sure to get a *petit taxi* and not a more expensive big Mercedes. The fare into central Guéliz is 5dh-6dh; to the Medina 10dh. Alternatively, if you can be bothered with the wait, bus Nos.3 and 8 pass by the station en route to the place de Foucault for Jemaa El Fna.

### By bus

The *gare routière* is just outside the Medina walls at Bab Doukkala. Most long-distance buses terminate here, including those operated by national carrier **CTM** (044 43 39 33). Both the central Medina and Guéliz are walkable from the station; alternatively a *petit taxi* will cost 5dh-6dh, or catch a local bus for place de Foucault (Jemaa El Fna). There is also a CTM office in Guéliz on boulevard Mohammed Zerktouni, a few doors along

from the Cinema la Colisée, where buses also halt and tickets can be bought.

The superior buses run by **Supratours** (044 43 55 25), to and from Essaouira, Agadir, Laayoune and Dakhla only, pull up at the forecourt of the company's own little terminus, next door to the railway station (*see above*). Note that Essaouira is a popular destination and the Supratour buses fill up fast, so it's wise to purchase your tickets at least a day in advance (for further details, *see p187*).

Marrakech has a limited city bus network radiating from the Medina out to the suburbs. Other than along avenue Mohammed V, no buses operate within the confines of the city walls – where streets are so narrow and tortuously twisted that donkey carts can barely pass in places. Few local bus services are of much use to visitors. The possible exception are those services that run between the Medina and Guéliz, which is a fairly long walk, but it's much less hassle (and still relatively inexpensive) to take a taxi.

### Buses

City buses (044 43 39 33) are regular coaches with no air-conditioning. They charge a flat fee of 3dh payable to the driver. Beware: the drivers never have any change. All these buses leave from place de Foucault, opposite the Hotel de Foucault, just 100m west of the Jemaa El Fna:

### Local bus routes

**No.1** to Guéliz along avenue Mohammed V
**No.2** to Bab Doukkala for the *gare routière*
**No.3** to Douar Laskar via avenue Mohammed V, avenue Hassan II and the train station
**No.4** to Daoudiate (a northern suburb) by avenue Mohammed V
**No.8** to Douar Laskar via avenue Mohammed V, avenue Moulay Hassan and the train station
**No.10** to boulevard de Safi via Bab Doukkala and the *gare routière*
**No.11** to the airport via avenue de la Menara and the Menara Gardens
**No.14** to the train station

## Taxis

Taxis are plentiful and there is rarely a problem finding one, whatever the time of day or night. They are also cheap enough that it makes little sense bothering with buses. The standard ride is known as a **petit taxi** (lettered on the side of the car as such) and is usually a little khaki-coloured four-door Fiat, Simca or similar. By law, they can only carry a maximum of three passengers. Drivers are reluctant to use the meter. Asking for them to switch it on sometimes works, otherwise it's just a question of knowing the right fare. From Jemaa El Fna to Guéliz costs around 6dh; from Jemaa El Fna to the Palmeraie around 40dh. Expect to pay about 50 per cent more after about 8pm (9pm in summer).

**Grand taxis** (again, lettered as such) are bigger cars that can squeeze six people in and are normally more expensive. They loiter outside hotels and the railway station. Avoid them, unless you are a group of four or more or are travelling long distance: some *grand taxis* operate like minibuses running fixed routes to outlying suburbs, villages and towns, and even as far as Essaouira and Agadir.

Note, seat belts are mandatory for front seat passengers in a taxi.

## Driving

A car can be useful for venturing out of the city, especially for trips to the south, but unless you are a resident (making shopping trips, running the kids to school) a car is of limited use within Marrakech itself. For short-term visitors taxis are cheap and plentiful and easily hired by the day for around 250dh (£15) in and around the city; ask your hotel for help in finding a reputable driver.

If you do drive, then traffic travels on the right. The French rule of giving priority to traffic from the right is observed at roundabouts and junctions, ie cars coming on to a roundabout have priority over those already on it. Speed limits are 40km/h (25mph) in urban areas, 100km/h (62mph) on main roads, 120km/h (74mph) on autoroutes. There are on-the-spot fines for speeding and other traffic offences. Seatbelts are mandatory.

Be very wary when driving at night as cyclists and moped riders often have no lights. Neither do sheep, goats and pedestrians. In the case of an accident, report to the nearest *gendarmerie* to obtain a written report, otherwise insurance will be invalid.

## Car hire

To hire a car, you must be over 21, have a full current driving licence and carry a passport or an identity card. Rental isn't cheap; daily rates with a local agency start at about 400dh (around £25 at the time of writing) for a Fiat Palio, Citroen Saxo or Peugeot 205 with unlimited mileage. A Peugeot 306 kicks in at about 700dh (£44) per day, a Peugeot 406 at 950dh (£60).

With the internationals like Avis, Budget or Hertz, expect to pay about 25 per cent more.

The drawback with many of the local hire firms is the back-up service – cars may be unreliable, breakdown support may be lacking and replacement vehicles may not always be forthcoming.

Be aware that payments made in Morocco by credit card often incur an additional five per cent fee. This is one of several reasons why it works out cheaper to arrange your car rental in advance through the travel agent booking your flight or via the internet.

The major companies allow you to rent a car in one city and return it in another. Rental cars in Morocco are delivered empty of petrol and returned empty. Almost all agencies will deliver cars to your hotel and arrange pick-up at no extra charge but this service must be booked in advance.

If you are heading south over the mountains, remember that you are responsible for any damage if you take a car off-road or along unsuitable tracks. Four-wheel drives are available from most hire companies and start at around 1,200dh, or £75, per day.

### Always Car

*15 rue Imam Chafi, Kawkab Centre, Guéliz (061 19 31 29).* **Open** 8am-noon, 2.30-7pm daily. **Credit** MC, V. **Map** p256 B3.
Can organise anything from a two-door Fiat to a 4WD to a minibus, along with English-language chauffeurs.

### Avis

*137 avenue Mohammed V, Guéliz (044 43 25 25/fax 044 43 12 65/ www.avis.com/avisrak@mail.net).* **Open** 8am-7pm Mon-Sat; 8am-noon Sun. **Credit** AmEx, DC, MC, V. **Map** p256 B2.
**Other locations:** Aéroport Marrakech Menara (044 43 12 65). **Open** 8am-noon, 2-11pm Mon-Sat; 8am-noon Sun.

### Budget

*68 boulevard Mohammed Zerktouni, Guéliz (044 43 11 80/www.budget rentacar.com).* **Open** 8am-noon, 2.30-7pm Mon-Fri; 9am-noon, 3-6pm Sat; 9am-noon Sun. **Credit** AmEx, MC, V. **Map** p256 A6.

Other locations: Aéroport
Marrakech Menara (044 43 88 75).
Open 7am-10pm daily.

### Concorde Cars

*154 avenue Mohammed V, Guéliz
(044 43 11 16/fax 044 44 61
29/concordecar@iam.ma).* Open
8.30am-7.30pm Mon-Sat. Credit
AmEx, DC, MC, V. Map p256 B2.

### Europcar

*63 boulevard Mohammed Zerktouni,
Guéliz (044 43 12 28/fax 044 31
02 30/www.europcar.com).* Open
8.30am-noon, 2.30-7pm Mon-Sat.
Credit AmEx, MC, V. Map p256 B2.
Other locations: Aéroport
Marrakech Menara (044 43 77 18).
Open to meet incoming flights.

### Fathi Cars

*183 avenue Mohammed V, Guéliz
(044 43 17 63).* Open 8.30am-
12.30pm, 2.30-7pm Mon-Sat. Credit
AmEx, DC, MC, V. Map p256 B2.

### Hertz

*154 avenue Mohammed V, Guéliz
(044 43 13 94/www.hertz.com).*
Open 8.30am-12.30pm, 2-6.30pm
Mon-Sat. Credit AmEx, DC, MC, V.
Map p256 B2.
Other locations: Aéroport
Marrakech Menara (044 44 72 30).
Open 8.30am-12.30pm, 2-6.30pm
daily. Club Med (061 36 75 37). Open
9-11.30am, 5-7.30pm Mon-Fri, Sun.

### Majestic

*21 rue Tarek Ibn Ziad, Guéliz
(044 43 65 00/fax 044 43 43 92/
majesticloc@yahoo.fr).* Open
8.30am-12.30pm, 2.30-7pm Mon-Sat.
Credit MC, V. Map p256 B2.

## Parking

Wherever there's space to park
vehicles you'll find a *gardien
de voitures.* They're licensed
by the local authority to look
after left vehicles and expect to
be tipped 10dh or so by way of
a parking fee (the local rate is
2dh during the day, 5dh at
night, but as a visitor you're
not going to get away with
paying that). Street-side
parking is easy enough in the
New City (look for the orange-
painted kerbs) but more
troublesome in the Medina:
the main parking spots are
opposite the Préfecture de la
Medina or on rue Ibn Rachid.
Red and white kerb markings
mean no parking.

## Repairs & services

The agents below should be
able to help get you back on
the road.

### Garage Ourika

*66 avenue Mohammed V, Guéliz
(044 44 82 66).* Open 8.30am-noon,
2.30-6.30pm Mon-Sat. No credit
cards. Map p256 A1.
BMW, Fiat, Honda and Toyota
specialist.

### Garage Renault

*route de Casablanca, Semlalia (044
30 10 08).* Open 8am-noon, 2-
6.30pm Mon-Sat. No credit cards.
Renault specialist.

## Cycling

It's not quite China but humble
bicycles, mopeds and motorbikes are a hugely popular
mode of local transport –
despite widespread potholes,
choking bus fumes and the
perils of having to share the
road with the average lunatic
Marrakchi motorist.

If you fancy mixing it
yourself, try one of the places
listed below for bike rentals.
In addition, there are also a
couple of hire outfits at the
northern end of **rue Beni
Marine**, the small street
running parallel to and
between rue Bab Agnaou and
rue Moulay Ismail. Guys with
bikes for hire can also be found
on the central grassy verge
outside **Hotel Imperial Borj**
(5 avenue Echouhada) and
across from the **Hotel El
Andalous** on avenue de Paris,
both in Hivernage, and at the
**Hotel de Foucault** (off place
de Foucault) in the Medina,
though none are affiliated to
the hotels mentioned. In Guéliz
try the **Hotel Toulousain** on
rue Tarek ibn Ziad behind the
old Marché Central. Prices are
roughly 20dh per hour with
negotiable daily rates.

Note that most rental places
do not offer helmets or any
kind of lock so if you want to
leave the bike or scooter
anywhere it'll have to be with

a *gardien de voitures* (*see above*
**Parking**). Before taking a bike
check the gears and brakes as
servicing is not always high
priority.

### Action Sports Loisirs

*1 boulevard El Mansour,
apartment No.4, Guéliz (tel/fax
044 43 09 31/mobile 061 240 145).*
Open 8am-7pm Tue-Sun. Bicycle
rental 140dh for 2hrs; 350dh per
half-day. No credit cards. Map
p256 A2.
Action Sports Loisirs has the best
bikes in town, both in terms of
quality of machines and attention
to maintenance. Owner Alain rents
bikes for all kinds of terrain, and
also organises excursions for 700dh
(including lunch and transport).

### Marrakech Motos

*31 avenue Abdelkarim El Khattabi,
Guéliz (044 44 83 59/mobile 061
31 64 13).* Open 9am-10pm daily.
Scooter rental 250dh-300dh per
day, depending on model. No credit
cards. Map p256 A2.
Also known as Chez Jamal Boucetta.

### Salah Eddine

*18 rue de la Recette, Medina (061
87 31 45).* Open 9am-9pm daily.
Bicycle rental 10dh per hr; 100dh
per day. No credit cards. Map
p254 C6.
Salah Eddine operates from a
basement room just around the
corner from the Hotel Galia, off
rue Bab Agnaou.

## Walking

Walking is absolutely the only
way to get around the Medina,
which is where most visitors
spend the bulk of their time.
It's a compact area, perfect for
exploring on foot. Besides,
many of the streets and alleys
are too narrow for anything
bigger than a motorcycle or
donkey cart.

Make sure to pack a pair
of comfortable, flat-soled
shoes because the streets in
the Medina are rarely paved
or surfaced and as a result
are badly rutted by passing
cars. For visits any time
from November to April
bring something cheap
and waterproof because the
slightest bit of rain turns the
whole of the Medina to mud.

# Resources A-Z

## Addresses

In the newer quarters of the city streets are well signed in both French and Arabic. This is not the case in the Medina: major streets do have dual-script signs but the majority of smaller alleyways have signs in Arabic only, or simply no signs at all. Most of the time, when looking for a specific street or place the only option is to ask the locals. If the person questioned doesn't know, they'll often put themselves out to find someone who does, and you'll probably end up with an escort.

When addressing an envelope, write the house number after the street name and place the postcode before the city, as in the following example:

Monsieur Ledoux
avenue Mohammed V, 57
Marrakech-Medina
1050 Marrakech

## Business

Casablanca is the country's economic centre, Rabat is the political capital and Marrakech is a modestly sized provincial city that trades largely in tourism. Big business is generally absent from the local scene, meaning facilities for the visiting powerbroker are few. If you are here doing business, don't expect deals to be closed in a single meeting, partly because of red tape, partly because haggling and hedging are standard practice, but also because getting to the point is often considered rude. Neither should you expect anyone to show up on time; why hurry when, as the local saying goes, 'A chance encounter is worth a thousand appointments'? Patience and flexibility will be rewarded. But not always.

## Business centres

Marrakech's few business centres are all in the large five-star hotels, including the Mamounia (*see p42*), the Kempinski Mansour (044 33 91 00) and Le Meridien N'Fis (044 33 94 00); *see p57* **The chain gang**. However, such services as there are tend to be reserved for guests. Faxes may be sent from some *téléboutiques* (*see p235* **Telephones**) and most cybercafés will offer word-processing and printing.

## Conferences

Marrakech has a fully equipped conference centre in the Palais de Congres, which is managed by the Hotel Kempinski Mansour (044 33 91 00). However, it's geared up for major events rather than small-scale presentations. Most other five stars also have more modest conference facilities.

## Couriers

Within Marrakech businesses use *petit taxis*. Note the number of the taxi (painted on the door) so if there's any problem later the police can track down the cabbie through the drivers' register – although this is rarely ever necessary. Pay as you would as a passenger. The following international couriers have offices in Marrakech:

### DHL
*133 avenue Abdelkarim El Khattabi, Guéliz (044 43 76 47/www.dhl.com).* **Open** 8am-12.30pm, 2.30-6.30pm Mon-Fri; 9am-1pm Sat. **Credit** MC, V. **Map** p256 A2.

### FedEx
*113 avenue Abdelkarim El Khattabi, Guéliz (044 44 82 57).* **Open** 8.15am-12.30pm, 2.15-6.30pm Mon-Fri; 8.30am-1pm Sat. **No credit cards. Map** p256 A2.

## Consumer

There are no such things as consumer rights. How could there be? You haggled for it and set your own price, in the course of which you examined the object in question to ascertain its value. If you feel cheated afterwards, you've only yourself to blame. However, if you do have a genuine grievance, take it to the tourist police, who are usually very good at settling matters promptly and usually in the favour of the visitor.

---

# Travel advice

For up-to-date information on travel to a specific country – including the latest news on safety and security, health issues, local laws and customs – contact your home country government's department of foreign affairs. Most have websites packed with useful advice for would-be travellers.

**Australia**
www.dfat.gov.au/travel

**Canada**
www.voyage.gc.ca

**New Zealand**
www.mft.govt.nz/travel

**Republic of Ireland**
www.irlgov.ie/iveagh

**UK**
www.fco.gov.uk/travel

**USA**
http://travel.state.gov

Directory

## Customs

The following allowances apply to people bringing duty-free goods into Morocco: 400g of tobacco, 200 cigarettes or 50 cigars, 1 litre of spirits and unlimited foreign currency.

Moroccan customs officials can be funny about electronic and photographic equipment. If it's just one or two items, obviously for your personal use, then you should be OK, but anyone with significant amounts of camera gear, for example, may have it written into their passports. Anything that can't be presented on leaving will be assumed to have been 'sold' and liable to a heavy duty tax. If the property has been stolen, you need police documentation to prove it. The best thing is to keep such items out of sight of customs officers.

Pets may be taken into Morocco as long as they have a medical certificate no more than ten days old and an anti-rabies certificate no more than six months old.

## Disabled

Marrakech is tough on anyone with a mobility problem. Roads and pavements are uneven and pitted, and frequently rutted. Routes through the Medina are narrow and crowded and it's necessary to be nimble to avoid the bicycles and donkeys. Outside of the bigger hotels (the Mamounia, the Royal Mirage Marrakech and the Sofitel all lay claim to disabled facilities), few buildings – if any – make concessions to the handicapped. In smaller hotels and riads, while facilities may be lacking, it's a given that people will try to make your stay as easy as possible but steps, if not stairs, are pretty much unavoidable. Problems may be compounded by the fact that banisters do not exist

in traditional Moroccan homes or in most riads and small hotels.

## Electricity

Morocco operates on 220V AC. Plugs are the European two-pin variety. If you forget to bring an adapter, they're available from electrical shops for around 25dh. Visitors from the USA will need to bring a transformer if they intend to use appliances from home.

## Embassies & consulates

There's just the one diplomatic office in Marrakech, and that's the French, of course. As a reminder of colonial days past, it occupies the most prominent site in the city, next to the Koutoubia Mosque. Its high blank wall fringes the place de Foucault. You'll find other embassies and consulates in Rabat and Casablanca.

### British Consulate

*17 boulevard de la Tour Hassan, Rabat (037 72 96 96/fax 037 70 45 31/www.britain.org.ma/consular/services.html).* **Open** 8.30am-12.30pm, 1.30-4pm Mon-Thur; 8.30am-12.30pm Fri.
Also handles Irish and New Zealand consular affairs. In the event of an emergency in Marrakech, contact **Residence Jaib** (55 boulevard Mohammed Zerktouni, 044 43 60 78, mobile 061 14 84 44). Britain also has consulates in Casablanca and Tangier.

### Canadian Consulate

*13 rue Jaafar Es Sadiq, Agdal, Rabat (037 68 74 00/fax 037 67 21 87).* Also handles Australian consular affairs.

### French Consulate

*rue Ibn Khaldun, Medina, Marrakech (044 38 82 00).* **Open** 8.30-11.45am Mon-Fri. **Map** p254 B6.

### US Consulate

*2 avenue de Marrakech, Rabat (037 76 22 65/fax 037 76 56 61/www.usembassy.ma).* **Open** 8.30am-5.30pm Mon-Fri.
The US also has a consulate in Casablanca (8 Boulevard Moulay Youssef, 022 26 45 50).

## Emergencies

**Police** 19
**Fire service** 15 or 044 43 04 15
**Ambulance service** 044 44 37 24

## Health

Morocco doesn't have any reciprocal health care agreements with other countries, so taking out your own medical insurance is advisable. No vaccinations are required for Marrakech, although inoculation against hepatitis is a good idea. Travellers commonly complain of stomach upsets, but this is more often due to the change in diet than food poisoning. Make sure you bring along anti-diarrhoeal capsules, such as Imodium, and play safe by avoiding tap water: bottled water is inexpensive and available at all restaurants and cafés.

Should you get ill, then be warned that the Moroccan healthcare system is ropey. While good doctors can be found and pharmacies are surprisingly well stocked and knowledgeably staffed, for anyone afflicted with serious illness the best route to take is the one leading straight to the airport and home.

### Contraception & abortion

You can purchase condoms as well as birth control pills over the counter at any pharmacy. If you aren't currently using birth control, bring an emergency morning-after pill kit with you as this is not available in Morocco.

Abortion is not openly discussed. It is unavailable to unmarried women; any doctor practising an abortion on an unmarried woman can be arrested and disbarred. However, married women who already have children seem to be able to have abortions discreetly without any problems. For non-Moroccans the best bet is to contact an abortion clinic in Spain.

## Dentists

Dental care in Marrakech is of a reasonable standard – discounting the wizened old guys on Jemaa El Fna with the trays of pliers and loose false teeth (although an otherwise perfectly sensible English friend of ours swears one of these guys cured her abscess). Offices and equipment may not be state of the art, but the practitioners are usually competent. However, getting appointments with the best guys isn't always easy.

### Docteur Youssef Dassouli

*Résidence Asmae, apartment No.6, 1st floor, above Pâtisserie Yum Yum, route de Targa (044 43 53 03, emergency contact 064 90 65 14).* **Office hours** 9am-noon, 3.30-7pm Mon-Fri. **No credit cards.** English spoken.

## Doctors

There's no shortage of doctors and specialists in Marrakech, but the trick is to find a good one. We can recommend the following:

### Doctor Béatrice Peiffer Lahrichi

*Résidence Lafrasouk, 1st floor, 10 rue Oued El Makhazine, Guéliz (044 43 53 29).* **Office hours** 9am-12.30pm, 3.30-6.30pm Mon-Fri; 9am-12.30pm Sat. **No credit cards.** **Map** p256 B3.
French doctor (speaks no English) working out of a very modern surgery with full lab facilities.

### Doctor Frederic Reitzer

*Above Café Zohra, Immeuble Moulay Youssef, 4th floor, rue de la Liberté, Guéliz (044 43 95 62/emergency contact 061 17 38 03).* **Office hours** 9.30am-noon, 3.30-7pm Mon-Fri; 10am-noon Sat. **No credit cards. Map** p256 B2.
Speaks English.

### Docteur Samir Bellmezouar

*Polyclinique du Sud, rue Yougoslavie, Guéliz (061 24 32 27).* **Office hours** *Emergency team* 24hrs daily. **No credit cards. Map** p252 A2.
Doesn't speak English but does make house calls.

### Docteur El Oufir (gynaecologist)

*125 avenue Mohammed V, Guéliz (044 43 18 28).* **Office hours** 8.30am-1pm, 3.30-7pm Mon-Fri; 8.30am-1pm Sat. **No credit cards.** **Map** p256 B2.
Speaks English.

## Hospitals

The only place to go is the Polyclinique du Sud. This private clinic is frequented by the expat community and used by most insurance companies if their clients experience problems. Avoid at all costs public hospitals, where the severe lack of personnel, equipment and funding is frighteningly apparent.

### Polyclinique du Sud

*rue Yougoslavie, Guéliz (044 44 79 99).* **Open** 24hr emergency service. **Credit** MC, V. **Map** p256 A2.

## Pharmacies

Pharmacies are clearly marked with a green cross and/or green crescent. There's at least one in every neighbourhood. The drugs may have different names from those you're used to, but ask and you'll find staff well informed. Most pharmacies are open 9am to 6-7pm Monday to Friday. Some may also open on Saturday mornings or afternoons. When closed, each pharmacy should display a list of alternative pharmacies open after hours. For addresses of some pharmacies, *see p134.*

## Prescriptions

Next to anything can be bought over the counter without a prescription; about the only thing that raises eyebrows are condoms.

## STDs, HIV & AIDS

Sexually transmitted diseases, including HIV and AIDS, are here as everywhere in the world. However, due to the cultural context, these problems are not readily discussed. There has been talk of free AIDS tests but, as with all things sexual, the problem in Morocco is largely ignored.

The Association de Lutte Contre le Sida (ALCS, or in English, the Association for the Fight Against AIDS) was set up in 1988, the first of its kind in the Maghreb and Middle East. Its headquarters are in Casablanca but it is active in 11 Moroccan cities, including Marrakech. The ALCS can provide advice, prevention information and screening, as well as organise care for people living with HIV.

### ALCS

*17 avenue Massira El Khadra Maarif, Casablanca (022 99 42 42/ www.alcsmaroc.org).*

## ID

You are meant to carry some ID at all times. Moroccans have identity cards but a passport is fine for foreign visitors, or better still, just photocopies of the information pages so you can leave the actual document safely stashed back at the hotel. Valid ID is essential when checking into a hotel, hiring a car, changing or paying with travellers' cheques (and sometimes just changing foreign currency) and collecting poste restante.

## Insurance

All travellers should take out personal travel insurance to cover trip cancellation, emergency medical costs and loss or theft of baggage or money. If you're planning to take part in horse-riding, skiing or mountaineering, for

Directory

# No hassle

Hassle in a Marrakech? In a word: gone. While visitors to the city used to be plagued by the 'orrible aitches of hustlers, hassle and hard sell, all that's very much a thing of the past. Since the new king came on the scene in 1999 life has got so much easier for the visitor. Tourism is vitally important to the local economy and mindful of the damage aggressive touts and *faux* guides were doing to the city's reputation action had to be taken. Hence the formation of the 'brigade touristique', or tourist police.

Throughout the city plain clothes agents patrol the souks and alleys of the Medina benignly watching over all foreigners. They even haunt the alleyways by night, lurking in shadowy doorways around riads and hotels. Should any rash local approach a foreign tourist with a view to waylay, cajole or entreat then wham, the brigade are in there like a shot and the miscreant is dragged off for a good talking to down at the station. It's a bit draconian, particularly when you're being accompanied by a local who is a genuine friend and some officious type halts them and demands to see their papers, but by God, it's effective.

example, you should also consider additional 'dangerous sports' cover.

Keep a record of your policy number and the emergency telephone number with you.

## Internet

Computers are expensive in Morocco, so most people resort to private internet centres, which are becoming ever easier to find. In the Medina they're concentrated along rue Bab Agnaou, with at least half a dozen in a 200-metre stretch; in Guéliz the best are up around place Abdel Moumen. Prices are about 10dh an hour. The cheapest – and unlikeliest – internet access is offered at the Arset Abdelsalam, Marrakech's 'internet park', opposite the Ensemble Artisanal (*map p254 A5*), which has several public-access terminals in a glass building at the park entrance charged at 5dh per hour. ISPs tend to be oversubscribed and, with one or two notable exceptions, download times are

painfully slow. You might want to take along a book. We're not kidding.

If you are lugging around your own laptop, then you can get connected in some of the better hotels by using an RJ-11 standard telephone connector. However, few of the major ISPs have any sort of local access number for Morocco and you will have to call long distance to log on. Between high telephone tariffs and lengthy download times this can prove costly.

## Internet service providers (ISPs)

**Ménara** (Maroc Télécom's ISP, www.menara.ma) is available to those with a landline. To subscribe, visit the Maroc Télécom office (*see p235* **Telephones**). The other option is **Wanadoo** (081 00 63 63, www.wanadoo.ma) prepaid cards (10hrs for 50dh; 20hrs for 70dh). These cards don't include the telephone communications needed to access the server. Wanadoo

cards can be purchased at Marjane (route de Casablanca, 044 31 37 24), Magawork (1 Résidence Maniss La Youne, boulevard Aila Fassi (044 33 13 92) or Buraliste Bouargan (168 avenue Mohammed V, Guéliz, 044 43 02 57).

## Internet access

### Askmy
*6 boulevard Mohammed Zerktouni, Guéliz (044 43 06 02)*. **Open** 8am-2am daily. **No credit cards.** **Map** p256 A2.
The best internet centre in Marrakech bar none, with 14 state-of-the-art computers hooked up with ultra-fast 128kbps connections. Rates are slightly higher here, at 12dh per hour but it's worth the extra expense.

### Cyber Club
*avenue Mohammed V (next to Café Koutoubia), Medina (no phone)*. **Open** 9.30am-1pm, 3-10.30pm daily. **No credit cards. Map** p252/254 B5.
Right across from the Koutoubia, a small sign points down a flight of steps to this basement room with 11 online terminals.

### Mohammed Yasin Cyber Café
*38 rue Bab Agnaou, Medina*. **Open** 7am-midnight daily. **Map** p254 C6.
Close to the Pâtisserie des Princes, this is maybe the best of the street's internet providers courtesy of its super-fast connection speeds. And with 16 terminals it's rare that you have to wait for a free computer.

## Left luggage

There are no left luggage facilities at Marrakech's international airport. Bags can be left at the railway station for 10dh per day, and staff insist that they are padlocked.

## Legal help

Embassies and consulates (*see p229*) can assist nationals in emergencies and provide a list of English-speaking lawyers.

## Lost property

In general, if you've lost it, forget it. Recovering lost property depends on the good nature of the person who finds your belongings. If you've lost something on public transport, call the transport operator, who should, in principle, hang on to lost property – but don't hold your breath.

## Maps

There is no commercially available map of Marrakech. A small city plan is inset on most of the Morocco maps but while these are good for overviews of the city they lack the detail required for navigating the Medina. At present, the maps in this book are as good as it gets.

The best overall map of the country is the Michelin sheet 959, on a scale of 1:1,000,000 with a 1:600,000 inset of the Marrakech area, useful for anyone heading over the Atlas. Decent alternatives include Hildebrand's (1:900,000) and GeoCenter (1:800,000).

## Media

### Foreign publications

English-language publications are easy to come by. Expect to find the major dailies (usually just 24 hours old) including the *Guardian*, *Telegraph*, *The Times*, *Daily Mail* and *Sun*, plus the Sundays and those weekly international digests put out by some of the broadsheets. There will also usually be the *International Herald Tribune*, *Time*, *Newsweek* and *The Economist* plus sundry fashion, style and interiors mags. Details of newsagents stocking foreign papers is given in the **Shops & Services** chapter: *see p133*.

### Magazines

Most mags are in French, and anyone who can read the language should look out for *Medina* and *Maison du Maroc*: the former is Morocco travel

with places that will interest tourists, the latter is the local equivalent of *Homes & Gardens*.

## Newspapers

There are both French and Arabic papers. Though there is increasing editorial freedom, national dailies tend to restrict their coverage to the goings on of the royal family, sports and local events (sounds familiar, no?). There's little in the way of foreign news. If you read French, the best paper is the daily *Le Figaro*, printed in Casablanca.

## Television

Most hotels and riads that offer TV have satellite with BBC World, CNN, French TV5 and occasionally Sky channels.

## Money

Local currency is the Moroccan dirham, abbreviated dh (in this book) and sometimes MDH, or MAD. There are 100 centimes to a dirham. Coins come in denominations of 5, 10, 20 and 50 centimes (all useless) and 1, 2, 5 and 10dh. Note that there are two different types of 5dh coin in circulation: a large silver-coloured version and a smaller new bi-metal issue (which, in turn, is similar to the 10dh coin but smaller). It's confusing. Small change is useful for things like tips and taxi fares and should be hoarded. Banknotes come in denominations of 20, 50, 100 and 200dh. (There is also a 10dh note but this is being phased out.)

Excess dirhams can be exchanged for euros or dollars (pounds sterling are often not available) at a bank. You may be asked to show the exchange receipts from when you converted your hard currency into dirhams – this is because banks will only allow you to

change back up to half the amount of Moroccan currency originally purchased.

At the time of writing, conversion between currencies is easy, as 10dh = US$1 = €1.

## ATMs

Cashpoints, or *guichets automatiques*, are common in most Moroccan towns and cities, and it's perfectly possible to travel on plastic – although it's always wise to carry at least a couple of days' 'survival money' in cash. Most ATMs are connected to the international banking systems and issue dirhams on most European and US debit and credit cards. If the ATM carries only a Visa symbol, don't go there; it will only process locally issued Visa cards and may well swallow the international variety (we've heard tales of this happening). Instead look for machines bearing the Cirrus, Link and Maestro symbols.

Most banks set a daily withdrawal limit of 2,000dh (currently around £125) per day on ATM withdrawals. If you need more, just go to an exchange bureau with your card and passport and get a cash advance.

ATMs are concentrated along rue Bab Agnaou in the Medina and around place Abdel Moumen in Guéliz. Beware of Monday mornings; machines are often empty after the weekend.

## Banks

The main local banks are Banque Commerciale du Maroc (BCM), Banque Marocaine du Commerce Extérieur (BMCE), Banque Marocaine du Commerce et de l'Industrie (BMCI) and Crédit du Maroc. All have agreements with major international banks. The heaviest concentration of bank branches is around place

Abdel Moumen in Guéliz. For opening hours, *see below*. Note that the BMCI on boulevard Mohammed Zerktouni (round the corner from Café Atlas) is open at weekends and on public holidays, when most other banks are closed.

## Bureaux de change

Almost all banks have a bureaux de change counter, as do most major hotels of three stars and up. The exchange rate is set by the Bank of Morocco and is uniform. No commission is charged. When changing money you will usually be asked to show your passport. There's a convenient exchange window on rue Bab Agnaou, 100 metres along from Jemaa El Fna.

## Credit cards

MasterCard and Visa are widely accepted at shops, restaurants and hotels; American Express less so. Places that accept AmEx often add five per cent to cover the cost of the transaction. It's wise to carry cash back-up because management will often claim that the machine is 'broken' or that your card won't go through – they aren't keen on the delay in payment that processing a credit card entails. Most establishments can do a manual transaction ('au sabot') and phone for an authorisation.

Credit card fraud is also a problem in Morocco, so keep all receipts to check against your statement. Chip and PIN, needless to say, has yet to reach Morocco.

BMCE banks will give cash advances on MasterCard and Visa up to around 5,000dh.

American Express is represented in Marrakech by Voyages Schwartz (044 43 33 21), whose offices are in the Immeuble Moutaouskil, 1 rue Mauritanie, Guéliz (*map p256*

B3). It won't give cash advances but it will issue a letter of credit that you can then use to get cash at any Crédit du Maroc bank.

### Lost/stolen credit cards

All lines have English-speaking staff and are open 24hrs daily.
**American Express** *00 973 256 834*
**Barclaycard** *00 44 1604 230 230*
**Diners Club** *022 99 455/00 44 1252 513 500*
**MasterCard** *00 1636 722 7111*
**Switch** *00 870 000459*

## Travellers' cheques

Travellers' cheques are accepted by most banks, though you may be bounced around between counters or branches before finding someone to cash them. Stick to well-known brands like Thomas Cook and American Express. A commission is usually charged of around 20dh-25dh per transaction, irrespective of the number of cheques or amount cashed. The Banque El Maghreb is an exception in charging nothing. Some hotels and shops will also accept travellers cheques as payment.

## Opening hours

Opening times listed in this book should be taken more as guidelines than gospel. Many places close in the afternoon for a siesta, which is not always reflected in the times we have given. As a rule of thumb the working week is Monday to Friday, with a half-day on Saturday. Note that hours vary in summer (from around 15 June to the end of September) and during Ramadan (*see p234* **Islamic holidays**), when business open and close later.

**Banks** 8.30-11.30am, 2.30-4.30pm Mon-Fri.
**Shops** 9am-1pm, 3-7pm Mon-Sat.
**Museums & tourist sights** Usually closed Tue.

## Police

Crime against visitors is low and physical violence almost unheard of. You do need to watch your pockets and bags, though, particularly around Jemaa El Fna. If you are robbed or have a complaint against an unscrupulous taxi driver or souk merchant, the place to go is the office of the Brigade Touristique.

Note, if you are the victim of crime outside Marrakech, then you must make a report to the local police wherever the incident occurred – do not wait until your return to the city.

### Police stations

The main police station (Hôtel de Police; *map p252 B3*) is on rue Oued El Makhazine in Guéliz near the Jnane El Harti park. There's also an office of the tourist police (Brigade Touristique; 044 38 46 01) on the north side of Jemaa El Fna.

## Postal services

The main post office (PTT Centrale) is on place du 16 Novembre, Guéliz, halfway along avenue Mohammed V (across from the McDonald's). It's open 8am-2pm Mon-Sat. There is a second, smaller PTT in the Medina on rue Moulay Ismail, between Jemaa El Fna and the Koutoubia Mosque, open 8am-noon and 3-6pm Mon-Fri in the winter and 8am-3pm in the summer. Stamps are sold at a dedicated *timbres* counter, but can also be bought at a *tabac* or at the reception desks of larger hotels. Parcels should be taken unwrapped for examination.

Mail delivery is painfully slow. Post offices provide an express mail service (EMS), but also known as *poste rapide*). For really urgent mail, it's probably safer to use one of the international courier companies, *see p227*.

# Islamic holidays

Of all the Islamic holidays, **Ramadan** is the most significant and the one that has the greatest impact on the visitor. This is the Muslim month of fasting. Many Moroccans abstain from food, drink and cigarettes between sunrise and sunset. Many cafés and restaurants will close during the day. It's also bad form to flaunt your non-participation by smoking or eating in the street. Ramadan nights are some of the busiest of the year as, come sundown, eateries are packed with large groups communally breaking their fast, a meal known as *iftar*. Jemaa El Fna gets particularly wild.

The end of Ramadan is marked by the two-day feast of **Eid El Seghir** ('the small feast'). A few months later the feast of **Eid El Kebir** ('the big feast') commemorates Abraham's sacrifice of a ram instead of his son. It's not a good time for sheep as every family that can afford to emulates the Patriarch's deed by slaughtering an animal.

Three weeks after Eid El Kebir is **Moharram**, the Muslim New Year. The other big Muslim holiday is **Mouloud**, a celebration of the birthday of the Prophet Mohammed.

Islamic religious holidays are based on a lunar calendar, approximately 11 days shorter than the Gregorian (Western) calendar. This means that Islamic holidays shift forward by 11 days each year.

|              | **2005** | **2006**       | **2007**  |
|--------------|----------|----------------|-----------|
| **Ramadan**      | 3 Oct    | 24 Sept        | 13 Sept   |
| **Eid El Seghir**| 3 Nov    | 28 Oct         | 13 Oct    |
| **Eid El Kebir** | 21 Jan   | 11 Jan/31 Dec  | 20 Dec    |
| **Moharran**     | 10 Feb   | 31 Jan         | 20 Jan    |
| **Mouloud**      | 19 Apr   | 8 Apr          | 27 Mar    |

Note, these dates are approximate as the exact start of the celebrations depends on the sighting of the full moon.

## Poste restante

Poste restante is not always reliable, but if you want to give it a go, have the letters addressed to 'Poste Restante, PTT Centrale, Marrakech', and make sure that the surname is clear. A passport will be needed to pick up any mail.

## Religion

Islam underpins society, places of worship are prominent and religious festivals are a highlight of the annual calendar. Sex before marriage is taboo. Islam may be tougher on alcohol, but the Moroccans have always been notably more liberal when it comes to drugs (*see p236* **Kif and majoun**). Although every neighbourhood has its mosque, few Moroccans perform the required five daily cycles of prayer. Many of those who do attend the mosque are content to limit their visits to noon Friday, the main weekly prayer session. Most Moroccans, however, do make an effort to observe Ramadan, at least for the first week; *see above* **Islamic holidays**.

## Christian

### Church of St Anne
*rue El Imam Ali, Guéliz (044 43 05 85)*. **Map** p256 B3.

Catholic services are held in French, but there is an interdenominational service delivered in English at 10.30am Sunday (9.30am during July) with tea and coffee afterwards.

## Smoking

Morocco is firmly in thrall to nicotine. Non-smokers are outcasts and few cafés and restaurants recognise the concept of a clean-air environment. So why buck the trend? If you don't smoke, then Marrakech is the perfect place to start. Foreign cigarette brands cost 32dh, or about £2, for 20, while the best of the domestic product goes for even less. Passive smoking or active, it's your choice, but you've got to inhale some time.

## Study

The Institut Français de Marrakech offers a selection of reasonably priced classes in Arabic to foreigners and can recommend tutors for private study. An intensive 40-hour summer course is available for 700dh. Marrakech also has the Cadi Ayyad University but this is of little interest to the average foreign visitor.

### Institut Français de Marrakech
*route de Targa, Jebel Guéliz (044 44 69 30/fax 044 44 74 97)*.

### Cadi Ayyad University
*avenue Prince Moulay Abdellah, BP 511, Guéliz (044 43 48 13/fax 044 43 44 94/www.ucam.ac.ma)*.

## Telephones

Telephoning abroad from Marrakech is no problem. Either use the cardphones that are liberally dotted around town (cards are bought from post offices, *tabacs* or news vendors) or one of the numerous *téléboutiques*. The latter are identified by a large blue and white sign depicting a telephone receiver. They are small premises with anything from two to a dozen coin-operated phones in booths. The overseer supplies change. International calls require a minimum of three 5dh coins. In the Medina there's at least one *téléboutique* on every main streets.

Off-peak rates apply from midnight to 7am weekdays, from 12.30pm Saturday and all day Sunday.

## Dialling & codes

To call abroad dial 00, then the country code followed by the telephone number. When calling within Morocco you need to dial the three-digit area code even if you are calling from the same area. For instance, if you are making a local call within Marrakech, you must still dial 044. Mobiles began with the prefix 06 or 07.

### Morocco country code 212

### Area codes
**Casablanca** 022
**Essaouira** 044
**Fès** 055
**Marrakech** 044
**Ouarzazte & the south** 044
**Rabat/Tangier** 033

## Faxes

Most, but not all, *téléboutiques* will send a fax for you. Faxes to international destinations will cost around 70dh.

## Mobile phones

There are two main mobile service providers offering a pay-as-you-go option: the national operator Maroc-Télécom and Méditel. Most European networks have arrangements with one of the two so that visitors can use their mobiles in Morocco (but bear in mind that it's expensive). Alternatively, mobile users can buy a pre-paid SIM card from either of the Moroccan network operators. For a charge of

around 200dh you are provided with a local number through which calls can be made at more favourable rates.

### Maroc-Télécom (Agence Guéliz Mobile)
*avenue Mohammed V (opposite McDonald's), Guéliz (044 43 44 53/fax 044 43 10 23/www.iam.ma).* **Open** 8.30am-noon, 2-7pm Mon-Fri; 8.30am-1pm Sat. **Credit** MC, V. **Map** p256 B2.

### Méditel
*279 avenue Mohammed V, Guéliz (044 42 74 44).* **Open** 9am-noon, 3-9.30pm daily. **No credit cards**. **Map** p256 B2.

### Aloha
*15 avenue Mohammed V, Guéliz (044 42 00 34/fax 044 42 00 32).* **Open** 9am-9pm Mon-Sat. **No credit cards**. **Map** p256 A1. Méditel franchise.

### Ilaicom
*117 avenue Houmann El Fetouaki, Medina (044 38 59 63).* **Open** 10am-1pm, 3.30-7.30pm Mon-Sat. **Credit** MC, V. **Map** p254 C7. Méditel franchise.

### Kent 2
*40 avenue Abdelkarim El Khattabi, Guéliz (044 44 84 38/fax 044 42 00 32).* **Open** 9.30am-9pm Mon-Sat. **No credit cards**. **Map** p252 A2. Méditel franchise.

### Le Portable
*8 rue Fatima Zohra, Medina (044 44 22 28).* **Open** 9.30am-1pm, 3.30-8pm daily. **No credit cards**. **Map** p252 B4. Méditel franchise.

## Operator services

The international operator can be accessed by dialling 120, and to make a reverse charge call say *'Je voudrais téléphoner en PCV'* but be prepared for a wait. To get the domestic operator dial 10. For directory enquiries dial 16, but don't expect English to be spoken.

## Time

Morocco follows GMT all year round, which means that it's on the same time as Britain and Ireland in winter but an

hour behind during British Summer Time (late March to late October).

## Tipping

Tipping is expected in cafés and restaurants (round up the bill or add 10-15 per cent), by guides and porters, and by anyone else that renders you any sort of small service. Five or ten dirhams is sufficient. It is not necessary to tip taxi drivers, who can just be content with overcharging.

## Toilets

Public toilets are a rarity – use the facilities when in bars, hotels and restaurants. They're usually decent enough (and occasionally stunning, as at Comptoir). It's a good idea to carry some tissues as toilet paper is not always available; the traditional method here is to use the water hose to sluice yourself clean. A wastebasket beside the toilet is for used tissues, which the plumbing generally isn't up to digesting. At cafés the toilet attendant expects a few dirhams as a tip; it's bad form not to oblige.

## Tourist information

The **ONMT** (Office National Marocain du Tourisme) has a fairly useless presence in Marrakech. Basic tourist info can also be found at its website www.visitmorocco.com.

### ONMT
*ONMT, place Abdel Moumen, Guéliz (044 43 61 31).* **Open** 8.30am-noon, 2.30-6.30pm Mon-Fri; 9am-noon, 3-6pm Sat. **Map** p256 A1.

## International offices

**London** *205 Regent Street, W1R 7DE (+44 20 7437 0073).*
**New York** *20 East 46th Street, suite 1201, 10017 (+1 212 55 72 520).*
**Paris** *161 rue Saint Honoré, 75001 (+1 42 60 63 50).*

**Directory**

# Kif and majoun

Recreational marijuana use filtered into the Maghreb from the Middle East sometime around the 12th century and has been a part of Moroccan life ever since. Discreet use is tolerated and a significant minority still consume the stuff. It's smoked as *kif* (grass) in a long pipe called a *sebsi* or less tradtionally as hash mixed with tobacco in European style joints. It's also eaten in the notoriously hallucinogenic jam- or cake-like form of *majoun*.

But Morocco is the world's largest cannabis producer and most of it is exported. In the area around Ketama in the Rif Mountains, up to 1,000 sq km are under cultivation bringing up to $3 billion a year back into the Moroccan economy.

That cash is one reason why the authorities pay little more than lip service to US and European pressure to stamp this trade out. But there are also practical problems. The Berbers of the Rif are fiercely independent and have successfully resisted assimilation since Roman times. One mid-1990s attempt to burn the *kif* crop was met with armed resistance. Government attempts to introduce crop substitution have proved useless as nothing else of value will flourish in the rocky landscape.

Moroccan law maintains stiff penalties for sale or consumption and however much you might want to sample the local produce treat all approaches with caution. It's not just that dealers will supply poor quality at inflated prices. It's also that some double as police informers, angling for a share of the *baksheesh* you'll later pay to buy yourself out of trouble.

There are 600 or so Europeans in Moroccan jails and nearly all of them have been banged up for cannabis-related offences. To reduce the risk of joining them, follow these simple guidelines:

● Leave any transaction for a few days until you've got a feel for how things work.
● Avoid street dealers. If you don't know any locals, the best bet is a younger souk stallholder who might have a bit under the counter. Don't ask. Wait for their approach.
● Never buy more than a small amount for personal use, and don't travel with any in your possession.

## Visas & immigration

All visitors to Morocco need a passport to enter the country, which should be valid for at least six months beyond the date of entry. No visas are required for nationals of Australia, Britain, Canada, Ireland, New Zealand, the US and most EU countries. If in doubt check with your local Moroccan embassy.

Travellers can stay in Morocco for three months from the time of entry. Extensions require applying for an official residence permit, which is a lengthy and tedious procedure. First it's necessary to open a bank account in Morocco for which you will need a minimum of 20,000dh (£1,250) deposited in your account and an *attestation de résidence* from your hotel or landlord.

Then you need to go to the Bureau des Etrangers equipped with your passport, seven passport photos, two copies of the *attestation*, two copies of your bank statement, and a 60dh stamp (available from any *tabac*). Once all the requisite forms have been filled out in duplicate you should receive a residence permit a few weeks later.

A simpler option may be to leave the country for a few days and re-enter, gaining a new three-month stamp.

### Bureau des Etrangers
*Comissariat Central, Guéliz.* **Open** 8am-noon, 2-6pm Mon-Thur; 8am-noon Fri.

## When to go

The tourist office claim that Marrakech receives 350 days of sunshine a year is stretching it a bit, but the weather is rarley a talking point – it's typically expressed with one of three adjectives: hot, hotter or hottest. December and January can be afflicted with overcast skies and rain showers, but Marrakech still makes for a good winter retreat with daily temperatures of around 15-20°C (59-68°F). Evenings can be chilly and you need to be in a hotel that has heating.

March to May is the perfect time to visit but beware of high-season price hikes at Easter. Summers can be oppressive with temperatures averaging 30-35°C (86-95°F) and frequently pushing up towards 40°C (104°F). The heat is a drain on energy and poolside lounging suddenly seems more attractive than sightseeing. It's not until September that things start to cool off again, with autumn being another climatically attractive season. Hotel rates soar over Christmas.

Directory

## Public holidays

Morocco's six secular holidays occupy a day each. Banks, offices and civil service institutions close, but many shops stay open and public transport runs as usual.

**1 January** New Year's Day
**1 May** Labour Day (Fête du Travail)
**30 July** Feast of the Throne (Fête du Trône), commemorating the present king's accession
**14 August** Allegiance Day
**6 November** Day of the Green March (Marche Vert), commemorating the retaking of Spanish-held Saharan territories
**18 November** Independence Day

Religious holidays occupy two or three days and if these happen to fall midweek then the government commonly extends the holiday to cover the whole working week.
*See also p234* **Islamic holidays**.

## Festivals

Four years old in 2005, the **Marrakech International Film Festival** has established itself as the city's most prestigious and glitzy cultural event. In past years the festival has been held in both September and December but it looks likely to settle in

November: *see p141*. The only other Marrakech jamboree of note is June's two-week **Festival of Folk Art and Music**. Now in its 40th year, the festival annually takes on a different theme, played out by dozens of troupes from around Morocco. At the time of writing the people behind Kasbah Agafay (*see p62*) were promising a **Marrakech Fashion Week** 2005 with international designers, celebs and a focus on UK fashion, but no further details were available. There is also talk of a literary festival for 2006 but again, no firm details as yet.

Outside of Marrakech, there's the annual **Festival d'Essaouira** (*see p181*), held each June in the pretty Atlantic port town. It attracts a host of international performers and is well worth heading out to the coast for if you happen to be in Morocco in June.

## Women

Though Marrakech is Islamic, few special rules apply. With some provisos, you needn't dress any differently here than at home. However, if you've a liking for minis and micros, leave those behind. Shorts are out too. To avoid causing

offence or being stared at, wear trousers or dresses and skirts that reach the knee or lower. Loose and baggy light cotton is the way to go. In more conservative areas such as the northern Medina, women should keep their shoulders covered (though a headscarf is *not* necessary).

In touristy areas such as around Jemaa El Fna and the main souks, you may get hit on. It's usually harmless and nothing more than you could expect to experience in Greece or Italy, but all the same it can be annoying. It's also generally easy to shrug off. Avoid direct eye contact. Don't beam wide smiles at men. Don't respond to invitations, come-ons or obnoxious comments. If a man is persistent and in your face, raise your voice so others around know you're being bothered. Chances are someone will intervene on your behalf.

## Work

Although Marrakech is welcoming of foreign residents, most are retired or living on incomes derived in their home countries. In such cases, as long as you can prove regular transfers of funds are being made into a Moroccan bank account, then it's a relatively easy matter to obtain a *carte de séjour* (residence permit). Earning your keep as a foreigner in Marrakech is harder. International companies setting up in Morocco (hotels, for instance) tend to do their hiring abroad.

Teachers with recognised qualifications (CELTS) could make inquiries at the American Language Center where English is taught to local students.

### American Language Centre (ALC)
*3 impasse des Moulins, boulevard Mohammed Zerktouni, Guéliz (044 44 72 59).* **Open** 9am-noon, 3-7pm Mon-Fri; 9am-noon Sat.

# Weather report

| | Temperature(°C/°F) Average high | Rainfall (in/mm) |
|---|---|---|
| Jan | 21/70 | 1.1/28 |
| Feb | 22/72 | 1.2/30 |
| Mar | 23/73 | 1.2/30 |
| Apr | 26/79 | 1.1/28 |
| May | 29/84 | 0.7/18 |
| June | 30/86 | 0.3/7.6 |
| July | 33/91 | 0.1/2.5 |
| Aug | 36/97 | 0.1/2.5 |
| Sept | 31/88 | 0.3/7.6 |
| Oct | 28/82 | 1.0/25 |
| Nov | 24/75 | 1.3/33 |
| Dec | 21/70 | 1.3/33 |

**Directory**

# Vocabulary: French

In French, as in other Latin languages, the second person singular (you) has two forms. Phrases here are given in the more polite *vous* form. The *tu* form is used with family, friends, young children and pets; you should be careful not to use it with people you do not know sufficiently well, as it is considered rude. You will also find that courtesies such as *monsieur, madame* and *mademoiselle* are used much more than often their English equivalents.

## General expressions

good morning/hello *bonjour*
good evening *bonsoir*
goodbye *au revoir*
hi (familiar) *salut*
OK *d'accord*; yes *oui*; no *non*
How are you? *Comment allez vous?/vous allez bien?*
How's it going? *Comment ça va?/ça va?* (familiar)
Sir/Mr *monsieur* (M)
Madam/Mrs *madame* (Mme)
Miss *mademoiselle* (Mlle)
please *s'il vous plaît*; thank you *merci*; thank you very much *merci beaucoup*
sorry *pardon*; excuse me *excusez-moi*
Do you speak English? *Parlez-vous anglais?*
I don't speak French *Je ne parle pas français*
I don't understand *Je ne comprends pas*
Speak more slowly, please *Parlez plus lentement, s'il vous plaît*
how much?/how many? *combien?*
Have you got change? *Avez-vous de la monnaie?*
I would like... *Je voudrais...*
it is *c'est*; it isn't *ce n'est pas*
good *bon* (m)/*bonne* (f); bad *mauvais* (m)/*mauvaise* (f)
small *petit* (m)/*petite* (f); big *grand* (m)/ *grande* (f)
beautiful *beau* (m)/*belle* (f); well *bien*; badly *mal*
expensive *cher*; cheap *pas cher*

a bit *un peu*; a lot *beaucoup*; very *très*; with *avec*; without *sans*; and *et*; or *ou*; because *parce que*
who? *qui?*; when? *quand?*; which? *quel?*; where? *où?*; why? *pourquoi?*; how? *comment?*
at what time/when? *à quelle heure?*
forbidden *interdit/défendu*
out of order *hors service/ en panne*
daily *tous les jours (tlj)*

## Getting around

When is the next train for...? *C'est quand le prochain train pour...?*
ticket *un billet*; station *la gare*; platform *le quai*
bus/coach station *gare routière*
entrance *entrée*; exit *sortie*
left *gauche*; right *droite*; interchange *correspondence*
straight on *tout droit*; far *loin*; near *pas loin/près d'ici*
street *la rue*; street map *le plan*; road map *la carte*
bank *la banque*; is there a bank near here? *est-ce qu'il y a une banque près d'ici?*
post office *La Poste*; a stamp *un timbre*

## Sightseeing

museum *un musée*
church *une église*
exhibition *une exposition*; ticket (for museum) *un billet*; (for theatre, concert) *une place*
open *ouvert*; closed *fermé*
free *gratuit*; reduced price *un tarif réduit*

## Accommodation

Do you have a room (for this evening/for two people)? *Avez-vous une chambre (pour ce soir/pour deux personnes)?*
full *complet*; room *une chambre*
bed *un lit*; double bed *un grand lit;* (a room with) twin beds *(une chambre) à deux lits*
with bath/(room)/shower *avec (salle de) bain/douche*
breakfast *le petit déjeuner*
included *compris*
lift *un ascenseur*
air-conditioned *climatisé*

## At the café or restaurant

I'd like to book a table (for three/at 8pm) *Je voudrais réserver une table (pour trois personnes/à vingt heures)*
lunch *le déjeuner*; dinner *le dîner*
coffee (espresso) *un café*; white coffee *un café au lait/café crème*; tea *le thé*; wine *le vin*; beer *la bière*
mineral water *eau minérale*; fizzy *gazeuse*; still *plate*
tap water *eau du robinet/une carafe d'eau*
the bill, please *l'addition, s'il vous plaît*

## Behind the wheel

no parking *stationnement interdit/stationnement gênant*; speed limit 40 *rappel 40*; petrol *essence*; unleaded *sans plomb*

## Numbers

0 *zéro*; 1 *un* (m), *une* (f); 2 *deux*; 3 *trois*; 4 *quatre*; 5 *cinq*; 6 *six*; 7 *sept*; 8 *huit*; 9 *neuf*; 10 *dix*; 11 *onze*; 12 *douze*; 13 *treize*; 14 *quatorze*; 15 *quinze*; 16 *seize*; 17 *dix-sept*; 18 *dix-huit*; 19 *dix-neuf*; 20 *vingt*; 21 *vingt-et-un*; 22 *vingt-deux*; 30 *trente*; 40 *quarante*; 50 *cinquante*; 60 *soixante*; 70 *soixante-dix*; 80 *quatre-vingts*; 90 *quatre-vingt-dix*; 100 *cent*; 1,000 *mille*; 1,000,000 *un million*.

## Days, months & seasons

Monday *lundi*; Tuesday *mardi*; Wednesday *mercredi*; Thursday *jeudi*; Friday *vendredi*; Saturday *samedi*; Sunday *dimanche*.

January *janvier*; February *février*; March *mars*; April *avril*; May *mai*; June *juin*; July *juillet*; August *août*; September *septembre*; October *octobre*; November *novembre*; December *décembre*.

Spring *printemps*; summer *été*; autumn *automne*; winter *hiver*.

# Vocabulary: Arabic

Within Marrakech (and other main towns and cities) you can get by in French, which is widely spoken by all educated Moroccans. However, a little effort with Arabic goes a long way, even if it is just a few stock phrases like 'hello' and 'goodbye'. Moroccan Arabic is a dialect of the standard Arabic language and is not the same as that spoken elsewhere in North Africa and the Middle East, although there are some words and phrases in common. We should point out that transliteration from Arabic into English is a highly inexact science and a wide variety of spellings are possible for any given word (for example Koran vs Quran). In this guide we've tended to plump for whatever seemed the most straightforward. You are also likely to encounter Berber, which comes in three distinct dialects. Most Berber speakers will also be fluent in Arabic.

## Arabic pronunciation

Arabic has numerous sounds that non-speakers have trouble in pronouncing but nobody is going to knock you for trying.

*gh* - like the French 'r', slightly rolled
*kh* - like the 'ch' in loch

## Emergencies

leave me alone *esmahli la*
help! *tekni!*
help me, please *awenni afak*
call the police *ayyet el bolice*
thief *sheffar*
I'm lost *tweddert*

## General expressions

good morning/hello *sabah el kheir/salaam aleikum*
good evening *masr el kheir*
goodbye *masalaama*

please *min fadlak* (to a male); *min fadlik* (to a female)
yes *aywa/anam*; no *la*
How are you? *labas/kifhalak (to a male)/kifhalik (to a female)*
thank you *shukran*
no thanks *la shukran*
sorry/excuse me *esmahli*
Do you speak English? *Itkelim Ingleezi?*
I don't speak Arabic *Metkelimsh Arabi*
I don't understand *Mafayimtish*
who? *shkun?*; why? *lash?*; which? *ashmen?*; where? *feyn?*
today *el youm*; tomorrow *ghedda*; yesterday *imbara*
God willing *inshalah*
never mind/so it goes *malish*
tips *baksheesh*
let's go *yalla*
passport *passeport*

## Shopping

how much?/how many? *bekam?*
Do you have...? *Wahesh andakum...?*
Have you got change? *Maak sarf?*
credit card *kart kredi*
travellers' cheques *shek siyahi*
good *mleah*; bad *mish imleah*
small *seghir*; big *kebir*
beautiful *jameel*
that's expensive *ghali bezzaf*
enough *kafi*

## Getting around

Where is...? *Feyn keyn...?*
Where is the hotel? *Feyn keyn el otel?*
airport *el mattar*
station *el mahatta*
bus/coach station *mahatta d'el ottobisat*
ticket office *maktab el werka*; ticket *werka*
train station *el gar*
bus stop *plasa d'el ottobisat*
museum *el mathaf*
embassy *el sifara*
pharmacy *farmasyan*
bank *el banka*
post office *el busta*; stamp *etnaber*
restaurant *el mattam*
mosque *jamaa*
left *yassar*; right *yemeen*
stop here *haten hinayer*
here *hina;* there *hinak*

## Accommodation

Do you have a room? *Andak beit?*
key *srout*
room *beit*
sheet *eyzar*
shower *doush*
toilet *vaysay*
breakfast *iftar*

## At the café or restaurant

table for... *tabla dyal...*
what's that? *shnu hada?*
I'm a vegetarian *makanakulsh elham*
I don't eat... *makanakulsh...*
meat *leham*
chicken *dzhazh*
fish *elhut*
bread *elkhobz*
coffee *qahwa*; tea *atay*
beer *birra*; wine *shshrab*
mineral water *sidi ali*
the bill, please *lahsab afak*

## Numbers

0 *sifer*; 1 *wahid*; 2 *itnehn*; 3 *telata*; 4 *arbaa*; 5 *khamsa*; 6 *setta*; 7 *seba*; 8 *tamanya*; 9 *tesa*; 10 *ashra*; 11 *hadasha*; 12 *itnasha*; 13 *teltash*; 14 *arbatash*; 15 *khamstash*; 16 *settash*; 17 *sebatash*; 18 *tamantash*; 19 *tesatash*; 20 *eshreen*; 21 *wahid w'eshreen*; 22 *itnehn w'eshreen*; 30 *telateen*; 40 *arba'een*; 50 *khamseen*; 60 *setteen*; 70 *seba'een*; 80 *tamaneen*; 90 *tesa'een*; 100 *mea*; 1,000 *alef*.

## Days, months & seasons

Monday *el itnehn*; Tuesday *el teleta*; Wednesday *el arbaar*; Thursday *el khemis*; Friday *el jomaa*; Saturday *el sebt*; Sunday *el ahad*.

January *yanayir*; February *fibraiyir*; March *maris*; April *abril*; May *mayu*; June *yunyu*; July *yulyu*; August *aghustus*; September *sibtimber*; October *oktobir*; November *nufimbir*; December *disimbir*.

# Glossary

## Architecture

**bab** gate
**dar** house
**fundouk** medieval merchants' inn arranged around a central courtyard with stabling on the gound floor, sleeping quarters above
**hammam** traditional bathhouse
**kasbah** traditional Berber fortress/palace
**koubba** domed tomb
**mashrabiya** fretworked wooden screens traditionally used for windows
**Mauresque** French colonial version of neo-Moorish architecture
**méchouar** parade ground
**medersa** Koranic school for the teaching of Islamic law and scriptures
**mihrab** prayer niche facing towards Mecca in a mosque
**minbar** pulpit in a mosque for the reading of the Koran, usually free-standing
**muqarna** Moorish ceiling ornamentation resembling stalactites
**pisé** mud reinforced with straw and lime, and the primary building material of Marrakech
**riad** house with a central courtyard garden
**tadelakt** moisture-resistant polished plaster wall surface
**zaouia** shrine of a holy man, usually also doubling as a theology school
**zelije** coloured tilework typical of Moorish decoration

## Around town

**agdal** walled garden
**arset** quarter
**calèche** horse-drawn carriage
**derb** alley
**hôtel de ville** city hall
**jnane** market garden
**maison d'hôte** guest house
**medina** Arabic for 'city', often used to mean the 'old city'
**marché** market
**mellah** traditional Jewish quarter
**place** square
**souk** bazaar or market

## Culture

**babouche** traditional leather slippers, typically yellow
**baksheesh** a tip or kickback
**baraka** blessings
**ben** son of (also spelled ibn)
**Berber** the indigenous tribes people of southern Morocco
**bidonvilles** unplanned slum dwellings on the outskirts of town
**douar** tribe
**Fassi** adjective for someone from Fès
**gnawa** semi-mystical brotherhood of muscians descended from black African slaves. Also the name of the music they play
**haj** pilgrimage to Mecca which observant Muslims are expected to perform at least once during their lifetime. Also the honorific title of someone who has made the pilgrimage
**hijab** headscarf warn by some Muslim women
**imam** priest of a mosque
**jellaba** traditional men's robe
**jinn** souls without bodies, usually malevolent (also spelled djinn)
**kif** the local marijuana, cultivated extensively in the Rif Mountains
**leila** all-night gnawa music performance (the word literally means 'night')
**maalim** master craftsman or master of any profession, including musician
**majoun** a cake or jam of marijuana
**Marrakchi** adjective for someone from Marrakech
**muezzin** the man who makes the call to prayer
**oud** musical instrument, like a lute
**sidi** saint
**Souari** adjective for someone from Essaouira
**wali** regional governor appointed by the king

## Food

**briouettes** little envelopes of paper-thin *ouarka* (filo) pastry wrapped around ground meat, rice or cheese and deep fried, served as an hors d'oeuvre
**chakchouka** dessert of light pastry filled with fruit
**couscous** coarse-ground semolina flour. Also the name of the cooked dish
**harira** Moroccan vegetable soup
**pastilla** *ouarka* (filo) pastry typically filled with a mixture of shredded pigeon, almonds and spices, served as an hors d'oeuvre
**tajine** slow-cooked stew of meat (usually lamb or chicken) and/or vegetables. Also the name of the conically lidded dish it's cooked in
**trid** shredded pigeon wrapped in a crêpe soaked in broth

## History

**Almohads** Berber dynasty (1147-1269) that ruled out of Marrakech before relocating to Rabat
**Almoravids** Berber dynasty (1062-1147) that founded Marrakech
**Green March** Action by which Morocco seized the Spanish colony of Rio del Oro in the western Sahara in 1975
**Merenids** Berber dynasty (1248-1554) that ruled from northern Morocco
**Saadians** Arab dynasty (1549-1668) that oversaw a brief renaissance of imperial Marrakech
**Treaty of Fès** The act that formalised the imposition of French rule over Morocco in 1912

# Further Reference

Some of these books, DVDs and CDs are out of print or deleted but try a websearch on bookfinder.com or ebay.com.

## Books

### Fiction

**Ben Jelloun, Tahar** *This Blinding Absence of Light* (2004) Novel concerning the desert concentration camps in which King Hassan II held his political enemies, by Morocco's most acclaimed writer.

**Binebine, Mahi** *Welcome to Paradise* (2002) A ragtag group of the hopeful and the hopeless cower on a north Atlantic beach waiting for the boat that's to smuggle them into Europe. Highly moving.

**Bowles, Paul** *The Sheltering Sky* (1949) There's little in the writings of Morocco's most famous expat writer that relates to Marrakech, but his best-known novel hauntingly portrays the untamed tribal life and sandy expanses of desert North Africa.

**Brady, James** *Paris One* (1977) The thud of a body toppled off a roof into a dirt alley in Marrakech triggers bitching, sex and bloodletting in the Parisian fashion world.

**Burroughs, William** *The Naked Lunch* (1959) Compiled in Tangier from hoarded scraps of stories and typed up in a hotel room by Kerouac, who suggested the title.

**Eggers, Dave** *You Shall Know Our Velocity* (2003) Two whiney naïve American dopes set off round the world to give away $38,000, stopping in on Marrakech along the way.

**Freud, Esther** *Hideous Kinky* (1992) A child's view of hippy life in the Marrakech of the early 1970s; mum wants to be a Sufi, her two young girls just want to go home.

**Goytisolo, Juan** *Makbara* (1980) 'Spain's greatest living writer' is a long-standing resident of Marrakech. He also exhibits a cavalier way with grammar and punctuation.

**Grenier, Richard** *Marrakech One-Two* (1983) Slight comedy about an international crew in Morocco to film a life of the Prophet. Includes obligatory hostage taking and sex-crazed female Arab radicals.

**Grimwood, Jon Courtenay** *Stamping Butterflies* (2004) A would-be assassin holed up in a future version of Marrakech plots to kill the US president. Cutting edge Moroccan-tinged sci-fi from Britain's answer to William Gibson.

**Taylor, Debbie** *The Fourth Queen* (2003) Scots lass rises through the ranks of the harem in 18th-century Marrakech and has sex with a dwarf called Microphilius. Based on a true story, apparently.

**Watkins, Paul** *In the Blue Light of African Dreams* (1990) Lyrical tale of Foreign Legion flyers based in Mogador (Essaouira) who desert desert patrols to attempt the first aerial crossing of the Atlantic.

### Non-fiction

**Bowles, Paul** *Their Heads Are Green* (1963) Non-fiction bits of travelogue in Mexico and Turkey but also in Morocco, up in the Rif and down in the Sahara.

**Busi, Aldo** *Sodomies in Eleven Point* (1988) Travels through Morocco and Tunisia in which museums and monuments take a back seat to gay sex.

**Canetti, Elias** *The Voices of Marrakech* (1967) A Nobel Prize winner's highly impressionistic tales and thumbnail sketches of the city. Yes, it's highly lyrical, but it's also a bit dull really.

**Harris, Walter** *Morocco That Was* (1921) Correspondent of *The Times* who witnessed the downfall of the sultans and arrival of the French (1912) and documented all in a wickedly funny style.

**Hopkins, John** *The Tangier Diaries 1962-1979* (1997) 'Bill Willis calls my house "Scorpion Hall" there are so many. I keep viper serum and scorpion serum in the ice box in case someone gets bitten.' Magic stuff.

**Maxwell, Gavin** *Lords of the Atlas* (1966) The single best book on Marrakech – an account of the rise and fall of the despotic Glaoui clan.

**Mayne, Peter** *A Year in Marrakesh* (1953) Recently reprinted account by a loafing Englishman of local alley life with drugs, casual sex and garden picnics. A bit of a wheeze.

**Rogerson, Barnaby** *Marraekch, the Red City* (2003) Terrific anthology of non-fiction writings on the city, from Ibn Battuta in 1325 to BBC radio reporters chasing down story tellers on the Jemaa El Fna in 2002.

## Film

For films shot in, but not necessarily about, Morocco, see p140 **The joy of sets**.

**Hideous Kinky** *dir. Gillies Mackinnon (1998)* Solid adaptation of the novel with Kate Winslet romanced by Moroccan-born Said Tagmaoui and loads of gorgeous local scenery.

**The Man Who Knew Too Much** *dir. Alfred Hitchcock (1955)* Hitchcock's second take on the title begins with a slow 30-minute travelogue shot entirely on location in Marrakech.

**Moroccan Chronicles** *dir. Moumen Smihi (1999)*

Haunting portmanteau of three fables: one shot in Marrakech, one in Essaouira and one in Tangier.

**Morocco**
*dir. Josef von Sternberg (1930)*
Marlene Dietrich vamps it up in Marrakech and elsewhere with legionnaire Gary Cooper. No plot to speak of.

**Othello**
*dir. Orson Welles (1951)*
Shot in fits and starts over four years, on a dozen locations including, notably, Essaouira, where the film crew's prolonged stay was a huge boost to the local economy.

**Our Man In Marrakesh**
*dir. Don Sharp (1996)*
Light hearted, stereotypical 1960s comedy spy romp concerning fixed UN votes and starring the excellent Terry-Thomas as a Moroccan caid. Almost entirely shot on location in Marrakech.

**The Road to Morocco**
*dir. David Butler (1942)*
Like Webster's dictionary Bing (Crosby) and Bob (Hope) are Morocco bound, quipping and gagging as they vie for the hand of Dorothy Lamour.

**The Sheltering Sky**
*dir. Bernardo Bertolucci (1990)*
Adaptation of the Bowles novel in which a travelling American couple go down the drain in the desert losing life/sanity against dramatic Moroccan backdrops.

## Discography

For more general information *see pp145-7* **Music**

## Classical

**Amina Alaoui** *Alcanaera* (Auvidis Ethnic)
The great diva of Arab-Andalous music accompanied by three classical musicians. Ethereal and beautiful.

**Moroccan Ensemble of Fès** *Andalucian Music from Morocco* (Harmonia Mundi)

Good recordings of Moroccan classical music performed by one of Morocco's finest orchestras.

## Berber & gnawa

**B'net Marrakech** *Chamaa* (Empreinte Digitale)
All-female ensemble from Marrakech who've been making a big impression on the European world music circuit.

**Jil Jilala** *Chamaa* (Blue Silver)
One of the most revered of all North African bands and this album illustrates why their sound remains so influential.

**Lemchaheb** *La Chanson Populaire Marocaine* (Club Du Disque Arabe)
A CD that captures the band raw before they went West.

**Najat Aatabou** *The Voice Of The Atlas* (Globestyle)
Outspoken female Berber vocalist who sings in Berber, Arabic and French and has risen to major star status.

**Nass El Ghiwane** *Le Disque d'Or* (Blue Silver)
Classic album from the early 1970s features Nass at their finest.

**Various** *Gnawa Music of Marrakech: Night Spirit Masters* (Axiom US)
Great recording of gnawa musicians in the Medina, featuring Brahim El Belkani.

**Various** *Maroc: Musique Populaire* (Club du Disque Arabe)
CD of *grika* (improvised) folk music. Spookily intense.

**Various** *Morocco: Jilala Confraternity* (Ocora)
An important recording of a small Jilala ensemble who perform rituals in rural Morocco on request.

## Fusion

**Aisha Kandisha's Jarring Effects** *Shabeenisation* (Barbarit) This album comes with a high-tech Bill Laswell

sheen and effectively marries hip-hop and electro influences to Moroccan music.

**Gnawa Diffusion** *Algeria* (7 Colours Music)
Reggae, ragga and funk fused courtesy of the hugely popular band from Grenoble in France.

**Hassan Hakmoun** *Trance* (Real World)
Produced by Afro-Celt leader Simon Emmerson, a jazz- and funk-influenced take on gnawa.

**Horowitz, Richard & Deyhim, Sussan** *Majoun* (EMI Classical)
Extraordinary collaboration between an Iranian vocalist, an American composer and a slew of Moroccan musicians.

**Lemchaheb & Dissidenten** *Sahara Elektrik* (Exile Music)
A collaboration between leading Moroccan *chaabi* (roots) and German world experimentalists Dissidenten.

**Master Musicians of Jajouka** *Apocalypse Across the Sky* (Axiom US)
Bill Laswell captures all the elemental power of the Jajouka orchestra. Not to be filed under easy listening.

**Momo** *The Birth Of Dar* (Apartment 22)
Rockin' live but Momo's mixing of gnawa riffs over breakbeats falls a little flat in the studio.

**Nass Marrakech** *Boubera* (Harmonia Mundi)
A gifted gnawa group based in Barcelona. They are joined here by Latin jazz musicians Omar Sosa and Jorge Pardo.

## Rock & pop

**Blur** *Think Tank* (Food)
Recorded in Marrakech and all the better for it as Britpop is superseded by 'soukpop'.

**Crosby, Stills and Nash** *Crosby, Stills and Nash* (Warner) CSN's 1969 debut album and the hippies are converging on Morocco.

**Page and Plant** *No Quarter* (Fontana) Jimmy and Robert reunite and go to Morocco.

# Index

Note: page numbers in
**bold** indicate section(s)
giving key information
on a topic; *italics*
indicate photographs.

## a

Abdel Aziz, sultan 14
Abdel Moumen, sultan
199
Abdel Rahman, sultan
*10*, **13**, 31
abortion 229-230
accommodation *see*
hotels
addresses 227
Agdal Gardens 11,
**90-92**
Agdz 218
Aghmat 201
Ahmed El Mansour
**12**, 30, 83-84, 90
AIDS/HIV 230
air travel 224
Essaouira 187
Aisha Kandisha's
Jarring Effects 146,
242
Aït Benhaddou *204*,
205
Aksar Soual 196
Alaouites **12-13**, 213,
214, 215
Almohads **11**, 28-29,
30, 68, 70, 90, 93, 199
Almoravids **11**, 28, 29,
70, 75, 90, 199, 201,
219
Amanjena 25, **61-62**
The Thai Restaurant
114
Amazrou **219**, 220
ambulance 229
American Language
Centre 237
Amizmiz 191
Amridil 208
antiques **119-120**, 126
architecture **28-31**,
34-36
arches 28, *78*
colour 29, 80
glossary 240
tiles 29
woodwork 29-30
argan oil 122, 199
Arhbalou 201-202

Arset Abdelsalam 90
art *see* galleries
Asni 196
athletics 156
Atlas, High 190-192,
194, 196-204, 208
climbing 156
tours & activities 195
Atlas Corporation
Studios 206-207, *207*
Atlassides, Les 144

## b

Bab Agnaou 11, 29, **82**
Bab Debbagh 81
Bab Doukkala 80
Bab Doukkala Mosque
80
Bab Er Rob 82
Bab Es Salam market
85, **131**
Bab Laksour 76
Bab Taghzout 77-79
*babouches* 72, 121,
**122**, 125
babysitting 137
Badii Palace 12, 30, *83*,
**83-84**, 90
bags 123, 126-127
Bahia Palace 14, 31,
**85-86**, *86*
balloon flights **160**
Balmain, Pierre 80, 99
banks 232-233
Barrage Lalla
Takerkost 191
Barrage Moulay
Youssef 191
bars 148-154
Essaouira 184-185
*see also p247 Bars
& clubs index*
Beatles, The 19, 147
beauty salons 134
beer-drinking 149
Beldi Country Club 160
Belkahia, Farid 142
Belkani, Brahim El 147
Ben Abdellah,
Abdelatif 23-25
Ben Abdellah, Sidi
Mohammed 13
Ben Moussa, Ba
Ahmed 14, 85
Ben Tachfine, Youssef
68
tomb 68

Ben Youssef Medersa
12, 30, **74-75**, *77*
Ben Youssef Mosque
72
Berbers 10-11, 29, 30,
32, 192, 199, 202
jewellery 211
linguistic jokes 212
music 145-146, 242
Bergé, Pierre 92
Best of Morocco 195
bicycle hire 198, **226**
Bigman, Sydney 18
Binebine, Mahi 142,
241
birdwatching 210, 211,
212, 216
Bizzarri, Fabrizzio 36
Blur 147, 242
B'net Marrakech 146,
242
Boccara, Charles 31,
**34**, 61, 88
bookshops **132-133**,
144
Boumalne Dadès
210-211
Bowles, Paul 19, 145,
241
bureaux de change 233
Burroughs, William 19,
87, 145, 241
buses 224-225
Amizmiz 191
Drâa Valley 218
Essaouira 187
Ouarzazate 203
Ourika Valley 201
Taroudant 196
business services 227

## c

cafés 114-116
Essaouira **184-185**
internet 187, **231**
*see also p247
Restaurants &
cafés index*
*calèches* 65, 66, 137-138
camels **220**, 222
campsites 191
candles 127
cannabis 19, **236**
carpets **120**, **122-123**
carriages *see calèches*
cars & driving 194-195,
**225-226**

hire 194, 225-226
parking 226
repairs 226
Casa Lalla 47
restaurant 103
Cascades d'Ouzoud 191
cashpoints 232
Centre Artisanal 120
ceramics & pottery
**123**, 128, **132**, *133*,
191, 201, 221
Chigaga 222
children's services &
activities 136-138
chocolates 127
Chrob ou Chouf 77
churches 87-88
St Anne 88, **234**
Churchill, Winston **15**,
22, 42, 43, 79, 158
cinemas 140-141
classes *see* courses
climbing 156
clothes 121-125
children's 138
Club Med 138
clubs 148-149,
**154-155**
*see also p247 Bars
& clubs index*
conference facilities
227
consulates 229
consumer rights 227
contraception 229
couriers 227
courses 234
cookery 116
crafts 34, **120**
credit cards 98, 118,
**233**
Criée Berbère 72
currency 232-233
customs & excise 229
cycling 94, **226**

## d

Dadès Gorge
**210-211**, 212
Dadès Valley 192,
**208-212**
Daoudiate Stadium 156
Dar Aït Sidi El Mati
208
Dar Bellarj 75
Dar Cherifa **76**, *143*,
**144**, 147

Dar El Bacha (Dar El Glaoui) 14, 31, **79-80**
Dar El Hajar 68
Dar Si Said Museum 30, **86**
Dar Tamsna 36
dates 218, 219
day trips 191
Delacroix, Eugène 19, 142
dentists 230
design 32-36
Destination Evasion 195
Deux Tours, Les 34, **61**
Diabat 174, 177
disabled facilities 229
doctors 230
Drâa Valley 12, 192, **218-222**
drink 148-149
  shops 127
driving *see* cars & driving
drugs 19, **236**
Dufy, Raoul 142
Dyers' Quarter 72-74

**e**

electricity 229
emergencies 229
Ensemble Artisanal 120
Erfoud 213-214
Essaouira 166-187
  accommodation 174-181
  beaches 173-174, 177
  cafés & bars **184-185**, 187
  cemeteries 171
  changes of name 169
  as film location 167, 170, **184**
  galleries 186-187
  history 12, 13, **166-169**
  Jews & Mellah 167, 170, 171
  map *172-173*
  museum 171
  music festivals **147**, 166, **181**, 237
  Place Moulay Hassan *167*, 169
  port *168*, 170
  resources 187
  restaurants 181-183
  shops 185-186
  sightseeing 169-174
  Skala de la Ville 170
  souks 171-173

tourist information 187
transport **187**, 224
windsurfing 177

**f**

fabrics 128
faxes 235
Festival d'Essaouira 147, **181**, 237
festivals 237
  film **141**, 237
  music **147**, 166, **181**, 237
films & film industry **139-141**, 206-207
  cinemas 140-141
  costumes & props 34
  International Film Festival **141**, 237
  shot in Morocco 42, 75, 76, 77, 139, **140**, 191, 197, 205, **241-242**
  studio tour 206-207
fitness 160-164
florists 127
food
  cookery lessons 116
  dates 218, 219
  markets 131
  Moroccan cuisine & menus **108**, 240
  shops 118, 127
football 156, 158
Fossaic, Jacqueline 23, **34-35**
fossils 214
*fundouks* 77
furniture 128-131

**g**

Galerie Bleue 144
galleries 86, 128, **142-144**, 212
  Essaouira 186-187
gardens 90-94
  Agdal 11, **90-92**
  Koutoubia 68, 90
  Majorelle 88, **92-93**
  Mamounia 93
  Menara 11, 90, *91*, **93-94**, 138
gay scene 152
Getty family 19, 33
*Gladiator* 139, 140, 205, 207
Glaoua clan 14, 204, 205, 206
Glaoui, El *see* Thami El Glaoui

glassware 131
glossary 240
gnawa **146**, 147, 167, **181**, 217, 242
golf 156-158, 161
Goundafi clan 198-199
Goytisolo, Juan 70, 71, 241
Grand Méchouar 83
Grand Tazi **55**, 82, 150
grika 145
Guéliz 17, 65, **87-89**
  accommodation 57-59
  bars 151-153
  cafés 116
  galleries 144
  Marché Central 88, **131**
  restaurants 107-111
guides **65-66**, 118
gyms 160-161
Gysin, Brion 87, 147

**h**

haggling 119
hairdressers 134
Hakmoun, Hassan 146, 242
hammams 161-162
hang-gliding 160
Harti Stadium, El 156
Hassan II, king **18-20**, 33, 94, 161
  portraits 20-21
health 229-230
  centres & spas 160-164
Hendrix, Jimi 147, 167, 174
herbalists 79, **134**
*Hideous Kinky* (Esther Freud)
  book 137, 241
  film 75, 77, 139, 191, 241
hiking *see* trekking
hippies 19, 167-169
history 10-21, 22-23, 66, 85, 166-169, 199, 204, 206, 214-215
  pre-1900 10-14
  French rule 14-17, 23
  post-independence 18-21
Hitchcock, Alfred 42, 76
Hivernage 65
  accommodation 59
  bars 153
  café 116
  restaurants 111

holidays
  Islamic 234
  public 237
home accessories 127-132
horse-drawn carriages *see calèches*
horse-riding 159
Hotel Es Saadi 59
  spa 164
  Théatro (club) 154
Hotel Toulousain 87
hotels 38-62
  architecture 34-35, 36
  the best for… 38
  budget 53-59
  chains 57
  child-friendly 136
  deluxe 41, 59, 61-62
  Essaouira 181-183
  expensive 41-47, 61, 62
  further afield 61-62
  hammams & spas 162, 164
  moderate 47-53, 57, 59, 62
  new development 27
  pools 160
  riads explained 38
  *see also p247 Accommodation index*

**i**

Ibn Toumart 199
Ijoujak 198
Imi-n-ifri 191
Imlil 191, **196-197**
Institut Français de Marrakech 234
insurance 230-231
internet 231
Islam 10-11, 234
Islam, Yusuf *see* Stevens, Cat
Istiqlal Party 17, 18

**j**

Jardins de la Koutoubia 41
  Piano Bar 151
  pool 160
  restaurant 105
Jebel Kissane 218
Jebel Toubkal 192, 197
Jemaa El Fna 27, 64, *69*, **70-71**, 138
  food stalls 101
  map *68*

jewellery **125-126**,
211
Jewish Market *see*
Marché Couvert
Jews
Essaouira 167, 170,
171
exodus 85
jewellers 211
Mellah *84*, 84-85
Zagora 219
*jinn* 79
Jnane El Harti **88**, 138
Jnane Tamsna 36, **59**
Joans, Ted 18
Jones, Brian 19, 147

**k**

Kabbaj, Mohammed
Amine 31
karting 159-160
Kasbah Mosque 29, *29*,
**82**
kasbahs 30-31, 193
Aït Benhaddou 31,
**205**
Amridil 208
in Dadés Valley 208,
211
in Drâa Valley 218,
219
Marrakech 82
Oumnast 191
around Rissani 214,
215
in Skoura *31*, 31, 208
Tamandot 164, **198**
Tamdaght 205
Tamesloht 191
Taouirt 31, **205**
Telouet 14, 31, **204**
Tiffoultoute 31, **206**
around Tin Mal
198-199
du Toubkal 197
Kawkab FC 156, **158**
Kawkab Jeu 138
Kechmara 88, **109**, 151
Kelaa M'Gouna, El
209-210
Khamlia 217
Koubba El Badiyin 11,
28, **75**, *76*
Koubba of Lalla Zohra
68
Koutoubia Gardens 68,
90
Koutoubia Mosque 11,
29, 64, *67*, **67-68**
ksars 214, 215
Ksour Agafay 22, 76
ksours 30-31, 193, 219

**o**

lakes 191
lanterns **123**, 128, 132
leather goods 123, 126-
127
left luggage 231
legal help 231
Liberté, rue de la 88
library (Tamegroute)
221
Lippini, Alessandra 36
literature 241
*Lords of the Atlas*
(Gavin Maxwell) 66,
241
lost property 231-232
Loum-Martin,
Meryanne 35-36
Lyautey, Louis *13*, 14,
17, 167

**m**

Madani El Glaoui 14, 16
magazines 232
Maison Arabe 43
hammam 162, *163*
restaurant **103**, 116
Maison Tiskiwin 86
Majorelle, Jacques 92,
142
Majorelle Gardens 88,
**92-93**
Mamounia 15, 17, **42**,
92, 133
Gardens 93
Trois Palmiers **107**
*Man Who Knew Too
Much, The* 42, 76,
140, *141*, 241
Mansour, El *see* Ahmed
El Mansour; Yacoub
El Mansour
Mansour Mosque, El
*see* Kasbah Mosque
maps 249-256
Essaouira 172-173
Jemaa El Fna 68
recommended 232
souks 73
marathon 156, *157*
marble, black 214
Marché Centrale 88,
**131**
Marché Couvert 85,
**131**
marijuana *see* cannabis
markets 85, 88, **131**
out of town 194
*see also* souks
Marrakech Art Gallery
144

massage 162-164
Master Musicians of
Jajouka 145-146, 147,
242
Matisse, Henri 19, 142
*medersas* 30, 221
Ben Youssef Medersa
12, 30, **74-75**, *77*
Medina 23-27, **64-65**,
**67-86**
accommodation 41-57
bars 149-151
cafés 114
restaurants 98-107
southern 82-86
walls 66
*see also* Jemaa El
Fna; Koutoubia
Mosque; souks
Melehi, Mohammed
142
Mellah, The *84*, 84-85
markets 85, **131**
Menara Gardens 11, 90,
*91*, **93-94**, 138
Meranids **11-12**, 29-30
Merzouga 192, 213,
**216**, *217*
metalwork 74, 126,
**131-132**
M'Hamid 220,
**221-222**
microlight flights 160
Ministerio del Gusto
76, **144**
mobile phones 235
Mohammed IV, sultan
90
Mohammed V, avenue
65, 87, 88, *89*
Mohammed V, king
**17-18**, 85
Mohammed VI, king
**20-21**, **27**, 82, 86,
141, 184
money 232-233
Morabiti, Mohammed
143
mosques
Bab Doukkala 80
Ben Youssef 72
Kasbah (El Mansour)
29, *29*, **82**
Mouassine 76
*see also* Koutoubia
Mosque
Mouassine 76-79
Mouassine fountain 76
Mouassine Mosque 76
Moulay Brahim
(village) 196
Moulay Hafid, sultan
14

Moulay Hassan, sultan
13-14, 213
Moulay Ismael, sultan
12-13, 30, 200
Mouvement Populaire
18
Mouyal, Elie 31, **34-35**
museums
Dar Si Said Museum
30, **86**
Maison Tiskiwin 86
Musée de Marrakech
**75-76**, 133, 144
Musée des Arts et
Traditions
Populaires
(Essaouira) 171
Museum of Islamic
Art **92**, 144
music, live 145-147
festivals **147**, 166,
**181**, 237
gnawa **146**, 147, 167,
**181**, 217, 242
grika 145
music, recorded
discography 242
stalls selling 133
Western musicians
147

**n**

Nass El Ghiwane 146
newsagents 133-134
newspapers 232

**o**

oases 193, 208, 209,
213-217, 219-220
Oliveraie de Marigha
160
opening hours 118,
**233**
Orientalism 142
*Othello* (film) 140, 167,
170, **184**
Ouarzazate 139, 140,
192, 203, **205-207**,
208, 218
Ouirgane 196, **198**
Oukaimeden 160, 201,
**202**
Ouled Driss 222
Ourika Valley 191, 192,
**201-202**

**p**

Pacha 27, **148-149**,
**154**
restaurants 113

Palais des Congrès 88
Palais Rhoul 162
Palmeraie 65, *94*, **94**
  accommodation 59-61
  ancient irrigation
    pipes 90
  restaurants 111-113
Palmeraie Golf Palace
  136, 137, **158**
  Club Equestre 159,
    *159*
  sports facilities 138,
    160
parks 88, 138
parties 25
Penny, Joanne 25
Perez, Lynn 25
Perry, Maggie 18, 23
pharmacies 134, 230
photography services
  134
place Abdel Moumen
  88
place de Foucault 90
place du 16 Novembre
  88
Plant, Robert 147
police 229, **233**
  tourist **231**, 233
Polisario 19
Polyclinique du Sud
  230
postal services 233-234
pottery *see* ceramics &
  pottery
poverty 27
property 23-27
Prost, Henri 17, 87
prostitution 149

**q**

Qoubba Galerie d'Art,
  La 144
quad-biking 159-160
Quartier Industriel 118

**r**

Rahba Kedima 72
railways 88, **224**
  left luggage 231
Relais du Lac, Le 138
residence permits 236
restaurants 96-114
  the best for… 96
  child-friendly 138
  Essaouira 181-183
  French 106, 107, 109,
    111
  further afield 113-114
  Indian 109
  Moroccan 98-103, 107

Moroccan cuisine
  & menus **108**, 240
  pizzerias/Italian 106,
    108, 109, 111
  Thai 105, 113, 114
  vegetarian-friendly
    98, 111, **113**, 216
  *see also p247*
    *Restaurants index*
Rhode School of
  Cuisine 116
Riad Magi 23, 55
Riad Tamsna 86
riads
  as accommodation 38
  design 36
  exclusive hire 25
  foreign purchasers
    23, 25, 27
  *see also* hotels
Rissani *214*, 214-216
rock carvings 202
Rolling Stones 19, 33,
  59, 147
Roosevelt, Franklin D.
  15, 17, 22
rosewater 209-210
Route d'Amizmiz 191
Royal Golf Club 158
  kids' club 138
Royal Opera House 34,
  **88**
running 156

**s**

Saadian Tombs 12, 30,
  *82*, **82-83**
Saadians **12**, 30, 200,
  219
Sahara Desert 190,
  **193**, 221-222
  camel treks **220**, 222
  Merzouga dunes 216,
    *217*
Saint Laurent, Yves 22,
  23, 33, **92**
Semarine, rue 72
Semlalia 57
Setti Fatma 201, **202**
shipping services 118
shoes 127
shops 117-134
  children's 138
  Essaouira 185-186
  haggling 119
  opening hours 118
  *see also* markets;
    souks
Shrine of Sidi Abdel
  Aziz 77
Shrine of Sidi Bel
  Abbas 77-79

Shrine of Sidi Ben
  Slimane El Jazuli 17,
    **79**
Sidi Kaouki 177
sightseeing, the best
  65, 190
Sijilmassa 214-215
skiing **160**, 202
Skoura *31*, 31,
  **208-209**
slippers *see babouches*
smoking 234
snake charmers 70
Sofitel 57
  pool 160
  spa 164
Souk des Babouches
  72, 122
Souk des Teinturiers
  **74**, 77
Souk El Attarin 72
Souk El Kebir 72-76
Souk El Khemis 36,
  **131**
Souk Haddadin 74
Souk Laghzel 72
souks **72-81**, 117-118
  Dar El Bacha 79-80
  Dyers' Quarter 72-74
  *fundouks* 77
  historic sights 74-76,
    79-80
  map *73*
  Mouassine 76-79
  saints & shrines
    77-79
  Semarine & the Great
    Souk 72-76
  standard purchases
    122-123
  tanneries 80-81
  *see also* markets;
    shops
Source des Poissons
  Sacrés 212
souvenirs 120, 122-123
Spanish quarter 88
spas 164
sports 156-164
  active 156-160
  children's 138
  health & fitness
    160-164
  spectator 156
  *see also specific*
    *sports*
stationery 133
STDs 230
Stevens, Cat 147, 169
storks 75
Sugar Factory 25
Sultana 45, *46*
  spa 164

Sunset Club 111, 154
supermarkets 118
swimming 160
synagogues 85

**t**

Taddert 203
*tadelakt* **34**, 36, 132
Tafilelt Oasis 192,
  **213-217**
Tahanaoute 196
tajines (food) 108
tajines (pottery) 132
Tamegroute 220-221
Tamesloht 191
Tamnougalk 218
tanneries 80-81
Tansift Garden 138
Taouz 217
Taroudant 12, 196,
  **200**
taxis 65, 194, **225**
Taylor, Villa 22-23
telephones 234-235
television 232
Telouet 14, 191,
  **204-205**, 206
tennis 160
textiles 132
Thami El Glaoui 14,
  *16*, 17, 79, 204, **206**
time, local 235
Timiderte 218
Tin Mal 11, 191, 196,
  *198*, **198-200**
Tinejdad 212
Tinerhir 211-212
Tinfou 221, *221*
tipping 235
Tizi-n-Test 191-192,
  193, 196, *200*, **200**
Tizi-n-Tichka 16, 192,
  193, **203**
Tnine de l'Ourika *201*,
  201
Todra Gorge 156, **212**
toilets 76, 80, **235**
Tomb of Youssef Ben
  Tachfine 68
Toundoute 208
tourism 27
tourist information 235
tours 195
transport 65, 194-195,
  **224-226**
  with children 137
  to Essaouira 187
  *see also* buses;
    railways; taxis
travel advice 227
trekking 197, 202
  camels **220**, 222

**u**

university 234

**v**

Valley of the Almonds 208
Valley of the Birds 210
Valley of the Kasbahs *see* Dadès Valley
Valley of the Roses 210
visas 236
vocabulary 238-240

**w**

Walk of the Seven Waterfalls 202
walking 226
*see also* trekking
weather 193, **236, 237**
Wholesale Market 131
Wilbaux, Quentin 23
Willis, Bill 23, **32-34**, 92, 99, 111
windsurfing 177
wine 149
  shops 127
women
  Berber jewellery 211
  dress & safety 237
  and gnawa 146
  restaurant run by 107
  rights 21
  work 237
Worldsoft 118

**y**

Yacoub El Mansour 68, 82
yoga **164**, 195

**z**

Zagora 219-220
zelije 29, 30, 36

**Accommodation in Marrakech**

Amanjena 61
Caravanserai *61*, 62
Casa Lalla 47
Coralia Club Palmariva 136, 137
Dar Atta 47
Dar Attajmil 47
Dar Doukkala 47
Dar Fakir 53
Dar les Cigognes 47
Deux Tours 34, 61
Grand Tazi 55, 82, 150

Hotel du Pacha 57
Hotel El Andalous 160
Hotel Es Saadi 59, 164
Hotel Gallia 55
Hotel Hivernage 164
Jardins de la Koutoubia 41, 160
Jnane Mogador 55
Jnane Tamsna 59
Kasbah Agafay 62
Ksar Char-Bagh *54*, 59
Maison Arabe 43
Mamounia 42
Meridien N'Fis 57
Palmeraie Golf Palace 136, 137
Riad Azzar 49
Riad El Cadi 49
Riad El Fenn 43, *45*
Riad Enija 43
Riad Farnatchi *39*, 41
Riad Hayati 49
Riad Ifoulki 49, 136
Riad Kaiss 50, *50-51*
Riad Lotus Ambre 43
Riad Mabrouka 50
Riad Magi 55
Riad Noga 51
Riad 72 51
Royal Mirage Marrakech 57
Sherazade 55
Sofitel Marrakech 57, 160, 164
Sultana 45, *46*, 164
Tchaikana 53, *53*
Tichka Salam 57
Tigmi 62
Villa des Orangers 41
Villa El Arsa 57

**Restaurants & Cafés in Marrakech**

Abyssin, L' 111
Alizia 111
Amandine 116
Argana *71*, 98
Bagatelle 107
Bar L'Escale 107
Bô-Zin 113
Boule de Neige 116
Café Arabe 77
Café Atlas 88
Café de France 114
Café Glacier 71
Café les Négociants *87*, 88, 116
Casa Lalla 103
Catanzaro 108, 138
Chez Chegrouni 98
Comptoir 111
Dar Moha 99

Dar Yacout *97*, 99
Fassia, El 107
Foundouk *98-99*, 103
Jacaranda 109
Jad Mahal 153
Jardins de la Koutoubia 105
Jnane Tamsna 59
Kawkab Jeu 138
Kechmara 109
Ksar Char-Bagh *54*, 59
Ksar Es Saoussan 99
Lolo Quoi 109
McDonald's 138
Maison Arabe 103
Marrakchi 103, *112*
Narwama 105
Pâtisserie des Princes 114
Pavilion *105*, 106
Pizzeria Niagra 109
Pizzeria Venezia *102*, 106
Restaurant Toubkai 103
Riad Tamsna 86
Rôtisserie de la Paix *106-107*, 109
Salam Bombay 109
Sunset Club 111, *114-115*
Table du Marché 116
Tansift Garden 138
Terrasses de l'Alhambra 106
Thai Restaurant, The 114
Tobsil 103
Trattoria de Giancarlo 111
Trois Palmiers 107

**Bars & Clubs in Marrakech**

Alanbar 150
Bar L'Escale 151
Bodega *148*, 151
Café Atlas 151
Casa, La 153
Chesterfield Pub 151
Churchill Piano Bar *150*, 150
Club, Le 150
Comptoir 153, *153*
Diamant Noir 154
Grand Tazi 150
Jad Mahal 153
Kechmara 151
Ksour Agafay 22, 76
Lounge, Le 151
Montecristo 152
Moualamid Bar, El 152
Musica Bar 153
Narwama 150

New Feeling 154
Pacha 154
Paradise Club 154
Piano Bar 151
Samovar 153
Strada, La 153
Sunset Club 154
Théatro 154, *155*
VIP Room 155
White Room 155

# Advertiser's Index

Please refer to relevant pages for full details

GB Airways/British Airways    **IFC**

## In Context

| | |
|---|---|
| L'Heure Bleue Palace | **8** |
| Riyad El Mezouar | **26** |
| Morocco Experience & Projects | **26** |
| Marrakech 3000 | **26** |

## Where to Stay

| | |
|---|---|
| Maroc Sélection | **40** |
| Riad Kniza | **44** |
| Jnane Tamsna | **48** |
| ALCS | **52** |
| Time Out City Guides | **56** |
| La Mamounia | **58** |
| Riads Morocco | **60** |
| Riad Kaiss | **60** |

## Restaurants & Cafés

| | |
|---|---|
| Le Comptoir Paris-Marrakech | **100** |
| bo-zin | **104** |
| Jnane Tamsna | **104** |
| La Sultana | **104** |
| Café Arabe | **108** |

## Shops & Services

| | |
|---|---|
| Al Badii Gallery | **124** |
| Artisanat Babftouh Marrakech | **130** |

## High Atlas & Sahara

| | |
|---|---|
| Journeys Elite | **188** |
| Rediscover The World | **188** |
| Kasbah du Toubkal | **188** |

## Directory

| | |
|---|---|
| Always Car | **228** |
| Avis | **228** |
| Riad Ifoulki | **IBC** |

| | |
|---|---|
| Place of interest and/or entertainment . . . . . . . . . | ▮ |
| Railway station . . . . . . . . . . . . . . . . . . . . . . . . . . . . . | ▮ |
| Park . . . . . . . . . . . . . . . . . . . . . . . . . . . . . . . . . . . . . . . | ▮ |
| City wall . . . . . . . . . . . . . . . . . . . . . . . . . . . . . . . . . . . | ▬ |
| Area name . . . . . . . . . . . . . . . . . . . . . . . . . . . . . . . | GUÉLIZ |
| Mosque . . . . . . . . . . . . . . . . . . . . . . . . . . . . . . . . . . . . | ☪ |
| Church . . . . . . . . . . . . . . . . . . . . . . . . . . . . . . . . . . . . | ✚ |
| Post office . . . . . . . . . . . . . . . . . . . . . . . . . . . . . . . . . | ✉ |
| Hotels . . . . . . . . . . . . . . . . . . . . . . . . . . . . . . . . . . . . . | ● |
| Restaurants . . . . . . . . . . . . . . . . . . . . . . . . . . . . . . . | ● |

# Maps

| | |
|---|---|
| **Marrakech Overview** | **250** |
| **Marrakech Medina** | |
| **– North** | **252** |
| **Marrakech Medina** | |
| **– South** | **254** |
| **Guéliz/Hivernage** | **256** |

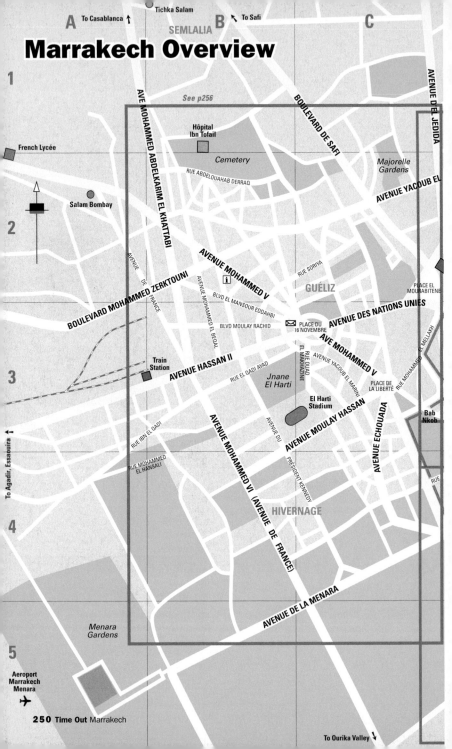

# Marrakech Overview

A    B    C

To Casablanca ↑

To Safi ↗

Tichka Salam

SEMLALIA

See p256

AVE MOHAMMED ABDELKARIM EL KHATTABI

BOULEVARD DE SAFI

AVENUE DEL JEDIDA

French Lycée

Hôpital Ibn Tofail

Cemetery

RUE ABDELOUAHAB DERRAQ

Majorelle Gardens

AVENUE YACOUB EL

Salam Bombay

AVENUE DE FRANCE

AVENUE MOHAMMED V

RUE SORIYA

GUÉLIZ

PLACE EL MOURABITENE

BOULEVARD MOHAMMED ZERKTOUNI

AVENUE MOHAMMED EL BECAL

BLVD EL MANSOUR EDDAHBI

BLVD MOULAY RACHID

PLACE DU 16 NOVEMBRE

AVENUE DES NATIONS UNIES

AVE MOHAMMED V

RUE MOHAMMED EL MELLAH

Train Station

AVENUE HASSAN II

RUE EL QADI AYAD

Jnane El Harti

RUE OUAD EL MAKHAZINE

AVENUE YACOUB EL MARINI

PLACE DE LA LIBERTÉ

El Harti Stadium

RUE IBN EL QADI

AVENUE MOHAMMED VI (AVENUE DE FRANCE)

AVENUE DU PRÉSIDENT KENNEDY

AVENUE MOULAY HASSAN

AVENUE ECHOUADA

Bab Nkob

RUE MOHAMMED EL HANSALI

To Agadir, Essaouira ↑

HIVERNAGE

RUE

AVENUE DE LA MENARA

Menara Gardens

Aeroport Marrakech Menara ✈

To Ourika Valley ↓

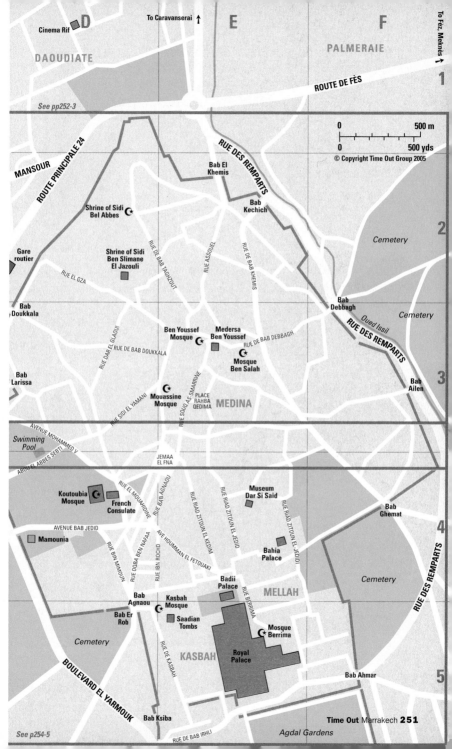

**D**

Cinema Rif

DAOUDIATE

**E**

To Caravanserai ↑

**F**

To Fès, Meknès →

PALMERAIE

ROUTE DE FÈS

**1**

*See pp252-3*

0       500 m
0       500 yds
© Copyright Time Out Group 2005

MANSOUR

ROUTE PRINCIPALE 24

RUE DES REMPARTS

Bab El Khemis

Bab Kechich

Shrine of Sidi Bel Abbes ☾✶

Cemetery

**2**

Gare routier

RUE EL GZA

Shrine of Sidi Ben Slimane El Jazouli

RUE DE BAB TAGHZOUT

RUE ASSOUEL

RUE DE BAB KHEMIS

Bab Debbagh

Cemetery

Oued Issil

RUE DES REMPARTS

Bab Doukkala

RUE DAR EL GLAOUI

RUE DE BAB DOUKKALA

Ben Youssef Mosque ☾✶

Medersa Ben Youssef ☾✶

RUE DE BAB DEBBAGH

Mosque Ben Salah ☾✶

Bab Ailen

**3**

Bab Larissa

RUE SIDI EL YAMANI

Mouassine Mosque ☾✶

RUE SOUQ AS-SMARRINE

PLACE RAHBA QEDIMA

MEDINA

AVENUE MOHAMMED V

Swimming Pool

ABOU EL ABBES SEBTI

JEMAA EL FNA

Koutoubia Mosque ☾✶

RUE EL MOUAHIDINE

French Consulate

RUE BAB AGNAOU

RUE RIAD ZITOUN EL KEDIM

RUE RIAD ZITOUN EL JEDID

Museum Dar Si Said

RUE RIAD ZITOUN EL JEDIDI

Bab Ghemat

**4**

AVENUE BAB JEDID

Mamounia

RUE BIN MMOUN

RUE OQBA BEN NAFAA

RUE BIN ROCHD

AVE HOUMMAN EL FETOUAKI

Bahia Palace

Bab Agnaou

Badii Palace

RUE BERRIMA

MELLAH

Cemetery

RUE DES REMPARTS

Bab Er Rob

Kasbah Mosque ☾✶

Saadian Tombs

Mosque Berrima ☾✶

Cemetery

RUE DE KASBAH

KASBAH

Royal Palace

Bab Ahmar

**5**

BOULEVARD EL YARMOUK

Bab Ksiba

RUE DE BAB IRHLI

Agdal Gardens

*See p254-5*

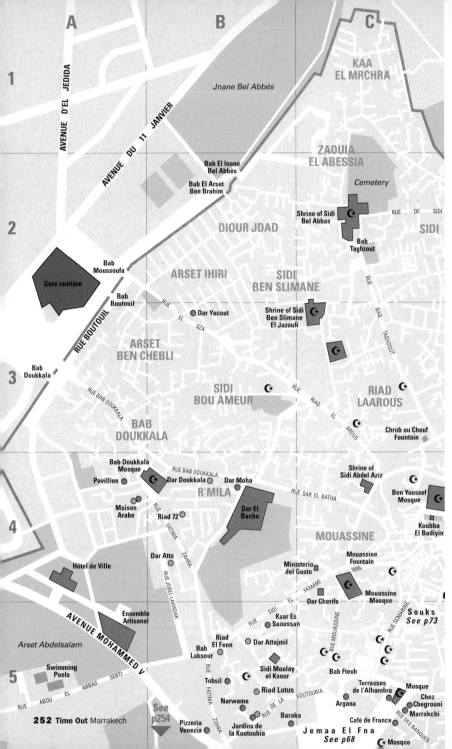

A

B

C

1

2

3

4

5

AVENUE D'EL JEDIDA

AVENUE DU 11 JANVIER

*Jnane Bel Abbés*

KAA
EL MRCHRA

ZAOUIA
EL ABESSIA

*Cemetery*

RUE    DE    SIDI

Bab El Inane
Bel Abbès

Bab El Arset
Ben Brahim

DIOUR JDAD

Shrine of Sidi
Bel Abbas

Bab
Taghzout

SIDI

Gare routière

Bab
Moussoufa

Bab
Boutouil

Bab
Doukkala

ARSET IHIRI

Dar Yacout

SIDI
BEN SLIMANE

Shrine of Sidi
Ben Slimane
El Jazouli

RUE

BAB

TAGHZOUT

RUE

EL

GZA

ARSET
BEN CHEBLI

RUE BOUTOUIL

RUE BAB DOUKKALA

SIDI
BOU AMEUR

BAB
DOUKKALA

RUE

RIAD

EL

AROUS

RIAD
LAAROUS

Chrob ou Chouf
Fountain

Bab Doukkala
Mosque

Pavillion

Maison
Arabe

Riad 72

RUE BAB DOUKKALA

Dar Doukkala

R'MILA

Dar Moha

Dar El
Bacha

RUE SAR EL BATHA

Shrine of
Sidi Abdel Aziz

Ben Youssef
Mosque

Koubba
El Badiyin

RUE

FATIMA

ZAHRA

Dar Atta

RUE

JEBEL

LAKHDAR

Hôtel de Ville

Ensemble
Artisanal

MOUASSINE

Ministerio
del Gusto

Mouassine
Fountain

EL

YAMAMI

Dar Cherifa

Mouassine
Mosque

RUE MOUASSINE

RUE SEMARINE

Souks
See p73

AVENUE MOMMED V

*Arset Abdelsalam*

Swimming
Pools

RUE

ABOU

EL

ABBAS

SEBTI

RUE

Ksar Es
Saoussan

RUE

SIDI

Riad
El Fenn

Bab
Laksour

Dar Attajmil

RUE

FATIMA

Tobsil

Sidi Moulay
el Ksour

Riad Lotus

RUE

DE

LA

KOUTOUBIA

Bab Fteuh

Terrasses
de l'Alhambra

Mosque

Chez
Chegrouni
Marrakchi

RUE DES BANQUES

Narwama

See
p254

ZOHRA

Pizzeria
Venezia

Jardins de
la Koutoubia

Baraka

Argana

Café de France

Jemaa El Fna
See p68

Mosque

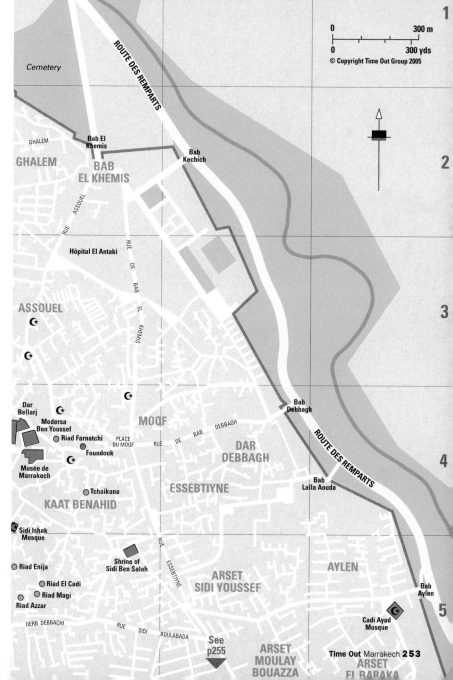

# Marrakech Medina - North

D     E     F

1

0        300 m
0        300 yds
© Copyright Time Out Group 2005

*Cemetery*

ROUTE DES REMPARTS

GHALEM

Bab El Khemis

GHALEM

BAB EL KHEMIS

Bab Kechich

2

RUE ASSOUEL

Hôpital El Antaki

RUE DE BAB EL KHEMIS

ASSOUEL

3

Dar Bellarj

Medersa Ben Youssef

Riad Farnatchi

MOQF

PLACE DU MOQF

RUE DE BAB DEBBAGH

DAR DEBBAGH

Bab Debbagh

Foundouk

Musée de Marrakech

ROUTE DES REMPARTS

ESSEBTIYNE

Bab Lalla Aouda

4

Tchaikana

KAAT BENAHID

Sidi Ishak Mosque

Shrine of Sidi Ben Salah

RUE ESSEBTIYNE

Riad Enija

Riad El Cadi

Riad Magi

Riad Azzar

DERB DEBBACHI

RUE SIDI BOULABADA

ARSET SIDI YOUSSEF

AYLEN

Bab Aylen

Cadi Ayad Mosque

5

See p255

ARSET MOULAY BOUAZZA

ARSET EL BARAKA

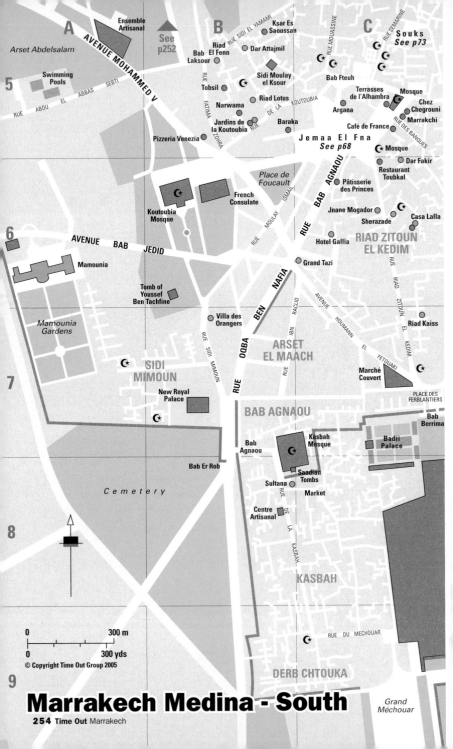

# Marrakech Medina - South

Riad Enija

Riad El Cadi

Riad Magi

Riad Azzar

DERB DEBBACHI

RUE SIDI BOULABADA

RUE ESSEBTIYNE

Shrine of
Sidi Ben Salah

See
p253

ARSET
SIDI YOUSSEF

AYLEN

Bab
Aylen

5

Cadi Ayad
Mosque

ARSET
MOULAY
BOUAZZA

ARSET
EL BARAKA

Riad Noga

Villa El Arsa

Riad Ifoulki

DOUAR
GRAOUA

RUE RIAD ZITOUN

Dar Si Said
Museum

Moulay Idriss
Palace

JNANE
BEN CHEGRA

RUE BA HMAD

RUE EL CADI AYAD

JNANE
BOUSSEKRI

6

Maison
Tiskiwin

Riad Mabrouka

EL JEDID

Riad Hayati

RIAD ZITOUN
EL JEDID

Bahia
Palace

RUE IMAM EL RHEZALI

Bab
Ghemat

Po
Ma

Shrine of Sidi
Youssef Ben Ali

7

Bab Es Salam
Market

MELLAH

Jewish
Cemetery

PLACE
SOUWEKA

Dar les
Cigognes

Cemetery

BERIMA

Berima
Mosque

JNANE EL AFIA

8

Royal
Palace

Bab Jnane
El Afia

Méchouar
Intérieur

BAB
HMAR

Bab
Hmar

QUARTIER
SIDI YOUSSEF
BEN ALI

9

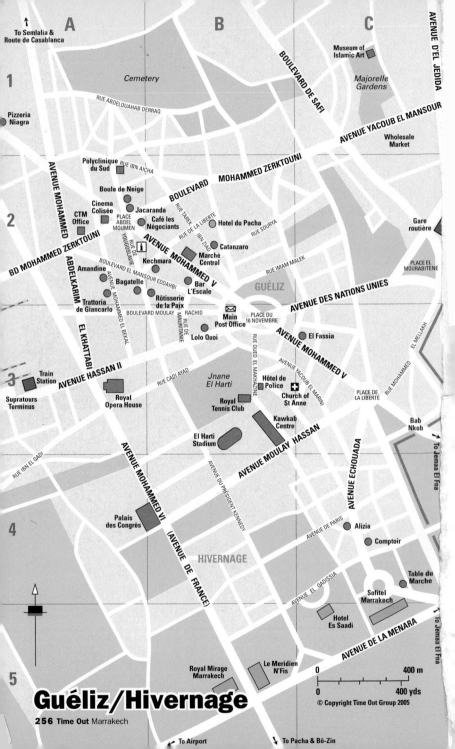

# Guéliz/Hivernage

© Copyright Time Out Group 2005